Preliminary Edition Notice

You have been selected to receive a copy of this book in the form of a preliminary edition. A preliminary edition is used in a classroom setting to test the overall value of a book's content and its effectiveness in a practical course prior to its formal publication on the national market.

As you use this text in your course, please share any and all feedback regarding the volume with your professor. Your comments on this text will allow the author to further develop the content of the book, so we can ensure it will be a useful and informative classroom tool for students in universities across the nation and around the globe. If you find the material is challenging to understand, or could be expanded to improve the usefulness of the text, it is important for us to know. If you have any suggestions for improving the material contained in the book or the way it is presented, we encourage you to share your thoughts.

Please note, preliminary editions are similar to review copies, which publishers distribute to select readers prior to publication in order to test a book's audience and elicit early feedback; therefore, you may find inconsistencies in formatting or design, or small textual errors within this volume. Design elements and the written text will likely undergo changes before this book goes to print and is distributed on the national market.

This text is not available in wide release on the market, as it is actively being prepared for formal publication. Accordingly, the book is offered to you at a discounted price to reflect its preliminary status.

If you would like to provide notes directly to the publisher, you may contact us by e-mailing studentreviews@cognella.com. Please include the book's title, author, and 7-digit SKU reference number (found below the barcode on the back cover of the book) in the body of your message.

Contemporary World Problems

Preliminary Edition

Edited by Glenn R. Storey

University of Iowa

Bassim Hamadeh, CEO and Publisher
Kassie Graves, Director of Acquisitions and Sales
Jamie Giganti, Senior Managing Editor
Jess Estrella, Senior Graphic Designer
Angela Schultz, Acquisitions Editor
Michelle Piehl, Project Editor
Stephanie Kohl, Licensing Associate
Christian Berk, Associate Production Editor
Robyn Allan, Production Assistant

Printed in the United States of America

ISBN: 978-1-5165-2192-0 (pbk) / 978-1-5165-2193-7 (br)

Contents

Chapter 1
Malicious Gossip?

OBJECTIVES

- Learn where the original meaning of the word anthropology comes from (Aristotle).
- Determine the significance of the anthropological approach to contemporary world problems.
- Explain how anthropology works to come to grips with how people in other cultures think about the world and its problems.
- Analyze an ancient anthropological effort (Herodotus) and a more modern attempt to connect with another culture (Bohannan).

KEY TERMS

Anthropology: the study of humankind (did it start with malicious gossip?). There are two central concepts of anthropology: 1) humans are a product of evolution (change through time); and 2) all humans are part of groups that possess culture. There are 5 sub-disciplines in anthropology: 1) socio-cultural anthropology (the founding discipline, in which anthropologist study human cultures in the present by dealing with living people); 2) biological anthropology (once called "physical anthropology") which studies humans as a biological organism (and studies our closes primate relatives); 3) archaeological anthropology (study of the socio-cultural anthropology of past societies through the study of material remains and people who are dead); 4) linguistic anthropology (the study of human cultural beliefs behavior as revealed in human languages, which number about 6,000); and 5) applied anthropology (the newest sub-discipline which studies how to apply anthropology to address contemporary world problems). In a word, anthropology is the scientific study of human beings, approached scientifically (both in the biology of humans and in the social science of human behavior), and in terms of the humanities.

Culture: the complex of beliefs, behaviors and customs that characterize and are shared by a distinct cultural group. There is no single definition of culture accepted by all anthropologists, who, nevertheless, continue to believe the concept is a useful one. Two anthropologists in 1952 listed over 160 definitions of culture. There are 6 features of culture generally agreed upon by anthropologists: 1) It is made up of learned behaviors; 2) it involves the use of language and symbols (something that stands for something else); 3) it is patterned and integrated; 4) it is shared in a framework of interaction; 5) it is in some way adaptive (but not necessarily perfectly functional in every way); 6) it is subject to change.

Ethnography: an anthropological description of how another culture works.

Culture shock: the natural troubled reaction and surprise at being immersed in another culture which acts and views things in a different way than the way it is done in one's own culture.

Ethnocentrism: the belief that one's own culture is superior to all other cultural systems.

SCHEMA ACTIVATION ACTIVITY

Write down the words that occur to you when answering the question: *What do you think of when you hear the term "anthropology?"*

(Save these to share later in your discussion sections.)

INTRODUCTION

There are four short readings for you in this chapter. Three are translations from Ancient Greek and one is an engaging tale of an anthropologist in the field. The readings are designed to give you an idea of how anthropology works and how anthropology approaches contemporary world problems.

READING #1: ARISTOTLE, NICHOMACHEAN ETHICS IV.III.30-33

*The great-souled person is not used to fawning, nor is anything "the greatest!" in their eyes. Such a one is completely without malice; for it is not particularly characteristic of great-souled individuals to keep harboring in mind personal injuries, but rather it is their trait to overlook them. Neither are such individuals prone to talk about people (**anthropologos**) in gossip, either about themselves or about other people. The great-soul cares neither to be commended, nor to hear others belittled, but is not also lavish with praise. For that reason, he or she is not a speaker of evil, not even about enemies, unless striving to be insolent on purpose. Least of all does such a one complain or ask pitifully for help in adverse circumstances or when faced with trifling setbacks. So much for being overly-anxious concerning such things. Interested only in possessing beautiful and useless things, rather than productive and useful ones, the great-soul thus demonstrates complete self-sufficiency.*

Aristotle, the student of Plato and founder of "the Academy" (a grove outside Athens where philosophers went to learn and practice philosophy), is also the founder of much rational Western thought. In almost any field of academia (named after his grove!), Aristotle had something to say by way of studying a topic in a scientific, systematic manner. In his *Nichomachean Ethics*, Aristotle laid the foundation for the discipline we call moral philosophy. As an exemplar of the morally good individual (at least to the Greeks), Aristotle described the characteristics of the "great-souled" person. Within this long description, Aristotle used the word that we have adapted for the discipline of anthropology.In a description of the "great-souled" individual, Aristotle uses the word "anthropology" for the first time, in a surprising— but perhaps very accurate, at least in one sense—meaning of the word.

Anthropologia-Talk about People

So, the term anthropology, in its first use in Greek, literally means "gossip," in the sense of its root meaning, "talking about people"—anthropos was usually in the past translated as "man" but it really means "human." When anthropology was founded as an academic discipline, the methodology was simple: just ask people from other cultures to talk about their culture, and explain the way they do things in that culture. So, anthropology starts as "talk about people"— literally.

In European languages, when technical language began to be needed, in the last 400 years or so, Greek and Latin were frequently the source for new words. The Greek word logia, which meant basically "talk," was extended to mean the kinds of things it had also meant to the Greeks: "logic of," "study of." So, when the early academics of the discipline that was to become anthropology adopted that term, they meant it to indicate: "the study of humans."

This passage not only uses the term anthropology for the first time, it also describes the kind of person that the anthropologist tries to be. To be an anthropologist, to look beyond your own culture and try desperately to understand why other people in other cultures do things differently and accepts them—one has to be something of a "great-soul." And, it may seem paradoxical that an anthropologist should focus on beautiful and non-utilitarian objects, but that is an important aspect of coming to understand another culture, especially in terms of its material culture, the objects that people use in their everyday lives. The other paradoxical feature of the passage is the admission that one can talk evil about enemies, if one is being human and acting with hubris, or "overbearing pride"—you will consider this again in Chapter 10. To the Greeks, morality consisted of "helping your friends and harming your enemies." It simply happens that people, when dealing with adversaries, slip into a mode of acting above themselves—to the point even of offending the gods—which is what hubris really means. Aristotle excuses even the great-souled person when they slip into this very human mode. Perhaps it is also a recognition that human interactions can be messy and problematic, which every anthropologist knows and has to try and navigate as they live and work among the people of the culture they are studying.

Holism

Plenty of other disciplines study aspects of humanity, but none of them do so as comprehensively as modern anthropology, which has been called "the most scientific of the humanities" and "the most humanistic of the sciences." What makes anthropology special is its application of the principle of "holism"—humans can only be properly studied "as a whole" or "in totality." All aspects of human behavior and nature are interrelated, and so humans should be studied "in holistic perspective."

READING #2: HERODOTUS, HISTORIES III.38

The Greek historian Herodotus, who lived and wrote in the latter half of the 5th c. BCE, is sometimes called "The Father of History." In this extract, he lays the foundation for anthropology's understanding of the concept of ethnocentrism. This passage virtually defines it. The context is an incident at the court of the Persian King Darius, in the 6th c. BCE.

For, if someone were to pose a question to all people, directing them to choose the finest out of all the customs in the world; everyone, after considering the question carefully from all angles, would invariably choose those of their own culture. So much so does everyone, by quite a wide margin, consider the customs of their own people to be the very best. Therefore, it is not reasonable for anyone but a madman to make fun of custom. Therefore, in the face of so much thoughtful consensus about the issues surrounding custom, one can come to that conclusion by many additional indications, but especially with reference to the following story: Darius, while King of the Persians, when he had summoned the Greeks present at his court, he asked them how much money they would be willing to take to eat their own parents when they had died. The Greeks said that for no amount of money would they do such an immoral thing. After that, when he had called in ambassadors from the Indian people known as Kallatiae, who do eat their parents, Darius asked (with the Greeks present and informed of what was being said through interpreters) how much money it would take to get the Kallatiae to burn their parents after death on a funeral pyre. They, crying out loudly in protest, demanded that Darius cease speaking of such a sacrilege. Therefore, this belief that all people think their own culture's customs are the best, is a well-established conclusion, and rightly, it seems to me, Pindar said poetically that "Custom is the King of All."

Ethnocentrism

This passage beautifully illustrates the challenge of ethnocentrism because every culture "thinks it is right." And, to define our identities, we like to think that we ARE right. But one person's meat is another person's poison, as illustrated here more than two thousand years ago.

Cannibalism

Cannibalism is one of the most challenging of all topics that anthropology has to talk about, the act of eating human flesh. We strongly believe that this is done, but it has rarely been observed, and when it has, the describer and the description are not universally believed. It does seem common that members of one culture will accuse the members of another culture of doing this, as a way of insulting them and belittling them (and thus proving that one's own culture's customs are better than anyone else's). Most anthropologists do believe that cannibalism exists, but it is very rare. It is also true that a number of cultures practice endocannibalism, the "eating of one's own," as an act of great respect. Christians (many of whom would severely condemn the practice of eating of human flesh) should reflect that the sacrament of the Mass is a ritual doing the same thing as eating of relatives: to show great respect. No other comment is really needed on this amazing passage.

READING #3: HERODOTUS, HISTORIES II.35-37

Book II of Herodotus' histories is devoted to the Egyptians, whom the Greeks recognized as a far older, and in some ways far superior, culture to their own. Book II may well be the first "ethnography"—the anthropologist's write-up of the study of another culture. That being the case, Herodotus, "the Father of History," deserves his other nickname: "The Father of Anthropology." Here is an excerpt of his ethnographic observations on the Egyptian "Other."

Because of a different kind of climate prevailing among themselves, plus a river possessing a nature completely distinct from all other rivers, the Egyptians have acquired customs and laws wholly and in many ways opposite to those among other peoples. Among them, the women buy and sell in the marketplace, while the men, staying at home, do the weaving. While others weave pushing the weft upwards, the Egyptians push it downwards. While men carry burdens on their heads, the women do so on their shoulders. It is the women who urinate standing up, while the men do it sitting down. They evacuate their bowels inside the houses, but they eat outside in the streets, arguing that disgraceful necessary acts must be done in secret, while acts that are not disgraceful can be done openly. No woman serves as a priestess, either of a male god or a female deity, but men are priests of all gods and all goddesses. There is no rule compelling boys to support their parents if they are not willing to, but every compulsion applies to daughters to do so, even if unwilling.

The priests of the gods in the rest of the world wear their hair long, but in Egypt they are shaved. For other people, the custom for whom it most concerns in mourning is to shave their heads, but the Egyptians, just after deaths, allow hair to grow, both on the head and on the chin. Until then, they are shaved. For other peoples, daily life is carried on separate from animals, but to Egyptians, daily life is close to beasts. Other people live dependent on wheat and barley, but the greatest reproach is put on an Egyptian who derives sustenance from those grains, but they make food from a kind of grain that some people call rye. They knead their flour with their feet, but they take up mud and dung with their hands. Other people leave their genitals as they are in nature, except for those who have learned it from the Egyptians, who practice circumcision. Each man owns two cloaks, but each woman just one. The rope-holes and ropes for sails other people attach to the outside of the ship, while the Egyptians do it on the inside. The Greeks write their letters and calculate their numbers bearing the hand from left to right; the Egyptians do so from right to left. Doing it this way, yet they themselves say that they do it to the right "rightly," whereas the Greeks do it "wrongly," that is, to the left. They employ two kinds of writing, and they call the one sacred, the other, common.

Being the most religious of all people, they employ the following kinds of customs. They drink from bronze drinking cups, rinsing them out every day—not just the one doing it, the other not—but all doing this. They wear linen cloaks always newly-washed, making this most of all their business; they practice circumcision for the sake of cleanliness. They esteem being clean to being more attractive. Their priests shave their entire bodies every third day, lest lice or any other filthy things should breed in themselves while they are serving the gods. The priests wear only clothing of linen and footwear of papyrus; it is not allowed to them to wear another material for clothing, nor other material for their footwear. They bathe two times each day in cold water and twice each night. In a word, they discharge a myriad array of religious observances.

The priests experience not just a few benefits. They do not waste or spend anything of their own property, but even sacred loaves of special white bread are baked for them. For each priest, there is quite a large abundance of beef and poultry meat every day. There is also given to them wine from the vine. They are not allowed to eat fish. The Egyptians do not at all sow beans much in their country; they do not nibble on them as they grow, nor do they eat them by cooking them up. The priests do not even endure looking upon them, considering them to be a kind of pulse that is unclean. There is not just one who serves as a priest for each of the gods, but many. One of these is the High Priest. If any High Priest should die, his son is installed in his place.

What Herodotus Got Right

There are several commentaries for Herodotus' work which try to determine how accurate his reporting may have been. Generally, the commentators give Herodotus fairly high marks for getting things right. However, scholars have pointed out that Herodotus writes with a model in mind, in which he contrasts everything with the practices of his own culture and he likes to do what is called "symmetry and inversion"—whatever the Greeks did was done exactly the opposite by the Egyptians. One commentator calls this his tendency to "over-schematization" and "oversimplification." Thus Herodotus insists that the Greeks and Egyptians did the opposite from each other regarding gender practices. We know that Egyptian men and women both kept shops and did the marketing and that they carried loads on their heads or shoulders indifferently, so his "over-schematization" here leads him astray. One commentator suggests that Herodotus got the idea that women carried burdens on the shoulders because they frequently would have carried babies and small children that way.

Egyptologists agree that there is some evidence for men squatting to urinate, and even that Egyptians used a kind of indoor toilet. But where did Herodotus get the idea that women stood up to urinate? Egyptian women probably squatted to urinate as much as men did, but there has been a long-standing tradition throughout the centuries in contexts in which women have to wear heavy skirts and, in emergencies (or as a common practice, as in the French Court of Versailles because of the monumentally inconvenient dresses worn), those women have to stand up to urinate and then move away from the spot. It is from this practice that Herodotus may have gotten the idea that Egyptian women stood to urinate. New Kingdom iconography does show women in dresses that appear as tight as body suits and so thus were hard to remove quickly for bodily functions.

It is also said by scholars that Herodotus was right about the differing parental responsibilities of sons and daughters. One commentator, however, thought that the point of mentioning this was indicative of the comparative independence of Egyptian women. After all, to say that they were responsible for support of parents indicates that Egyptian women were more independent than Greek women because they could incur obligations on their own account, apart from their husbands.

What Herodotus Got Wrong

Herodotus also got a couple of things wrong about how Egyptians wrote. Their characters are not necessarily read only right to left. The key to Egyptian hieroglyphs is that they are read from the direction in which the signs face. If the vulture (the sign for "a") is facing to the left, one reads from left to right. Egyptian signs follow that order in being read, and from top to bottom when arranged vertically. Even the Greeks knew how to read from right to left. In the 6th c. BCE, Greek inscriptions were often read boustrophedon (literally, as the cattle turn in plowing). The inscription starts from left to right but when it got to the end of the line, it simply started on the next line being read from right to left. Think about that; it is like an algorithm that uses the least amount of energy in doing a task. One doesn't plow a field by getting to the end, stopping, going back to the starting spot and plowing again in the same direction. You save distance by turning around and going back in the other direction. The Greeks (and certainly Herodotus) would have been familiar with this. And, Herodotus mentions only two forms of writing, the sacred, and that of the people. The Egyptians called their hieroglyphs "Gods' Words" so Herodotus is right, and "hieroglyph" does mean "sacred incising." The other form of Egyptian writing we call "demotic" (that "of the people") partly thanks to this passage of Herodotus. He did miss the other form of writing, which we call "hieratic." It is a form of hieroglyphs but in script. In a way, the block hieroglyphs are like our printing, whereas the hieratic was like our script, and because both words are from the Greek word for "sacred," Egyptian scribes had to learn both forms of "sacred" writing.

Herodotus claims that non-Egyptians do not live as closely to their animals as the Egyptians do. That is certainly wrong. In many cultures, the "longhouse" is a common form of dwelling and portions of it often were for animals. Romano-Batavian farmhouses in Holland in ancient times were longhouses that held both humans and their animals. Until recently in the Greek countryside, farmhouses commonly held donkeys, mules, sheep and goats on the first, ground floor, while the family lived in the second floor upstairs. Egyptian models of bakeries and potteries at work show that the kneading of dough and clay were done, without preference, by the hands and feet. Because Egypt was so short of wood for fuel, as in other such places, dried dung was used for fires, especially for cooking, which would mean that people handled animal "chips" frequently while carrying out tasks at the hearth or oven.

The interesting thing about the prohibition on fava beans is that commentators have come up with two reasons for it: 1) eating beans leads to unseemly flatulence (not good for a priest!) and 2) the shape of the beans was objectionable (they look like genitals, hence priests should not even look at them). Most commentators agree that Egyptians ate lots of beans, so they were only taboo for priests. The Greeks who followed the teachings of Pythagoras also regarded beans as taboo, probably for similar reasons. The other taboo shared by the Pythagoreans and Egyptian priests was the prohibition on eating fish. Inasmuch as secular Egyptians all ate lots of fish, this prohibition is unfathomable for both the priests and the Pythagoreans; but, perhaps an anthropologist should refrain from characterizing that result as "unfathomable?!"

Finally, Herodotus claimed that the Egyptians were the most religious of all peoples. That is simply false: all humans are about equally religious, so claims of this kind are specious.

Shakespeare in the Bush

by Laura Bohannan

Just before I left Oxford for the Tiv in West Africa, conversation turned to the season at Stratford. "You Americans," said a friend, "often have difficulty with Shakespeare. He was, after all, a very English poet, and one can easily misinterpret the universal by misunderstanding the particular."

I protested that human nature is pretty much the same the whole world over; at least the general plot and motivation of the greater tragedies would always be clear—everywhere—although some details of custom might have to be explained and difficulties of translation might produce other slight changes. To end an argument we could not conclude, my friend gave me a copy of *Hamlet* to study in the African bush: it would, he hoped, lift my mind above its primitive surroundings, and possibly I might, by prolonged meditation, achieve the grace of correct interpretation.

It was my second field trip to that African tribe, and I thought myself ready to live in one of its remote sections—an area difficult to cross even on foot. I eventually settled on the hillock of a very knowledgeable old man, the head of a homestead of some hundred and forty people, all of whom were either his close relatives or their wives and children. Like the other elders of the vicinity, the old man spent most of his time performing ceremonies seldom seen these days in the more accessible parts of the tribe. I was delighted. Soon there would be three months of enforced isolation and leisure, between the harvest that takes place just before the rising of the swamps and the clearing of new farms when the water goes down. Then, I thought, they would have even more time to perform ceremonies and explain them to me.

I was quite mistaken. Most of the ceremonies demanded the presence of elders from several homesteads. As the swamps rose, the old men found it too difficult to walk from one homestead to the next, and the ceremonies gradually ceased. As the swamps rose even higher, all activities but one came to an end. The women brewed beer from maize and millet. Men, women, and children sat on their hillocks and drank it.

People began to drink at dawn. By midmorning the whole homestead was singing, dancing, and drumming. When it rained, people had to sit inside their huts: there they drank and sang or they drank and told stories. In any case, by noon or before, I either had to join the party or retire to my own hut and my books. "One does not discuss serious matters when there is beer. Come, drink with us." Since I lacked their capacity for the thick native beer, I spent more and more time with *Hamlet*. Before the end of the second month, grace descended on me. I was quite sure that *Hamlet* had only one possible interpretation, and that one universally obvious.

Early every morning, in the hope of having some serious talk before the beer party, I used to call on the old man at his reception hut—a circle of posts supporting a thatched roof above a low mud wall to keep out wind and rain. One day I crawled through the low doorway and found most of the men of the homestead sitting huddled in their ragged cloths on stools, low plank beds, and reclining chairs, warming themselves against the chill of the rain around a smoky fire. In the center were three pots of beer. The party had started.

The old man greeted me cordially. "Sit down and drink." I accepted a large calabash full of beer, poured some into a small drinking gourd, and tossed it down. Then I poured some more into the same gourd for the man second in seniority to my host before I handed my calabash over to a young man for further distribution. Important people shouldn't ladle beer themselves.

"It is better like this," the old man said, looking at me approvingly and plucking at the thatch that had caught in my hair. "You should sit and drink with us more often. Your servants tell me that when you are not with us, you sit inside your hut looking at a paper."

The old man was acquainted with four kinds of "papers": tax receipts, bride price receipts, court fee receipts, and letters. The messenger who brought him letters from the chief used them mainly as a badge of office, for he always knew what was in them and told the old man. Personal letters for the few who had relatives in the government or mission stations were kept until someone went to a large market where there was a letter writer and reader. Since my arrival, letters were brought to me to be read. A few men also brought me bride price receipts, privately, with requests to change the figures to a higher sum. I found moral arguments were of no avail, since in-laws are fair game, and the technical hazards of forgery difficult to explain to an illiterate people. I did not wish them to think me silly enough to look at any such papers for days on end, and I hastily explained that my "paper" was one of the "things of long ago" of my country.

"Ah," said the old man. "Tell us." I protested that I was not a storyteller. Storytelling is a skilled art among them; their standards are high, and the audiences critical—and vocal in their criticism. I protested in vain. This morning they wanted to hear a story while they drank. They threatened to tell me no more stories until I told them one of mine. Finally, the old man promised that no one would criticize my style, "for we know you are struggling with our language." "But," put in one of the elders, "you must explain what we do not understand, as we do when we tell you our stories." Realizing that here was my chance to prove *Hamlet* universally intelligible, I agreed.

The old man handed me some more beer to help me on with my storytelling. Men filled their long wooden pipes and knocked coals from the fire to place in the pipe bowls; then, puffing contentedly, they sat back to listen. I began in the proper style, "Not yesterday, not yesterday, but long ago, a thing occurred. One night three men were keeping watch outside the homestead of the great chief, when suddenly they saw the former chief approach them."

"Why was he no longer their chief?"

"He was dead," I explained. "That is why they were troubled and afraid when they saw him."

"Impossible," began one of the elders, handing his pipe on to his neighbor, who interrupted, "Of course it wasn't the dead chief. It was an omen sent by a witch. Go on."

[pagebreak]

Slightly shaken, I continued. "One of these three was a man who knew things"—the closest translation for scholar, but unfortunately it also meant witch. The second elder looked triumphantly at the first. "So he spoke to the dead chief saying, 'Tell us what we must do so you may rest in your grave,' but the dead chief did not answer. He vanished, and they could see him no more. Then the man who knew things—his name was Horatio—said this event was the affair of the dead chief's son, Hamlet."

There was a general shaking of heads round the circle. "Had the dead chief no living brothers? Or was this son the chief?"

"No," I replied. "That is, he had one living brother who became the chief when the elder brother died."

The old men muttered: such omens were matters for chiefs and elders, not for youngsters; no good could come of going behind a chief's back; clearly Horatio was not a man who knew things.

"Yes, he was," I insisted, shooing a chicken away from my beer. "In our country the son is next to the father. The dead chief's younger brother had become the great chief. He had also married his elder brother's widow only about a month after the funeral."

"He did well," the old man beamed and announced to the others, "I told you that if we knew more about Europeans, we would find they really were very like us. In our country also," he added to me, "the younger brother marries the elder brother's widow and becomes the father of his children. Now, if your uncle, who married your widowed mother, is your father's full brother, then he will be a real father to you. Did Hamlet's father and uncle have one mother?"

His question barely penetrated my mind; I was too upset and thrown too far off-balance by having one of the most important elements of *Hamlet* knocked straight out of the picture. Rather uncertainly I said that I thought they had the same mother, but I wasn't sure—the story didn't say. The old man told me severely that these genealogical details made all the difference and that when I got home I must ask the elders about it. He shouted out the door to one of his younger wives to bring his goatskin bag.

Determined to save what I could of the mother motif, I took a deep breath and began again. "The son Hamlet was very sad because his mother had married again so quickly. There was no need for her to do so, and it is our custom for a widow not to go to her next husband until she has mourned for two years."

"Two years is too long," objected the wife, who had appeared with the old man's battered goatskin bag. "Who will hoe your farms for you while you have no husband?"

"Hamlet," I retorted, without thinking, "was old enough to hoe his mother's farms himself. There was no need for her to remarry." No one looked convinced. I gave up. "His mother and the great chief told Hamlet not to be sad, for the great chief himself would be a father to Hamlet. Furthermore, Hamlet would be the next chief: therefore he must stay to learn the things of a chief. Hamlet agreed to remain, and all the rest went off to drink beer."

While I paused, perplexed at how to render Hamlet's disgusted soliloquy to an audience convinced that Claudius and Gertrude had behaved in the best possible manner, one of the younger men asked me who had married the other wives of the dead chief.

"He had no other wives," I told him.

"But a chief must have many wives! How else can he brew beer and prepare food for all his guests?"

I said firmly that in our country even chiefs had only one wife, that they had servants to do their work, and that they paid them from tax money.

It was better, they returned, for a chief to have many wives and sons who would help him hoe his farms and feed his people; then everyone loved the chief who gave much and took nothing— taxes were a bad thing.

I agreed with the last comment, but for the rest fell back on their favorite way of fobbing off my questions: "That is the way it is done, so that is how we do it."

I decided to skip the soliloquy. Even if Claudius was here thought quite right to marry his brother's widow, there remained the poison motif, and I knew they would disapprove of fratricide. More hopefully I resumed, "That night Hamlet kept watch with the three who had seen his dead father. The dead chief again appeared, and although the others were afraid, Hamlet followed his dead father off to one side. When they were alone, Hamlet's dead father spoke."

"Omens can't talk!" The old man was emphatic.

"Hamlet's dead father wasn't an omen. Seeing him might have been an omen, but he was not." My audience looked as confused as I sounded. "It was Hamlet's dead father. It was a thing we call a 'ghost.'" I had to use the English word, for unlike many of the neighboring tribes, these people didn't believe in the survival after death of any individuating part of the personality.

"What is a 'ghost?' An omen?"

"No, a 'ghost' is someone who is dead but who walks around and can talk, and people can hear him and see him but not touch him."

They objected. "One can touch zombis."

"No, no! It was not a dead body the witches had animated to sacrifice and eat. No one else made Hamlet's dead father walk. He did it himself."

"Dead men can't walk," protested my audience as one man.

I was quite willing to compromise.

"A 'ghost' is the dead man's shadow."

But again they objected. "Dead men cast no shadows."

"They do in my country," I snapped.

[pagebreak]

The old man quelled the babble of disbelief that arose immediately and told me with that insincere, but courteous, agreement one extends to the fancies of the young, ignorant, and superstitious, "No doubt in your country the dead can also walk without being zombis." From the depths of his bag he produced a withered fragment of kola nut, bit off one end to show it wasn't poisoned, and handed me the rest as a peace offering.

"Anyhow," I resumed, "Hamlet's dead father said that his own brother, the one who became chief, had poisoned him. He wanted Hamlet to avenge him. Hamlet believed this in his heart, for he did not like his father's brother." I took another swallow of beer. "In the country of the great chief, living in the same homestead, for it was a very large one, was an important elder who was often with the chief to advise and help him. His name was Polonius. Hamlet was courting his daughter, but her father and her brother . . . [I cast hastily about for some tribal analogy] warned her not to let Hamlet visit her when she was alone on her farm, for he would be a great chief and so could not marry her."

"Why not?" asked the wife, who had settled down on the edge of the old man's chair. He frowned at her for asking stupid questions and growled, "They lived in the same homestead."

"That was not the reason," I informed them. "Polonius was a stranger who lived in the homestead because he helped the chief, not because he was a relative."

"Then why couldn't Hamlet marry her?"

"He could have," I explained, "but Polonius didn't think he would. After all, Hamlet was a man of great importance who ought to marry a chief's daughter, for in his country a man could have only one wife. Polonius was afraid that if Hamlet made love to his daughter, then no one else would give a high price for her."

"That might be true," remarked one of the shrewder elders, "but a chief's son would give his mistress's father enough presents and patronage to more than make up the difference. Polonius sounds like a fool to me."

"Many people think he was," I agreed. "Meanwhile Polonius sent his son Laertes off to Paris to learn the things of that country, for it was the homestead of a very great chief indeed. Because he was afraid that Laertes might waste a lot of money on beer and women and gambling, or get into trouble by fighting, he sent one of his servants to Paris secretly, to spy out what Laertes was doing. One day Hamlet came upon Polonius's daughter Ophelia. He behaved so oddly he frightened her. Indeed"—I was fumbling for words to express the dubious quality of Hamlet's madness—"the chief and many others had also noticed that when Hamlet talked one could understand the words but not what they meant. Many people thought that he had become mad." My audience suddenly became much more attentive. "The great chief wanted to know what was wrong with Hamlet, so he sent for two of Hamlet's age mates [school friends would have taken a long explanation] to talk to Hamlet and find out what troubled his heart. Hamlet, seeing that they had been bribed by the chief to betray him, told them nothing. Polonius, however, insisted that Hamlet was mad because he had been forbidden to see Ophelia, whom he loved."

"Why," inquired a bewildered voice, "should anyone bewitch Hamlet on that account?"

"Bewitch him?"

"Yes, only witchcraft can make anyone mad, unless, of course, one sees the beings that lurk in the forest."

I stopped being a storyteller and took out my notebook and demanded to be told more about these two causes of madness. Even while they spoke and I jotted notes, I tried to calculate the effect of this new factor on the plot. Hamlet had not been exposed to the beings that lurk in the forests. Only his relatives in the male line could bewitch him. Barring relatives not mentioned by Shakespeare, it had to be Claudius who was attempting to harm him. And, of course, it was.

For the moment I staved off questions by saying that the great chief also refused to believe that Hamlet was mad for the love of Ophelia and nothing else. "He was sure that something much more important was troubling Hamlet's heart."

"Now Hamlet's age mates," I continued, "had brought with them a famous storyteller. Hamlet decided to have this man tell the chief and all his homestead a story about a man who had poisoned his brother because he desired his brother's wife and wished to be chief himself. Hamlet was sure the great chief could not hear the story without making a sign if he was indeed guilty, and then he would discover whether his dead father had told him the truth."

The old man interrupted, with deep cunning, "Why should a father lie to his son?" he asked.

I hedged: "Hamlet wasn't sure that it really was his dead father." It was impossible to say anything, in that language, about devil-inspired visions.

"You mean," he said, "it actually was an omen, and he knew witches sometimes send false ones. Hamlet was a fool not to go to one skilled in reading omens and divining the truth in the first place. A man-who-sees-the-truth could have told him how his father died, if he really had been poisoned, and if there was witchcraft in it; then Hamlet could have called the elders to settle the matter."

The shrewd elder ventured to disagree. "Because his father's brother was a great chief, one-who-sees-the-truth might therefore have been afraid to tell it. I think it was for that reason that a friend of Hamlet's father—a witch and an elder—sent an omen so his friend's son would know. Was the omen true?"

"Yes," I said, abandoning ghosts and the devil; a witch-sent omen it would have to be. "It was true, for when the storyteller was telling his tale before all the homestead, the great chief rose in fear. Afraid that Hamlet knew his secret he planned to have him killed."

The stage set of the next bit presented some difficulties of translation. I began cautiously. "The great chief told Hamlet's mother to find out from her son what he knew. But because a woman's children are always first in her heart, he had the important elder Polonius hide behind a cloth that hung against the wall of Hamlet's mother's sleeping hut. Hamlet started to scold his mother for what she had done."

There was a shocked murmur from everyone. A man should never scold his mother.

"She called out in fear, and Polonius moved behind the cloth. Shouting, 'A rat!' Hamlet took his machete and slashed through the cloth." I paused for dramatic effect. "He had killed Polonius."

[pagebreak]

The old men looked at each other in supreme disgust. "That Polonius truly was a fool and a man who knew nothing! What child would not know enough to shout, 'It's me!'" With a pang, I remembered that these people are ardent hunters, always armed with bow, arrow, and machete; at the first rustle in the grass an arrow is aimed and ready, and the hunter shouts "Game!" If no human voice answers immediately, the arrow speeds on its way. Like a good hunter, Hamlet had shouted, "A rat!"

I rushed in to save Polonius's reputation. "Polonius did speak. Hamlet heard him. But he thought it was the chief and wished to kill him to avenge his father. He had meant to kill him earlier that evening...." I broke down, unable to describe to these pagans, who had no belief in individual afterlife, the difference between dying at one's prayers and dying "unhousell'd, disappointed, unaneled."

This time I had shocked my audience seriously. "For a man to raise his hand against his father's brother and the one who has become his father—that is a terrible thing. The elders ought to let such a man be bewitched."

I nibbled at my kola nut in some perplexity, then pointed out that after all the man had killed Hamlet's father.

"No," pronounced the old man, speaking less to me than to the young men sitting behind the elders. "If your father's brother has killed your father, you must appeal to your father's age mates: *they* may avenge him. No man may use violence against his senior relatives." Another thought struck him. "But if his father's brother had indeed been wicked enough to bewitch Hamlet and make him mad that would be a good story indeed, for it would be his fault that Hamlet, being mad, no longer had any sense and thus was ready to kill his father's brother."

There was a murmur of applause. Hamlet was again a good story to them, but it no longer seemed quite the same story to me. As I thought over the coming complications of plot and motive, I lost courage and decided to skim over dangerous ground quickly.

"The great chief," I went on, "was not sorry that Hamlet had killed Polonius. It gave him a reason to send Hamlet away, with his two treacherous age mates, with letters to a chief of a far country, saying that Hamlet should be killed. But Hamlet changed the writing on their papers, so that the chief killed his age mates instead." I encountered a reproachful glare from one of the men whom I had told undetectable forgery was not merely immoral but beyond human skill. I looked the other way.

"Before Hamlet could return, Laertes came back for his father's funeral. The great chief told him Hamlet had killed Polonius. Laertes swore to kill Hamlet because of this, and because his sister Ophelia, hearing her father had been killed by the man she loved, went mad and drowned in the river."

"Have you already forgotten what we told you?" The old man was reproachful. "One cannot take vengeance on a madman; Hamlet killed Polonius in his madness. As for the girl, she not only went mad, she was drowned. Only witches can make people drown. Water itself can't hurt anything. It is merely something one drinks and bathes in."

I began to get cross. "If you don't like the story, I'll stop."

The old man made soothing noises and himself poured me some more beer. "You tell the story well, and we are listening. But it is clear that the elders of your country have never told you what the story really means. No, don't interrupt! We believe you when you say your marriage customs are different, or your clothes and weapons. But people are the same everywhere; therefore, there are always witches and it is we, the elders, who know how witches work. We told you it was the great chief who wished to kill Hamlet, and now your own words have proved us right. Who were Ophelia's male relatives?"

"There were only her father and her brother." Hamlet was clearly out of my hands.

"There must have been many more; this also you must ask of your elders when you get back to your country. From what you tell us, since Polonius was dead, it must have been Laertes who killed Ophelia, although I do not see the reason for it."

We had emptied one pot of beer, and the old men argued the point with slightly tipsy interest. Finally one of them demanded of me, "What did the servant of Polonius say on his return?"

With difficulty I recollected Reynaldo and his mission. "I don't think he did return before Polonius was killed."

"Listen," said the elder, "and I will tell you how it was and how your story will go, then you may tell me if I am right. Polonius knew his son would get into trouble, and so he did. He had many fines to pay for fighting, and debts from gambling. But he had only two ways of getting money quickly. One was to marry off his sister at once, but it is difficult to find a man who will marry a woman desired by the son of a chief. For if the chief's heir commits adultery with your wife, what can you do? Only a fool calls a case against a man who will someday be his judge. Therefore Laertes had to take the second way: he killed his sister by witchcraft, drowning her so he could secretly sell her body to the witches."

I raised an objection. "They found her body and buried it. Indeed Laertes jumped into the grave to see his sister once more—so, you see, the body was truly there. Hamlet, who had just come back, jumped in after him."

"What did I tell you?" The elder appealed to the others. "Laertes was up to no good with his sister's body. Hamlet prevented him, because the chief's heir, like a chief, does not wish any other man to grow rich and powerful. Laertes would be angry, because he would have killed his sister without benefit to himself. In our country he would try to kill Hamlet for that reason. Is this not what happened?"

"More or less," I admitted. "When the great chief found Hamlet was still alive, he encouraged Laertes to try to kill Hamlet and arranged a fight with machetes between them. In the fight both

18

the young men were wounded to death. Hamlet's mother drank the poisoned beer that the chief meant for Hamlet in case he won the fight. When he saw his mother die of poison, Hamlet, dying, managed to kill his father's brother with his machete."

"You see, I was right!" exclaimed the elder.

"That was a very good story," added the old man, "and you told it with very few mistakes." There was just one more error, at the very end. The poison Hamlet's mother drank was obviously meant for the survivor of the fight, whichever it was. If Laertes had won, the great chief would have poisoned him, for no one would know that he arranged Hamlet's death. Then, too, he need not fear Laertes' witchcraft; it takes a strong heart to kill one's only sister by witchcraft.

"Sometime," concluded the old man, gathering his ragged toga about him, "you must tell us some more stories of your country. We, who are elders, will instruct you in their true meaning, so that when you return to your own land your elders will see that you have not been sitting in the bush, but among those who know things and who have taught you wisdom."

It is helpful to know a summary of Shakespeare's *Hamlet* if you have not read or seen the play. Here are links to summaries on Cliff Notes and Spark Notes: https://www.cliffsnotes.com/literature/h/hamlet/play-summary and http://www.sparknotes.com/shakespeare/hamlet/summary.html

You could Google this article and find a wide range of comments on it, from both professionals and non-professionals alike.

Universal Artistic Truths?

The main theme is that, although we believe there are some universal truths about human nature, experience of the world views of another culture can create some amazing surprises that challenge that belief. Anthropologists have a name for this which we call "cultural relativism." Bohannan had an English colleague who said that Shakespeare "was a very English poet, and one can easily misinterpret the universal by misunderstanding the particular." She disagreed and thought that "Human nature is pretty much the same the whole world over." There is some truth to the idea that certain famous works in one culture do not work in another. My Mexican mother understood Cervantes' *Don Quixote* in a way that I never could. I remember when the movie "Topsy-Turvy" came out (about the career of Gilbert and Sullivan) and I was in Holland working with archaeologists of the city of Nijmegen, which started out as a Roman legionary camp. My Dutch colleagues were excited to see the movie and then came to me terribly disappointed. I just pointed out that only native-English speakers could easily appreciate the niceties of the Gilbert and Sullivan partnership and that their famous expressions would lose something in translation. A Chinese musician I studied theory with once confessed that he loved all of Western music but simply could not figure out Western opera. I sympathized, given that Chinese opera seems very challenging even for a Western opera-lover.

Here is a little schematic of the problems between English Shakespeare's *Hamlet*, and the way that the Tiv in Africa could not figure it out.

Hamlet's Difficulties	Tiv Beliefs
Whether to believe a Ghost	There are no individual personalities after death
Marriage was too quick	One should marry a brother's wife quickly at death, "he did well"
Royal monogamy	Royal polygyny
I must avenge my father!	Avenging a death is not for a son but for the age mates

Oddly enough (or perhaps not!), the Tiv believe in the same universals as Bohannan: "We believe you when you say your marriage customs are different, or your clothes and weapons. But people are the same everywhere."

And, just as all peoples world-wide can be, the Tiv can also be ethnocentric: "Sometime you must tell us some more stories of your country. We, who are the elders, will instruct you in their true meaning."

Topsy-Turvydom

Commentators take the last quote and offer two opinions about it: 1) she told the story to the elders, but if she had told it to children or ordinary "citizens," it might have been accepted more favorably at face value. After all, most of us do not believe in ghosts, but we still understand and enjoy the story, accepting it that people in Shakespeare's time were more likely to have believed in ghosts; 2) the anthropologist Laura Bohannan was desperately trying to understand how the Tiv think about things, but it seems that the Tiv were not as interested in Western beliefs—at least the elders just wanted to "set straight" the outsider, perhaps thinking of themselves as guardians of Tiv cultural beliefs. There are people in our culture who are just as uninterested in other cultural beliefs and want to "set outsiders straight." We call that attitude "ethnocentrism," and it will come up again and again in later chapters.

On the other hand, the article does show us that there ARE some universals that we all share as humans. One commentator suggested that Bohannan's essay is "bursting with cultural convergences" and it is clear that what we find of interest in Hamlet: kinship, fratricide, revenge, justice, and madness are issues other cultures, such as the Tiv, also find interesting. Folklorists tell us that there are about 20 themes that are found cross-culturally in much story-telling. Everyone loves stories and finding out what they mean, because humans are creatures that attribute meaning to the world constantly. It also seems that another universal is ethnocentrism—probably no cultural group lacks it. Another characteristic that seems universal is the striving for morality, the recognition of "right" and "wrong." The biggest surprise was how different this could be in terms of the story of Hamlet. Marrying too quickly is often considered "wrong" in Judeo-Christian belief, but was considered "right" to the Tiv, who were concerned that a man's line should continue through his brother, so no delay is warranted.

But one anthropological commentator suggests that the whole question can be quite topsy-turvy. How appropriate that Gilbert and Sullivan were considered the kings of "topsy-turvydom!"

CONCLUSION: WRAP-UP

The heart of anthropology is the realization that people do things differently in other cultures and that people in every culture also think that the way they do things is the best way. Anthropology is practiced by human beings who are just as surprised by the first element as anyone else, and also have to admit that they probably ultimately believe the same thing about the second element as other people do. So, the central task of anthropology is to accept the realization of the first element and courageously face the admission of the second element. The key to modern anthropology is a concept called "reflexivity" which calls upon anthropologists to reflect on the motivations for all their actions and the way they carry out their studies. So, anthropologists must constantly take "selfies" of their own state of mind and how it might influence their approach to "the Other," the academic summary concept of individuals different from ourselves. However, consider how both elements, understood as a general failure to accept it that other cultures do things differently, coupled with the general attitude that the way one's own cultures do things is the best way, constitute two very crucial reasons for why there are such intransigent world problems facing us today. It doesn't take a lot of imagination to figure out how, in international affairs, if one nation says "our way is best and your way is not good" is going to be a recipe for trouble. That is the issue we will turn to in Chapter 10, and appreciate how a Greek writer understood and wrote about this 2,500 years ago. In the next unit, Chapter 2, we will continue with the theme of understanding that cultures do things differently, and consider how the study of other cultures might be carried out and what it sounds like when completed.

ACTIVITIES

Activity for Readings #1 and #2: as a class, refer to your Schema activation responses and discuss them in light of the two ancient authors to answer the following question: *did Aristotle and Herodotus provide the foundation for anthropology according to your impressions of what anthropology does? Why or why not?*

Activity for Reading #3: split into small groups and come up with two to three answers to the following questions: Herodotus seemed to view the Egyptians as the complete opposite of non-Egyptians.

- What mistakes do you think Herodotus made because of this "opposite" way of viewing people? That is, in what way did he most go wrong?
- Do you think it is a good general approach to view things as opposites, or in opposition, to one another when trying to compare them? Why or why not?
- What are some examples of this "opposite" approach in our world today?
- In your opinion, what happens when people view things as "the opposite" to themselves?

Activity for Reading #4: in small groups, come up with three characteristics of the Hamlet story that might be universal after all (consult the play summaries if necessary), and come up with three characteristics that seem clearly NOT to be universal. Lastly, brainstorm three ways in which this article reflects how some current world problems arise.

SOURCES

The text for Aristotle is from the 1939 edition of the Nichomachean Ethics, Harvard University Press, Loeb Classical Library, edited by H. Rackham. The text for Herodotus is from the 1926-1938 Histories, Harvard University Press, Loeb Classical Library, volume II, edited by A.D. Godley. The information on Herodotus comes from three main sources: 1) a draft of a translation and commentary on Herodotus being produced by Peter Green; 2) the work of of W. W. How and J. Wells *A Commentary on Herodotus*, Oxford, Clarendon Press, 1928; and 3) David Asheri, Alan Lloyd and Aldo Corcella, edited by Oswyn Murray and Alfonso Moreno, with a contribution by Maria Brosius, translated by Barbara Graziosi, Matteo Rossetti, Carlotta Dus, and Vanessa Cazzato: *A Commentary on Herodotus Books I-IV*, Oxford University Press, 2007. An important commentary on Shakespeare in the Bush (which is quoted) is Michelle Scalise Sugiyama 2003 Cultural Variation is Part of Human Nature: Literary Universals, Context-Sensitivity, and "Shakespeare in the Bush" *Human Nature* 14(4): 383-396. The variety of definitions of culture are found in Alfred Kroeber and Clyde Kluckhohn 1952 *Culture ; a critical review of concepts and definitions* Papers of the Peabody Museum of American Archaeology and Ethnology, Harvard University v. 47, no. 1.

Chapter 2

The Anthropological Approach: Expect the Unexpected

OBJECTIVES

- Experience what happens when one's own culture is put under the microscope in the way that anthropology has traditionally analyzed another culture.
- Examine whether the supposedly dispassionate analytic consideration of another culture may inadvertently cause problems.
- Analyze the significance of cultural relativism in terms of the modern concern with universal human rights and how anthropologists work to try to identify problems and solutions in a proper understanding of cultural context, and how all contexts are subject to the need to respect human rights.
- Analyze whether humor is an effective way to consider an important theoretical concept, or whether it seems like trivializing something important.

KEY TERMS

Cultural relativism: the key anthropological belief that elements of every culture need to be understood in terms of the culture itself, and not be judged in terms of outside value systems.

Critical Cultural Relativism: the idea that, although anthropologists accept the necessity for cultural relativism, it is not absolute; cultural features must be assessed against the standard of whether or not a particular cultural features promotes, or works against, basic human rights.

Emic: approaching elements of a culture through the eyes of members of that culture.

Etic: approaching elements of culture through the eyes of an outside, neutral observer.

Culture Shock: the discomfort experienced when exposed to another culture, usually felt upon arrival in another cultural context.

Reverse Culture Shock: seeing one's own culture in a surprising and disconcerting new light, that as seen by an outside observer, and being shocked at that portrait of one's own culture.

SCHEMA ACTIVATION ACTIVITY

Write down your thoughts in answer to the following question: ***Why do you think we enjoy talking about another culture in exotic terms? Is it because it's a form of "gossip"?***

(Save these to share later in your discussion sections.)

INTRODUCTION

In this Chapter, you will start with a classic article on the culture called the "Nacirema." That article is pretty old, but still a favorite for readers such as this one. But here, we include another article updating current anthropology's take on that classic article. Then, we will explore cultural relativism and come to appreciate why that concept in anthropology is both necessary and needs to be tempered by the realization that anthropologists ultimately must come to be advocates for their main subject of study—human being. Exploring the problems of the contemporary world requires that anthropologists once and for all make it clear that the sole standard of approach to humans is one in which there is respect for universal human rights.

The University of Michigan anthropologist Horace Miner wrote a famous article about a mystery culture called the "Nacirema." The tone of the article was a very professional ethnographic etic account of this unfamiliar culture. See what you think. Then, a recent anthropological consideration of the Nacirema phenomenon is presented. The two readings should be discussed together.

BODY RITUAL AMONG THE NACIREMA
By Horace Miner

The anthropologist has become so familiar with the diversity of ways in which different peoples behave in similar situations that he is not apt to be surprised by even the most exotic customs. In fact, if all of the logically possible combinations of behavior have not been found somewhere in the world, he is apt to suspect that they must be present in some yet undescribed tribe. This point has, in fact, been expressed with respect to clan organization by Murdock. In this light, the magical beliefs and practices of the Nacirema present such unusual aspects that it seems desirable to describe them as an example of the extremes to which human behavior can go.

Professor Linton first brought the ritual of the Nacirema to the attention of anthropologists twenty years ago, but the culture of this people is still very poorly understood. They are a North American group living in the territory between the Canadian Creel the Yaqui and Tarahumare of Mexico, and the Carib and Arawak of the Antilles. Little is known of their origin, although tradition states that they came from the east....

Nacirema culture is characterized by a highly developed market economy which has evolved in a rich natural habitat. While much of the people's time is devoted to economic pursuits, a large part of the fruits of these labors and a considerable portion of the day are spent in ritual activity. The focus of this activity is the human body, the appearance and health of which loom as a dominant concern in the ethos of the people. While such a concern is certainly not unusual, its ceremonial aspects and associated philosophy are unique.

The fundamental belief underlying the whole system appears to be that the human body is ugly and that its natural tendency is to debility and disease. Incarcerated in such a body, man's only hope is to avert these characteristics through the use of the powerful influences of ritual and ceremony. Every household has one or more shrines devoted to this purpose. The more powerful individuals in the society have several shrines in their houses and, in fact, the opulence of a house is often referred to in terms of the number of such ritual centers it possesses. Most houses are of wattle and daub construction, but the shrine rooms of the more wealthy are walled with stone. Poorer families imitate the rich by applying pottery plaques to their shrine walls. While each family has at least one such shrine, the rituals associated with it are not family ceremonies but are private and secret. The rites are normally only discussed with children, and then only during the period when they are being initiated into these mysteries. I was able, however, to establish sufficient rapport with the natives to examine these shrines and to have the rituals described to me.

The focal point of the shrine is a box or chest which is built into the wall. In this chest are kept the many charms and magical potions without which no native believes he could live. These preparations are secured from a variety of specialized practitioners. The most powerful of these are the medicine men, whose assistance must be rewarded with substantial gifts. However, the medicine men do not provide the curative potions for their clients, but decide what the ingredients should be and then write them down in an ancient and secret language. This writing is understood only by the medicine men and by the herbalists who, for another gift, provide the required charm.

The charm is not disposed of after it has served its purpose, but is placed in the charm box of the household shrine. As these magical material s are specific for certain ills, and the real or imagined maladies of the people are many, the charm-box is usually full to overflowing. The magical packets are so numerous that people forget what their purposes were and fear to use them again. While the natives are very vague on this point, we can only assume that the idea in retaining all the old magical materials is that their presence in the charm-box, before which the body rituals are conducted, will in some way protect the worshipper.

Beneath the charm-box is a small font. Each day every member of the family, in succession, enters the shrine room, bows his head before the charm-box, mingles different sorts of holy water in the font, and proceeds with a brief rite of ablution. The holy waters are secured from the Water Temple of the community, where the priests conduct elaborate ceremonies to make the liquid ritually pure.

In the hierarchy of magical practitioners, and below the medicine men in prestige, are specialists whose designation is best translated "holy-mouth-men." The Nacirema have an almost pathological horror of and fascination with the mouth, the condition of which is believed to have a supernatural influence on all social relationships. Were it not for the rituals of the mouth, they believe that their teeth would fall out, their gums bleed, their jaws shrink, their friends desert them, and their lovers reject them. They also believe that a strong relationship exists between oral and moral characteristics. For example, there is a ritual ablution of the mouth for children which is supposed to improve their moral fiber.

The daily body ritual performed by everyone includes a mouth-rite. Despite the fact that these people are so punctilious about care of the mouth, this rite involves a practice which strikes the uninitiated stranger as revolting. It was reported to me that the ritual consists of inserting a small bundle of hog hairs into the mouth, along with certain magical powders, and then moving the bundle in a highly formalized series of gestures.

In addition to the private mouth-rite, the people seek out a holy-mouth-man once or twice a year. These practitioners have an impressive set of paraphernalia, consisting of a variety of augers, awls, probes, and prods. The use of these objects in the exorcism of the evils of the mouth involves almost unbelievable ritual torture of the client. The holy-mouth-man open the client's mouth and, using the above mentioned tools, enlarges any holes which decay may have created in the teeth. Magical materials are put into these holes. If there are no naturally occurring holes in the teeth, large sections of one or more teeth are gouged out so that the supernatural substance can be applied. In the client's view, the purpose of these ministrations is to arrest decay and to draw friends. The extremely sacred and traditional character of the rite is evident in the fact that the natives return to the holy--mouth-men year after year, despite the fact that their teeth continue to decay.

It is to be hoped that, when a thorough study of the Nacirema is made, there will be careful inquiry into the personality structure of these people. One has but to watch the gleam in the eye of a holy-mouth-man, as he jabs an awl into an exposed nerve, to suspect that a certain amount of sadism is involved. If this can be established, a very interesting pattern emerges, for most of the population shows definite masochistic tendencies. It was to these that Professor Linton referred in discussing a distinctive part of the daily body ritual which is performed only by men. This part of the rite involves scraping and lacerating the surface of the face with a sharp instrument. Special women's rites are performed only four times during each lunar month, but what they lack in frequency is made up in barbarity. As part of this ceremony, women bake their heads in small ovens for about an hour. The theoretically interesting point is that what seems to be a preponderantly masochistic people have developed sadistic specialists.

The medicine men have an imposing temple, or *latipso*, in every community of any size. The more elaborate ceremonies required to treat very sick patients can only be performed at this temple. These ceremonies involve not only the thaumaturge but a permanent group of vestal maidens who move sedately about the temple chambers in distinctive costume and head- dress.

The *latipso* ceremonies are so harsh that it is phenomenal that a fair proportion of the really sick natives who enter the temple. The concept of culture ever recover. Small children whose indoctrination is still incomplete have been known to resist attempts to take them to the temple because "that is where you go to die." Despite this fact, sick adults are not only willing but eager to undergo the protracted ritual purification, if they can afford to do so. No matter how ill the supplicant or how grave the emergency, the guardians of many temples will not admit a client if he cannot give a rich gift to the custodian. Even after one has gained admission and survived the ceremonies, the guardians will not permit the neophyte to leave until he makes still another gift.

The supplicant entering the temple is first stripped of all his or her clothes. In everyday life the Nacirema avoids exposure of his body and its natural functions. Bathing and excretory acts are performed only in the secrecy of the household shrine, where they are ritualized as part of the body-rites. Psychological shock results from the fact that body secrecy is suddenly lost upon entry into the *latipso*. A man, whose own wife has never seen him in an excretory act, suddenly finds himself naked and assisted by a vestal maiden while he performs his natural functions into a sacred vessel. This sort of ceremonial treatment is necessitated by the fact that the excreta are used by a diviner to ascertain the course and nature of the client's sickness. Female clients, on the other hand, find their naked bodies are subjected to the scrutiny, manipulation and prodding of the medicine men.

Few supplicants in the temple are well enough to do anything but lie on their hard beds. The daily ceremonies, like the rites of the holy-mouth-men, involve discomfort and torture. With ritual precision, the vestals awaken their miserable charges each dawn and roll them about on their beds of pain while performing ablutions, in the formal movements of which the maidens are highly trained. At other times they insert magic wands in the supplicant's mouth or force him to eat substances which are supposed to be healing. From time to time the medicine men come to their clients and jab magically treated needles into their flesh. The fact that these temple ceremonies may not cure, and may even kill the neophyte, in no way decreases the people's faith in the medicine men.

There remains one other kind of practitioner, known as a "listener." This witchdoctor has the power to exorcise the devils that lodge in the heads of people who have been bewitched. The Nacirema believe that parents bewitch their own children. Mothers are particularly suspected of putting a curse on children while teaching them the secret body rituals. The counter-magic of the witchdoctor is unusual in its lack of ritual. The patient simply tells the "listener" all his troubles and fears, beginning with the earliest difficulties he can remember. The memory displayed by the Nacirema in these exorcism sessions is truly remarkable. It is not uncommon for the patient to bemoan the rejection he felt upon being weaned as a babe, and a few individuals even see their troubles going back to the traumatic effects of their own birth.

In conclusion, mention must be made of certain practices which have their base in native esthetics but which depend upon the pervasive aversion to the natural body and its functions. There are ritual fasts to make fat people thin and ceremonial feasts to make thin people fat. Still other rites are used to make women's breasts larger if they are small, and smaller if they are large. General dissatisfaction with breast shape is symbolized in the fact that the ideal form is virtually outside the range of human variation. A few women afflicted with almost inhuman hyper-mammary development are so idolized that they make a handsome living by simply going from village to village and permitting the natives to stare at them for a fee.

Reference has already been made to the fact that excretory functions are ritualized, routinized, and relegated to secrecy. Natural reproductive functions are similarly distorted. Intercourse is taboo as a topic and scheduled as an act. Efforts are made to avoid pregnancy by the use of magical materials or by limiting intercourse to certain phases of the moon. Conception is actually very infrequent. When pregnant, women dress so as to hide their condition. Parturition takes place in secret, without friends or relatives to assist, and the majority of women do not nurse their infants.

Our review of the ritual life of the Nacirema has certainly shown them to be a magic-ridden people. It is hard to understand how they have managed to exist so long under the burdens which they have imposed upon themselves. But even such exotic customs as these take on real meaning when they are viewed with the insight provided by Malinowski when he wrote:

"Looking from far and above, from our high places of safety in the developed civilization, it is easy to see all the crudity and irrelevance of magic. But without its power and guidance early man could not have mastered his practical difficulties as he has done, nor could man have advanced to the higher stages of civilization."

Social-Science Fiction: The Genesis and Legacy of Horace Miner's "Body Ritual among the Nacirema"

Mark Burde

ABSTRACT In this article, I present the first comprehensive examination and analysis of what remains, nearly sixty years after its initial publication, not only one of the most frequently read articles in the history of *American Anthropologist* but also one of the more widely circulated English-language pieces of 20th-century social science. Combining archival research at Horace Miner's home institution, interviews with family members and former colleagues, and examination of over 50 partial or full anthological reproductions of the piece spanning five decades, I examine the genesis and reception of the work with an eye to unpacking the reasons for its extraordinary longevity. My conclusions are, first, that the work has been read in a surprisingly atomized rather than holistic manner, resulting in a misunderstanding of Miner's likely intentions. Second, the work has accumulated diametrically opposed readings as either illustrative of or, since the late 1960s, radically skeptical of basic ethnographic method. Third, this and other paradoxes inherent in the composition and reception of the work, combined with its comic traits, qualify it as a latter-day example of the carnivalesque. [*Horace Miner, "Body Ritual among the Nacirema," reception study, ethnographic critique, the carnivalesque*]

RÉSUMÉ Ce travail propose la première analyse de fond de l'article qui, presque soixante ans après son apparition dans cette revue, figure souvent parmi les plus lus de l'histoire de cette publication. Au vingtième siècle, ce texte est aussi l'un de ceux dans le champ des sciences sociales en langue anglaise ayant connu la plus large diffusion. J'examine la genèse et la réception de « Body Ritual among the Nacirema » à l'aide de documents originaux, à partir de l'examen détaillé d'une cinquantaine de reproductions anthologiques du texte. Celles–ci furent publiées durant cinq décennies. Il fut réalisé sur la base également d'entretiens avec d'anciens collègues de Miner et de membres de sa famille. J'ai cherché à déceler les raisons de sa remarquable longévité. J'en conclus, tout d'abord, que le texte a souvent été interprété aux dépens d'une compréhension globale. En second lieu, que furent attribuées à l'article des significations diamétralement opposées. Celui–ci illustrerait, ou remettrait radicalement en cause, selon le cas, les préceptes de base de la méthode ethnographique. Enfin, cette réception paradoxale du texte refléterait en quelque sorte une réalité inhérente à sa composition qui, jointe à sa dimension comique, confère à l'ouvrage une dimension carnavalesque moderne. [*Horace Miner, "Body Ritual among the Nacirema," étude de réception, critique ethnographique, le carnavalesque*]

RESUMEN En este artículo, presento la primera examinación exhaustiva y el análisis de lo que permanece, cerca de 60 años después de su publicación inicial, no sólo uno de los artículos más frecuentemente leídos en la historia del *American Anthropologist* sino también una de las piezas más ampliamente circuladas en lenguaje inglés de las ciencias sociales del siglo XX. Combinando investigación de archivos en la institución base de Miner, entrevistas con miembros de la familia y antiguos colegas, y examinación de más de 50 reproducciones antológicas parciales o totales de la pieza abarcando cinco décadas, examino la génesis y recepción del trabajo enfocado en lograr examinar de cerca las razones por su extraordinaria longevidad. Mis conclusiones son, primero, que el trabajo ha sido leído de una manera sorprendentemente atomizada en vez de una manera holística resultando en una mala interpretación de las intenciones probables de Miner. Segundo, el trabajo ha acumulado diametralmente opuestas lecturas como ilustrativas de o, desde finales de los 1960s, radicalmente escépticas del método etnográfico básico. Y tercero, ésta y otras paradojas inherentes a la composición y recepción del trabajo, combinadas con sus características cómicas, lo cualifica como un ejemplo de lo carnavalesco de nuestros días. [*Horace Miner, "Rito del cuerpo entre los Nacirema," estudio recepción, crítica etnográfica, lo carnavalesco*]

We have, with no little success, sought to keep the world off balance; pulling out rugs, upsetting tea tables, setting off firecrackers. It has been the office of others to reassure; ours to unsettle. Australopithecenes, Tricksters, Clicks, Megaliths—we hawk the anomalous, peddle the strange. Merchants of astonishment.
—Clifford Geertz, Distinguished Lecture: Anti Anti-Relativism [1984]

THE ACCIDENTAL CLASSIC

In the most recent year for which figures are available (2012), the second-most frequently downloaded article from the AnthroSource database was Lila Abu-Lughod's "Do Muslim Women Really Need Saving?" of September 2002. More than 5,000 users read or were instructed to read this prominent Columbia University ethnographer's meditation on the intersections of anthropology, gender politics, cultural identity, and interreligious conflict composed at a particularly tense moment in world affairs. Topping the list, however, with more than double the number of downloads as Abu-Lughod's piece, was Horace Miner's 1956 classic, "Body Ritual among the Nacirema."[1] No single data point, to be sure, should ever be overinterpreted ("Nacirema" was only seventh on the list the previous year), and, in any case, different evaluative criteria render different rankings, with far more citations attributed to Abu-Lughod's article than to Miner's by Google Scholar, for example.

Miner himself, a 44-year-old tenured professor at the University of Michigan when the article appeared, would not have minded being surpassed by Abu-Lughod. Several of his former colleagues recall him expressing dismay and even exasperation later in life at being known more for the accidental success of his 2,300-word humor piece than for his three major monographs and numerous articles. Walter Goldschmidt—who as newly appointed editor-in-chief of *American Anthropologist* had decided after some hesitation to publish the spoof, effectively overruling the decision of his predecessor, Sol Tax, to reject it—testified shortly before his recent death to having heard Miner voice similar sentiments (Goldschmidt 2012:119). Presumably the immediacy of the reactions elicited in the popular press in particular took Miner aback and portended a stylistic albatross around his neck. By 1950s standards, the piece (as we would say today) went viral within weeks.[2]

Readers unfamiliar with "Body Ritual among the Nacirema" may wish to consult Miner's article before proceeding, lest the bluntly prosaic nature of the following synopsis spoil the author's intended effect. Sandwiched between an application of Durkheimian notions of the sacred to the behavior of the mentally ill (Goffman 1956) and a reassessment of intercontinental diffusion patterns of aboriginal fish poisons (Quigley 1956), the seventh article of the June 1956 issue of *American Anthropologist* promised readers a description of the people of its title, whose mores were said to illustrate "the extremes to which human behavior can go" (Miner 1956:503). Over the course of 20 paragraphs of disciplined deadpan delivery, Miner proceeded to describe contemporary American ("Nacirema") culture from the standpoint of a zealous and overearnest ethnologist.[3] The article presents cherished national myths, various hygienic practices, and visits to doctors, dentists, pharmacists, psychiatrists, hospitals, and hairdressers as though they were startling ethnographic discoveries being described and interpreted for the first time.[4]

Nearly 60 years later, the Nacirema *charm-box* (medicine cabinet) and daily *mouth-rite* (tooth brushing), their *holy-mouth-men* (dentists) and *listeners* (therapists), along with Notgnihsaw, the *latipso*, and other exotic-sounding anadromes of exceedingly familiar terms have not aged excessively and continue to find broad new nonspecialist readerships. Assuredly the work's staying power lies first and foremost in its instructional value. It is entertaining and witty, with gag upon gag carried off in deft parody of the participant-observer form being imitated. These traits, along with the article's capacity to initiate mass audiences to a key concept of ethnographic analysis—cultural relativism as an antidote to ethnocentrism—give the text uncommon didactic utility. The icing on the pedagogical cake has long been the rare chance "Nacirema" affords to orchestrate moments of sudden Gestalt shift, of abrupt reassignment of signifiers to signifieds in young adult minds, often before the very eyes of the knowing instructor, momentary merchant of astonishment. The force of the mental tea-tables upset has been enough to drive young people the world over to web chronicle the nature of the firecracker moment and to plaster the Internet with their amazement.[5]

The work has almost never been taken seriously, however, in the research literature, including, as noted above, by its author. To be sure, the piece spawned a subgenre of noncomic inquiry premised on the use of the Nacirema motif as a stock heuristic device of defamiliarization (e.g., Kimmel 2006), but more representative of learned opinion is the assertion that the article is "a sleight of hand" with "the feel of a trick" resulting in naught but "a flash of defamiliarizing amusement" (Marcus and Fischer 1986:140), or that it constitutes mere in-group hijinks or "intramural japes" (Geertz 1988:108), or that it typifies an ahistorical anthropological "gambit" in which "a set of cute references" are substituted for nuanced cultural understanding (Di Leonardo 1998:60).

Yet "Body Ritual among the Nacirema" can legitimately stake a claim to a role in the history of the discipline. It built upon and probably accelerated, however facetiously, a number of major developments in the anthropology of the early to mid–20th century—from what might be termed the corporeal turn in cultural inquiry, best exemplified by the work of Mary Douglas (1966) and Michel Foucault (1963) and already implicit in the work of Robert Hertz (1928) and Margaret Mead and Frances Macgregor (1951), to the greater formalization of the autoethnography performed on U.S. society (Hayano 1979; Spradley and Rynkiewich 1975), a mode of inquiry exemplified by Allison Davis and colleagues (1941) and Hortense Powdermaker (1950) that dates back to the 1910s (Di Leonardo 1998:27–28). The article also presciently anticipated the countercultural moment of the 1960s and 1970s—in spelling common terms in reverse, for example, it ironically literalized the denigration of unindustrialized cultures as "backward"—as well as the poststructuralist preoccupation with the subject positionality of the anthropological observer and rejection of the premise of transparently self-evident cultural or behavioral acts. Insofar as it appears (though probably was not intended) to question some foundational precepts of the discipline that it invokes, it could also be counted as an important early expression of a key precept of public anthropology.[6]

The premise of this investigation, which presents the first detailed examination of the genesis and reception of one of the most widely read and distributed pieces of social science writing of the past 75 years, is that any learned journal article having known hundreds of thousands of readers is performing important cultural work deserving of closer inspection. On the basis of examination of approximately fifty of the one hundred or so partial or full reprints of the piece that have appeared since 1956, complemented by archival research done at Miner's home institution, as well as by interviews with surviving colleagues and family members, I have come to three interrelated findings. The first is that, like most classics, "Nacirema" means different things to different people, anthologized as the case may be for its lessons on social structure (Henslin 1988:xv), the importance of culture (Ogburn and Nimkoff 1958:69), the socially constructed nature of the normal (Branaman 2001:11), pathology and illness (Folta and Deck 1979:297), and criminal deviance (Hagan 2011:93), or, most idiosyncratically, for its putative New Age valorization of magic (Burrill and Fast 1983:339). As an unfortunate consequence, a multifaceted text has been greatly singularized over six decades, sometimes pruned down in any given presentation to monovocal extracts, with thematically essential components like the article's three mock references treated with some frequency as ancillary at best.

Second, almost all published readings of "Nacirema" fall into one of two opposing camps: the work is held to be illustrative of the promise of anthropological inquiry or, antithetically, as a challenge to its basic claims. Although the former stance is considerably more common ("Nacirema," for example, illustrates "in parody form how an anthropological perspective can help us see ourselves in a new light" [Dundes 1968:433] or how the ethnocentrism of U.S. readers "prevents them from seeing their own culture as anything other than normal and natural" [Ferraro 2004:1], or it simply demonstrates "the utility of the ethnographic approach" [Bonder et al. 2002:11]), the piece has also been regularly interpreted since the late 1960s as either a cautionary tale or an out-and-out indictment of ethnology's presumed failings and questionable presuppositions. To one anthologist, it is a demonstration of "how inferences appear when they are presented as reality" (Abrahamson 1969:2); to another, it is "a test case of the objectivity of ethnographic description" (Angeloni 2005:ix); and, to a third, it is an example of how U.S. anthropologists tend to substitute "alleged correlation" for actual causation (P. Rose 1972:45).[7] Yet another commentator finds in "Nacirema" a reminder that "even seasoned outside ethnographers, such as Malinowski and Mead, have misunderstood, misinterpreted, or inaccurately described important features of native life and culture" (Hayano 1979:102).

Last, this dualistic reception, combined with the tenor and contents of the article itself, argues in favor of granting "Nacirema" the status of latter-day carnivalesque work as the term is used in pre- and early-modern European cultural studies (e.g., Bakhtin 1984a, 1984b; Burke 1978:191).[8] The piece is most evidently carnivalesque in its form and content: it momentarily and ostentatiously suspends norms of professional seriousness; satirically exaggerates, among other things, U.S. hyperhygienism and the alleged cupidity and sadism of the medical and dental professions, respectively; parodically imitates from its title onward a highly codified and instantly recognizable official discourse (in this case, the participant-observer ethnographic report); relies on sudden and radical shifts of perspective; and temporarily inverts habitual power relationships, with the dominant Anglo-American culture being discussed in analytical terms ordinarily reserved for cultural Others such as aboriginal peoples. At the center of it all is a grotesque body defined variously by its decay, defecatory excretions, or hypermammary development.[9]

Less self-evidently, however, when read in the broader context of its creation and reception, "Nacirema" also shows the oxymoronic mixture of frivolity and seriousness, of evanescent comic meaning and trenchant social bite, that constitute the two sides to the historical carnivalesque in the Western tradition. As a result, the work has managed to meld comedy with consequence in a manner rarely— if ever—achieved by other examples of the scientific spoof genre that Miner helped popularize.[10] In the following pages, I shall make the case in support of these first and second claims and briefly explore the implications of the third. As a tribute to Miner between the 20th anniversary of his having succumbed to Alzheimer's disease in November of 1993 at age 81 and the 60th anniversary of the publication of the piece in 1956, I shall argue that when resituated in the context of Miner's life and career "Nacirema" deserves consideration not, of course, as a serious piece of research in itself but, rather, as a more evocative reflection than is generally acknowledged on the profession whose practices it ludically evokes.

HORACE MINER, PLAYFUL PRAGMATIST

Horace Mitchell Miner was born in St. Paul, Minnesota, in 1912 but soon moved with his family to Louisville, where his father had been appointed professor of psychology at the University of Kentucky. There the younger Miner studied zoology and archaeology, receiving his B.A. in 1933, and immediately thereafter moved on to the University of Chicago to pursue a Ph.D. in anthropology under the direction of Robert Redfield. Initially hired as an instructor in 1937 by what is now known as Wayne State University in Detroit, Miner moved to the University of Michigan after World War II—during which he had served for three years as a counter-intelligence officer—becoming a tenured associate professor of sociology and anthropology at Michigan in 1947 (Griffin 1995:290). During his brief stay in Detroit, Miner may well have had occasion to familiarize himself with a social organization founded in the 1920s by the city's black bourgeoisie and monied class, the Nacirema Club, conceived of as an Afro-American analogue to the city's leading all-white social clubs. (It seems unlikely, on the other hand, that he would have had reason to be familiar with the Nacirema Steamship Corporation, a Delaware company at least as old as the social club.) Between 1951 and his 1980 retirement, which was hastened by the onset of the dementia that would lead to his death 13 years later, Miner held a joint appointment in sociology and anthropology at Michigan.

While at Chicago, Miner met and married Agnes Murphy, a fellow graduate student in Germanic philology who would become a research partner in many of his projects, including his doctoral dissertation and first book, entitled St. Denis: A French-Canadian Parish (republished in 1963), and his second and third major monographs, The Primitive City of Timbuctoo (Miner 1953) and Oasis and Casbah: Algerian Culture and Personality in Change, coauthored by Miner's colleague George A. De Vos (Miner and De Vos 1960). Secondary work of Miner's included a 100-page study of 1940s rural U.S. culture entitled Culture and Agriculture: An Anthropological Study of a Corn Belt County (Miner 1949a), underwritten by a division of the U.S. Department of Agriculture, and numerous articles.

Miner worked within the functionalist paradigm in which he had been trained at Chicago, and in this sense his studies were representative of the Malinowskian ethnographic method ascendant in early to mid–20th century U.S. cultural anthropology, with a heavy admixture of A. R. Radcliffe-Brown's influence. The St. Denis book, for example, investigated rural Quebec life from a multitude of cultural angles (territorial versus genealogical moieties, religion, control of nature, and so on) and was replete with descriptive detail. ("No farmer even wants a car, because of the upkeep. The work horse can be hitched to the buggy at no expense whatever and can draw the sleigh when autos cannot be used at all" [Miner 1963:43]). Miner was especially influenced by his advisor's interest in the polar binary of rural versus urban as a heuristic device, and both the Quebec book of 1939 and the Timbuktu ("Timbuctoo") study of 1953 were deemed by reviewers of the time, with few exceptions, to be admirably innovative in applying and rethinking this classic division.

By all accounts a man of a pleasantly even temperament, neither charismatic nor given to self-aggrandizement (he appears not to have directed a single doctoral dissertation), Miner earned a reputation among colleagues as down-to-earth and self-effacing. His personnel file at the University of Michigan reveals a man of playful disposition: a postcard Miner sent to his close friend and fellow anthropologist James B. Griffin on arrival in Morocco for a research visit, for example, has a color photo of a buxom belly dancer reclining on a divan in skimpy performance regalia; on the text side, Miner provides his new address, requests some extra copies of his Algeria book for distribution to local functionaries, and then concludes with the following line: "As you can see from the picture, I can hardly wait to get to work" (Miner 1967). Miner was also capable of a deft verbal pirouette when the situation called for it: later in his career, one of his reports on a recent set of students' seminar evaluations opens self-deprecatingly with "I recognize that the average opinion of my students is that I am no better than an average teacher" (Miner 1973). All evidence suggests that he loved performing fieldwork and had a streak of the adventurer in him: his daughter and only child Denise, named after the Quebec hamlet in which she was conceived, reports that her father once described fieldwork to her as, in essence, "being paid to be a grown-up Eagle scout" (conversation with author, January 23, 2013), and the research for his Algeria book was in many respects a continuation of his movements throughout North Africa as an aide to General Omar Bradley during World War II.

Miner's inclinations thus tended more toward the applied than the theoretical, more the social and cultural than the coldly empirical, more the interdisciplinary than the disciplinarily doctrinaire. He had in fact been hired at Michigan by the then-chairman of the sociology department Robert Angell for his competence in social anthropology in hopes that the broad interweaving of various social science disciplines that Angell had come to value at Harvard could be replicated at Michigan (Steinmetz 2007:345). Likewise, the federal government had recruited Miner shortly after the war to write *Culture and Agriculture* (Miner 1949a) so that policy decisions might be made on the ostensibly sound basis of fact. He reputedly mailed a copy of *Oasis and Casbah* (Miner and De Vos 1960) to Charles de Gaulle at the end of the Algerian war for independence in the early 1960s to offer an evidence-based analysis of the myriad problems that had beset the colonial power there (Griffin 1995:290). His composition of "Body Ritual among the Nacirema" probably coincided with his tenure as president of the Society for Applied Anthropology (1954 to 1955). In the preface to the reissued edition of his Quebec book, moreover, he briefly rebutted a critic by asserting that his research had not been undertaken "to illustrate or to 'test' any social typology" (Miner 1963:vii), thereby foregrounding his preference for pragmatics over theory.

MINER THE PARODIST

All of the common threads of Miner's proclivities are well illustrated by what is in many respects the largely unknown twin to the "Nacirema" piece, a wittily satirical commentary on the status of the social sciences in the Cold War–era university published in *Human Organization* in 1960. Parodying the form of both the newspaper advice column and the 1950s instructional film, "Researchmanship: The Feedback of Expertise" insouciantly mocks and ridicules the naked instrumentalization of U.S. social science in "meeting the Soviet threat" (Miner 1960:1) by purporting to instruct the reader in how to play the grant-procurement game facetiously named in the title. In the process, the narrating "advisor" takes aim at a broad array of targets, including the shift to competitively procured foundation-funded research and the concomitant increase in competition and turf wars among researchers, as well as the increasing quantification of research output, the rise of the collaborative research model at the expense of individual work, the incessant invocation of national need in a context of ideological struggle, and, perhaps most tellingly, the creeping technophilia and mania for quantitative analysis that were, needless to say, at odds with Miner's propensity toward the cultural, the historical, and the qualitative.

For example, the ambitious researcher, the reader is told, must first understand some pecuniary basics: "The relationship between the cost of a project and the significance of the research results has been well established in the physical sciences. If the social sciences are to produce comparable results in these critical times, they must conduct more basic and expensive research" (1960:1). An ancillary concern, logically enough, is equipment: "If possible, research plans should include data analysis involving the use of electronic computers, which are both very scientific and very expen-

sive" (1960:1–2). As far as the question of actual topic is concerned, the researcher is advised to stake a claim to a suitably unexplored field and aggressively to fend off colleagues trying to encroach on it: "A few well-placed, devastating reviews should divert the talents of his competitors into more fruitful research channels" (1960:2).

Yet Miner was also perfectly happy to direct some of the ribbing toward himself. "As it is generally conceded that the best research is done when the scientist is in his normal family setting," he wrote, "it is desirable to decide travel aims in cooperation with one's wife" (1960:2). Once such domestic desiderata have been attended to, the reader is told, the researcher can then identify a problem researchable only in the target country. The exact humoristic valence of other intradisciplinary references is harder to assess: for example, does the following allusion to Mead's work hold up a jovial mirror to collective foibles of the profession as a whole or single out for the charge of vulgarization a few of its most successful practitioners and their acolytes?

> The key to writing for the general public lies in the selection of an appropriate title for the monograph. With such a title and hard covers, a monograph becomes a Book. A variety of title forms are available. The resounding success of *Pubescence in Puerto Rico* set a pattern of titles referring to emergent adolescence. Sexy titles have also done well ever since the publication of the classic, *Sin and Sincerity in Seven Societies*, and more than one general reader has found himself immersed in pure research data hidden behind a jacket illustration of a buxom savage. [1960:3]

Miner's tacit acknowledgment of the necessity to engage in a bit of academic marketing may in fact here shade over into a lament at those who push it toward sensationalism.

One could justifiably conclude from such excerpts as I have quoted that "Researchmanship" amounts to nothing more than a jesting session with colleagues, a ritualized and fleeting facetiousness that might just as well have been delivered within the sanctioned silliness of a roast or a well-watered banquet—the frivolously comedic, in other words. Yet, in its trenchant tongue-in-cheek spoof of the evolution of academic research funding under Cold War imperatives, the same article also concealed an insightful barb of considerable import. In tearing the covers off inappropriate institutional bedfellows, "Researchmanship" presciently foresaw and portended trends that culminated, for example, in the intradisciplinary uproar caused when news of Project Camelot—the U.S. federal government's plan to study and tame leftist insurrections overseas with the help of domestic social scientists (sociologists in particular)—leaked out in 1964 (Solovey 2001). Considering that a mere decade and a half prior to Miner's "Researchmanship" piece the height of patriotic duty for anthropologists like Ruth Benedict was to provide patterned analyses of national adversaries posing existential threats to the U.S. way of life (Miner himself had served as a counterintelligence officer for three years in World War II), the shift is remarkable. It is precisely this oxymoronic mix of, on the one hand, ephemeral in-group insouciance (the "intramural japes" of Geertz's formulation) and, on the other hand, trenchant social commentary on the state of the academy at a specific historical moment that found its most felicitous mix in the "Nacirema" article.

"NACIREMA": PLAY . . . WITH A PURPOSE

"Nacirema" came about through a double dose of editorial happenstance. The newly appointed editor-in-chief of *American Anthropologist*, as previously noted, hesitated before eventually publishing the article, but according to Miner's daughter Denise, the piece had already been submitted and rejected for inclusion in the humor section of a general-interest publication of the day similar to *The Saturday Evening Post* (conversation with author, January 23, 2013). Presumably lines like "were it not for the rituals of the mouth, they believe that . . . their friends [would] desert them, and their lovers reject them" (Miner 1956:504) and the assertion that "the fundamental belief underlying the whole system appears to be that the human body is ugly" (1956:503) were originally supposed to comment wryly on the swarms of hortatory advertisements for mouthwash, breath mints, dandruff shampoo, and deodorant soap that would have inevitably resided in close typographic proximity to the piece in its intended environment. The change in publication venue must necessarily have occasioned an inward disciplinary shift in the article's referentiality. To be sure, the sendups performed on U.S. hyperhygienism, worship of material progress, and ethnocentric exceptionalism presumably present in the original version remained intact, but now the focus shifted to a more methodical targeting of the anthropological idiom and method themselves.

The tip offs are legion from the first sentence: What neutral scientific meaning is being conveyed by the word *exotic* (the anthropologist "is not apt to be surprised by even the most exotic customs" [1956:503])? As the essay develops, moreover, one senses one is in the hands of an author in winking dialogue with his colleagues, men (mainly) likely to sense the uproarious literalization that was being performed on the two lofty words that most defined the postevolutionist ethnographic method: "my people."[11] Nowhere is Miner's method more clearly on display, however, than in his succession of three mock scientific references, often regrettably excised in reprints and extracts. Far from being bibliographical pixie dust meant merely to connote scientific rigor, they point in meaningful, if facetious, ways to actual publications by eminent anthropologists and hence carry specific meaning germane to the text. Miner cites, in order, a passage from *Social Structure*, the Yale professor George Peter Murdock's 1949 milestone project in kinship studies; a wry section on diffusion from Ralph Linton's 1936 textbook *The Study of Man*; and, most consequentially, Bronislaw Malinowski's "Magic, Science, and Religion," originally published in 1925 (republished in 1948). Each, it turns out, is contributing a slightly different tile to the mosaic of the article's disciplinary commentary, with Murdock probably being ribbed in a manner akin to the oblique treatment of Mead in the

"Researchmanship" article, Linton tacitly acknowledged as a fellow master of mockery, and Malinowski treated with tantalizing indeterminacy.

Murdock and Linton

The first sentence of "Nacirema" expresses the fact of human cultural variety ("the diversity of ways in which different peoples behave in similar situations" [1956:503]), the second shoves the reader onto the ground of suspiciously comprehensive mathematical analysis ("if all the logically possible combinations of behavior have not been found somewhere in the world, [the anthropologist] is apt to suspect that they must be present in some yet undescribed tribe" [1956:503]), and the third credits Murdock with the insight ("This point has, in fact, been expressed with respect to clan organization by Murdock [1949:71]" [1956:503]). Tracking down the citation in Murdock's *Social Structure* catches a man in the act of striving with such enthusiasm to catapult his field beyond what one of his reviewers called "the inescapable immaturity of the social sciences" (L. Gross 1950:498) as to be carried off by his model.

More precisely, Murdock's chapter 4, "The Clan," tackles the data set of family structure for 250 societies worldwide with a classificatory gusto that can only be described as hyper-Linnaean. After having established the first possibility in clan formation as patrilocal residence, the second as matrilocal residence, and the third as "localizing a matri-sib around its male rather than its female members" (1949:70), Murdock ventures into the realm of what he freely admits is speculation, extrapolating from real-world experience into the domain of logical exigency by positing a fourth and final possibility of clan formation, "as yet purely hypothetical" (1949:71). In this model, unmarried women would move in with their paternal aunts and be joined there by any future husband. The familiar mother's brother "avunculate" relationship thus finds itself symmetrically and, presumably, to the anthropologist, satisfyingly mirrored through a kinship chiasmus, the "amitate" of the father's sister bond giving rise to an "*amitalocal*" (Murdock's coinage) rule of residence (1949:71). One senses here a scientist reserving a future ledger entry in the annals of ethnographic description, to which gesture Miner, as the self-appointed master of ceremonies of the roast he has called, has seemingly decided to respond by bestowing the prize for the most earnest recent application and extension of a scientific paradigm.

Whereas the Murdock reference likely constitutes good-natured ribbing, the Linton citation pays homage, as noted, to a fellow wit. "Professor Linton," the second paragraph begins, "first brought the ritual of the Nacirema to the attention of anthropologists twenty years ago" (1956:503). Contrary to ill-informed assumptions that Linton preceded Miner in the use of the concept-term *Nacirema* (cf. Clausen 1981:20), Miner is actually pointing the reader toward a clever twist in the diffusion chapter of Linton's textbook. After a sober and straightforward exposition of the concept, leading to the proposition that every culture of the day, despite a recent explosion of technological innovation, probably owes at least 90 percent of its substance to inventions made by other civilizations, Linton slips in a 600-word humorous illustration of this point by following a "solid American citizen," subsequently labeled "our friend," throughout a typical day: the cotton, wool, or silk in the man's bedding owe their domestication to ancient Indians, Near Easterners, or Chinese, respectively, whereas his soap can be traced back to ancient Gaul, and his shaving, for its part, constitutes "a masochistic rite which seems to have been derived from either Sumer or ancient Egypt" (Linton 1936:326). It is worth noting in passing that Miner pays explicit homage to this line in "Nacirema": "It was to these [masochistic tendencies] that Professor Linton referred in discussing a distinctive part of the daily body ritual which is performed only by men" (1956:505).

If Miner took inspiration from Linton, however, it was probably more through this mild version of his predecessor's satirical impulse than from the expanded and much more trenchant reworking of the same piece that appeared a year later in a general-interest monthly edited by H. L. Mencken (Linton 1937). *The American Mercury* version of the essay that has become well known as "100% American" reads like an anthropologist having a go at Sinclair Lewis's assault on Babbittry: "There can be no question about the average American's Americanism or his desire to preserve this precious heritage at all costs. Nevertheless, some insidious foreign ideas have already wormed their way into his civilization without his realizing what was going on," writes Linton acidly; "dawn finds the unsuspecting patriot garbed in pajamas, a garment of East Indian origin; and lying in a bed built on a pattern which originated in either Persia or Asia Minor" (1937:427). Ethnocentrism is reformulated here as insidious jingoism finding expression in prewar nativism and isolationism, which the anthropologist appears constitutionally inclined to denounce and ridicule. By contrast, the mockable ideologies of contemporary U.S. society selected by Miner for his commentary—hyperhygienism and material excess—are treated in "Nacirema" to the gentler defamiliarization strategy used to great comic effect already by such Enlightenment proto social scientists as the baron de Montesquieu in his *Persian Letters* (Montesquieu 2008). No doubt as a reward for its greater subtlety and more accessible humor, it is Miner's rather than Linton's lesson on ethnocentrism that has been widely anthologized—and hence canonized—by introductory textbooks and readers.

Malinowski's Ghost: A Twist, a Tweak, or a Tip of the Hat?

Miner's third and final citation is the most important reference and the most open to interpretation. The final paragraph of "Nacirema" reads as follows:

> Our review of the ritual life of the Nacirema has certainly shown them to be a magic-ridden people. It is hard to understand how they have managed to exist so long under the burdens which they have imposed upon themselves. But even such exotic customs as

these take on real meaning when they are viewed with the insight provided by Malinowski when he wrote (1948:70): "Looking from far and above, from our high places of safety in the developed civilization, it is easy to see all the crudity and irrelevance of magic. But without its power and guidance early man could not have mastered his practical difficulties as he has done, nor could man have advanced to the higher stages of civilization." [Miner 1956:507]

For Walter Goldschmidt (2012:119), these lines give the article "a twist that exposed Malinowski's prejudices," an assessment shared by a number of the article's anthologists and constituting a substantial portion of its staying power in some pedagogical circles. Has the reader not just been treated to a humorous and witty demonstration of the culturally constructed nature of the category of "magic," in contrast to which the great Malinowski seems to be promoting an out-of-date evolutionary paradigm that condescendingly places an essentialized notion of magic before the advent of civilization on the continuum of progress?

It is unlikely that Miner had anything so subversive in mind, however, because in point of fact he was recycling the Malinowski quotation from a book review he himself had written seven years prior to "Nacirema." In this earlier instance, significantly, Malinowski had been lauded as an authoritative predecessor. Specifically, Miner was evaluating a 500-page compilation of ethnographic materials on magic by a retired University of Nebraska anthropologist, Hutton Webster, which Miner found acceptably encyclopedic but theoretically retrograde. He wrote as follows:

> The final chapter on "The Role of Magic" restates functions of magic which may be found in many older discussions of the subject. While Dr. Webster recognizes that magic may be an important "integrating and organizing factor in primitive society," he obviously disapproves of magic because it operates "to discourage intellectual acquisitiveness . . . and to substitute unreal for real achievement in the natural world." The reviewer can not better state his reaction to this point than by quoting the concluding remarks of Malinowski's essay "Magic, Science and Religion." [1949b:300]

Miner then ended his review with the same two lines from Malinowski's essay as conclude the "Nacirema" article.

Seen in this context, Malinowski's characterization of magic, from Miner's perspective, clearly stood on the enlightened side of history against an outmoded tendency, evident in the approach taken by late Victorians like J. G. Frazer and followed by Webster, to dismiss the magical out of hand as the antithesis of progress and unrecuperably lacking all cultural and social value. A physician commenting on "Nacirema" several years after its appearance came to a similar conclusion in his summary of the piece for the readership of the *New England Journal of Medicine*: "As [Miner] notes, at the close of his essay, this magic-ridden native tribe has burdened itself with an incredible hocus-pocus of medical customs. Appropriately, he recalls an observation by Malinowski, an anthropologist of great reknown [*sic*], who saw meaning in such behavior and once wrote: 'Looking from far and above . . .'" (P. Gross 1959:758), the ellipsis here standing in for Gross's full reproduction of the two-sentence Malinowski quotation that concludes "Nacirema."

In other words, for at least one 1950s reader, Miner did not subversively turn Malinowski's words against him at all but, rather, standing on the shoulders of his predecessor, carried the "Nacirema" joke to its logical conclusion: If it is we who can be viewed as primitive savages, why not take advantage of this useful shift in perspective and perform the same intellectual salvage operation on our own behavior as has benefited other magic-practicing societies? Why our fascination for exotic otherness to the exclusion of our own supposedly unmarked and unremarkable zero-degree culture? The seeming haughtiness of Malinowski's stance disappears when seen from this angle, and what initially might seem to be Miner's distancing himself from a foundational thinker of the ethnographic method is replaced implicitly by a more inclusive gesture—the call to break down the barriers between what a later commentator would term "zones of cultural visibility and invisibility" (Rosaldo 1988:78).

In an oral interview conducted in the late 1980s by Susan Trencher, Walter Goldschmidt had in fact offered a similar interpretation prior to voicing the much later anti-Malinowskian assessment cited above (e-mail to author, December 13, 2012). Goldschmidt explained to Trencher that his decision to publish "Nacirema" was rooted in what he saw as its implicit exhortation to contemporary anthropologists, particularly in the United States, to rethink their tendency to overexoticize the seemingly strange and marvelous practices of the peoples they studied; they should strive instead, to paraphrase T. S. Eliot, to make the unfamiliar familiar (Spiro 1990:47). It was no coincidence, according to this point of view, that Miner chose for his mock descriptions those very hygienic and corporeal practices that seemed at once most unremarkable and normative to those living in the United States and most obsessively extraordinary to outsiders—a double lesson, in effect. Private stashes of travel toilet paper, sterilization rituals performed on eating utensils on camping trips—the list of quirky U.S. hygiene traits remains long to this day in the minds of outsiders, as anyone who has traveled extensively outside of the United States knows. To the extent that "Nacirema" contains what Goldschmidt called a "twist," it might arguably be the fact that the article takes the tried-and-true defamiliarization technique that writers have performed satirically on their home cultures since antiquity (Dalnekoff 1973) and brings it full circle: "Nacirema" implicitly points to the duty of anthropologists to find the recognizable and the ordinary in another people's unfamiliar and superficially strange behavior. Let us thus be hawkers of familiarity as much as merchants of astonishment. May the exoticizing cease.

Intriguing Duality

Nonetheless, Goldschmidt's reading of veiled subversion in the concluding lines of "Nacirema" has long had the upper hand over Miner's likely intended use of the quotation, and it meshes well with the related but distinct idea, hinted at by several anthologists and explicitly stated by Renato Rosaldo (1987:94; cf. Note 6), that "Nacirema" can and should be read as an indictment of the misprisions inherent to ethnographic method itself. The editor of a reader devoted to perspectivism in the study of religion, for example, points readers of his "Nacirema" reprint toward "the ironic way in which the famous anthropologist Bronislaw Malinowski is quoted at its close"; "apparently neutral description," after all, "often carries with it both interpretation and evaluation" (McCutcheon 1999:19). Similarly, a 1974 introduction to sociology, summarizing objections to ethnographic theory, set the laudable insights of "Nacirema" against Malinowski's alleged condescension: "Perhaps it takes more than a touch of ethnocentrism to look at primitive culture in the condescending way of Malinowski" (J. Rose 1974:510), and an even-earlier editor lamented the use of "such name-calling categories as 'civilized' and 'primitive' peoples" (Dundes 1968:433). Much more recently, Serena Nanda and Richard Warms's widely used *Cultural Anthropology* textbook, for example, encourages students to turn their skeptical attention to Malinowski's phrasing: "Have we really 'advanced to the higher stages of civilization'? What does that mean anyway?" (2014:41).

The broader point of interest here is the resemblance, as previously mentioned, between "Nacirema" and carnivalesque forms, particularly in their pre- and early-modern European manifestations. A recurring conundrum in carnival studies is how to evaluate consequence and political valence (Humphrey 2001). In a word, is any given festive or ritualistically parodic production innocuous or antagonistic toward the power hierarchies in which it operates and whose language it often appropriates? One very early form of in-group joking that "Nacirema" resembles—the Carmina Burana–style play with the learned language of the 12th-century clerical class—is almost wholly devoid of subversive intent, for all its possible moment-specific dissatisfaction (Bayless 1996). Which is to say that Miner most probably did not intend for "Nacirema" to attack the founders and foundations of his discipline any more than his distant forebears intended a parodic Latin Gospel satirizing the social ill of clerical cupidity to attack the fundamental legitimacy of their theocratic institutions (Bayless 1996:138–139, 197). Over time, however, to complete the parallel, later observers of premodern in-group parodic satires read into their caustic intramural joking a radically reformist agenda that had not been intended at the time of their creation.[12] It seems plausible, based on the evidence presented above, that Miner's spoof has in similar fashion been retroactively interpreted in light of a critical ethos that "Nacirema" itself may have assisted in generalizing but that did not, in fact, inform the production of the work.

CONCLUSION

The spring of 1956 was a time for revelations and new directions. Just as Miner's article began to circulate in June, the U.S. public was introduced to Caribbean cultural otherness by a singer of Jamaican and Martiniquan descent named Harry Belafonte, whose *Calypso* album of the same month featured an instant hit song about banana boat dock workers greeting the rising sun with a memorable cry of "Day-O." Also in June, President Eisenhower signed legislation creating the interstate highway system that would restructure U.S. conceptions of space and time sufficiently for the automobile-highway-hour to have displaced the mile as the normative unit of conversational travel measurement in our day ("we live two hours north of Boston"). Three months earlier, Nikita Khrushchev had introduced delegates at a closed session of the Russian Communist Party Congress to a daring denunciation of the crimes of Stalin (Robinson 2002:43–44), and the year before Sputnik sailed upward and sent a smug sense of self-confidence and exceptionalism dipping downward in the United States, Horace Miner introduced his compatriots to a familiar people unflatteringly depicted from an unfamiliar standpoint. The piece immediately escaped the bounds of its learned publication venue and, unlike the nearly contemporaneous New Math project, which did not successfully introduce the country's youth to the concepts of perspectivism and contingency, has proven hugely successful ever since at popularizing broadly similar tenets from an ethnographic standpoint.

Nearly 60 years later, ideology, international conflict, and cultural difference have all assumed configurations of which Miner's contemporaries probably never dreamed, as illustrated by the success of "Do Muslim Women Really Need Saving?" (Abu-Lughod 2002). That "Body Ritual among the Nacirema" continues to hold its own in the readership ratings despite this radically changed environment might cynically be dismissed as an accident of the high value accorded to entertainment in North American pedagogical traditions. As I have acknowledged, one cannot assume that the author of the work would have defended it against such a charge. One affirmative approach to giving "Nacirema" its due might have been to probe, in the manner of Erve Chambers (1989), the unsuspected organic links between ethnography and comedy.

Based on my extensive examination of the genesis and reception of the work in the context of Miner's professional inclinations, however, I have concluded that much of the surprising staying power of "Nacirema" lies in its carnivalesque duality as both elaborately coded in-group joke and seeming act of radical and far-reaching disciplinary insubordination, at once evanescent and consequential. Between these two poles, the work has flourished in the vast middle ground of pedagogical utility by illustrating, to the satisfaction of most professional readers, the basic ethnographic precept that cultural relativism should serve as an antidote to the malady of ethnocentrism and by delivering a Montaignesque message in a Woody Allen–esque package. The famous lessons of "On Cannibals" ("everyone calls barbarous whatever is not part of his own practice" and "we have no other model for truth and reason than the example and pattern of the opinions and customs of the country we live in" [Montaigne 1958:152;

translation modified]) find form in a narrative as insouciantly inventive as those concocted by the sometime–*New Yorker* humorist.

Viewed from this perspective, there may be more commonality between Abu-Lughod's "Muslim Women" and Miner's "Nacirema" than initially meets the eye. Granted, Miner's piece can be viewed as celebrating cultural relativism, whereas Abu-Lughod's (2002:787–788) overtly probes its limits. Yet to the extent that "Nacirema" arguably helped make the academic world safe for such metadisciplinary questions as the reflexivity debate of the late 1960s and 1970s, it served as indirect precursor to Abu-Lughod's work (e.g., 1991). Both pieces also pose challenges, albeit in completely different ways, to the legitimacy and reliability of what has come to be called the ethnographic gaze. But perhaps most significantly, the two most consulted AnthroSource articles of 2012, Miner's and Lughod's, represent two noteworthy examples of anthropology fulfilling its promise to provide trenchant, apposite, and timely critique of a specific cultural moment.

Mark Burde   *Residential College, University of Michigan, Ann Arbor, Ann Arbor, MI 48109; MBurde@umich.edu*

NOTES

Acknowledgments.   For giving generously of their time and making numerous invaluable suggestions, I wish to thank the four anonymous reviewers of my manuscript, the family of Horace Miner, and the anthropologists and sociologists who kindly allowed me to query them for hours on end. My gratitude extends particularly deeply to Professors David McCurdy and Susan Trencher. I also thank the interlibrary loan departments of the University of Michigan, Ann Arbor, and Wayne State University for expeditious fulfillment of countless loan and scan requests. Finally, readers should note that I did not invent but, rather, borrowed the first portion of my title, as indicated in Note 7.

1. The figure was 11,413 downloads, to be precise (telephone inquiry by author, June 6, 2013). Investigating independently, Rocks-Macqueen (2013) established the same rank (first) for Miner's article in the same year, measuring by views rather than downloads (30,309).
2. Immediately following its publication in *American Anthropologist*, "Body Ritual among the Nacirema" had been summarized in the general readership publication *Science News Letter* (June 16, 1956, p. 24). Similar unsigned digests and short extracts followed in Upjohn Pharmaceuticals's *Scope Weekly* (July 11, 1956, p. 13), the University of Michigan alumni magazine (October 20, 1956, p. 59), the dental journal *Contact Point* (November 1956, p. 65), and *Science Digest* (December 1956, p. 24). Additionally, *Harper's Magazine* published an archaeological analogue to "Nacirema" five months after the appearance of Miner's piece (Nathan 1956).

3. In the interests of simplicity, the term *American* will be used sporadically here in the sense it had for Miner and his contemporaries—that is, as a the adjectival form for the country known as the United States and in divergence from usual *AA* style.

4. Miner was not the first to use a reversed ethnological perspective in the service of comico-satirical commentary. Grant Allen's *The British Barbarians* and H. G. Wells's *The Wonderful Visit*, both of 1895, presented unflattering views of humankind from the standpoint of a visiting anthropologist and an angel, respectively; for this and other examples of the form prior to Miner, see Stableford 2003:xlii and 2006:166.

5. Take, for example, the following April 16, 2012, blog posting to Tumblr made by a self-described anthropology student proficient in both Chinese and English:

> Well, I felt cheated. But it was awesome. For those who have yet to read this wonderfully grotesque piece of ethnographic essay by Horace Miner, please do [. . .] Those who had read it, did you feel as cheated as I was? Maybe you'd realized what Miner was talking about right away (smartass) but I didn't, so I spent the first couple of readings going WTF IS WRONG WITH THESE PEOPLE and then when I did realize I was like . . . shit. Brownie points for you Prof. Miner, you made me feel like a loser. But like I said, it was an awesome read. [. . .] I had my word document opened ready to write the essay as I was reading it, and before even writing anything, I typed out "The author is a big fat ethnocentric man." Lawl. When I look at that sentence now, it's just, gold. I'm gonna keep it till the very end when writing the essay, so I can remind myself how much of a oblivious moron I had been. I'm sorry Prof. Miner. So after finally realizing that Nacirema, when flipped backwards, spells American, (SURPRISE!!!XD) I went on and read the whole thing a few more times and was greatly entertained for the rest of the day and the next. [CatchAnThro 2012]

6. "[Public anthropology] asks: Why can't anthropologists be followers of Gramsci as well as Malinowski, Foucault as well as Boas, by generating not only field data *but analyses of the framings that frame their collection?*" (Borofsky 2000:9). Compare Rosaldo (1987:94), for whom Miner's article evokes "a scathing critique of ethnographic discourse."

7. I borrow the phrase *social-science fiction* from P. Rose 1972:45.

8. The term is used in two related but distinct senses, one limited to calendrically bounded festivities and the other referring to broader representational practices and worldviews. My use falls into the latter camp.

9. I allude to Bakhtin (1984a:303–367).

10. Cf. *The Journal of Irreproducible Results* founded by two Israeli scientists in 1955 and *The Worm Runner's Digest*, initiated in the early 1960s by Miner's University of Michigan colleague James V. McConnell, a research psychologist. For a useful overview of a number of works that could be considered the successors to "Nacirema," see Jarvis 2003. I exclude from consideration here the numerous outright imitations elicited by the work, which, with the possible exception of Walker (1970), miss the mark of the original by varying degrees.

11. "The archetypal 'tribe' of nineteenth-century evolutionary anthropology might best be called the 'Amongtha'—as in the characteristic Frazerian comparativist refrain, 'Among the Arunta . . . . Among the Fuegians . . . .' But with the accomplishment of the ethnographic revolution, it was more appropriately called 'My People'—the group among whom the fieldworker carried on 'participant observation,' from whom were generated ethnographic 'data' for subsequent interpretation, and who became the lifelong reference point for all the ethnographer's comparative anthropological statements" (Stocking 2001:317). I thank Professor Susan Trencher for drawing this point to my attention.

12. For example, a 19th-century British specialist of satire and caricature wrote the following assessment of a famous group of medieval intraecclesiastical parodists: "The spirit of the goliards continued to exist long after the name had been forgotten; and the mass of bitter satire which they had left behind them against the whole papal system, and against the corruptions of the papal church of the middle ages, were a perfect godsend to the reformers of the sixteenth century, who could point to them triumphantly as irresistible evidence in their favour" (Wright 1875:174).

REFERENCES CITED

Abrahamson, Mark, ed.
1969 Introductory Readings on Sociological Concepts, Methods, and Data. New York: Van Nostrand Reinhold.

Abu-Lughod, Lila
1991 Writing against Culture. *In* Recapturing Anthropology: Working in the Present. Richard G. Fox, ed. Pp. 137–162. Santa Fe: School of American Research Press.
2002 Do Muslim Women Really Need Saving? Anthropological Reflections on Cultural Relativism and Its Others. American Anthropologist 104(3):783–790.

Allen, Grant
1895 The British Barbarians: A Hill-Top Novel. New York: G. P. Putnam.

Angeloni, Elvio
2005 Annual Editions: Anthropology 06/07. 29th edition. New York: McGraw-Hill.

Bakhtin, Mikhail
1984a[1965] Rabelais and His World. Hélène Iswolsky, trans. Bloomington: University of Indiana Press.
1984b[1929] Problems of Dostoevsky's Poetics. Caryl Emerson, ed. and trans. Minneapolis: University of Minnesota Press.

Bayless, Martha
1996 Parody in the Middle Ages: The Latin Tradition. Recentiores: Later Latin Texts and Contexts series. Ann Arbor: University of Michigan Press.

Bonder, Bette, Laura Martin, and Andrew W. Miracle
2002 Culture in Clinical Care. Thorofare: SLACK.

Borofsky, Robert
2000 Commentary—Public Anthropology: Where To? What Next? Anthropology News 41(5):9–10.

Branaman, Ann, ed.
2001 Self and Society. Blackwell Readers in Sociology series. Malden: Blackwell.

Burke, Peter

1978 Popular Culture in Early Modern Europe. New York: Harper and Row.

Burrill, Richard L., and Howard Fast

1983 The Human Almanac: People through Time. Sacramento: Sierra Pacific.

CatchAnThro

2012 Review: Body Ritual among the Nacirema. CatchAnThro: Musings of an Anthropology Student, April 16. http://catchanthro.tumblr.com/post/21205186366/review-body-ritual-among-the-nacirema, accessed March 24, 2014.

Chambers, Erve

1989 Thalia's Revenge: Ethnography and Theory of Comedy. American Anthropologist 91(3):589–598.

Clausen, Joy P.

1981 Review of Culture and Childrearing. Medical Anthropology Newsletter 13(1):20.

Contact Point, The

1956 Anthropologist Describes Curious Rites of "Primitive" Tribe Now Inhabiting U.S. Contact Point, November: 65.

Dalnekoff, Donna Isaacs

1973 A Familiar Stranger: The Outsider of Eighteenth Century Satire. Neophilologus 57(2):121–134.

Davis, Allison, Burleigh B. Gardner, and Mary R. Gardner

1941 Deep South: A Social Anthropological Study of Caste and Class. Southern Classics series. Chicago: University of Chicago Press.

Di Leonardo, Micaela

1998 Exotics at Home: Anthropologies, Others, American Modernity. Chicago: University of Chicago Press.

Douglas, Mary

1966 Purity and Danger: An Analysis of Concepts of Pollution and Taboo. Routledge Classics series. London: Routledge and Kegan Paul.

Dundes, Alan, ed.

1968 Every Man His Way: Readings in Cultural Anthropology. Englewood Cliffs, NJ: Prentice Hall.

Ferraro, Gary, ed.

2004 Classic Readings in Cultural Anthropology. Belmont: Wadsworth.

Folta, Jeannette R., and Edith S. Deck, eds.

1979[1966] A Sociological Framework for Patient Care. Second edition. New York: Wiley.

Foucault, Michel

1963 Naissance de la clinique. Une archéologie du regard médical [The birth of the clinic: An archaeology of medical perception]. Paris: Presses Universitaires de France.

Geertz, Clifford

1984 Distinguished Lecture: Anti Anti-Relativism. American Anthropologist 86(2):263–278.

1988 Works and Lives: The Anthropologist as Author. Stanford: Stanford University Press.

Goffman, Erving

1956 The Nature of Deference and Demeanor. American Anthropologist 58(3):473–502.

Goldschmidt, Walter

2012 Anthropology and the Business Cycle (or, The Rise from Student Rags to Academic Riches). In Expanding American Anthropology, 1945–1980: A Generation Reflects. Alice Beck Kehoe and Paul L. Doughty, eds. Pp. 110–122. Tuscaloosa: University of Alabama Press.

Griffin, James B.

1995 Horace Mitchell Miner (26 May 1912–26 November 1993). Proceedings of the American Philosophical Society 139(3):288–292.

Gross, Llewellyn

1950 Review of Social Structure. American Journal of Sociology 55(5):498–500.

Gross, Paul A. M.

1959 Body Ritual among the Nacirema: A Note on Medical Anthropology and Magic in Medicine. The New England Journal of Medicine 261(15):757–758.

Hagan, Frank E.

2011 Introduction to Criminology: Theories, Methods, and Criminal Behavior. Seventh edition. Thousand Oaks: SAGE.

Hayano, David M.

1979 Auto-Ethnography: Paradigms, Problems, and Prospects. Human Organization 38(1):99–104.

Henslin, James M.

1988 Down to Earth Sociology: Introductory Readings. Fifth edition. New York: Free Press.

Hertz, Robert

1928[1909] La prééminence de la main droite. Etude sur la polarité religieuse [The preeminence of the right hand: A study of religious polarity]. In Mélanges de sociologie religieuse et folklore [Miscellany of religious sociology and folklore]. Robert Hertz, auth. and ed. Pp. 99–129. Paris: Alcan.

Humphrey, Chris

2001 The Politics of Carnival: Festive Misrule in Medieval England. Manchester Medieval Studies. Manchester: Manchester University Press.

Jarvis, William E.

2003 Time Capsules: A Cultural History. Jefferson: McFarland.

Kimmel, Michael

2006 Ritualized Homosexuality in a Nacirema Subculture. Sexualities 9(1):95–105.

Linton, Ralph

1936 The Study of Man. New York: D. Appleton-Century.

1937 One Hundred Per Cent American. The American Mercury 40(160):427–429.

Malinowski, Bronislaw

1948 Magic, Science and Religion and Other Essays. Garden City: Doubleday.

Marcus, George E., and Michael M. J. Fischer

1986 Anthropology as Cultural Critique: An Experimental Moment in the Human Sciences. Chicago: University of Chicago Press.

McCutcheon, Russell T., ed.

1999 The Insider/Outsider Problem in the Study of Religion: A Reader. London: Cassell.

Mead, Margaret, and Frances Cooke Macgregor
  1951 Growth and Culture, a Photographic Study of Balinese Child-hood. New York: Putnam.
Michigan Alumnus, The
  1956 The Editor's Scratch Pad. The Michigan Alumnus 20:59.
Miner, Horace
  1949a Culture and Agriculture: An Anthropological Study of a Corn Belt County. Ann Arbor: University of Michigan Press.
  1949b Review of Magic: A Sociological Study. American Anthropologist 51(2):300.
  1953 The Primitive City of Timbuctoo. Princeton: Princeton University Press.
  1956 Body Ritual among the Nacirema. American Anthropologist 58(3):503–507.
  1960 Researchmanship: The Feedback of Expertise. Human Organization 19(1):1–3.
  1963[1939] St. Denis: A French-Canadian Parish. Chicago: University of Chicago Press.
  1967 "As you can see from the picture." Untitled postcard, James B. Griffin Papers: Box 16, folder "Correspondence 1930–75, Miner, Horace, 1934–71." Bentley Historical Library, University of Michigan, Ann Arbor.
  1973 "I recognize." Untitled memo to Howard Schuman, Department of Sociology Records, 1929–87: Box 8, folder "Horace Miner." Bentley Historical Library, University of Michigan, Ann Arbor.
Miner, Horace M., and George De Vos
  1960 Oasis and Casbah: Algerian Culture and Personality in Change. Ann Arbor: University of Michigan Press.
Montaigne, Michel de
  1958[1943] The Complete Essays of Montaigne. Donald M. Frame, trans. Stanford: Stanford University Press.
Montesquieu, Charles de Secondat, baron de
  2008 [1721] Persian Letters. Margaret Mauldon, trans. Introduction and notes by Andrew Kahn. Oxford: Oxford University Press.
Murdock, George Peter
  1949 Social Structure. New York: Macmillan.
Nanda, Serena, and Richard Warms
  2014 Cultural Anthropology. Eleventh edition. Belmont: Wadsworth/Cengage.
Nathan, Robert
  1956 Digging the Weans. Harper's Magazine 213(1278):46–49.
Ogburn, William F., and Meyer F. Nimkoff
  1958 Sociology. Third edition. Boston: Houghton Mifflin.
Powdermaker, Hortense
  1950 Hollywood, the Dream Factory: An Anthropologist Looks at the Movie-Makers. Boston: Little, Brown.
Quigley, Carroll
  1956 Aboriginal Fish Poisons and the Diffusion Problem. American Anthropologist 58(3):508–525.
Robinson, Neil
  2002 Russia: A State of Uncertainty. London: Routledge.
Rocks-Macqueen, Doug

  2013 What Is the Deal with the Nacirema?!?—AAA Viewer Stats and the Relevance of #Anthropology. Doug's Archaeology, July 30. http://dougsarchaeology.wordpress.com/2013/07/30/what-is-the-deal-with-the-nacirema-aaa-viewer-stats-and-the-relevance-of-anthropology/, accessed May 24, 2014.
Rosaldo, Renato
  1987 Where Objectivity Lies: The Rhetoric of Anthropology. In The Rhetoric of the Human Sciences: Language and Argument in Scholarship and Public Affairs. John S. Nelson, Allan Megill, and Donald N. McCloskey, eds. Pp. 87–110. Madison: University of Wisconsin Press.
  1988 Ideology, Place, and People without Culture. Cultural Anthropology 3(1):77–87.
Rose, Jerry D.
  1974 Introduction to Sociology. Second edition. Chicago: Rand McNally.
Rose, Peter Isaac, ed.
  1972 Seeing Ourselves: Introductory Readings in Sociology. New York: Knopf.
Science Digest
  1956 Rituals of the "Nacirema" Tribe. Science Digest 40: 24.
Science News Letter
  1956 U.S. Society Described. Science News Letter 69(24):372.
Scope Weekly
  1956 American Culture—A View from the Future. Scope Weekly, July 11:13.
Solovey, Mark
  2001 Project Camelot and the 1960s Epistemological Revolution: Rethinking the Politics-Patronage-Social Science Nexus. Social Studies of Science 31(2):171–206.
Spiro, Melford E.
  1990 On the Strange and the Familiar in Recent Anthropological Thought. In Cultural Psychology: Essays on Comparative Human Development. James W. Stigler, Richard A. Shweder, and Gilbert Herdt, eds. Pp. 47–61. Cambridge: Cambridge University Press.
Spradley, James P., and Michael A. Rynkiewich, eds.
  1975 The Nacirema: Readings on American Culture. New York: Little, Brown.
Stableford, Brian
  2003 Introduction. In Deluge. Sydney Fowler Wright, auth. Brian Stableford, ed. Pp. xi–lviii. Middletown: Wesleyan University Press.
  2006 Science Fact and Science Fiction: An Encyclopedia. New York: Routledge.
Steinmetz, George
  2007 American Sociology before and after World War II: The (Temporary) Settling of a Disciplinary Field. In Sociology in America: A History. Craig Calhoun, ed. Pp. 314–366. Chicago: University of Chicago Press.
Stocking, George W., Jr.
  2001 Delimiting Anthropology: Historical Reflections on the Boundaries of a Boundless Discipline. In Delimiting Anthropology: Occasional Essays and Reflections. George W. Stocking

Jr., auth. Pp. 303–329. Madison: University of Wisconsin Press.

Wells, H. G.
1895 The Wonderful Visit. New York: Macmillan.

Walker, Willard
1970 The Retention of Folk Linguistic Concepts and the ti´ yĉɨr Caste in Contemporary Nacireman Culture. American Anthropologist 72(1):102–105.

Wright, Thomas
1875 A History of Caricature and Grotesque in Literature and Art. London: Chatto and Windus.

Miner's article spawned a whole reader, in which several authors expanded on what he did, considerably less successfully (one even described NASCAR as a "planetarium for racs" = cars— it loses its force if overdone). An activity for this article will ask you to consider whether Burde is right, that Miner's article was a form of "carnavalesque" in the same spirit as *Carmina Burana,* the bawdy songs written by frustrated monks in the Middle Ages. The question is: does this humor hold up? Why would Miner's article continue to be a "crowd-pleaser."

A Case of Missing Persons:
Cultural Relativism in Today's World

by Barbara D. Miller

Introduction

In the nineteenth century, ethnologists quite regularly documented "exotic" customs such as human sacrifice, infanticide, and ritual suicide. In the early twentieth century, as cultural relativism emerged as a strong value in the discipline, cultural anthropologists, for the most part, avoided writing about such practices. Rather than debating the moral issues that one encounters when learning about another culture, anthropologists concentrated on topics like kinship systems, agricultural practices, leadership patterns, and myths. Today, a growing interest in defining universal human rights has ignited a lively debate within anthropology about cultural relativism.

Cultural relativism, the principle that cultural traits are best understood in the context of the cultural system of which they are a part and, therefore, not subject to external or absolute standards, became a central tenet of cultural anthropology, particularly as anthropologists sought to dispel notions of racism and ethnocentrism in the early twentieth century. Cultural relativism asks us to engage in a "suspension" of our values so that we might interpret other peoples' customs in the context of their cultures. To do otherwise -- to judge other peoples' customs from our own culture's viewpoint -- often leads to ethnocentrism, or the belief that one's own culture and its values are superior to that of others.

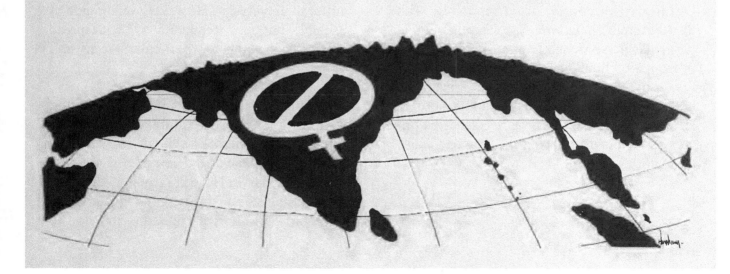

Many anthropologists still hold to some form of "absolute cultural relativism" by which anything that is acceptable in any one culture has to be viewed as acceptable by an outsider seeking to understand the practice. My study of contemporary patterns of female infanticide, sex-selective abortion, and general neglect and abuse of females in India has led me to a revised view that I call "critical cultural relativism."

Studies in Mortality

Population dynamics can be grouped under three major areas of study: fertility (reproduction and population growth), mortality (death), and migration (population movements). Both population anthropology and medical anthropology address these topics, but population anthropologists have paid far more attention to studying fertility and migration than to studying mortality, until recently.

Mortality is more difficult to research in a typical fieldwork period (one year) and within the traditional fieldwork setting of a village or urban neighborhood. In one year's time, several births might occur in a village of 1,000 people, and many people may migrate in and out. But only one infant death may occur, and no murders or suicides.

Death may, of course, occur randomly, with no discernible pattern associated with a particular person's death, at a particular time, or from a particular cause. Death is often the result of biological factors that impair the body's functioning, such as a malformation in an infant's heart. In short, there often are non-cultural factors determining the time and cause of death.

Culture and Mortality

In many cases, culturally-shaped patterns play a key role in putting certain people more "at risk" of dying from a particular cause, or at a particular age, than otherwise. We only have to look at statistics on mortality from car accidents in the United States, and especially from car accidents in which alcohol is involved, to see that such deaths are not evenly spread throughout the population. Culturally prescribed roles for adolescent males that involve "macho" type display behavior, excessive alcohol consumption, and otherwise dangerous lifestyle features are obviously implicated in the much higher mortality rates they experience, compared to females and older age groups.

Starting even before birth, an infant's chances of survival are influenced by culture. In societies where women are overworked and undernourished because of culturally constructed patterns of discrimination, infants are likely to be smaller and therefore less likely to survive infancy than in societies where prenatal care receives more attention.

In some societies, once a baby is born, culture plays an immediate and direct role in deciding whether or not the child will live. Abundant evidence from around the world documents the deliberate killing of offspring as almost a cultural universal. However, infanticide is usually not a frequent or widespread phenomenon within any particular society as a whole.

The mechanisms of infanticide differ, historically and cross-culturally. Infanticide refers to deliberate killings of juvenile offspring, but the word "deliberate" is not easy to define. Marvin Harris, a leading American anthropologist of the cultural materialism tradition, has contributed much to contemporary thinking on infanticide. He distinguishes between direct and indirect infanticide.

Direct infanticide is the intentional killing of a child, by such common methods as poisoning, exposure to weather, smothering, or strangling. Indirect infanticide is more subtle and may not be exactly "deliberate." Indirect infanticide results in the death of a child through such practices as neglect in care and treatment. For example, not feeding a baby enough leads to malnutrition and lack of resistance to disease, and not taking the child to the clinic for treatment of an illness may allow the illness to progress to a terminal stage.

In different cultures, different children are at risk of infanticide. For example, it may be children born with teeth, since they are believed to be witches, or one of a set of twins since twins are widely believed to be inauspicious, or firstborn boys. Considering all the evidence we have for infanticide cross-culturally, we can say that the preponderant cases of systematic infanticide -- infanticide that is practiced by comparatively many people in the society, through history -- are systems of female infanticide.

In the United States, there are substantial numbers of infant murders and untold cases of fatal child abuse each year. But victims do not seem to be consistently more of one gender than another, as far as current statistics indicate (although cases of sexual abuse tend to involve far more cases of female children as victims).

Rural India: A Case Study

Information about son preference and daughter neglect in rural India (80 percent of India's population lives in rural areas) provides solid

clues to the problem of why and how so many girls die. However, there is still much that is not known, and cultural anthropology can play an important role in generating further knowledge that might be useful to health planners. In addition, there are people in India who do not support the discrimination against females, who are working to encourage new social policies to promote equality between the sexes in Indian society today.

We know that the most extreme and widespread scarcity of girls is seen in the northwestern region of India. This pattern is similar to the distribution of direct infanticide as revealed through a study of reports from the 1800s. For more contemporary periods, census data collected by the government of India every ten years, throughout the nation, allow us to calculate "sex ratios" (that is, the number of boys per girls, so that "perfect" balance -- although this rarely occurs -- would be 100 boys for every 100 girls).

Biologists have shown that in humans, the sex ratio at conception is 120:100, with more boys than girls. Despite the fact that female embryos have a higher mortality rate than males within the first two weeks of conception, the mortality rate of males is greater than that of females at every age thereafter. By birth, the sex ratio has fallen to about 106:100 in most documented populations, and throughout the life span, the ratio continues to fall. The result is that there are more males than females in the younger generations, but increasingly more females than males in the older population.

Research on juvenile sex ratios (for under ten-year-olds) in India shows that in some areas of the northwestern plains, ratios exist of 115-120 boys for every 100 girls. This means that one of every five or six girls dies an excess death compared to boys.

Daughters and Dowries

One might guess that the poverty of India drives people to kill female infants or to let them die through neglect. But in India, the scarcity of daughters has consistently been greatest among the "propertied" class -- farmers who own their land, as compared to landless agricultural wage-workers -- and upper caste groups in the north. This social pattern causes perplexity among many people in the United States, since most Euro-Americans have a "rationality" model of "child investment," a model which sees poverty, not wealth, as a force driving people to do difficult and unpleasant things to other people.

Why, then, does female infanticide and neglect make sense from the perspective of the propertied class? North Indian propertied-class cultural rules of marriage, in conjunction with the limitations for women's wage earning in this class, make daughters a very costly burden to raise. It is essential that a girl be married, since spinsterhood is a great stigma for her and her family, and she must be married to a boy of a somewhat higher socioeconomic status, requiring a very expensive dowry. North Indian-style dowry includes goods such as furniture (refrigerator, bed, motorcycle, watch, clothing, jewelry) and, increasingly, large sums of cash. The better the dowry, the "better" the groom's family will be. If a family seeks to marry off a daughter well, the expenses will put them in debt for many years. That burden is even greater if there is more than one daughter to be married.

Therefore, having a limited number of daughters is a poverty *avoidance* strategy for those who are *not* poor. The problem with having more than one daughter is not that the family cannot afford to feed them as children, but that they cannot afford to get them married properly later on.

Consider in the North Indian propertied group context the difference between having sons versus daughters. If you have a son, you can expect that he will "bring in" with his bride a

48

substantial sum of money and goods, because in this kinship system, daughters "marry out" of their natal family (exogamy) and take up residence in their husband's natal home or village.

As dowry is evolving in India in the 1990s, more and more of its contents goes to the groom's family rather than to the newly-married couple. If a family has several sons, it is likely to be in very good financial shape. Incoming dowry through one's sons' marriages can be used, in turn, to pay for the dowry of one's own daughter(s). Given this system, a parent wants to have more sons than daughters.

Among the poor, although dowry has become more common since the 1970s, daughters were traditionally married with no dowry, or even with the transfer of bridewealth or brideprice. Bridewealth is usually a cash amount of a fixed rate which is transferred from the family of a groom to the father of the bride. Compared to dowry, brideprice is a much smaller amount, and a prospective groom can work to earn it himself rather than being totally dependent on his family to provide it. Imagine, in this system, if you were the parent of several daughters; the prospect of receiving bridewealth would make a big difference in your attitude about having daughters.

Impact of Modernization

Modernization theorists claim that with increasing urbanization, industrialization, and education, discrimination against girls and women declines. But over the past several decades, the scarcity of girls in India has been spreading, both regionally and socially. Comparison of unbalanced juvenile sex ratios from the decade 1961-1971 revealed that a substantially greater number of districts had "suspiciously high" sex ratios in 1971 than in 1961: from one fourth of all India's districts up to one-third. Geographically, the problem is spreading outward from the northwestern core area into all directions.

Another major change since the 1980s is the increasing use of medical technology to learn the sex of a fetus and to seek an abortion in the case of a female fetus. This technology is now widely available in India, even though its use for sex-selection purposes was recently banned by the national government. Statistics from a large study of births in northwestern India reveal that people are aborting female fetuses in large numbers. Sex ratios at birth are reaching 115-120 boys per 100 girls, similar to what was previously the result of indirect infanticide in the same area. (Compare the expected "normal" ratio of about 106 boys to 100 girls.)

Recent evidence of direct female infanticide has also emerged in several rural areas of the state of Tamil Nadu in far southern India. It is not currently known whether this is a new practice or whether it has been going on for a long time and simply unnoticed by researchers and health care workers. The state government of Tamil Nadu, which is relatively progressive concerning women's issues, has taken several steps to help stop this practice, including setting up "drop boxes" for unwanted female babies who can then be adopted, and offering to pay marriage costs for daughters once they are grown.

The Anthropologist and Social Policy

Should anthropologists who study groups made vulnerable by societally defined conditions of inequality become involved in policy and action that alleviates such inequalities? Emphasis on key areas of research can add much to our understanding of how and why people are systematically disadvantaged by their culture and anthropologists can suggest ways to improve their situation.

According to absolute cultural relativism, anything that goes on in any culture is "just fine" because, it is said, no one has the right to judge the rightness or wrongness of any behavior or belief, and such judgment would be ethnocentric. According to this view, anthropologists should maintain their objectivity and remain uninvolved in policy or social action.

Consider where this position leads by looking at one of the horrors of the twentieth century: the Holocaust during World War II. Millions of Jews and other minorities in much of Eastern and Western Europe were killed as part of the German Aryan supremacy campaign. The absolute cultural relativist position would hold that the Holocaust was undertaken according to the values of the culture in which it occurred, so who are we to say anything about it?

Can anyone feel truly comfortable with such a position? We have to ask, "Whose culture supported the values that killed millions of people on the grounds of racial purity?" It was not the culture of the Jews and the Gypsies. It was the culture of Aryan supremacists, who were a subgroup primarily of Germans. We have a much more culturally complex picture than a simple absolute cultural relativist statement can take into account. There was not "one" culture and its values involved. Rather, we see an example of cultural imperialism at work, whereby one culture claims supremacy over minority cultures and proceeds to exterminate the latter in the interests of the former. We can perceive oppressors and victims.

---••••---

Critical Cultural Relativism

An alternative conceptual option is what I term *critical cultural relativism*. This perspective is situated within the general framework of cultural relativism, whereby we try to view all cultures empathically from the inside. But it is more specific. It prompts us to understand the plural interests within any society (whether it is between Nazis and Jews, the old and the young, the rich and the poor, men and women, the able and the less able) and to understand the power relationships between these interest groups. We must critique the behavior of these groups from the standpoint of some set of more or less generally agreed upon human rights.

French anthropologist Claude Lévi-Strauss commented that "No society is perfect," even when considered from what that society claims as moral values. He pinpoints the difficult position of the anthropologist who looks from one culture to another. The predicament is how to maintain what could be called scientific objectivity. Lévi-Strauss claims that the task of the anthropologist is to study "the other" without passing judgment. Other anthropologists claim, to the contrary, that since one cannot ever achieve true objectivity, the best we can do is examine and expose our own biases, and then try to treat all cultures equally, to look equally critically at all cultures -- one's own and "others." Critical cultural relativism tries to do this in terms of a set of universal human rights.

Cultural anthropologists following a path of critical cultural relativism face the challenge of what might be considered universal human rights; that is, rights that should be guaranteed to all people everywhere regardless of their culture. Defining human rights in a cross-cultural perspective may seem like an easy task. For example, we might argue that the right to food and health care should be universal. But the case of India's missing millions of girls illustrates just how difficult this might be.

Extreme cultural relativists argue that a balanced sex ratio, or even gender equality in health and welfare, is ethnocentric, and since they do not seem to apply to India, then they are not appropriately applied there. In such a view, an unbalanced sex ratio -- achieved through female infanticide and neglect and sex-selective abortion -- is culturally appropriate and acceptable.

Indian Activists

One can argue to the contrary, though, because many people in India are "egalitarianists" and do not support the inequality that does exist. As the following story, told to me by a long-time medical doctor serving in the rural areas of northern India, indicates, little girls who are discriminated against are also able to express their unhappiness with the situation, at least through their tears:

> In one village, I went into a house to examine a young girl, and I found that she had an advanced case of tuberculosis. I asked the mother why she hadn't done something sooner about the girl's condition because now, at this stage, the treatment would be very expensive. The mother replied, "then let her die, I have another daughter." At the time, the two daughters sat nearby listening, one with tears streaming down her face.

In India, activists are working on many fronts to try to equalize life chances for males and females, from political lobbying against sex-selective abortion to grassroots work with parents, teaching them the value of daughters.

Cultural anthropologists can contribute to a more precise understanding of just where, and in which groups, little girls are at most risk of dying so that appropriate action might be taken to remedy the situation. And they can help with better understanding of how and why this happens, so that policies might go to the root of the problem and not just the surface. Cultural anthropologists could carry on research in the following arenas, showing:

1. How schooling affects attitudes toward sons and daughters and other matters such as dowry marriage and women's work. While many scholars insist that "education is the key," ironically the data for India show that, in northern India, the poorest and least educated people are less discriminatory toward daughters than many more well-off and educated people. In India, being educated goes with middle and upper class lifestyles, and such are not necessarily egalitarianist; indeed, they may be extremely conservative when it comes to women's rights.

2. How more and better health care provisions might affect female child health and survival. Some scholars argue that if more clinics were available, then parents would care for children of both genders more equally. Currently, however, studies show that parents in the northern part of the country are using better health care facilities for their sons, not their infant daughters, even when the distance to the clinic is not great.

3. How women's work affects gender patterns of child survival. Development studies demonstrate that, worldwide, children's welfare responds more positively to an increase in maternal earning power compared to an increase in paternal earning power, because mothers more than fathers use their income for household welfare expenditures. In northern India, where strong negative

sanctions exist about women's work for rural middle and upper-class families, it is difficult to know how women's earnings could be enhanced and if women would have the intrahousehold power to allocate earnings toward equal treatment of children.

4. How mothers deal psychologically with the loss of children. Is maternal grief a Western luxury that rural Indian mothers are socialized against? How do parents and other household members speak about the deaths of children, wanted or unwanted? And how is this changing, given the now widespread availability of television with its international messages about behavior, emotion, and discourse?

Although more is known now than fifty years ago about the cultural dynamics of India's missing females, the entire story is only slowly and unevenly unfolding. Much more needs to be known. In the United States, in addition, we must face the fact that increasing numbers of parents are seeking sex-selective abortion. The problem of gender-specific reproductive wishes is not just "over there," but increasingly in our own culture. Critical cultural relativism helps us to better understand cultural practices and actions desirable to take, given certain norms of universal moral behavior and universal human rights.

Barbara D. Miller
George Washington University
Department of Anthropology
Director, Women's Studies Program

About Barbara Miller

Barbara Miller first became interested in India in elementary school and as a senior in high school took a course in cultural anthropology at a local college. While an undergraduate at Syracuse, she participated in a year-long study program in Banaras, India. She received her PhD, with distinction, from Syracuse University in 1978. She plans to return to India for extended research in the future.

Barbara's research interests include child survival, women's health status, the cultural construction of morbidity and mortality, migration and mental health, intrahousehold dynamics, public policy regarding the household, and rural development in relation to population dynamics. She has done field research in India, Bangladesh, and Jamaica, and has coauthored a book on Sri Lanka.

For Further Reading

Jeffery, Patricia, Roger Jeffery and Andrew Lyon, *Labour Pains and Labour Power: Women and Childbearing in India*, London: Zed Books, 1988.

Miller, Barbara D. *The Endangered Sex: Neglect of Female Children in Rural North India*, Ithaca: Cornell University Press, 1981.

Rohner, Ronald P. and Manjustri Chaki-Sircar, *Women and Children in a Bengali Village*, Hanover, NH: University Press of New England, 1988.

Waldron, Ingrid. "Why Do Women Live Longer than Men?" *Social Science and Medicine* 10:349-362, 1976.

One possible complaint with anthropology is its adoption of the standard of cultural relativism. That standard suggests that it is wrong to criticize another culture's features without taking into account that culture's context. In other words, most cultural features make sense in the overall context of the culture within which they are embedded. Cultures do tend to make sense, within their own systems. However, what if a culture practices human sacrifice, such as the Aztecs?[1] Many cultures in the past have done that, even though today human sacrifice is illegal worldwide. An anthropologist might reply that if the Aztecs practiced human sacrifice and made it work in their culture, we should not question it. Critics of anthropology might rightly point out that such a stance—accepting human sacrifice—might seem immoral. A debate over human sacrifice might be useful. There are some researches who compare capital punishment in the U.S. or the state-sanctioned death of a nation's soldiers in war in the name of patriotism as a possible form of human sacrifice for reasons not unlike the Aztecs' reason for their practice—to keep one's nation-state and culture going. We probably can agree that human sacrifice is not a cultural practice that we find praiseworthy and that it is difficult to be culturally relativistic when discussing that practice. Miller explains why anthropologists need a code of "Critical Cultural Relativism."

CONCLUSION: WRAP-UP

Horace Miner's little trick has entertained faculty and students for a couple of generations. But are Burde's doubts about whether it is still a useful exercise valid? Miner does talk about the Nacirema in the way that mid-twentieth century anthropologists talked about other "primitive" cultures. Does the patronizing tone ring distinctly out-of-date now? Or does the "scientific objectivity" that the piece tries to emulate successfully illustrate that, from an etic viewpoint, many American cultural traits do seem as odd as the "primitive" traits anthropologists have attributed to other cultures? (Note that I have put primitive in quotations; this is a word with pejorative connotations that most anthropologists distinctly like to avoid nowadays.)

Finally, Miller suggests that the anthropological tool of cultural relativism needs some updating. It is clear that many anthropologists would agree that the real, appropriate standard to be applied in today's world is the appeal to human rights. That should be easy for all participants in the debate to understand and appreciate. The Golden Rule, found in many cultures, would seem to be a standard that most people can agree upon. And, contemporary world problems, in

---

[1] Full Disclosure: I am half-Mexican on my mother's side. Many of the people where she came from (including herself) probably are descendants of the Matlazinca people. These people were probably Otomí speakers, not Nahua speakers as were the Aztecs. (Aztec is an incorrect term, but too common to try and eliminate; the Aztec proper name is *Mexica* [pronounced "Meshica," in Nahautl, hence the name of the country]. The Aztecs conquered the Matlazinca and forced them to fight in Aztec armies. Although we are shocked at the level of Aztec human sacrifice, most all of the people of Mesoamerica at that time, understood it and accepted it. Many practices humans have indulged in that require the ritualized death of adult humans may well count as humans sacrifice [Roman gladiatorial combat, for example]. So, we must be careful about how we treat the subject.

many cases, would not be problems if the actors had simply agreed to respect human rights. Protection of human rights is probably the central concern of anthropology in its modern form, and the guide to solving current problems flows through the UN Universal Declaration of Human Rights. It is also probably a good reason for us to consider ourselves "global citizens."

ACTIVITIES

General Activity: bringing your Schema activation responses to class, discuss as a class whether it is appropriate for anthropology to be gossip or talk about exotic things.

Activity for Readings 5 and 6: split into small groups and come up with answers to the following questions:

- How long did it take you to figure out who the Nacirema are?
- Do you consider Miner's summary to be old-fashioned or out-of-date in any way?
- Do you think that Burde's recent comments make you feel less entertained by Miner's piece, or do you agree that it is "carnavalesque" in the spirit of Carl Orff's famous music quoting monks complaining about their constrained lives, *Carmina Burana* {heard frequently in movie soundtracks}?
- What is the effect of having Miner describe the Nacirema in such an outsider, etic fashion? As a member of the "target" culture, do you feel that his portrayal is "fair"?
- Do you think it is possible that an etic, neutral, dispassionate portrayal of other cultures is fair to them? Does that kind of description tend to offend other cultures to the point that attempts at mutual understanding are impeded and thus contemporary world problems may be exacerbated?
- Do you agree with Burde's point that "Nacirema" shows how cultural relativism serves as an antidote to ethnocentrism?

Activity for Reading 7: Let us look at another controversial cultural practice: male circumcision. Run an in-class debate addressing the following question:

- {Pro} is male circumcision a legitimate cultural practice that should be respected from a cultural relativistic viewpoint, or
- {Con} male circumcision is a form of genital mutilation concerning which a critical cultural relativistic viewpoint should be adopted and the practice discouraged on the grounds of human rights.

SOURCES

On human rights, a good recent review is Peter W. Van Arsdale 2017 *Global Human Rights: People, Processes, and Principles* Long Grove, IL: Waveland Press. The Nacirema book is by James P. Spradley and Michael A. Rynkiewich, editors 1975 *The Nacirema: readings on American culture* Boston: Little Brown.

Chapter 3
The Role of Elites

OBJECTIVES

- Explore the origins of the change from egalitarian foragers to modern hierarchically organized humans, by seeing what happened when an anthropologist tried to give a gift to the foraging people he was studying.
- Explore a debate on how elites operate in a complex society between a critic of elites and another commentator.
- Debate whether it is better to be a *chief* or a *commoner* in the modern world.

KEY TERMS

Reverse Hierarchy Dominance: how effective leveling mechanisms in egalitarian societies are applied that keep someone from getting more resources than anyone else.

Social Stratification: differential access to resources; which means institutionalized inequality, whereby elites, solely by virtue of their ascribed (given at birth) status, are entitled to more basic necessities and luxuries than common people in the society. Abraham Lincoln characterized this situation, in addressing the issue of slavery, as the "Tyrannical Principle": "You make bread, and I'll eat it!"

Egalitarian society: society in which people are treated differently based only on age and gender.

Ranked: society in which there are fewer positions of prestige and status than the number of people who can hold them.

Achieved status: situation in which individuals, by their talents and skills, can achieve a particular status or position.

Ascribed status: situation in which individuals, merely by birth, are ascribed a certain status or position.

Magnanimity payments: in ancient cultures, elites provide "services" to the common mass of people—such as free banquets on holidays, paying for public buildings and temples—to defuse the natural resentment of commoners as they observe the consumption of wealth by elites.

SCHEMA ACTIVATION ACTIVITY

Write down your thoughts in answer to the following question: *Is all gift-giving motivated solely by the desire to be generous? List some of the reasons that people give gifts.*

(Save these to share later in your discussion sections.)

INTRODUCTION

In this Chapter, you will start by reading about another surprising experience for an anthropologist. You read in Chapter 1 an article about one anthropologist getting a "comeuppance" when dealing with an African culture. This reading is the classic tale of another anthropologist in Africa experiencing the same thing. Both articles should convey the impression of how difficult it is to go into another culture where things are very different. Both anthropologists were a little bit ethnocentric. But, both learned the lesson of why that is problem. There are two main points to think about while reading this article: 1) what is it that makes gift-giving far from a straightforward proposition? and 2) is it realistic to think that cultural elements can be used to belittle skill and talent and still have the culture function? We will do another take on gifts in Chapter 12.

Eating Christmas in the Kalahari

Richard Borshay Lee

The !Kung Bushmen's knowledge of Christmas is thirdhand. The London Missionary Society brought the holiday to the southern Tswana tribes in the early nineteenth century. Later, native catechists spread the idea far and wide among the Bantu-speaking pastoralists, even in the remotest corners of the Kalahari Desert. The Bushmen's idea of the Christmas story, stripped to its essentials, is "praise the birth of white man's god-chief"; what keeps their interest in the holiday high is the Tswana-Herero custom of slaughtering an ox for his Bushmen neighbors as an annual goodwill gesture. Since the 1930's, part of the Bushmen's annual round of activities has included a December congregation at the cattle posts for trading, marriage brokering, and several days of trance-dance feasting at which the local Tswana headman is host.

As a social anthropologist working with !Kung Bushmen, I found that the Christmas ox custom suited my purposes. I had come to the Kalahari to study the hunting and gathering subsistence economy of the !Kung, and to accomplish this it was essential not to provide them with food, share my own food, or interfere in any way with their food-gathering activities. While liberal handouts of tobacco and medical supplies were appreciated, they were scarcely adequate to erase the glaring disparity in wealth between the anthropologist, who maintained a two-month inventory of canned goods, and the Bushmen, who rarely had a day's supply of food on hand. My approach, while paying off in terms of data, left me open to frequent accusations of stinginess and hard-heartedness. By their lights, I was a miser.

The Christmas ox was to be my way of saying thank you for the cooperation of the past year; and since it was to be our last Christmas in the field, I determined to slaughter the largest, meatiest ox that money could buy, insuring that the feast and trance-dance would be a success.

Through December I kept my eyes open at the wells as the cattle were brought down for watering. Several animals were offered, but none had quite the grossness that I had in mind. Then, ten days before the holiday, a Herero friend led an ox of astonishing size and mass up to our camp. It was solid black, stood five feet high at the shoulder, had a five-foot span of horns, and must have weighed 1,200 pounds on the hoof. Food consumption calculations are my specialty, and I quickly figured that bones and viscera aside, there was enough meat—at least four pounds—for every man, woman, and child of the 150 Bushmen in the vicinity of /ai/ai who were expected at the feast.

Having found the right animal at last, I paid the Herero £20 ($56) and asked him to keep the beast with his herd until Christmas day. The next morning word spread among the people that the big solid black one was the ox chosen by / ontah (my Bushman name; it means, roughly, "whitey") for the Christmas feast. That afternoon I received the first delegation. Ben!a, an outspoken sixty-year-old mother of five, came to the point slowly.

"Where were you planning to eat Christmas?"

"Right here at /ai/ai," I replied.

"Alone or with others?"

"I expect to invite all the people to eat Christmas with me."

"Eat what?"

"I have purchased Yehave's black ox, and I am going to slaughter and cook it."

"That's what we were told at the well but refused to believe it until we heard it from yourself."

"Well, it's the black one," I replied expansively, although wondering what she was driving at.

"Oh, no!" Ben!a groaned, turning to her group. "They were right." Turning back to me she asked, "Do you expect us to eat that bag of bones?"

"Bag of bones! It's the biggest ox at / ai/ai."

"Big, yes, but old. And thin. Everybody knows there's no meat on that old ox. What did you expect us to eat off it, the horns?"

Everybody chuckled at Ben!a's one-liner as they walked away, but all I could manage was a weak grin.

That evening it was the turn of the young men. They came to sit at our evening fire. /gaugo, about my age, spoke to me man-to-man.

"/ontah, you have always been square with us," he lied. "What has happened to change your heart? That sack of guts and bones of Yehave's will hardly feed one camp, let alone all the Bushmen around ai/ai." And he proceeded to enumerate the seven camps in the /ai/ai vicinity, family by family. "Perhaps you have forgotten that we are not few, but many. Or are you too blind to tell the difference between a proper cow and an old wreck? That ox is thin to the point of death."

"Look, you guys," I retorted, "that is a beautiful animal, and I"m sure you will eat it with pleasure at Christmas."

"Of course we will eat it; it's food. But it won't fill us up to the point where we will have enough strength to dance. We will eat and go home to bed with stomachs rumbling."

That night as we turned in, I asked my wife, Nancy: "What did you think of the black ox?"

"It looked enormous to me. Why?"

"Well, about eight different people have told me I got gypped; that the ox is nothing but bones."

"What's the angle?" Nancy asked. "Did they have a better one to sell?"

"No, they just said that it was going to be a grim Christmas because there won't be enough meat to go around. Maybe I'll get an independent judge to look at the beast in the morning."

Bright and early, Halingisi, a Tswana cattle owner, appeared at our camp. But before I could ask him to give me his opinion on Yehave's black ox, he gave me the eye signal that indicated a confidential chat. We left the camp and sat down.

"/ontah, I'm surprised at you: you've lived here for three years and still haven't learned anything about cattle."

"But what else can a person do but choose the biggest, strongest animal one can find?" I retorted.

"Look, just because an animal is big doesn't mean that it has plenty of meat on it. The black one was a beauty when it was younger, but now it is thin to the point of death."

"Well I've already bought it. What can I do at this stage?"

"Bought it already? I thought you were just considering it. Well, you'll have to kill it and serve it, I suppose. But don't expect much of a dance to follow."

My spirits dropped rapidly. I could believe that Ben!a and /gaugo just might be putting me on about the black ox, but

Halingisi seemed to be an impartial critic. I went around that day feeling as though I had bought a lemon of a used car.

In the afternoon it was Tomazo's turn. Tomazo is a fine hunter, a top trance performer… and one of my most reliable informants. He approached the subject of the Christmas cow as part of my continuing Bushman education.

"My friend, the way it is with us Bushmen," he began, "is that we love meat. And even more than that, we love fat. When we hunt we always search for the fat ones, the ones dripping with layers of white fat: fat that turns into a clear, thick oil in the cooking pot, fat that slides down your gullet, fills your stomach and gives you a roaring diarrhea," he rhapsodized.

"So, feeling as we do," he continued, "it gives us pain to be served such a scrawny thing as Yehave's black ox. It is big, yes, and no doubt its giant bones are good for soup, but fat is what we really crave and so we will eat Christmas this year with a heavy heart."

The prospect of a gloomy Christmas now had me worried, so I asked Tomazo what I could do about it.

"Look for a fat one, a young one… smaller, but fat. Fat enough to make us /gom ('evacuate the bowels'), then we will be happy."

My suspicions were aroused when Tomazo said that he happened to know of a young, fat, barren cow that the owner was willing to part with. Was Tomazo working on commission, I wondered? But I dispelled this unworthy thought when we approached the Herero owner of the cow in question and found that he had decided not to sell.

The scrawny wreck of a Christmas ox now became the talk of the /ai/ai water hole and was the first news told to the outlying groups as they began to come in from the bush for the feast. What finally convinced me that real trouble might be brewing was the visit from u!au, an old conservative with a reputation for fierceness. His nickname meant spear and referred to an incident thirty years ago in which he had speared a man to death. He had an intense manner; fixing me with his eyes, he said in clipped tones:

"I have only just heard about the black ox today, or else I would have come here earlier. /ontah, do you honestly think you can serve meat like that to people and avoid a fight?" He paused, letting the implications sink in. "I don't mean fight you, /ontah; you are a white man. I mean a fight between Bushmen. There are many fierce ones here, and with such a small quantity of meat to distribute, how can you give everybody a fair share? Someone is sure to accuse another of taking too much or hogging all the choice pieces. Then you will see what happens when some go hungry while others eat."

The possibility of at least a serious argument struck me as all too real. I had witnessed the tension that surrounds the distribution of meat from a kudu or gemsbok kill, and had documented many arguments that sprang up from a real or imagined slight in meat distribution. The owners of a kill may spend up to two hours arranging and rearranging the piles of meat under the gaze of a circle of recipients before handing them out. And I also knew that the Christmas feast at /ai/ai would be bringing together groups that had feuded in the past.

Convinced now of the gravity of the situation, I went in earnest to search for a second cow; but all my inquiries failed to turn one up.

The Christmas feast was evidently going to be a disaster, and the incessant complaints about the meagerness of the ox had already taken the fun out of it for me. Moreover, I was getting bored with the wisecracks, and after losing my temper a few times, I resolved to serve the beast anyway. If the meat fell short, the hell with it. In the Bushmen idiom, I announced to all who would listen:

"I am a poor man and blind. If I have chosen one that is too old and too thin, we will eat it anyway and see if there is enough meat there to quiet the rumbling of our stomachs."

On hearing this speech, Ben!a offered me a rare word of comfort. "It's thin," she said philosophically, "but the bones will make a good soup."

At dawn Christmas morning, instinct told me to turn over the butchering and cooking to a friend and take off with Nancy to spend Christmas alone in the bush. But curiosity kept me from retreating. I wanted to see what such a scrawny ox looked like on butchering and if there *was* going to be a fight, I wanted to catch every word of it. Anthropologists are incurable that way.

The great beast was driven up to our dancing ground, and a shot in the forehead dropped it in its tracks. Then, freshly cut branches were heaped around the fallen carcass to receive the meat. Ten men volunteered to help with the cutting. I asked /gaugo to make the breast bone cut. This cut, which begins the butchering process for most large game, offers easy access for removal of the viscera. But it also allows the hunter to spot-check the amount of fat on the animal. A fat game animal carries a white layer up to an inch thick on the chest, while in a thin one, the knife will quickly cut to bone. All eyes fixed on his hand as /gaugo, dwarfed by the great carcass, knelt to the breast. The first cut opened a pool of solid white in the black skin. The second and third cut widened and deepened the creamy white. Still no bone. It was pure fat; it must have been two inches thick.

"Hey /gau," I burst out, "that ox is loaded with fat. What's this about the ox being too thin to bother eating? Are you out of your mind?"

"Fat?" /gau shot back, "You call that fat? This wreck is thin, sick, dead!" And he broke out laughing. So did everyone else. They rolled on the ground, paralyzed with laughter. Everybody laughed except me; I was thinking.

I ran back to the tent and burst in just as Nancy was getting up. "Hey, the black ox. It's fat as hell! They were kidding about it being too thin to eat. It was a joke or something. A put-on. Everyone is really delighted with it!"

"Some joke," my wife replied. "It was so funny that you were ready to pack up and leave /ai/ai."

If it had indeed been a joke, it had been an extraordinarily convincing one, and tinged, I thought, with more than a touch of malice as many jokes are. Nevertheless, that it was a joke lifted my spirits considerably, and I returned to the butchering site where the shape of the ox was rapidly disappearing under the axes and knives of the butchers. The atmo-

sphere had become festive. Grinning broadly, their arms covered with blood well past the elbow, men packed chunks of meat into the big cast-iron cooking pots, fifty pounds to the load, and muttered and chuckled all the while about the thinness and worthlessness of the animal and /ontah's poor judgment.

We danced and ate that ox two days and two nights; we cooked and distributed fourteen potfuls of meat and no one went home hungry and no fights broke out.

But the "joke" stayed in my mind. I had a growing feeling that something important had happened in my relationship with the Bushmen and that the clue lay in the meaning of the joke. Several days later, when most of the people had dispersed back to the bush camps, I raised the question with Hakekgose, a Tswana man who had grown up among the !Kung, married a !Kung girl, and who probably knew their culture better than any other non-Bushman.

"With us whites," I began, "Christmas is supposed to be the day of friendship and brotherly love. What I can't figure out is why the Bushmen went to such lengths to criticize and belittle the ox I had bought for the feast. The animal was perfectly good and their jokes and wisecracks practically ruined the holiday for me."

"So it really did bother you," said Hakekgose. "Well, that's the way they always talk. When I take my rifle and go hunting with them, if I miss, they laugh at me for the rest of the day. But even if I hit and bring one down, it's no better. To them, the kill is always too small or too old or too thin; and as we sit down on the kill site to cook and eat the liver, they keep grumbling, even with their mouths full of meat. They say things like, 'Oh this is awful! What a worthless animal! Whatever made me think that this Tswana rascal could hunt!'"

"Is this the way outsiders are treated?" I asked.

"No, it is their custom; they talk that way to each other too. Go and ask them."

/gaugo had been one of the most enthusiastic in making me feel bad about the merit of the Christmas ox. I sought him out first.

"Why did you tell me the black ox was worthless, when you could see that it was loaded with fat and meat?"

"It is our way," he said smiling. "We always like to fool people about that. Say there is a Bushman who has been hunting. He must not come home and announce like a braggard, 'I have killed a big one in the bush!' He must first sit down in silence until I or someone else comes up to his fire and asks, 'What did you see today?' He replies quietly, 'Ah, I'm no good for hunting. I saw nothing at all [pause] just a little tiny one.' Then I smile to myself," /gaugo continued, "because I know he has killed something big."

"In the morning we make up a party of four or five people to cut up and carry the meat back to the camp. When we arrive at the kill we examine it and cry out, 'You mean to say you have dragged us all the way out here in order to make us cart home your pile of bones? Oh, if I had known it was this thin I wouldn't have come.' Another one pipes up, 'People, to think I gave up a nice day in the shade for this. At home we may be hungry but at least we have nice cool water to drink.' If the horns are big, someone says, 'Did you think that somehow you were going to boil down the horns for soup?'"

"To all this you must respond in kind. 'I agree,' you say, 'this one is not worth the effort; let's just cook the liver for strength and leave the rest for the hyenas. It is not too late to hunt today and even a duiker or a steenbok would be better than this mess.'"

"Then you set to work nevertheless; butcher the animal, carry the meat back to the camp and everyone eats," /gaugo concluded.

Things were beginning to make sense. Next, I went to Tomazo. He corroborated /gaugo's story of the obligatory insults over a kill and added a few details of his own.

"But," I asked, "why insult a man after he has gone to all that trouble to track and kill an animal and when he is going to share the meat with you so that your children will have something to eat?"

"Arrogance," was his cryptic answer.

"Arrogance?"

"Yes, when a young man kills much meat he comes to think of himself as a chief or a big man, and he thinks of the rest of us as his servants or inferiors. We can't accept this. We refuse one who boasts, for someday his pride will make him kill somebody. So we always speak of his meat as worthless. This way we cool his heart and make him gentle."

"But why didn't you tell me this before?" I asked Tomazo with some heat.

"Because you never asked me," said Tomazo, echoing the refrain that has come to haunt every field ethnographer.

The pieces now fell into place. I had known for a long time that in situations of social conflict with Bushmen I held all the cards. I was the only source of tobacco in a thousand square miles, and I was not incapable of cutting an individual off for non-cooperation. Though my boycott never lasted longer than a few days, it was an indication of my strength. People resented my presence at the water hole, yet simultaneously dreaded my leaving. In short I was a perfect target for the charge of arrogance and for the Bushmen tactic of enforcing humility.

I had been taught an object lesson by the Bushmen; it had come from an unexpected corner and had hurt me in a vulnerable area. For the big black ox was to be the one totally generous, unstinting act of my year at /ai/ai, and I was quite unprepared for the reaction I received.

As I read it, their message was this: There are no totally generous acts. All "acts" have an element of calculation. One black ox slaughtered at Christmas does not wipe out a year of careful manipulation of gifts given to serve your own ends. After all, to kill an animal and share the meat with people is really no more than Bushmen do for each other every day and with far less fanfare.

In the end, I had to admire how the Bushmen had played out the farce—collectively straight-faced to the end. Curiously, the episode reminded me of the *Good Soldier Schweik* and his marvelous encounters with authority. Like Schweik, the Bushmen had retained a thorough-going skepticism of good intentions. Was it this independence of spirit, I wondered, that had kept them culturally viable in the face of generations of contact with more powerful societies, both black and white? The thought that the Bushmen were alive and well in the Kalahari was strangely comforting. Perhaps, armed with that independence and with their superb knowledge of their environment, they might yet survive the future.

Richard Borshay Lee is a full professor of anthropology at the University of Toronto. He has done extensive fieldwork in southern Africa, is coeditor of Man the Hunter *(1968) and* Kalahari Hunter-Gatherers *(1976), and author of* The !Kung San: Men, Women, and Work in a Foraging Society.

Lee here illustrates for us how human beings have dealt with one another for the vast majority of our evolutionary history as humans or proto-humans. Foraging was our way of life for millions of years, to be replaced only recently by agriculture (a phenomenon we will take up in the next chapter). So intent were we once on maintining an equal standing among us that this interesting method of rewarding talent developed. One question would be is whether this is what all foragers do, or is it more specific to the San peoples of Africa? The other question is whether this is a development on the part of the foragers in response to encroachment by agriculturalists, or does it go back to the time when all there were in the world were foragers. In our world, would not the good hunters be treated as the elites of society? What about the actual elites in our modern world? What is their role and significance? The next two readings take up that question and should be discussed together.

WHY ELITES FAIL

They're hyper-educated, ambitious and well rewarded. So why are our elites so incompetent?

by CHRISTOPHER HAYES

In 1990, at the age of 11, I stood in a line of sixth graders outside an imposing converted armory on Manhattan's Upper East Side, nervously anticipating a test that would change my life. I was hoping to gain entrance to Hunter College High School, a public magnet school that runs from grades seven through twelve and admits students from all five boroughs. Each year, between 3,000 and 4,000 students citywide score high enough on their fifth-grade standardized tests to qualify to take Hunter's entrance exam in the sixth grade; ultimately, only 185 will be offered admission. (About forty-five students, all from Manhattan, test into Hunter Elementary School in the first grade and automatically gain entrance to the high school.)

I was one of the lucky ones who made it through, and my experience there transformed me. It was at Hunter that I absorbed the open-minded, self-assured cosmopolitanism that is the guiding ethos of the current American ruling class. What animates the school is a collective delight in the talent and energy of its students and a general feeling of earned superiority. In 1982 a Hunter alumnus profiled the school in a *New York* magazine article called "The Joyful Elite" and

identified its "most singular trait" as the "exuberantly smug loyalty of its students."

That loyalty emanates from the deeply held conviction that Hunter embodies the meritocratic ideal as much as any institution in the country. Unlike elite colleges, which use all kinds of subjective measures—recommendations, résumés, writing samples, parental legacies and interviews—in deciding who gains admittance, entrance to Hunter rests on a single "objective" measure: one three-hour test. If you clear the bar, you're in; if not, you're out. There are no legacy admissions, and there are no strings to pull for the well-connected. If Michael Bloomberg's daughter took the test and didn't pass, she wouldn't get in. There are only a handful of institutions left in the country about which this can be said.

Because it is public and free, the school pulls kids from all over the city, many of whom are first-generation Americans, the children of immigrant strivers from Korea, Russia and Pakistan. Half the students have at least one parent born outside the United States. For all these reasons Hunter is, in its own imagination, a place where anyone with drive and brains can be catapulted from the anonymity of working-class outer-borough neighborhoods to the inner sanctum of the American elite. "I came from a family where nobody went to college. We lived up in Washington Heights. We had no money," says Jennifer Raab, who as president of CUNY's Hunter College oversees the high school as well. "It was incredibly empowering." When she surveys the student body, "it gets me very sappy about the American dream. It really can come true. These kids are getting an education that is unparalleled, and it's not about where they come from or who they are."

But the problem with my alma mater is that over time, the mechanisms of meritocracy have broken down. In 1995, when I was a student at Hunter, the student body was 12 percent black and 6 percent Hispanic. Not coincidentally, there was no test-prep industry for the Hunter entrance exam. That's no longer the case. Now, so-called cram schools like Elite Academy in Queens can charge thousands of dollars for after-school and

Eventually, the inequality produced by a meritocratic system will grow large enough to subvert the mechanisms of mobility.

weekend courses where sixth graders memorize vocabulary words and learn advanced math. Meanwhile, in the wealthier precincts of Manhattan, parents can hire $90-an-hour private tutors for one-on-one sessions with their children.

By 2009, Hunter's demographics were radically different—just 3 percent black and 1 percent Hispanic, according to the *New York Times*. With the rise of a sophisticated and expensive test-preparation industry, the means of selecting entrants to Hunter has grown less independent of the social and economic hierarchies in New York at large. The pyramid of merit has come to mirror the pyramid of wealth and cultural capital.

How and why does this happen? I think the best answer comes from the work of a social theorist named Robert Michels, who was occupied with a somewhat parallel problem in the early years of the last century. Born to a wealthy German family, Michels came to adopt the radical socialist politics then sweeping through much of Europe. At first, he joined the Social Democratic Party, but he ultimately came to view it as too bureaucratic to achieve its stated aims. "Our workers' organization has become an end in itself," Michels declared, "a machine which is perfected for its own sake and not for the tasks which it could have performed."

Michels then drifted toward the syndicalists, who eschewed parliamentary elections in favor of mass labor solidarity, general strikes and resistance to the dictatorship of the kaiser. But even among the more militant factions of the German left, Michels encountered the same bureaucratic pathologies that had soured him on the SDP. In his classic book *Political Parties*,

Christopher Hayes, editor at large of The Nation, *is the host of* Up With Chris Hayes *on MSNBC. This article is adapted from* Twilight of the Elites: America After Meritocracy, © *2012 by Christopher Hayes and published by Crown Publishers, a division of Random House Inc.*

he wondered why the parties of the left, so ideologically committed to democracy and participation, were as oligarchic in their functioning as the self-consciously elitist and aristocratic parties of the right.

Michels's grim conclusion was that it was impossible for *any* party, no matter its belief system, to bring about democracy in practice. Oligarchy was inevitable. For any kind of institution with a democratic base to consolidate the legitimacy it needs to exist, it must have an organization that delegates tasks. The rank and file will not have the time, energy, wherewithal or inclination to participate in the many, often minute decisions necessary to keep the institution functioning. In fact, effectiveness, Michels argues convincingly, requires that these tasks be delegated to a small group of people with enough power to make decisions of consequence for the entire membership. Over time, this bureaucracy becomes a kind of permanent, full-time cadre of leadership. "Without wishing it," Michels says, there grows up a great "gulf which divides the leaders from the masses." The leaders now control the tools with which to manipulate the opinion of the masses and subvert the organization's democratic process. "Thus the leaders, who were at first no more than the executive organs of the collective, will soon emancipate themselves from the mass and become independent of its control."

All this flows inexorably from the nature of organization itself, Michels concludes, and he calls it "The Iron Law of Oligarchy": "It is organization which gives birth to the dominion of the elected over the electors, of the mandataries over the mandators, of the delegates over the delegators. Who says organization says oligarchy."

The dynamic Michels identifies applies, in an analogous way, to our own cherished system of meritocracy. In order for it to live up to its ideals, a meritocracy must comply with two principles. The first is the Principle of Difference, which holds that there is vast differentiation among people in their ability and that we should embrace this natural hierarchy and set ourselves the challenge of matching the hardest-working and most talented to the most difficult, important and remunerative tasks.

The second is the Principle of Mobility. Over time, there must be some continuous, competitive selection process that ensures performance is rewarded and failure punished. That is, the delegation of duties cannot simply be made once and then fixed in place over a career or between generations. People must be able to rise and fall along with their accomplishments and failures. When a slugger loses his swing, he should be benched; when a trader loses money, his bonus should be cut. At the broader social level, we hope that the talented children of the poor will ascend to positions of power and prestige while the mediocre sons of the wealthy will not be charged with life-and-death decisions. Over time, in other words, society will have mechanisms that act as a sort of pump, constantly ensuring that the talented and hard-working are propelled upward, while the mediocre trickle downward.

But this ideal, appealing as it may be, runs up against the

reality of what I'll call the Iron Law of Meritocracy. The Iron Law of Meritocracy states that eventually the inequality produced by a meritocratic system will grow large enough to subvert the mechanisms of mobility. Unequal outcomes make equal opportunity impossible. The Principle of Difference will come to overwhelm the Principle of Mobility. Those who are able to climb up the ladder will find ways to pull it up after them, or to selectively lower it down to allow their friends, allies and kin to scramble up. In other words: "Who says meritocracy says oligarchy."

Consider, for example, the next "meritocracy" that graduates of Hunter encounter. American universities are the

While a small group of über-rich have captured an unprecedented share of the American economy, social mobility has been declining.

central institution of the modern meritocracy, and yet, as Daniel Golden documents in his devastating book *The Price of Admission*, atop the ostensibly meritocratic architecture of SATs and high school grades is built an entire tower of preference and subsidy for the privileged:

At least one third of the students at elite universities, and at least half at liberal arts colleges, are flagged for preferential treatment in the admissions process. While minorities make up 10 to 15 percent of a typical student body, affluent whites dominate other preferred groups: recruited athletes (10 to 25 percent of students); alumni children, also known as "legacies" (10 to 25 percent); development cases (2 to 5 percent); children of celebrities and politicians (1 to 2 percent); and children of faculty members (1 to 3 percent).

This doesn't even count the advantages that wealthy children have in terms of private tutors, test prep, and access to expensive private high schools and college counselors. All together, this layered system of preferences for the children of the privileged amounts to, in Golden's words, "affirmative action for rich white people." It is not so much the meritocracy as idealized and celebrated but rather the ancient practice of "elites mastering the art of perpetuating themselves."

A pure functioning meritocracy would produce a society with growing inequality, but that inequality would come along with a correlated increase in social mobility. As the educational system and business world got better and better at finding inherent merit wherever it lay, you would see the bright kids of the poor boosted to the upper echelons of society, with the untalented progeny of the best and brightest relegated to the bottom of the social pyramid where they belong.

But the Iron Law of Meritocracy makes a different prediction: that societies ordered around the meritocratic ideal will produce inequality without the attendant mobility. Indeed, over time, a society will become more unequal and less mobile as those who ascend its heights create means of preserving and defending their

privilege and find ways to pass it on across generations. And this, as it turns out, is a pretty spot-on description of the trajectory of the American economy since the mid-1970s.

The sharp, continuous rise in inequality is one of the most studied and acknowledged features of the American political economy in the post-Carter age. Paul Krugman calls it "The Great Divergence," and the economist Emmanuel Saez, who has done the most pioneering work on measuring the phenomenon, has written: "The top 1% income share has increased dramatically in recent decades and reached levels which had not been seen... since before the Great Depression."

One of the most distinctive aspects of the rise in American inequality over the past three decades is just how concentrated the gains are at the very top. The farther up the income scale you go, the better people are doing: the top 10 percent have done well, but they've been outpaced by the top 1 percent, who in turn have seen slower gains than the top 0.1 percent, all of whom have been beaten by the top 0.01 percent. Adjusted for inflation, the top 0.1 percent saw their average annual income rise from just over $1 million in 1974 to $7.1 million in 2007. And things were even better for the top 0.01 percent, who saw their average annual income explode from less than $4 million to $35 million, nearly a ninefold increase.

It is not simply that the rich are getting richer, though that's certainly true. It is that a smaller and smaller group of über-rich are able to capture a larger and larger share of the fruits of the economy. America now features more inequality than any other industrialized democracy. In its peer group are countries like Argentina and other Latin American nations that once stood as iconic examples of the ways in which the absence of a large middle class presented a roadblock to development and good governance.

So: income inequality has been growing. What about mobility? While it's much harder to measure, there's a growing body of evidence that, at the same time income inequality has been growing at an unprecedented rate, social mobility has been declining. In a 2012 speech, Alan Krueger, chair of President Obama's Council of Economic Advisers, coined the term "The Gatsby Curve" to refer to a chart showing that over the past three decades, "as inequality has increased... year-to-year or generation-to-generation economic mobility has decreased."

The most comprehensive attempt at divining the long-term trends in social mobility over several generations is presented in "Intergenerational Economic Mobility in the US, 1940 to 2000," a complex paper by economists Daniel Aaronson and Bhashkar Mazumder of the Federal Reserve Bank of Chicago. After a series of maneuvers that qualify as statistical pyrotechnics, they conclude that "mobility increased from 1950 to 1980 but has declined sharply since 1980. The recent decline in mobility is only partially explained by education."

Another pair of economists, from the Boston Federal Reserve, analyzed household income data to measure mobility over a period of three decades rather than intergenerational mobility. They found that in the 1970s, 36 percent of families stayed in the same income decile; in the 1980s, that figure was 37 percent; and in the 1990s, it was 40 percent. In other words, over time, a larger share of families were staying within their class through the duration of their lives.

This is evidence that the Iron Law of Meritocracy is, in fact, exerting itself on our social order. And we might ask what a society that has been corrupted entirely by the Iron Law of Meritocracy would look like. It would be a society with extremely high and rising inequality yet little circulation of elites. A society in which the pillar institutions were populated and presided over by a group of hyper-educated, ambitious overachievers who enjoyed tremendous monetary rewards as well as unparalleled political power and prestige, and yet who managed to insulate themselves from sanction, competition and accountability; a group of people who could more or less rest assured that now that they have achieved their status, now that they have scaled to the top of the pyramid, they, their peers and their progeny will stay there.

Such a ruling class would have all the competitive ferocity inculcated by the ceaseless jockeying within the institutions that produce meritocratic elites, but face no actual sanctions for failing at their duties or succumbing to the temptations of corruption. It would reflexively protect its worst members; it would operate with a wide gulf between performance and reward; and it would be shot through with corruption, rule-breaking and self-dealing, as those on top pursued the outsized rewards promised for superstars. In the same way the bailouts combined the worst aspects of capitalism and socialism, such a social order would fuse the worst aspects of meritocracy and bureaucracy.

It would, in other words, look a lot like the American elite in the first years of the twenty-first century.

Of all the status obsessions that preoccupy our elites, none is quite so prominent as the obsession with smartness. Intelligence is the core value of the meritocracy, one that stretches back to the early years of standardized testing, when the modern-day SAT descended from early IQ tests. To call a member of the elite "brilliant" is to pay that person the highest compliment.

Intelligence is a vitally necessary characteristic for those with powerful positions. But it isn't just a celebration of smartness that characterizes the culture of meritocracy. It's something more pernicious: a Cult of Smartness in which intelligence is the chief virtue, along with a conviction that smartness is rankable and that the hierarchy of intelligence, like the hierarchy of wealth, never plateaus. In a society as stratified as our own, this is a seductive conclusion to reach. Since there are people who make $500,000, $5 million and $5 billion all within the same elite, perhaps there are leaps equal to such orders of magnitude in cognitive ability as well.

In *Liquidated: An Ethnography of Wall Street*, anthropologist Karen Ho shows how the obsession with smartness produces "a meritocratic feedback loop," in which bankers' growing influence itself becomes further evidence that they are, in fact, "the smartest." According to one Morgan Stanley analyst Ho interviewed, those being recruited by the firm "are typically told they will be working with 'the brightest people in the world. These are the greatest minds of the century.'" Robert Hopkins, a vice president of mergers and acquisitions at Lehman Brothers, tells her of those who inhabit Wall Street: "We are talking about the smartest people in the world. We are! They are the smartest people in the world."

And just as one would suspect, given the fractal nature of inequality at the top, hovering above those who work at big Wall Street firms is an entire world of hedge-fund hotshots, who see themselves as far smarter than the grunts on Wall Street. "There's 100 percent no question that most people on Wall Street, even if they have nice credentials, are generally developmentally disabled," a hedge-fund analyst I'll call Eli told me, only somewhat jokingly, one night over dinner. Hedge funds, according to Eli and his colleagues, are the real deal; the innermost of inner rings. "I was surrounded my whole life by people who took intelligence very seriously," Eli told me. "I went to good schools, I worked at places surrounded by smart people. And until now I've never been at

Without qualities like wisdom, judgment, empathy and ethical rigor, extreme intelligence can be extremely destructive.

a place that prides itself on having the smartest people and where it's actually true."

That confidence, of course, projects outward, and from it emanates the authority that the financial sector as a whole enjoyed (and in certain circles still enjoys). "At the end of the day," Eli says with a laugh, "America does what Wall Street tells it to do. And whether that's because Wall Street knows best, whether Wall Street is intelligently self-dealing, or whether it has no idea and talks out of its ass, that is the culture in America."

This is the Cult of Smartness at its most pernicious: listen to Wall Street—they've got the smartest minds on the planet.

While smartness is necessary for competent elites, it is far from sufficient: wisdom, judgment, empathy and ethical rigor are all as important, even if those traits are far less valued. Indeed, extreme intelligence without these qualities can be extremely destructive. But empathy does not impress the same way smartness does. Smartness dazzles and mesmerizes. More important, it intimidates. When a group of powerful people get together to make a group decision, conflict and argumentation ensue, and more often than not the decision that emerges is that which is articulated most forcefully by those parties perceived to be the "smartest."

It is under these conditions that destructive intelligence flourishes. Behind many of the Bush administration's most disastrous and destructive decisions was one man: David Addington, counsel and then chief of staff to Dick Cheney. Addington was called "Cheney's Cheney" and "the most powerful man you've never heard of." A former Bush White House lawyer told *The New Yorker*'s Jane Mayer that the administration's legal framework for the "war on terror"—from indefinite detention, to torture, to rejection of the 1949 Geneva Accords, to denial of habeas corpus—was "all Addington."

Addington's defining trait, as portrayed in numerous profiles, is his hard-edged, ideologically focused intelligence. "The boy seemed terribly, terribly bright," Addington's high school history teacher told Mayer. "He was scornful of anyone who said anything that was naïve, or less than bright. His sneers were almost palpable." A *US News and World Report* profile of Addington observed that "his capacity to absorb complex information is legendary." Co-workers referred to him as "extremely smart" and "sublimely brilliant."

What emerges in these accounts is a figure who used his dazzling recall, razor-sharp logical ability and copious knowledge to implacably push administration policy in a rogue direction. Because he knew the law so well, he was able to make legal arguments that, executed by anyone else, would have been regarded as insane. He would edit briefs so that they always reflected a maximalist interpretation of presidential power, and his sheer ferocity and analytic horsepower enabled him to steamroll anyone who raised objections. Pentagon lawyer Richard Schiffrin described Addington's posture in a meeting just after 9/11 to Mayer this way: "He'd sit, listen, and then say, 'No, that's not right.'… He didn't recognize the wisdom of the other lawyers. He was always right. He didn't listen. He knew the answers."

This is a potent articulation of the dark emotional roots of the Cult of Smartness: the desire to differentiate and dominate that the meritocracy encourages. Ironically, in seeking to stand apart, the Cult of Smartness can kill independent thought by subtly training people to defer to others whom one should "take seriously."

But fractal inequality doesn't just produce errors of judgment like those we saw during the run-up to Iraq; it also creates a system of incentives that produces an insidious form of corruption. This corruption isn't the obvious quid pro quo of the Gilded Age—there are precious few cases of politicians taking satchels of cash in exchange for votes. What's far more common is what Harvard Law professor Lawrence Lessig calls "institutional corruption," in which an institution develops an "improper dependency," one that "conflicts with the dependence intended."

This kind of corruption is everywhere you look. Consider a doctor who receives gifts and honorariums from a prescription drug company. The doctor insists plausibly that this has no effect on his medical decisions, which remain independent and guided by his training, instincts and the best available data. And he is not lying or being disingenuous when he says this: he absolutely believes it to be the case. But we know from a series of studies that there is a strong correlation between gifts from pharmaceutical companies and doctors' willingness to prescribe their drugs.

This basic dynamic infects some of our most important institutions. Key to facilitating both the monumental housing bubble and its collapse was the ratings agencies' habit of giving even extremely leveraged, toxic securities a triple-A rating. The institutional purpose of the rating agencies (and their market purpose as well) is to add value for investors by using their expertise to make judgments about the creditworthiness of securities. Originally, the agencies made their money from the investors themselves, who paid subscription fees in exchange for access to their ratings. But over time the largest agencies shifted to a model in which the banks and financial entities issuing the securities would pay the agencies for a rating. Obviously, these new clients wanted the highest rating possible and often would bring pressure to bear on the agencies to make sure they secured the needed triple A. And so the ratings agencies developed an improper dependence on their clients, one that pulled them away from fulfilling their original institutional purpose of serving investors. They became corrupt, and the result was trillions of dollars in supposedly triple-A securities that became worthless once the housing bubble burst.

We see a similar destructive example of this dynamic at work in two groups we entrusted to guard the public interest when it comes to the economy: federal regulators and elite economists. In a paper about the financial crisis, Rob Johnson and Thomas Ferguson tracked the salary trends for those working in finance and those in the federal agencies tasked with regulating them and found a striking divergence between the two. The authors note:

> At some point after incomes in the financial sector took off, lifetime earnings of the regulated far outstripped what any regulator could ever hope to earn. Rising economic inequality was translating into a crippling institutional weakness in regulatory structure. Not surprisingly, as one former member of a U.S. regulatory agency expressed it to us, regulatory agencies turned into barely disguised employment agencies, as staff increasingly focused on making themselves attractive hires to the firms they were supposed to be regulating.

In his film *Inside Job*, Charles Ferguson documents the insidious ways in which consulting fees and moonlighting gigs with financial companies created systematic conflicts of interest for some of the nation's most prominent economists. Ferguson's film parades through a number of the most admired names in the field, from Larry Summers to Martin Feldstein to Frederic Mishkin, who all had lucrative sidelines working for business interests with stakes in their academic work. Mishkin even took $124,000 from the Iceland Chamber of Commerce to write a paper endorsing the country's economic model, just a few years before it collapsed.

What we are left with is the confusion that arises from an ambiguity of roles: are our regulators attempting to rein in the excesses of those they regulate, or are they auditioning for a lucrative future job? Are economists who publish papers praising financial deregulation giving us an honest assessment of the facts and trends, or courting extremely lucrative consulting fees from banks?

In her book *Shadow Elite*, about the new global ruling class, Janine Wedel recalls visiting Eastern Europe after the fall of the Berlin Wall and finding the elites she met there—those at the center of building the new capitalist societies—toting an array of business cards that represented their various roles: one for their job as a member of parliament, another for the start-up business they were running (which was making its money off government contracts), and yet another for the NGO on the board of which they sat. Wedel writes that those "who adapted to the new environment with the most agility and creativity, who tried out novel ways of operating and got away with them, and sometimes were the most ethically challenged, were most rewarded with influence."

This has an eerie resonance with our predicament. We can never be sure just which other business cards are in the pocket of the pundit, politician or professor. We can't be sure, in short, just who our elites are working for.

But we suspect it is not us.

Tyranny of Merit

by SAMUEL W. GOLDMAN

Twilight of the Elites: America After Meritocracy, Christopher Hayes, Crown Publishers, 292 pages

"Elite" wasn't always a dirty word. Before the 19th century, the term described someone chosen for office. Because this typically occurred in the church, the word possessed distinctly ecclesiastical connotations. The pre-Victorians transformed a word imputing religious status to individual persons into a collective noun with class implications. By the 1830s, "elite" referred to

Equality of opportunity tends to be subverted by the inequality of outcome that meritocracy legitimizes.

the highest ranks of the nobility.

Those meanings are no longer primary. As invoked by followers of the Tea Party movement, for example, "elite" means essentially a snob. Not, however, a snob of the old, aristocratic breed. In this context, "elite" means men and women who think degrees from famous universities mean they know better than their fellow citizens.

Elites like these don't just look down on regular folks from provincial perches in Boston or Palo Alto. According to stump speeches, blogs, and TV commentators, They've been getting their way on Wall Street and in Washington for years, with disastrous results for the country.

MSNBC host Chris Hayes is no conservative. But he agrees that America is governed by a ruling class that has proved unworthy of its power. According to Hayes, the failures of the last decade created a deep crisis of authority. We counted on elites to do the right thing on our behalf. The Iraq War, steroid scandal in baseball, abuse cover-up in the Catholic Church, incompetent response to Hurricane Katrina, and, above all, financial crisis showed that they didn't know enough or care enough to do so.

Twilight of the Elites advances two explanations for these failures. The first emphasizes elite ignorance. People with a great deal of money or power aren't like the rest of us. Their schedules, pastimes, and even transportation are different to those of ordinary people. This isn't always because their tastes are distinctive, at least initially. It's often a job requirement.

In addition to their unusual lifestyles, elite types don't spend much time with averages Joes. At work, they're surrounded by subordinates. At home, they live in literally or metaphorically gated communities and socialize with people similar to themselves. Again, there's nothing sinister about this. Because of their distance from the rest of the population, however, members of the elite often have little idea what's going on in less rarefied settings.

One consequence, Hayes argues, is that elites have trouble making good decisions. Ignorant of the challenges that the poor and middle-class face and separated from the consequences of their actions, elites are susceptible to making policies that seem reasonable, but which on-the-ground experience would expose as ineffectual. Take the evacuation of New Orleans before Hurricane Katrina. It didn't succeed because many New Orleanians had nowhere to go, no money to get there, and no cars in which to escape—facts the mayor and governor should have known.

The distance of elites can also have moral consequences. When policies fail, isolated elites are more likely to blame their subjects than themselves. Politicians blamed poor New Orleanians for being too lazy to evacuate. Similarly, the sellers of toxic securities blamed their customers for being too stupid to appreciate the risks that they were accepting. In an especially revolting example, members of the national-security establishment blamed Iraqis for failing to appreciate invasion and occupation. For elites like these, it's always someone else's fault.

All elites risk falling out of touch, and always have. As Hayes notes, the Declaration of Independence argues that effective authority must be accountable authority. The other aspect of Hayes's theory of elite failure is more contemporary, though. The problem of ignorance, he argues, is exacerbated by the principle of selection used by our most influential institutions. According to Hayes, modern American elites are distinctive because they acquire status by means of ostensibly objective criteria. As a result, they think they deserve their wealth and power.

The ideal of meritocracy has deep roots in this country. Jefferson dreamed of a "natural aristocracy." But the modern meritocracy dates only to the 1930s, when Harvard President James Bryant Conant directed his admissions staff to find a measure of ability to supplement the old boys' network. They settled on the exam we know as the SAT.

In the decades following World War II, standardized testing replaced the gentleman's agreements that had governed the Ivy League. First Harvard, then Yale and the rest filled with the sons and eventually daughters of Jews, blue-collar workers, and other groups whose numbers had previously been limited.

After graduation, these newly pedigreed men and women flocked to New York and Washington. There, they took jobs once filled by products of New England boarding schools. One example is Lloyd Blankfein, the Bronx-born son of a Jewish postal clerk, who followed Harvard College and Harvard Law School with a job at a white-shoe law firm, which he left to join Goldman Sachs.

Hayes applauds the replacement of the WASP ascendancy with a more diverse cohort. The core of his book, however, argues that the principle on which they rose inevitably undermines itself.

The argument begins with the observation that meritocracy does not oppose unequal social and economic outcomes. Rather, it tries to justify inequality by offering greater rewards to the talented and hardworking.

The problem is that the effort presumes that everyone has the same chance to compete under the same rules. That may be true at the outset. But equality of opportunity tends to be subverted by the inequality of outcome that meritocracy legitimizes. In

short, according to Hayes, "those who are able to climb up the ladder will find ways to pull it up after them, or to selectively lower it down to allow their friends, allies and kin to scramble up. In other words: 'whoever says meritocracy says oligarchy.'"

With a nod to the early 20th-century German sociologist Robert Michels, Hayes calls this paradox the "Iron Law of Meritocracy."

In the most personal section of the book, he describes the way the Iron Law of Meritocracy operates at his *alma mater*, Hunter College High

School in New York City. Admission to Hunter is based on the results of a single test offered to 6th graders who did well on statewide tests in 5th grade. Because there are no preferences for legacies, donors, members of minority groups, or athletes, admission to Hunter seems like a pure application of the meritocratic principle.

It doesn't work that way. Although its student body once reflected the racial and economic proportions of the city, Hunter has grown increasingly wealthy and white. Why? In Hayes's view, rich parents have discovered strategies to game the system. By buying cognitive enhancements like foreign travel, music lessons, tutoring in difficult subjects, and outright test prep, these parents give their kids a substantial leg up.

These children are better prepared than rivals from poor or negligent families. But it's hard to conclude that they've earned their advantage. They're clearly bright and hardworking. Yet they've also been fortunate to have parents who know what it takes to climb the ladder and can pay for those advantages. The ideal of meritocracy obscures the accidents of birth. From Hunter to Harvard to Goldman Sachs, the meritocrats proceed through life convinced that they owe their rise exclusively to their own efforts.

This sense of entitlement is one reason meritocratic elites are particularly susceptible to pathologies of distance. They don't only have distinctive lifestyles. They're convinced that they really deserve their privileges.

Could a radicalized upper-middle class turn from the bulwark of meritocracy into its opponent?

Of course, most elites have fancied themselves a superior breed. The way meritocracy obscures the role of chance, however, encourages the modern elite to think of themselves as unusually deserving individuals rather than members of a ruling class with responsibilities to the rest of society.

Finally, Hayes argues, the selection of the elite for academic accomplishment leads to a cult of intelligence that discounts the practical wisdom necessary for good decision-making. Remember Enron? They were the smartest guys in the room.

Hayes oversells his argument as a unified explanation of the "fail decade." Although it elucidates some aspects of the Iraq War, Katrina debacle, and financial crisis, these disasters had other

causes. Nevertheless, the Iron Law of Meritocracy elucid why our elites take the form they do and how they fell so out touch with reality. In Hayes's account, the modern elite is caught in a feedback loop that makes it less and less open and more and more isolated from the rest of the country.

What's to be done? One answer is to rescue meritocracy by providing the poor and middle class with the resources to compete. A popular strategy focuses on education reform. If schools were better, the argument goes, poor kids could compete on an equal footing for entry into the elite. The attempt to rescue meritocracy by fixing education has become a bipartisan consensus, reflected in Bush's "No Child Left Behind" and Obama's "Race to the Top."

Hayes rejects this option. The defect of meritocracy, in his view, is not the inequality of opportunity that it conceals, but the inequality of outcome that it celebrates. In other words, the problem is not that the son of a postal clerk has less chance to become a Wall Street titan than he used to. It's that the rewards of a career on Wall Street have become so disproportionate to the rewards of the traditional professions, let alone those available to a humble civil servant.

Hayes's prescription, then, is simple: we should raise taxes on the rich and increase redistributive payments to the poor and middle class.

Raising taxes is surprisingly popular, at least in principle. According to one poll Hayes cites, 81 percent of Americans favor a surtax on incomes over $1 million a year. Nevertheless, these seem unlikely to be enacted. Among other reasons, the legislators who would have to approve them are either drawn from or depend on the same class that the taxes target.

Yet Hayes is optimistic about the prospects for egalitarian reform. He places his hopes on a radicalized up-

per-middle class. As recently as a decade ago, people with graduate degrees and six-figure incomes could think of themselves as prospective members of the elite. While the income and influence of the very rich has zoomed ahead, however, the stagnation of the economy has left the moderately well-off at risk of proletarianization.

Despite their ideological differences, both the Tea Party and Occupy Wall Street draw support from this class. It's just that the Tea Party appeals to the parents, while Occupy mobilizes the kids.

Could a radicalized upper-middle class turn from the bulwark of meritocracy into its opponent? That seems unlikely for three reasons.

First, the polls Hayes mentions do not document popular support for redistribution. They indicate that Americans want to tax the rich to cover the deficit. Americans like their current entitlements and want to keep them. But there's no evidence that they endorse the egalitarian agenda Hayes has in mind.

Second, there's a tension between this agenda and the social liberalism to which Hayes is committed. Social scientists have found that we're willing to share resources with others like ourselves. We're reluctant, however, to make sacrifices for people we consider different or objectionable.

In a section on the "two eras of equality," Hayes urges us to adopt the solidaristic norms that characterize relatively homogeneous societies, including the United States circa 1960. At the same time, he praises the diversity and freedom of contemporary America. These things don't go together, in practice if not in principle.

The tax regime of 50 years ago was legitimatized by a broad consensus about the proper uses of shared prosperity. The more libertarian views dominant today are also relatively consistent across economic and social realms. Hayes thinks that we can combine the economic virtues of the former era with the social virtues of latter. That's wishful thinking.

I mentioned at the beginning of this review that Hayes is not a conservative. That's no defect in itself. But this book would have been improved, in the end, by engaging with the conservative tradition.

The central insight of this tradition is that there is no society without a governing class. Whether they're selected by birth, intelligence, or some other factor, some people inevitably exercise power over others. Hayes mounts a powerful critique of the meritocratic elite that has overseen one of the most disastrous periods of recent history. He lapses into utopianism, however, when he suggests that we can do without elites altogether. Like the poor, elites will always be with us. As the word's original meaning suggests, the question is how they ought to be chosen.

Samuel Goldman is a postdoctoral fellow at Prince ton University and a contributor to TAC's State of the Union blog.

Americans pride themselves on being a nation that rewards merit (achieved status) and not just your position born into a hierarchy (ascribed status). Many American believe that the United States is a "classless society." Unfortunately, that is a myth. The United States is a state-level complex society. All such societies that have ever existed possess hierarchichal divisions. We know that there is the Upper Class (now often referred to as "the 1%"), the Middle Class (which all observers now agree is shrinking), and the Lower Class (many of whom have fallen below the poverty line, and are in a constant struggle for mere survival).

The Failure of Merit-based selection processes

Hayes illustrates the problems of the so-called "meritocracy," by revealling the selection process for the private school he attended in Manhattan, that shows how, via "institutional corruption," the merit based procedures relied upon in the United States have been subverted by the elites. They spend money on tutoring and training for their children, giving them an advantage in the standardized test-taking upon which American education is built, which in turn puts them into the replacement category for their parents. That, in essence, makes the system a hereditary one, short-circuiting the purpose of finding and rewarding merit wherever it may be found.

Snob?

The second article reviews the first author's conclusions, noting how the word "elite" has come to mean "snob," and that whatever the situation, elites will always be needed. Goldman, in the end, does not really gainsay most of Hayes' argument. But, he makes the most challenging point of all, which may be correct: elites in complex societies will always be there. Did Jesus, with his comment: "You shall have the poor with you always" recognize this truth about complex state-level societies? As all states have always had hierarchies, so will all states always have elites. Goldman doubts that Hayes' suggestion, to empower the Middle Class to challenge the merit selection processes, will ultimately work. The question for you, as the next generation to run things, is one that will come up in a number of contexts of this course: even if it was so in the past in complex societies, *must* it be so in the future?

CONCLUSION: WRAP-UP

Eating Christmas in the Kalahari is the second very popular article that demonstrates how anthropology can turn everything on its head, as we try to explore experience of the "Other" from a standpoint of our own cultural practices. Richard Lee was taught a very powerful lesson by his treatment and we gained an insight into the dynamics of human living (via foraging) for most of our existence. The modern world is very different from the world of the forager, but is there something valuable about the ancient ways from which we could profit? Perhaps the real lesson is that egalitarianism is fragile and easily lost. But, as we contemplate a world of increasing and problematic inequality, are there things that we could do to restore the better balance that our foraging ancestors possessed, or is that world gone forever? Something to think about.

The two pieces on elites are from different viewpoints. Historically, all complex societies have been dominated by their elites. The political philosophy of the United States, by abolishing a hereditary aristocracy, tries to uphold merit as the principle of advancement rather than heredity. Is this ultimately going to work? Or is Goldman right that elites are (as he suggests) a necessary evil. The idea is that the emulation of elites (a practice that can be traced back to 7th c. BCE Athens, and elsewhere, for example) has brought us to this state. You will see, how our lives are affected by the need to emulate in the next chapter.

What about the elites? Is Hayes right that a measured response from the middle classes can right the situation, or is Goldman right that Hayes is just "utopian"? Everyone should be aware that the coiner of that word, Thomas More, used a Greek phrase, *ou topia*, meaning "No Place," so utopias really don't exist anywhere. Given that social stratification produces elites and that all state-level societies have them, and that virtually all the cultures in the world are now state-level societies, are elites something that might go away, and we would cease to need to emulate them? Possibly, they will be with us always. But does that mean we cannot do things to avoid the problems of emulation and the stress that comes with it? Can you or your colleagues envision a world where elites are NOT automatically favored and that the ideal of American egalitarianism might actually prove the robust rule of the state?

ACTIVITIES

Activity Reading #8: split into small groups and come up with answers to the following questions: Start with your ideas on the motivations of gift-giving. Then, take up the following: the San People make fun of excellent hunting, while enjoying its benefits. That illustrates "reverse hierarchy dominance." We think that such leveling mechanisms must have been in play for most of human history because for most of human history, humans have been foragers— living by hunting and gathering. Although this is a modern context, it seems likely that humans (and our ancestor species) prevented inequality in a manner such as this.

- Do you think it is reasonable for the San to make fun of a good hunter?
- Do you think that a feature such as this one can prevent inequality from arising?
- Before the change of regime, the South African Defense Forces used San hunters to track down and capture African National Congress guerillas; the SADF officers praised the hunting skills of their San employees. What effect would that have had on the San cultural feature of belittling hunters?
- What did the San do to someone who refused to "cool their heart?"
- Is the San cultural feature "fair" to individuals? Why or why not?

Activity Readings #9 and #10: Chief or Commoner? Split into small groups and discuss the following quote:

> *...a person's view of elites in past societies depends on whether one feels he or she was a 'Chief' or a 'commoner' in any previous incarnation. The chiefs will point to the achievements of hierarchically organized societies: the technological inventions, the scientific discoveries, the great works of art and architecture, the invention of writing, the development of literature, the institutions of government, the rule of law. They see elites as benefactors, serving the community as a whole, presiding over harmony within and defending a united society against attack from the outside. The commoners, on the other hand, argue that for the mass of the population all the achievements of civilization are but a poor exchange for the loss of freedom, equality and control over their own economic means enjoyed by hunters and simple tribal farmers. They therefore regard elites as fundamentally exploitative – if not always grinding the faces of the poor, at least keeping them in perpetual economic servitude. Elites do not work in the interests of a united society, but in their own interests by domination of a divided society. As far as we can judge these views objectively, there seems to be some truth on both sides.*

- Do you think magnanimity payments (such as Bill Gates' charities) are sufficient to defuse the natural resentment of commoners?
- A class system often depends on social mobility (allowing achieved status) for success (to defuse the resentment of commoners?); does meritocracy improve the situation of "chiefs" so that mobility is overcome by inequality, leading to oligarchy?
- Goldman closes with the comment, paraphrased from the New Testament that "You shall have elites {or the poor} with you always." Does that seem to be a realistic assessment?
- Close with a general discussion of: "is increasing inequality the world over a contemporary world problem?

SOURCES

Reverse Hierarchy Dominance comes from an article by Christopher Boehm; Harold B. Barclay; Robert Knox Dentan; Marie-Claude Dupre; Jonathan D. Hill; Susan Kent; Bruce M. Knauft; Keith F. Otterbein; Steve Rayner 1993 Egalitarian Behavior and Reverse Dominance Hierarchy [and Comments and Reply] *Current Anthropology* 34: 227-254. Magnanimity payments are discussed by James L. Boone. 1998. The Evolution of Magnanimity: When Is It Better To Give Than To Receive? *Human Nature* 9: 1-21. The Chief or Commoner quote is adapted from Ruth Whitehouse and John Wilkins 1986 *The Making of Civilization: History Discovered Through Archaeology* New York: Harper Collins p. 93.

Chapter 4

Consumerism: Building Identities or Wasteful Potlatching?

OBJECTIVES

- Determine to what extent consumerism is a cause of some modern world problems.
- Explain how anthropology has viewed the human tendency to consume in two ways: 1) as a way to use material objects to establish identities within cultural context and 2) as a strategy in many societies which leads to competitive destruction of material goods in competition with other human groups.
- Explore ways to deal with the pressures of competitive consumerism.

KEY TERMS

Conspicuous Consumption: coined by the sociologist/economist Thorsten Veblen to characterize the wasteful and questionable destruction of wealth by North American and European elites, using goods to bolster their social position.

Clutter: the unprecedented piling up of material goods that are being accumulated in average North American homes that causes stress but is a sign of identity.

Potlatch: the deliberate public destruction of material wealth in order to assert dominance over rivals watching the event.

SCHEMA ACTIVATION ACTIVITY

Write down your thoughts in answer to the following prompt: *Make a list of the 10 material objects that you believe that you absolutely MUST possess in order to keep up with your peers.*

(Save these to share later in your discussion sections.)

INTRODUCTION

In this Chapter, we reconsider an old idea from an American economist: the idea of "conspicuous consumption," whereby the elites (in continuation from the previous chapter) use consumption as a way to establish identity (and possibly dominance over other elements of society). One issue that will become clear is that we emulate the consumption habits of the elites, so that, in many ways, the pattern they have established has carried over into defining what the rest of the population does in this regard. Are we all "conspicuous consumers"? That answer may be personally sobering to all of us, as the archaeologist Jeanne Arnold and her team demonstrate.

What Would Thorstein Veblen Say?

The Nagging Problem of Conspicuous Consumption

David Scott
Texas A&M University
College Station, Texas

There is an old saying, sometimes attributed to social psychologist Kurt Levin, that there is nothing so practical as a good theory. I use this maxim as a point of departure for exploring the relevance of Thorstein Veblen's *The Theory of the Leisure Class* [1] to contemporary leisure. Originally published in 1899, the book is a scathing attack on the greedy leisure class of the day.[2] The book also sheds light on how all people use wealth and goods to bolster their social position relative to their neighbors and peers. To this day, sociologists use Veblen's ideas about status seeking to illustrate how patterns of economic inequality, female subordination, and environmental abuse are perpetuated.[3, 4, 5, 6]

Surprisingly, few leisure scholars employ Veblen's ideas about status seeking to understand contemporary forms of leisure. One exception is Chris Rojek,[7] but he warns against assuming that styles of leisure and consumption among the upper classes trickle down to the rest of society. It could be that many students of leisure simply have never read *The Theory of the Leisure Class*, or perhaps they consider the work outdated and relevant only to the study of leisure of a bygone era. To be fair, many passages in the book are dense, and several of my graduate students over the years have struggled with Veblen's style of writing. Nevertheless, I believe Veblen's ideas are as relevant today as they were over 100 years ago when the book was first published.

My goal in this chapter is to elucidate some of Veblen's ideas and then illustrate how they illuminate leisure spending, emulation among bird watchers, display of books, boundary maintenance and social distance, and environmental destruction. I warn you that my examples are intended to poke fun at how many Americans (including myself) think and act. Veblen's style was analytic, but there was a strong moral undertone to his work.[8] He was also a bit of satirist, and many of his status-seeking examples are funny. It is in this spirit that I consider Veblen. His ideas inform our understanding of leisure as scholars and as human beings. I believe we will be better people if we read and understand his work.

Understanding The Theory of the Leisure Class

A key premise in *The Theory of the Leisure Class* is that people strive for status and to elevate their social position in the eyes of others. Veblen used the term "emulation" to describe a "pervading trait of human nature"[9] whereby individuals seek favorable comparisons with others. To Veblen, emulation was a deep-seated motive that drives individuals to grade themselves and others in regard to worth. Emulation involves people distancing themselves from others deemed to be unworthy, while striving to take on the attitudes and behaviors of individuals judged to be respectable or prestigious. Although Veblen's work is largely a criticism of the leisure class of nineteenth century America, he recognized that emulation was practiced across all socioeconomic levels in society: "Members of each stratum accept as their ideal of decency the scheme of life in vogue in the next higher stratum, and bend their energies to live up that ideal."[10]

Veblen's ideas about status seeking provide insight into the origins of stratification processes in society. Veblen argued that the beginning of class differences stem from importance ascribed to various employments. Employments held in high esteem were exploitive in nature; unworthy employments smacked of drudgery and were deemed "debasing and ignoble." Although distinctions in employment remained pervasive during Veblen's lifetime, he saw that status and social position were conferred increasingly simply on the basis of wealth. Veblen noted that wealth provided a "customary basis of repute and esteem"[11] and had become "intrinsically honourable."[12] Today, wealth is an important indicator of social class in the United States, and Americans can readily be arranged along a hierarchy from rich to poor.

Veblen, however, believed that status did not automatically accrue to individuals who had wealth. Rather, people obtained status by advertising or putting their wealth on display. Veblen noted, "Wealth or power must be put in evidence, for esteem is awarded only on evidence."[13] One way people advertise their wealth is by engaging in conspicuous leisure, which Veblen defined as "non-productive consumption of time."[14] This definition is a bit cryptic, but the idea is that people have sufficient time to pursue activities and develop skills that show they are exempt from productive work and they are able to afford a life of idleness. Having leisure stemmed from a belief that productive work was vulgar and debasing.

What kinds of skills and activities would indicate that one could afford to be idle? In Veblen's day, these included "knowledge of the dead languages and the occult sciences; of correct spelling; of syntax and prosody; of the various forms of domestic music and other household art; of the latest proprieties of dress, furniture, and equipage; of games, sports, and fancy-bred animals, such as dogs and race-horses."[15] They also advertised their social position via "manners and breeding, polite usage, decorum, and formal and ceremonial observances generally."[16] In sum, conspicuous leisure included a wide range of skills and knowledge that clearly demonstrated that one was excused from paid work.

It is important to note that the life of leisure that Veblen wrote about in *The Theory of the Leisure Class* required more than just time—conspicuous leisure required considerable effort. To have leisure was not the same thing as a life of sloth. People had to demonstrate tangible proof that they were exempt from a whole range of employments. Manners provided Veblen a vehicle for driving home his point. He stated that the display of good manners "requires time, application, and expense, and can therefore not be compassed by those whose time and energy are taken up with work. A knowledge of good form is *prima facie* evidence that portions of the well-bred person's life which is not under the observation of the spectator has been *worthily spent* [italics added] in acquiring accomplishments that are of no lucrative effect."[17] The acquisition of manners and other skills required a specialized education that involved "a laborious drill in deportment and an education in taste and discrimination as to what articles of consumption are decorous and what are the decorous methods of consuming them."[18] Thus, much sweat went into developing the skills and knowledge that come under the banner of conspicuous leisure.

A second way people advertise their wealth is through conspicuous consumption. Veblen did not provide a precise definition, but it can be understood as the purchase and display of goods and services for the express purpose of showing off one's wealth and social position. Goods obviously have practical value and provide comfort to the buyer. Veblen, however, recognized that many goods are purchased because they are "a mark of prowess and perquisite of human dignity."[19] Being able to buy and show off goods and services that are excessive and too expensive for others to acquire derives status. According to King,[20] the entire Gilded Age rested on conspicuous consumption. During this era, exclusivity and outward appearances drove elites to pay exorbitant sums of money for clothes, jewelry, artwork, servants, travel, carriages and yachts, homes, and hosting parties and balls.

Women's clothing provides a useful example of conspicuous consumption. During Veblen's lifetime, elite women were raised to be dependent on men and were objects of display. As such, their clothing was often highly impractical and adorned to give evidence that they were exempt from productive work and thus beholden to the men in their lives. According to Veblen, "the high heel, the skirt, the impracticable bonnet, the corset, and the general disregard of the wearer's comfort, which is an obvious feature of all civilized women's apparel"[21] reflected conspicuous consumption in the decoration of women's clothing. Today, many women continue to wear clothes that are impractical, astonishingly expensive, and provide evidence of their subservient position in society.[22] Furthermore, expensive clothing is often worn for a relatively short period of time and then discarded with the introduction of new fashions. Thus, for many women, clothing functions primarily as adornment and secondarily as affording comfort.

Although the display of status can be achieved by either conspicuous leisure or conspicuous consumption, there are several reasons why Americans today rely progressively more on the latter to advertise their social position. One reason is that most people have to work to make a living. Few Americans have independent means to spend their lives in pastimes that have little outward productive value. A related reason is that employment has become highly valued as an end in itself. Riesman observed that Veblen's book had immediate shock value in America and many elites sought to distance themselves from practices that smacked of pretentiousness.[23] A life of leisure thus became a sign of wealth unjustly earned.

Perhaps the most important reason for the ascent of conspicuous consumption is that we live in societies that are now highly mobile where interactions are often ephemeral. Veblen recognized over a century ago that as societies become differentiated and fast paced, conspicuous consumption would become far more efficient than conspicuous leisure to convey one's social position: "In order to impress these transient observers, and to retain one's self-complacency under their observation, the signature of one's pecuniary strength should be written in characters which he who runs may read."[24] For all these reasons, status seeking today is far more likely to be expressed through consumption than skills and knowledge acquired during leisure time.

This is enough summary for the time being. There are other points from *The Theory of the Leisure Class* that need to be made, but I will flesh them out as I seek to demonstrate the relevance of Veblen's work to contemporary leisure in America.

Stuff Girls Need

I was recently discarding some newspaper advertisements, which I do with annoying regularity, when my eye caught a two-page ad that read, "Stuff girls need ... for so much less!" This particular advertisement included two teenage girls striking relaxed poses while wearing comfortable and reasonably priced pajamas. The advertisement also included English Lavender bath and body soap, spring sandals and some very comfortable looking shoes, and a multicolored handbag that took me back to the 1960s. Like the pajamas, all of these items seemed affordable. The last set of items on the page really caught my attention. They were four pairs of "fashion readers" (also known as fashion reading glasses). The glasses were priced at $19.99 each and they came in red, pink, lime, and aqua. I suppose these, too, were reasonably priced, although I have never actually priced fashion readers.

Elites in Veblen's day would have giggled at the irony of the phrase, "Stuff girls need … for so much less!" Then again, advertisements like this are not intended for people who do not have to worry about their budget. What really stands out for me is the assumption that we consumers (not just girls) *need* stuff displayed in the advertisements. Do teenage girls really need a bright red pair of fashion readers?

Most Americans can differentiate between an authentic need and a transitory want. Yet we live our lives as if a bright red pair of fashion readers was something we truly need. I don't think Veblen would have been surprised. He argued that people begin to look upon many of the goods and service they buy as necessities and regard them as vital to their lifestyle. Our neighbors and friends provide us clues about what is fashionable and decorous. Likewise, advertisers remind us constantly about what products, services, and tourism destinations are *de rigueur*. Most of us, of course, have to settle for less, but we nonetheless make purchases of a whole range of goods and services as if we needed them. According to Veblen, once people achieve a particular standard of living, that standard takes on the form of "habit" and only reluctantly do people recede from it.

These so-called "habits" are formed early and are quite ingrained by the time we enter adulthood. In fact, many teenagers and young adults are growing up these days with the expectation that they are entitled to a whole range of goods, services, and opportunities that were simply unavailable to generations of teens before them. Many of my college students don't find it unusual that they own their own pickup trucks, have their own personal computers, have credit cards in their own names, live in luxury condominiums, belong to private fitness clubs, own pedigreed dogs, and travel to exotic places during spring break. Many of them would undoubtedly agree that all of these possessions are stuff they need.

Students graduate and move on to newer and higher standards of living and emulation. Veblen observed that standards for emulation are ever changing, which gives rise to a gradual dissatisfaction with our current goods: "But as fast as a person makes new acquisitions, and becomes accustomed to the resulting new standard of wealth, the new standard forthwith ceases to afford appreciably greater satisfaction than the earlier standard did."[25] This means that our current thoughts about sufficiency are challenged as new standards of fashion and emulation arise. The adage, "keeping up with the Joneses" gets at this idea neatly. The point here is that people are perpetually concerned about their social position relative to their peers and make new purchases, lest their social standing depreciate. Thus, my students have graduated to bigger houses, bigger boats, and bigger television sets. They have also graduated to more expensive trucks, golf clubs, and vacation destinations.

In her provocative book, *The Overworked American*,[26] Juliet Schor noted that productivity among Americans doubled between 1948 and 1990. Put differently, Americans in 1990 were able to reproduce the 1948 standard of living in half the time. This means we could work far less (as little as 20 hours per week) and still maintain the same standard of living we had a few generations ago. We could have used this gain in free time to learn a second language, take leisurely walks in the park with our children, till our gardens, learn how to play the guitar, learn our neighbors' names, and volunteer at the local food pantry. Schor recognized, however, that our lifestyles are oriented to an "insidious cycle of work-and-spend."[27] The simple truth is that we Americans prefer goods and services to free time. As Veblen observed over 100 years ago, our status in the community will be judged increasingly by our appearances and not by the skills we have obtained during our leisure time. Thus, my standing among my peers has little to do with my ability to identify bird songs, my knowledge about Abraham Lincoln, or my limited talent as a former thespian. Rather, my reputation has everything to do with the car I drive, the size of my house, the artwork I display in my home, the schools to which I send my children, and my choice of vacation destinations. I need all this stuff. My place in the community demands it.

I'm Forcing Myself

In the 2006 film, *Priceless*, Audrey Tautou plays a gold digger by the name of Irène who finds herself compromised when she confuses Jean, a poor bartender on the French Riviera, for a rich suitor. Without any immediate prospects, Irène callously allows Jean to spend his small life savings on her in a 24-hour self-indulgent spree. One of Irène's excesses is caviar, a food she tells Jean that she loathes: "I don't even really like caviar, but I'm forcing myself." Irène knows she should cultivate a taste for this delicacy because it is expensive and it is something rich people eat. Perhaps she will be expected to consume more of it if she can only find the right man to take care of her.

Irène's attitude about caviar is neither extraordinary nor surprising. Veblen understood that people's tastes and definitions of beauty are very much a product "of the expensiveness of the articles."[28] This means that products that are expensive and in relative scarce supply will be regarded as intrinsically more beautiful, tasteful, authentic, and fashionable. Veblen's classic example is his comparison between silver and wrought iron spoons. Although both are equally functional, the former is regarded by fashion-minded people as more beautiful and delicate simply on the basis of the expense that went into making it.

I suspect that many Americans make similar judgments with regard to a whole range of goods and services. The corned beef I purchase at a top gourmet food store seems tastier than the corned beef my neighbor routinely purchases at the delicatessen at our local grocery store. The designer jeans I bought in Houston appear lovelier and seem to have a better fit than the jeans I tried on at Kmart©. I keep telling my wife that the $3,000, 50" inch plasma television set that I have my eye on will offer us more enjoyment and better entertainment than the $300, 26" standard-definition television set we currently own. I also tell her that I will be able to enjoy bird watching so much more with a $2,000 pair of binoculars. She just rolls her eyes.

However, there have been times I have failed to keep up appearances, and this has caused me no small amount of embarrassment. On my first and only visit to the opera I fell sound asleep. What can I say? I like rock-and-roll! My outdoor friends continue to laugh at me because I think the sleeping bags at REI© are overpriced. And I always feel ridiculous being the only person at a wine and cheese party who isn't making a fuss over the great taste of the expensive pinot noir. However, like Irène, I'm forcing myself to drink it even though what I really want is an ice-cold beer.

Books by the Yard

There is an amusing episode in Richard Russo's book, *Straight Man*,[29] when the major character, William Henry Devereaux, Jr., visits Dickie Pope, the chief executive officer (CEO) at the western Pennsylvania university where he works. Devereaux, an English professor and interim chair, is left alone in Dickie's office and spends a few minutes browsing the hundreds of books on his tall built-in bookshelf. As Devereaux peruses Dickie's library, he recalls a colleague's story that all of the books had been purchased at local auctions and secondhand book stores just prior to the CEO taking over the office. The story goes that Dickie had moved to the college town without any books of his own and he "sensed that it wouldn't be a good idea to fill the shelves with family photos and ceramic knickknacks."[30]

Fearing academic derision, Dickie commissioned his accommodating secretary to fill up the bookshelf with appropriate looking volumes that "befitted the chief executive officer of an institution of higher learning."[31]

Veblen surely would have understood Dickie's predicament. It is very important that we exhibit tangible evidence of our social position. The books that many of us own and display reflect our inquiring nature and our many interests. From time to time, we academics even open some of our books as we write articles and seek answers to life's thorny questions. Even if we don't read books, most of us, like Dickie, need to maintain appearances. Thus, most of the books we own are for display purposes only. I own several of these books myself and I have them strategically positioned on the coffee table in my living room so visitors can see just what kind of person I am.

The good news for fashioned-minded Americans is there are businesses that specialize in helping us create eye-catching libraries. One such company specializes in selling leather-bound books that are "visually enhancing and their addition to any decorative scheme creates an immediate impact and gives lasting pleasure." Most of the books supplied by the business were "published and bound in the eighteenth and nineteenth centuries and are offered in a wide variety of colours." This company assumes buyers won't actually read the books, because it is appearances, not facts, which count.[32] The books are "approximately six to nine inches in height and are primarily chosen for their decorative bindings rather than their subject matter." Buyers on a budget or individuals who simply need to fill a lot of shelf space will be happy to know that this company sells books by the yard.

I Need that Bird!

Serious bird watchers across the United States no doubt celebrated their 15 minutes of fame in January 2004 when *Sports Illustrated* published an article by Mark Obmascik about three men's battle to list as many birds as they could in the United States and Canada in a single calendar year.[33] The event, called a Big Year, was chronicled further by Obmascik in his popular book, *The Big Year: A Tale of Man, Nature, and Fowl Obsession.*[34] A Big Year is not for the faint of heart. It is a marathon birding extravaganza that borders on the obsessive. Participants spend thousands of dollars, travel untold miles crisscrossing North America, endure seasickness, extreme temperatures, and biting mosquitoes, and forsake loved ones and careers in their attempt to amass large lists of birds.

Big Year participants belong to a group of bird watchers that describe themselves as birders. One of North America's most well-known birdwatchers, Ken Kaufman,[35] provided a useful definition of birders—they "are out to seek, to discover, to chase, to learn, to find as many different kinds of birds as possible—and in friendly competition, to try to find more of them than the next birder."[36] Importantly, most birders keep life lists of all the bird species they have identified by sight and sound. There are actually a multitude of life lists that people keep. Some birders keep a list of the birds they have identified worldwide. Most North American birders keep a life list of North American birds (which arbitrarily includes the birds of Alaska, Canada, and the lower 48 states). Many also maintain state and province lists, county lists, and yard lists. Some even keep lists of all the birds they have identified by sound when watching movies.

In their efforts to list birds, many serious birders will travel long distances, often at a moment's notice, to track down vagrants and accidentals. In 2004, for example, thousands of birders from across North America traveled to South Texas to see a Crimson-Collared Grosbeak, a Mexican species that strayed into the United States. Birders routinely make similar pilgrimages to other birding hotspots across North America in order to chase rarities that they can add to their life lists. It is common to hear serious birders say, "I need that bird," and off they go in fevered pursuit of their target bird.

The stakes pursued by serious birders are pretty minimal. None of the three birders chronicled by Obmascik are household names. Nevertheless, I think Veblen would understand that serious birders are motivated by standards of emulation that are clear and that lead to unambiguous patterns of conspicuous consumption. Seeing birds that others have not seen is a badge of honor. Simultaneously, although a life list is an imperfect measure of birding skill,[37] its length remains a point of comparison among birders and compels them to travel long distances and spend large sums of money to list new birds.

To be fair, serious bird watchers are not very different from participants in other leisure activities. Standards of emulation exist across a whole range of pastimes and inspire participants to spend lavishly as they seek conquests and enhanced reputations. Some golfers, for example, travel extensively to play at different golf courses. Their mentality is to "collect" golf courses,[38] and many, I'm sure, spend handsomely over their lifetime in their quest. A collecting mentality is similarly evident among hunters and anglers, whitewater rafters, mountain climbers and rock climbers, skiers, baseball fans, and even world travelers. It is no coincidence that the subtitle of Patricia Schultz's bestselling travel book, *1,000 Places to See Before You Die* reads *A Traveler's Life List*.[39] I wonder how many Americans treat the book like gospel and spend excessive amounts of money as they travel to places that Schultz says they need to see.

It Would Never Do

During the Gilded Age of New York, strict rules were in place with regard to membership in high society. Many aspired to inclusion, but few were deemed properly qualified. According to King, "exclusion provided this new elite with its *raison d'être*: to be desirable, society must be seen as something distinct."[40] Old English and Dutch families with money were judged eligible. New money could potentially buy a place in high society, but that was the exception rather than the rule. The nouveau riche lacked the proper pedigrees and most individuals with newly acquired wealth were derogated for their vulgar and working-class origins. Could people of color hope to penetrate elite society? Flamboyant socialite Mamie Fish of this era provided a frank answer: "I do not believe in being too democratic. ... I shall not like to have to eat with Negroes. ... It would never do. We cannot mix with the Negro at all, and Negro equality will never come about."[41]

Veblen's *The Theory of the Leisure Class* skirted issues of ethnic and racial ostracism as he was interested in how people used wealth to impress others. However, Veblen would not have been surprised by Mamie Fish's candid remark. Indeed, scholars have noted that Veblen's ideas about social status were impacted some by his marginal status as the son of Norwegian immigrant.[42, 43, 44] For my purposes, it seems clear that Veblen's ideas are relevant in understanding why people in the United States create boundaries in their leisure to distance themselves from Blacks and a whole lot of other groups they define as inferior.

Recall that Veblen believed "emulation" was a fundamental trait of human nature that motivated people to strive for social status among their neighbors and contemporaries. That means our attitudes and behaviors conform to those whom we admire. It also means that we separate ourselves from others deemed unworthy, unattractive or socially inferior. This view of Veblen's work coincides with social psychologists' certainty that we naturally assign people to social categories. According to Massey, we humans are "mentally hardwired to engage in categorical thought"[45] and "we hold in our heads schemas that classify people into categories based on age, gender, race, and ethnicity."[46]

The company we keep bolsters our social position. Elites in Veblen's time created exclusive clubs to avoid the tarnish of mixing with people of questionable repute.[47] Today elites and non-elites alike create boundaries around their leisure to ensure they mix with the "right" company. Doing otherwise can mean a soiled reputation. Fraternities and sororities on college campuses routinely screen would-be members on the basis of race, ethnicity, and physical appearance.[48] Likewise, Americans created thousands of residential swimming pools and private swim clubs after municipal pools were desegregated in the 1950s. According to Wiltse, private pools allowed middle-class Whites "to exercise greater control over whom they swam with than was possible at public pools."[49] Private pools continue to ensure that White Americans need not swim with Blacks and other people who would potentially damage their social standing among peers. I suppose my minority students and I would only make waves if we were to crash some all-white church on Sunday. I can hear several long-standing parishioners say, "It would never do."

Killers of Baby Birds!

In the late 1800s, a nascent Audubon Society formed and grew in response to the appalling destruction of birds for women's dress. According to Kastner, "The plumed hat, fan, and wrap, decorated with feathers of ostrich or egret or even songbirds, was the essential fashion at the end of the nineteenth century."[50] The long, showy plumes of herons and egrets were particularly valued as ornaments. Weidensaul notes that a single egret feather was "worth roughly twice its weight in gold in the late 1890s."[51] Weidensaul estimated that the plume trade resulted in the harvesting of 200 million birds a year. Early Audubon leaders were instrumental in bringing visibility to the impact that fashion had on the destruction of birds. Fashioned-minded women who wore plumes "were assailed with epithets: 'Murderers! Killers of baby birds!'"[52] The Audubon Society was ultimately instrumental in lobbying the government to pass strict laws (e.g., the 1918 Migratory Bird Treaty Act) and establish wildlife refuges that protected birds and other wildlife from wanton destruction.

Although issues regarding environmental exploitation were in their embryonic stage during Veblen's lifetime, sociologists are beginning to understand that his ideas "offer precious insights on the role of humanity in both causing and exacerbating global environmental crises."[53] (Remember this when reading Troy's chapter following mine.) Veblen clearly understood that people across all strata of society are wasteful in their efforts to maintain appearances: "In order to be reputable it [consumption] must be wasteful. No merit would accrue from the consumption of the bare necessaries of life, except by comparison with the abjectly poor who fall short even of the subsistence minimum."[54] Just how wasteful are we? Judging from what we have done to our planet in the last 100 years—unchecked deforestation, global warming, the thinning of the ozone layer, the draining of wetlands, the dumping of toxic wastes into our oceans, lakes and rivers, the decline of species diversity—I would say that we have been very wasteful indeed. Our waste is also reflected in our dependence on oil and continued abuse of the planet to wrestle every last drop we can from it. Were Veblen alive today, I think we would agree that we will continue to abuse the Earth and its resources as long as we remain obsessed with our appearances relative to our neighbors and peers.

The origins of conservation stem in part from recognition of our excesses as human beings. I noted above that early bird protection came about when ordinary people saw the connection between thoughtless destruction of avian wildlife and contemporary fashions. It is important to note that many of the leaders of the movement to end the plume trade were women who had themselves adorned their dress with skins and feathers. One of those women, Harriet Lawrence Hemenway, experienced what Weidensaul described as "a road-to-Damascus conversion and became a champion of conservation."[55]

Our excesses stem from our need to keep up appearances. I am convinced that we can quit fashion and live a more humane, ecologically friendly lifestyle. We can begin doing this by committing to reduce our carbon footprint. We can also live with less and say goodbye to many of the middle-class trappings that we call "needs." Finally, we can take jobs that provide us ample free time to pursue activities in our communities that give us pleasure and make us feel we are making a difference in the lives of others. The downside of doing all this is that some of our peers will judge us peculiar, out of step, and hopelessly unfashionable. We will be the object of derision. I can live with that judgment if I know my lifestyle is one that will help save baby birds. I hope you feel the same way.

Discussion Questions

1. David's chapter is based on a book written more than 100 years ago about conspicuous consumption. What does the book's relevance to contemporary times say about the core values underlying our way of life?
2. How do today's leisure pursuits reflect Veblen's idea of conspicuous consumption? Relate Veblen's ideas to the notions of "keeping up with the Joneses" and "wearing one's wealth on one's sleeve."
3. David implies that we are in many respects still very much an adolescent culture; that we are consumed by wanting to make a good impression on other people through the conspicuous consumption of recreation-related goods and services. Do you agree with him? Please share your thinking.
4. What are the implications for a culture obsessed with conspicuous consumption in a world of limited natural resources? What are the implications for a sustainable future?
5. David admits that it is difficult to scale down and to stand alone against conspicuous consumption, but he also argues for the necessity of doing just that to ensure a sustainable future. Discuss the parallels between David and Cheryl's chapters. Are you prepared to scale down and stand alone to ensure a more sustainable future?

Notes

1. Veblen, T. (1934). *The theory of the leisure class.* New York: The Modern Press. (Original work published in 1899)

2. Reisman, D. (1953). *Thorstein Veblen: A critical interpretation.* New York: Charles Scribner's Sons.

3. Edgel, S. (2001). *Veblen in perspective: His life and thoughts.* Armonk, NY: M. E. Sharpe.

4. Mestrovic, S. (2003). *Thorstein Veblen on culture and society.* London: Sage Publications.

5. Mitchell, R. (2001). Thorstein Veblen: Pioneer in environmental sociology. *Organization & Environment, 14,* 389-408.

6. Patsouras, L. (2004). *Thorstein Veblen and the American way of life.* Montréal: Black Rose Books.

7. Rojek, C. (1995). *Decentring leisure: Rethinking leisure theory.* London: Sage Publications

8. Coser, L. (1971). *Masters of sociological thought: Ideas in historical and social context.* New York: Harcourt Brace Jovanovich, Inc.

9. Veblen, p. 109.

10. Ibid, p. 84.

11. Ibid, p. 28.

12. Ibid, p. 29.

13. Ibid, p. 36.

14. Ibid, p. 43.

15. Ibid, p. 45.

16. Ibid, pp. 45-46.

17. Ibid, p. 49.

18. Ibid, p. 50.

19. Ibid, p. 69.

20. King, G. (2009). *A season of splendor: The court of Mrs. Astor in the gilded age.* New York. Hoboken, NJ: John Wiley & Sons Inc.

21. Veblen, p. 181.

22. Mestrovic.

23. Riesman.

24. Veblen, p. 87.

25. Ibid, p. 31.

26. Schor, J. (1992). *The overworked American: The unexpected decline of leisure.* New York: Basic Books.

27. Ibid, p. 9.

28. Veblen, p. 127.

29. Russo, R. (1997). *Straight man.* New York: Vintage Books.

30. Ibid, p. 155.

31. Ibid.

32. Dowd, D. (1964). *Thorstein Veblen.* New York: Washington Square Press, Inc.

33. Obmascik, M. (2004, January 19). A fowl obsession. *Sports Illustrated,* pp. 68-72, 74-76.

34. Obmascik, M. (2004). *The big year: A tale of man, nature, and fowl obsession.* New York: Free Press.

35. Kaufman, K. (1997). *Kingbird Highway: The story of a natural obsession that got a little out of hand.* Boston: Houghton-Mifflin.

36. Ibid, p. xi.

37. Cocker, M. (2001). *Birders: Tales of a tribe.* New York: Atlantic Monthly Press.

38. Petrick, J., Backman, S., Bixler, R., & Norman, W. (2001). Analysis of golfer motivations and constraints by experience use history. *Journal of Leisure Research, 33,* 56-70.

39. Schultz, P. (2003). *1,000 places to see before you die: A traveler's life list.* New York: Workman.

40. King, p. 5.

41. Ibid, p. 85.

42. Coser.

43. Dowd.

44. Edgel.

45. Massey, D. (2007). *Categorically unequal: The American stratification system.* New York: The Russell Sage Foundation.

46. Ibid, p. 10.

47. King.

48. Berry, B. (2008). *The power of looks: Social stratification of physical appearance.* Burlington, VT: Ashgate.

49. Wiltse, J. (2007). *Contested waters: A social history of swimming pools in America.* Chapel Hill: The University of North Carolina Press.

50. Kastner, J. (1986). *A world of watchers.* New York: Alfred A. Knopf.

51. Weidensaul, S. (2007). *Of a feather: A brief history of American birding.* Orlando, FL: Harcourt, Inc.

52. Kastner, p. 74.

53. Mitchell, p. 97.

54. Veblen, p. 97.

55. Weidensaul, p. 156.

Thorsten Veblen coined the phrase "conspicuous consumption," endowing it with a biting satire that amounted to a towering moral condemnation of individuals who proclaimed their position by an ostentatious display of wealth and leisure. As Scott looks at it, Veblen's analysis of 1899 is just as valid as today because it is not just the possession of wealth that factors into this, but putting it on display.

Mountains of Things

JEANNE E. ARNOLD

American families have more material goods per household than any society in history. Even middle-class families with modest incomes have for decades enjoyed the ability to acquire a dizzying variety of inexpensive goods from every corner of the world. During the early 2000s, U.S. incomes were generally robust, unemployment was low, credit was easy to obtain, and persuasive marketing stimulated Americans to accumulate objects at startling rates. These trends characterized much of the later twentieth century as well.

The levels of material affluence that families attain, whatever the culture or status, are most clearly expressed *within* in the home. This is where people display and use the particular sets of goods they have selected from all those available to them through the primary sources of shopping, gifting, and inheritance. Since the home is the main locus for self-expression through things, it is ironic that while any of us can see the clothes and cars owned by neighbors, coworkers, and strangers when they venture into public spaces, our opportunities to scrutinize and admire the great majority of their possessions are nonexistent unless we happen to be engaged in carpet installation or door-to-door sales.

Tucked behind closed doors in neighborhoods across the country, rooms full of possessions serve as a source of satisfaction to hardworking parents, constantly reaffirming through their very presence in the house the sense that the family has done well. Yet U.S. cultural norms exert incessant pressure to acquire more. Home-design programs on TV and commercial advertisements in glossy magazines show how the respectable home ought to look, with a new spa-like master bathroom or stainless steel kitchen appliances. Through conversations and the rumor mill, parents constantly gauge whether they are keeping up with peers in ongoing materialistic competitions among family and neighbors, typically centering on upscale renovations and the latest vehicles and electronics. The imperative emerging from these material contests is more often than not that the time is ripe to purchase another round of new cars, toys, and television sets.

Significant tension besets middle-class parents who are trying to respond to financial demands coming at them from many directions. On the one hand, they need to meet the basic economic challenges of raising a family, including clothing, educating, and entertaining their growing children; buying a house (or paying the rent); and provisioning themselves with the goods and knowledge to perform competently as parents. All the while, they must keep pace with cultural trends and the frenzied, shop-until-you-drop environment that has prevailed in the United States for decades. By the closing years of the twentieth century, things had ratcheted up to such a fever pitch that being a successful middle-class family entailed substantial purchasing of discretionary and luxury consumer goods and the accompanying dangers of serious indebtedness.

It is fair to say that this material affluence, truly a defining feature of the time, comes at a steep cost, affecting not only the pocketbooks but also the states of mind of American parents. Families routinely succumb to overwhelming pressure to try new fashions and shoes and foods and just-released electronic gadgets, not to mention the latest marketing icons from blockbuster films. Resistance is nearly futile. Witness the frenzy that surrounds the release of a new-concept laptop or gaming console; people actually camp outside stores for hours to be among the first buyers. Advertisers set enormously effective consumer traps for families with young children, pressuring parents primarily through marketing directed at kids to buy a whole new suite of products to replace last year's toys, clothes, and sweets with new styles, new colors, and new brands.[1] Ever the dutiful consumers, families respond just as they have been socialized to do, by purchasing enough to trump the neighbors. Heaps of older toys and passé jeans and furnishings are shuttled to closets and basements. It should come as no surprise that after a few short years families amass more than the house can hold.

Economists and consumer historians closely track global production and sales in hundreds of categories of goods, and the data on annual manufacturing volume and the purchasing habits of the U.S. population are widely available. Staggering quarterly profits garnered by retailers make clear to even the most casual observer that millions of U.S. families are buying mountains of things. We can count and measure in various ways the billions of dollars' worth of goods that go out retailers' doors. But we have a limited grasp of how America's consumer frenzy plays out in measurable ways family by family and within people's homes. Since the home is the repository for nearly everything families own—that is, if they do not rent an off-site storage facility to absorb excesses—it stands to reason that we must delve into home spaces to document how many possessions households have, the kinds of objects they own (including older goods), where they place them, and how they use them. We also need to be in the home and hear directly from home owners to assess how they are coping emotionally with such material abundance. As simple as it sounds, this kind of systematic documentation of assemblages of goods in ordinary homes has never been recorded for any global industrial or postindustrial society. The material world of Americans at home—perpetually occluded from view—is seriously underexamined.

I led a team of archaeologists setting out to close this gap in our record of middle-class American life by introducing a group of methods focused on documenting material culture within and around the thirty-two homes in the CELF study.[2] We systematically assembled data on possessions and their uses within the Los Angeles houses using digital photography, scan sampling, and filming. We collected detailed family commentaries on rooms and objects that shed light on the meanings of possessions for contemporary families through family-narrated video home tours.

The homes of most (but not all) families in our study are strikingly crowded with things. In some, toys and clothes overflow bedroom closets; in others, food is stockpiled in garages and pantries; electronic gadgets are everywhere; and indoor objects spill into backyards. In about half the L.A. households, a clutter crisis results from an imbalance between house size and sheer numbers of artifacts owned. High levels of accumulation swamp bedroom closets and other storage areas, leaving stuff with no (hidden) place to go. Add to this the propensity for youngsters to leave their things strewn around, and we have the perfect recipe for daily cluttering of the house.

Clutter—particularly if it is someone else's—fascinates us. We see impossibly crowded closets or garages of some hapless couple on TV and feel better about our own. Those who try to provide assistance to resolve the problem of clutter or who discuss it as a contemporary phenomenon, however, rarely if ever explicitly define what it is. In the current study, in order to compare households and spaces and people's behavior, we need to portray materiality and clutter in quantitatively meaningful ways such as in terms of the *density* of possessions in a given space. The numbers of accumulated objects *per square foot* tell us whether a family is absorbing material goods in numbers consonant with house capacity. In a small house, of course, high densities of objects are reached quickly, and a cluttered look is difficult to avoid. The White House, on the other hand, at 55,000 square feet, or Elvis Presley's Graceland, at 17,552 square feet, would take gargantuan shopping sprees to fill and transform into cluttered spaces.

Density plays a major role in what constitutes clutter, but it is not the whole story. We must recognize two other components, both difficult to quantify and thus largely subjective. These are whether objects are tidily or messily arranged and whether they are visible somewhere other than where they belong. People will always have different thresholds in defining and tolerating clutter in their own homes, but generally speaking we all know clutter when we see it. One thousand neatly arranged DVDs are a model of organization; the same items scattered about on the floor and on tabletops are a visual blight. Some individuals with extreme minimalist taste might even consider one thousand DVDs on a shelf an example of clutter, but everyone will agree on the case of the strewn disks because they are clearly *unkempt* and *out of place*. Among the L.A. families, it appears that most households are losing the clutter battle. Fully 75 percent of the families in our study, and across much of Los Angeles, have acquired so much stuff that they have shifted masses of household objects into garages and expelled one or all of their cars onto adjoining driveways and streets.

The consumer one-upsmanship that produces these high densities of goods in homes eats up as much time as it does money. On the work side of the equation, there is an obvious link between the desire to purchase more goods and the need to work more hours (or better-compensated hours) to pay for them. Many parents take second jobs, work overtime, or magnify their stress by extending their lines of credit. Yet the more hours they work, the fewer hours they have available for family time and especially for leisure time. Economists document that Americans have a lengthy history of working more hours per year than adults in other countries.[3] U.S. employers provide significantly fewer paid vacation days than in the European Union, for instance, and American workers often do not take all the vacation days available to them.

On the home front, heaps of prized possessions erode family time. Contributing mightily to the leisure deficits of U.S. adults are the great costs in labor and energy needed to *manage* all the furnishings and goods in a home, including cleaning, organizing, and maintaining them. Working parents certainly have some leisure hours—roughly 15 percent of their time at home—but much of it is experienced in front of the television or computer.[4] Not only is parents' leisure time indoors and sedentary, but it is fragmented into short segments, and mothers enjoy less leisure than fathers. It is striking how elusive outdoor leisure time has become for middle-class parents and children. This phenomenon—so much time spent indoors—is one of the more unfortunate end products of the intertwined elements in this self-perpetuating, complex story featuring escalating consumerism, increasing time spent at work, growing heaps of possessions at home, rising stress, and declining leisure.[5]

RECORDING LIFE AT HOME

Documenting the Material World

Recording the full, rich spectrum of the material culture inside middle-class Los Angeles houses has been fraught with practical challenges, among them how to cope with the tendency for certain objects to be shifted around the house and how to address the issue of objects tucked away in storage locales (dressers, closets, attics). The primary limiting factor in our documentation process is visibility: in the end, we can record only what we can see in our photographic archive. We photographed just about every square inch of wall and floor space, so in that sense the archive is quite comprehensive. Closet interiors were often but not always captured in photos; dresser contents were not visible. After untold hours of review and coding,[6] we are now armed with systematically recorded frequencies of all countable and visible objects in each room of each house, divided into categories such as furniture, media electronics, decoration, lighting, and toys. We provide estimates for aggregated, abundant items such as large collections of CDs or dense piles of toys on the floor. We have still barely tapped this rich data set, but a few examples illustrate what can be done and what we can learn.

Among our first investigations was an enumeration of possessions to illuminate the best means to measure clutter and densities of objects in these homes. At the first home we coded, the Roland-Santos house, the counts exceeded 2,000 visible possessions within just the first three rooms addressed (two bedrooms and the living room). This family purposefully acquired at least 2,260 artifacts—furniture, art, lamps, a book collection, a music collection, toys, decorative objects, photos,

Figure 4.1. Densely packed garages present challenges to the counting and coding of possessions. This is a typical garage with a wide array of household artifacts (tables, bed, couch, chairs, TV, books, art, over forty dolls/toys/games, sports gear, backpacks, sleeping bags, strollers, etc.) and dozens of yard/garden/automotive objects—but no car in sight.

and more—and placed them in these rooms somewhere *in sight* (on a table, cabinet, wall, etc.). This is certainly a robust figure, and in this portion (540 sq. ft.) of the modest house's (980 sq. ft.) cozy rooms, this corresponds to object densities of 4 per square foot. Tallies include all objects on floors, furniture surfaces, and walls as well as on shelves and hangers in open closets, but these counts *do not* include untold numbers of items tucked into closed dresser drawers, storage boxes, and cabinets or buried under piles of stuff. So our count is clearly a quite *conservative* measure of actual objects owned. Houses in our study average 1,750 square feet of living space, and many rooms in quite a few of the houses are similarly overstuffed and cluttered. Garages, which serve as the most popular relief valve for possession overflows from the house, are often so crammed with objects that they pose a serious challenge to our ability to arrive at reliable counts (Figure 4.1). The grand totals of possessions from the object-rich Roland-Santos household are clearly above average for the thirty-two-family sample but not by a large margin.

More than sixty parents in our study created self-recorded, videotaped home tour narratives, commenting individually on their home spaces and expressing thoughts about the artifacts these spaces hold. Such narratives are rich in information about the meaningfulness of our homes and possessions and provide a large sample of specific words and phrases that parents use to describe their homes. Analysis of word choices allows us to investigate, among other things, whether clutter and high densities of objects affect parents' enjoyment of their homes. For example, most mothers comment directly and with annoyance about messiness and clutter, and they typically highlight their central role in trying to keep household mess under control. Words such as *chaotic, messy, cramped,* and *clutter* pop up frequently—accompanied by *always, constantly,* and *usually* to characterize how often this state of affairs occurs.

But there is a much deeper layer embedded in this story. CELF researchers Darby Saxbe and Rena Repetti examined these linguistic data and discovered that a number of parents in the study experience measurable psychological stress associated with clutter and disarray.[7] Readings of the stress hormone cortisol, derived from participants' saliva samples, reveal a measurable physiological link to cluttered home environments. Mothers whose narratives say that the home feels messy, cluttered, or unfinished actually show elevated depressed mood as the day progresses, based on cortisol readings and self-reports. This suggests that living day-to-day in a home that is "stressful" due to ongoing struggles with clutter is a more serious problem than previously thought. The clutter crisis affects some women's long-term health. Mothers who use language indicating that the home is relaxing or pleasant, or who describe their outdoor spaces (and "nature") at some length, experience their home as a more "restorative" environment. These mothers have cortisol readings indicating less stress, and they report better mood during weekday evenings at home. The clear message is that intense consumerism and its primary manifestations— disorganization and a high density of objects and clutter in the home— present challenges to women's well-being. The effect on men's health is ambiguous, and men say little about clutter and mess in their home tours. Many of them appear to simply ignore the problem.

Why is this so? I suspect that the cumulative impact of thousands of visible objects on display in room after room of the high-density, cluttered home is much greater than once thought. This is particularly the case where objects are poorly organized. Disorder exacts a psychological toll because it so clearly taxes family labor. Dusting, cleaning, upkeep, repair, straightening, reorganization—all these chores consume parents' time and energy. Merely *anticipating* such work almost certainly generates anxiety and stress, and carrying it out is a measurable strain on the household time budget.

Documenting the Rhythm of Activities at Home

Several generations of scholars, albeit with different purposes than ours, have pondered how modern, Western families use their homes. One of the more interesting phases of study began during the 1880s, when home efficiency experts in the United States and northern Europe sought to understand how people used their kitchen facilities—the sink, the stove, the counters—so they could improve the efficiency of kitchen design. An engaging fictionalization of one of these studies is presented in the 2003 Norwegian film *Kitchen Stories*, which tells the tale of a paid observer who perched in the corner and traced, on paper, the pathways of movement in the kitchen of a Scandinavian bachelor for several months.

Our study of course has a far loftier goal: to capture a detailed record of all family members' activities in all spaces of the home throughout the day. We want to be able to address many current and future questions about American middle-class families' utilization of rooms (by gender, by age), uses of objects, frequency of multitasking, and intrafamily interactions. To systematically document complex sets of activities for four or five family members (and guests, if present) in real time, we introduced and adapted methods from other disciplines. Our main method is scan sampling (see Appendix), which has been used by scientists in various kinds of naturalistic observational studies. We conducted our research with a handheld computer in order to record all observations regularly and with precision. Every ten minutes, project ethnographers recorded what each at-home family member was doing, including the person, room or outdoor space, objects in use (computer, bike, cutting board), other people interacting, and secondary activity, if any, such as watching television while eating lunch.

The resulting 16,935 timed observations make it feasible to query the database with an array of complex questions. We can examine across all families or within any given family what fathers, mothers, or children of various ages do, and where they are doing it. We also can assess how much (or little) they are interacting, how much their behaviors vary across weekdays compared to weekends or mornings compared to evenings, and which possessions are most likely to be put to use. Moreover, we can assess important economic questions such as how much time mothers and fathers, respectively, devote to dinners, childcare, chores, and the like, and how much (or little) time they may have left over for leisure at home.

Among the questions we pursue, this chapter discusses findings about the vanishing outdoor leisure of middle-class parents and gender differences among parents in how they spend their limited indoor leisure time. We see a significant departure from the universal suburban ideal that emerged in the 1950s and 1960s that the backyard was a center for "outdoor living," meant to be used frequently for play and entertaining.[8] Families still articulate this ideal when talking about their lives at home, but more than 75 percent do not live this way.[9] Instead, the leisure of both parents and children is focused on the indoors, and mothers carve out considerably less free time than do fathers, with the most notable gender-based leisure deficit on weekdays.[10] Television, Internet use on computers, reading, and game playing indoors consume most of the open time of American families. Many of our findings regarding families and their time use find solid support when we compare the results from Los Angeles to those from a much larger-scale study on time use among five hundred middle-class families in eight regionally diverse U.S. cities.[11]

HAPPINESS IS (NOT) AN OVERSTUFFED HOME OFFICE

Our large archives of home tour narratives, videotaped naturalistic family interactions, and photographs of rooms demonstrate clearly that many parents in our study find the thousands of things they have in their homes exhausting to contemplate, organize, clean, and maintain. When family members narrating home tours comment on their possessions as they move through their homes, they frequently voice frustrations over an inability to contain or reduce the clutter that surrounds them. This widely felt frustration in the United States has spurred a whole industry of home organizing, devoted especially to closet organizing systems and garage overhauls. The problem of household clutter has also attracted considerable media attention, and during the 2000–2005 period we witnessed a flood of popular television shows on clutter clearing, home organizing, designing for better storage capacity, and house remodeling and expansion.

Garages and home offices appear anecdotally to be the most object-filled, impacted spaces in the majority of American middle-class houses, and this is true for most of the families in our study as well. Some children's bedrooms and family rooms are also viable contenders for clutter supremacy among the Los Angeles households. So many goods are flowing through these homes—and often ending up in garages and attics—that only one quarter of garages retain enough room for a car. When we code and count all visible objects in the garages in our sample, we find an average of about 225. This figure is *significantly* limited by the chaotic arrangement of goods in most garages, which hampers our ability to precisely count boxes, tools, soccer balls, bikes, clothes, cleaning products, furniture, and stockpiled food lurking underneath or behind the visible, counted items.

Plotting in a bar graph all objects that could be spotted and enumerated, we see three distinct peaks, suggesting that these garages fall into three emergent organizational types. Average garage size across the whole L.A. sample is 362 square feet. The very low density, neat garage, represented by five examples in the study, has an average count of 48 objects—including one or two vehicles regularly parked in the space! These garages, which average 340 square feet, contain fewer than 0.14 objects per square foot.

The prototypical garage (nineteen in the L.A. sample) is densely packed and/or chaotic in its distribution of items and averages 190 countable artifacts (range is 125 to 300 objects per garage) in a mean of about 350 square feet. These garages have object densities of roughly 0.5 per square foot. The six exceptionally overstuffed garages in the study are larger than average (mean = 528 sq. ft.) and average 435 visible artifacts (range of 320 to 625). The density is roughly 0.9 objects per square foot, or about six times the density in the tidy garages, and I must emphasize that far more objects are present that we cannot count due to piling and stacking. This is a problem that is exacerbated as object density rises; true densities in some of these garages likely exceed 2 to 3 items per square foot. In these packed and typically disorderly garages, the entire floor space is given over to a more or less solid block of stored or tossed items. Not surprisingly, since garages are now primarily storage loci for possessions that no longer fit in the house, they exhibit a high diversity of objects such as televisions, furniture, holiday items, clothes, boxes of paper documents, file cabinets, art, and food alongside scattered yard and

Figure 4.2. One corner of a high-density home office space.

car paraphernalia. Two households no longer have a garage space as such; their garages are now physically converted to bedroom or cabinet-lined computer/recreation room spaces.

Home offices, present in well over half the houses, reveal comparably high—if not higher—densities of objects, which are typically positioned on walls, shelves, desktops, and floor corners since the spaces must accommodate foot traffic. Six of the houses have small home offices (averaging about 60 sq. ft.) in various corners or cubbyholes, and another three families have established two home offices, the second of which is small. One third of the L.A. families have larger home offices, normally full rooms such as former bedrooms and measuring more than twice the size, or 120 square feet (Figure 4.2). Most observers would agree that they are visually stress-inducing rather than "restorative" or restful spaces, and home tour narratives verify that parents experience them this way (see discussion below).

These are spaces where job-related work, schoolwork, or record keeping mixes with recreational uses. Not counting loose papers, magazines, and newspapers, which we treated as ephemera not amenable to accurate counts, the average number of visible objects is 313. Densities in the home office spaces are fairly consistent across the range of room sizes. In the small offices, if we exclude the large music collection in the home office at one household (> 1,600 CDs and 350 vinyl albums), we find a mean number of 137 objects, or 2.3 per square foot. (If we were to include that case, the mean count jumps to 380, and the density rises to a whopping 6.3 objects per square foot. It is clearly an outlier in this sample, but an argument can be made that it is not unusual.) The larger office spaces yield a mean of 257 objects, or 2.1 per square foot. All these figures significantly underrepresent objects actually in home office locations since such spaces are burdened with a complex mix of (uncountable) papers (homework, bills, mail, schoolwork, etc.) as well as dense assemblages of family photos, sports memorabilia, books, binders, videos, computing gear, and furniture. A sense of clutter prevails.

The historian Peter Thornton uses density in a similar way when comparing visually "busy" interior design periods—such as Queen Anne Victorian—to the material signatures of other eras. Victorians filled every available inch of home space with furniture, mirrors, art, decorative items, dark woods, and floral fabrics, the classic high-density look.[12] At the other end of the density spectrum, a midcentury modern living room is simple, spare, and often but not always low density. Neat built-in wood shelving units filled with organized sets of books or record albums could transform it into a high-density but still uncluttered space.

Psychologists who study compulsive hoarding behaviors have developed sets of photographs of rooms in successive stages of clutter accumulation to help clinicians gauge the severity of hoarding.[13] These sequences of images culminate in extraordinary levels of density and clutter: kitchens or living rooms with stacks of newspapers, boxes, dishes, and clothes towering over a maze of dangerous, twisting paths, the floors totally covered. Such images of course represent pathological behaviors and are far more extreme than the simple shifting clutter situations of ordinary households. But they help to bring these terms and patterns to life. We might think of density as how many objects we see in a space and clutter as (largely) the neatness and arrangement of those objects. Thus higher densities make clutter increasingly and proportionally harder to control, but they do not always go hand in hand.

Turning back to our house inventories, we know from scan sampling data that kitchens and living rooms are the most heavily used spaces in the thirty-two L.A. homes (kitchens on weekdays, living rooms on weekends). Not surprisingly, they also reveal clutter. Whereas kitchen tables and other kitchen surfaces attract mostly shifting panoplies of foods, dishes, photos, schedules, newspapers, mail, backpacks, and the paraphernalia associated with schoolwork and bill-paying tasks, far more is hidden away (and thus uncountable) inside cabinets, pantries, and drawers. Clutter in the kitchen is common, but assemblages of objects are usually transitory. We do not count papers and magazines or the transitory food items and plates that are set out for meals. Thus densities of more or less permanently on-display objects such as magnets and photos on the refrigerator or dish racks, plants, cookbooks, and toasters on the counters are moderate in the kitchen. Counts average about 80, and the mean densities are well under one per square foot. Just seven households maintain more than 100 visible objects in the kitchen.

In family room and living room spaces, on the other hand, large furnishings create entertainment-friendly locales surrounded by a more stable set of decorative objects that reveal a great deal about family taste and identity. Common here are family photos, art, TV sets, game stations, music systems, remote controls, plants, books, DVDs, videos, decorative objects such as ceramics and mementos from travel, and of course toys of many varieties. The average number of visible objects in living rooms is 196, but the range is wide: from 30 to 1,282. The mean density is about 2 per square foot, but a few approach 5 per square foot. Eleven families have both living rooms and family rooms, with the latter adding just over 205 visible artifacts on average to those houses' assemblages. Although at least two-thirds of living rooms and family rooms are densely packed with goods, those of a handful of the families are far more spartan and tidy, each with well under 100 objects.

What is most important about these sets of numbers is how they translate into family experiences. Clutter demands the energy and attention of the households that are burdened by it. The majority of homes in our thirty-two-family sample harbor high counts of consumer goods and would be classified as cluttered by objective observers (Figure 4.3). A number of parents find the situation personally stressful, as our cortisol data and some of the home tour narratives show. Some parents try to direct their attention away from the mess, accepting that while the kids are young the situation is not going to resolve itself, and the ever-shifting masses of objects just need to be herded occasionally into closets and bins. In their narratives, about half the mothers comment on various concentrations of mess (piles of toys, mounds of books and mail) around the house. While several of these moms temper their frustration and view clutter as inevitable, others are clearly irritated—even bitter—about it.

Karita (mother, school aide) during her home tour:

Figure 4.3. A two-child bedroom displaying clutter and a high density of objects.

This is the office. It's a place that we turned into from part of the garage. It's a total mess. . . . We probably should, you know, organize it better. But it works out well. Here is where the computers are and the kids do homework. We are all on the computers here from time to time. . . . And here we have the garage, with everything. This is usually a total mess, and it's a total mess today again. This is where we have bikes and all the old furniture, sofas, and things that we don't use. It's—how can I say it, it's a mess. It's not fun. It should be cleaned up, and we should probably get rid of a whole bunch of stuff.

Susannah (mother, administrator) during her home tour:

This is the everyday mess I see when I walk into my house. I've chosen to video my house on a day that it's very messy because this is what it looks like every day, so why pretend it's clean. This is the kitchen where I spend a lot of my evenings cooking dinner, feeding the baby. The baby eats pretty much while I cook dinner because she's so impatient to eat dinner. And this is the mess that I have to clean up every day. Probably five, six times a day I am cleaning up after people. So beside my full-time job as a parent, this is my other full-time job in the kitchen. And this is my hang-drying right there. Normally I'd be embarrassed to have anybody over but . . . I figured it would be better to have my real everyday life. This dining area is for, as you can see, junk. This is where junk piles up. I won't name names of who leaves junk on the table, but as you can see it's a newspaper. I don't read the newspaper.

A number of fathers in the study seem oblivious or unconcerned and make no comment as they pass untidy areas in their homes. Fathers are more likely to describe cluttered rooms as simply cozy or in need of remodeling or expansion, and they may muse about various artifacts without saying anything about messiness or crowding. But fathers such as Thomas, a marketing director, are exceptions. Showing his master bedroom, he says:

> Anyway, suffice to say that we cram an awful lot into this bedroom. In fact about six months ago we repainted and redecorated and took out an amazing amount of stuff. We really quite like it in here except for this area here which is a mess again [points to wife's items on floor]. And here's my little pile on the floor where I throw my day clothes.

Despite parents' best efforts to maintain order and keep their houses neat, disruptive material elements infiltrate just about every room, led by toys, mail, and paper from school and work. Keys, phones, books, computers, shoes, and newspapers add to the chorus of stuff that is moved around every day and often fails to find a good, out-of-sight resting spot. American families also have multiples of so many categories of possessions such as DVDs, CDs, books, digital games, toys, and magazines that it is inevitable that things are routinely strewn around in an untidy fashion, often leading, we now know, to measurable stress.

Turning to one last space in the public parts of the house, as we examined the kitchens in the study, I identified an interesting parallel between high total numbers of objects *in the house as a whole* and high counts of objects affixed to refrigerators. The typical American family places quite a few items on the front (and sometimes side) panel of refrigerators. For the 32 L.A. households, the greatest number of items on a single refrigerator is 166, the mean is about 52, and the lowest is 2 (Figure 4.4). Common objects are magnets, snapshots of family and pets, phone numbers, memos, calendars, kids' art, bills, and menus.[14] I assessed how many objects are typically placed there, what kinds of artifacts are considered appropriate, and how these patterns vary across families. Middle-class Angelenos consistently display decorative magnets as well as unframed

Figure 4.4. A prototypical "refrigerator display" featuring decorative magnets, informal snapshots, phone numbers, schedules, lists, and more.

family snapshots from various informal moments of family history. But we also find a dozen or more kinds of reminders such as school menus, plumbers' phone numbers, and invitations that are hardly added for their aesthetic value. Many refrigerator postings clearly serve a scheduling and organizing function for the family. Altogether, about 12 percent of households use their refrigerator panels sparingly (9 or fewer items), and these are rather neat by default. Every other kitchen fridge has at least 16 to 20 affixed objects; about 10 percent of these are well-organized spatially, with tidy rows of magnets and snapshots. The rest of the refrigerators have quite high object densities and appear from the outsider's perspective to be palimpsests of randomly placed objects, producing a rather untidy look.

My analysis suggests that a family's tolerance for a busy, untidy refrigerator surface appears to be a good predictor of a relaxed attitude about high object density and clutter in public rooms of the house: family room, living room, dining room, and office. To examine this phenomenon more closely, we had coders tally everything on the refrigerators, and then I grouped the six households with the highest refrigerator display counts (all with at least 80 artifacts on the panels) and grouped the seven households with the lowest counts (all with fewer than 20 affixed objects). Next, I aggregated the object count data from a set of the main rooms of each of those houses. The rooms I used for this analysis are the living room, dining room, kitchen, family room, and home office. I calculated the average artifact counts for the two groupings. The six houses in the first group (high-density refrigerator display) yield an average aggregate count of 1,448 objects in these rooms. The seven houses in the low-density refrigerator display group have far lower total object counts in these sets of rooms—just 322, on average. By any measure, this is a striking difference, and one consistent with my conjecture that there is a relationship. But I had to explore further whether the first group simply consisted of much larger houses, where we might expect more total objects.

To judge whether house size shaped the results, I turned once more to the density figures. I pulled in house square footage for the two subgroups and found that the houses with the highest raw counts of household artifacts and the visually busy refrigerators are *smaller* on average (1,336 sq. ft.), not larger, than the latter group (1,744 sq. ft.). This surprising finding means the homes with high-density refrigerator assemblages have exceptionally high household object densities. The houses with tidy refrigerator panels contain lower raw counts of stuff overall, even though they are more spacious. Thus these houses exhibit very low object densities. So there is some support for the idea that a family's tolerance for crowded, artifact-laden refrigerator surfaces mirrors high densities of possessions in the main rooms of the house and that families that keep tidy and minimally decorated refrigerators tend to have more modest assemblages of objects elsewhere in the home.

When we extended the analysis to include all thirty-two households simultaneously and ran simple significance tests, however, we did not identify a statistically significant correlation. This outcome may stem from the very basic approach we have taken to the question to date. We have not yet incorporated other variables that could be relevant, such as the effects of major "spring" cleanings and the number of years families have occupied their current residence. I believe there is an important pattern here, but it must be tested with a larger sample drawn from other middle-class U.S. homes.

It is nonetheless intriguing is that one iconic place in the home—the refrigerator panel—at least in part anticipates overall family tendencies regarding materialism (predilection to buy; intensive consumerism; accumulations over lifetimes) and tidiness and object organization in the house (dense vs. spartan, chaotic vs. orderly). The cases at the two ends of the spectrum (the very spartan and tidy panels and the very high density panels), at the very least, seem to mirror behaviors in the rest of the house. If this idea ultimately finds broader confirmation, we should be able to go to a house and make reasonable projections about the household material assemblage just by documenting characteristics of the refrigerator display.

PERSONAL IDENTITY: THE LABELING OF SPACE

Compared to other historical times and other societies around the world, the extent to which contemporary American household spaces display family members' personal identity and taste is striking. Given the array of elaborated goods of all imaginable kinds available to purchase, it is no surprise that parents, teens, and even younger children find objects to arrange in their homes that announce, "This is who I am." Our objects are our biographers. Middle-class Americans typically select two or three main classes of objects as suitable to embody chosen self-identities. One is iconic images or symbols from popular culture with which they feel a strong affinity. This part of our family biography we purchase or inherit. Many kinds of entities are available, including posters of rock stars and sports heroes, Disney motifs, national flags, sports pennants, paintings by prominent artists, and the like. Display of these artifacts in our homes assigns them considerable implicit value: we feel a strong attachment, we admire them, they entertain us, they are part of our heritage, or they reflect core interests and values. Preteens and teens most frequently identify with musicians, film and television stars, and sports heroes, materialized by means of posters on their bedroom walls. Such images are close to universal among the L.A. families.

Another class of objects dominating walls, doors, and desktops in many bedrooms and home offices includes markers of our accomplishments and other paraphernalia trumpeting our existence such as blue ribbons, diplomas, engraved trophies, and commercially made or homemade signs with personal names ("Marcus," "Giselle") that effectively lay claim to that space. These represent a more overt announcement of the identity of room "owners." They say, I am an important member of this family, and this is my name and my room! Or, I am a middle-school graduate, a soccer player, a ballet pupil, an Honors student, or a champion dog breeder, and these are my accomplishments. Honors are materialized and projected; space is carved out. Achievement- and name-related artifacts are ubiquitous in the L.A. households. One child's room has no fewer than six name emblems. This seems more prevalent for girls than for boys. Children use these material markers alongside social networks materialized in displays of photos of friends and family to carve out emerging identities and justify control of their own spaces and artifacts. Parents do this, too, in places such as home offices, where they might post a diploma or a photo of themselves with a famous public figure.

And third, family photographs are everywhere, numbering in the triple digits in many Los Angeles homes. Informal snapshots plaster surfaces such as refrigerators and kitchen cabinets, and framed photographs are ubiquitous in living rooms, family rooms, bedrooms, offices, and hallways. Recent family histories are captured in photos that preserve memories of weddings, school days, vacations, and other happy times. Although such displays are both commonplace—averaging 85 photos per household—and highly visible in the U.S. home (sets of photos are almost always visible from the front door), they are not mirrored in the homes of the Swedish and Italian families studied by our sister research centers. A few formal photos of family ancestors may be present in the typical Roman home, but displays do not spread throughout the house or extend to other object types. This pattern is distinctively American.

Although it seems grounded in recent consumerism as much as anything, the personalization phenomenon actually has deep historical roots. Clifford Clark's analysis of American homes shows that even the earliest emergence of suburbia during the late 1800s was framed by a set of new expectations about what the American house should be.[15] The thinking was that houses for the middle-class family must become far more than simply shelters or places of refuge. The house needed to support and nurture the family and encourage "the growth of each family member's talents, capabilities, and health"; moreover, it was expected to enhance "individual self-expression and creativity."[16]

As if wives and mothers were not burdened enough with child-raising and house upkeep, they were also then saddled with the responsibility of developing an attractive home design that announced who they were to neighbors and visitors. The house was strongly identified as the women's sphere as early as 1880—and artistic and musical activities and training of children in the arts were expected to take place there—and it was particularly true starting in the 1900s that women needed to imbue the house interior with *things* that creatively conveyed family tastes and personal identities. The house became a place for artistic expression and the projection of family ideals through the careful selection of furnishings, china sets, front porch decorations, paintings, and the like. The house form itself—both the style (Queen Anne, bungalow, colonial, Greek revival) and the room layout—was also considered an embodiment of personal expression, materially reflecting the owner's ideas about family, comfort, and social standing.

Such strong encouragement to express individuality naturally led to a rather competitive approach to home furnishing and upkeep. Although people sought a distinctive look for their own homes, most yearned more than anything to conform with the highest-ranking arbiters of taste in the neighborhood, those most well-off or admired. Widespread emulation in turn led to much duplication of house styles and furnishings. Strong tensions arose between imitation and creativity in the home.

Social critics of the early 1900s labeled the increasingly prevalent middle-class need to show off the home and possessions a form of exhibitionism.[17] This thrust toward personal, individualistic display of objects has persisted unabated in the American ethos for more than 120 years, and the zeal to personalize home spaces is clearly still with us.

Considering the house as an instrument of display, a "museum" for preserving family memories and histories, and an arena of self-expression helps to frame our understanding of the intense personalization evident in American homes. Specific places such as the fireplace mantel and the front parlor or foyer have evolved into standard locations for family photos, art objects, and sophisticated or expensive artifacts suggesting worldliness. As early as 1880, material possessions became signs of refinement, achievement, and status, and thus the home became the place for family display.[18] Since we could hardly carry all these things around, we brought people to see them in our homes.

The pressure to decorate escalated significantly with the birth of advertising in magazines and newspapers in the 1880s, creating a culture of consumption fully accessible to the common woman and man. Values shaped by media depictions of house-decorating ideals contributed significantly to what people wanted. Commodities multiplied, and women were encouraged to furnish their homes with everything new. The emergence of glittering, fantastic, museum-like department stores with sumptuous choices (Macy's, Marshall Field's) was seductive,[19] and it placed Americans of modest to substantial means on a path of consumer frenzy from which we have rarely swayed. It was not long afterward that Thorstein Veblen made his renowned, scornful comments about conspicuous consumption and waste in American society.[20] So the house as an unusually expansive canvas of personal expression is a true American legacy, materialized by as many dazzling and identity-projecting possessions as can be afforded.[21]

Intergenerational transitions—the ways in which each new generation of householders perpetuates this legacy—are underexamined in studies of material culture and modern life. Little is known about the process by which young couples, who have been socialized by the distinct family traditions of their respective childhood homes, may struggle to articulate what they identify with as they create new material surroundings. Couples must negotiate and ultimately develop a strategy to furnish and personalize their home as they build inventories of goods through purchases and inheritance. In cultures with deeper and stronger material heritage (Italy, for example), young couples might inherit a few valued heirlooms around which to build the new household. Twenty-first-century American couples are more likely to purchase their new household identities at Ikea and Target.

Among the families in our sample, a few decorating choices appear nearly universal, and these cases tell us something important about U.S. culture. Nothing puts the stamp of "this is ours" on a home and celebrates the unity of the family more than depictions of the family itself, and almost all the thirty-two Los Angeles families make a strong effort to portray family history through the display of photographs in multiple rooms of the home. While numbers of visible photos of family members (and pets) vary from as few as 10 to as many as 210, most families display at least 70 person-centered photos, and the average per household is a robust 85 (Figure 4.5). Some families maintain veritable shrines of family member images.

Photos range from formal (weddings, annual school pictures) to casual snapshots from family vacations, and they may be found in living rooms (often on mantels, walls, and special tables), hallways, bedrooms, kitchens, home offices, and even garages and bathrooms. Favorite locations for informal, unframed snapshots are the children's bedrooms and the refrigerator. On average, families include about 9 or 10 photos among the many items they attach to the refrigerator door. Framed photos and images from formal occasions like studio portraits or weddings usually

Figure 4.5. A living room wall featuring family photos in a highly visible locus immediately inside the front door. These are part of a large assemblage of photographs of family members located throughout the house.

are matched to spaces that are the most formal in the house (e.g., living rooms) and rest on the nicest tables or mantels. Middle-class families clearly share certain values regarding the appropriate placement of photos and the formality of framing.

Also on display in 97 percent of the homes are diplomas, certificates, awards, trophies, and other insignia of personal accomplishments of the children. We see less emphasis on markers of personal accomplishment among parents (found in about one quarter of the homes). But quite a few sets of parents in the study strongly identify with a specific cultural group, ethnicity, religion, or sexual identity, and they make an effort to display one or more important material markers in the home that signal their membership in or affiliations with those groups. These can be of fundamental importance to family self-identity. A Swedish-born mom displays a Swedish flag over the front door and has a large framed painting of a seascape from Sweden in her living room. Japanese American parents show off delicate decorative figurines from Japan in a living room display case. One of the two-father families in our study has rainbow artwork and other art pieces that celebrate the gay rights movement.

Another way in which American families commonly express identity and announce their values and interests is through the display of school and professional sports teams logos. Allegiance to teams takes the form of pennants, caps, and other items. In our study, the storied franchises of the Los Angeles Lakers basketball team and the Dodgers baseball team, represented by flags, foam fingers, posters, and helmets (about 18 percent of households), clearly predominate over lesser franchises and more distant teams. These are important ways that families announce their support and participation as members of a locally significant community.

Beyond these materializations that help to express in very central ways who the families *are*, we see their attempts to reveal a sense of style, cultural refinement, or "taste." Families adopt aesthetic preferences pertaining to certain styles of furniture, paint colors, and art from formative life experiences (parents, college friends, neighbors, high-end hotels) or overt emulation of cultural icons (the rich and famous). However, most young middle-class families with limited means are more likely to acquire furniture and framed posters from big-box stores than gilded bath fixtures and original paintings like the ones their cultural heroes have. Emulation can go only so far. There is also the issue of a new household needing to blend and accommodate the disparate tastes of the couple. The results in middle-class U.S. homes are, as we would expect, not always coherent. Mixed styles, little formal art, vacation mementos, knickknacks, and clutter are more prevalent than clean, recognizable furnishing styles.

Some homes in our study are dominated by juvenile iconography, including large, framed Disney icons in living room spaces. Others eschew Disney art but cannot wrestle free of children's materials in every room of the house. To say the least, it is challenging to have a stylish living room with blankets, Barbies, and Legos all over the tables and floor. Some families buy low-end furniture that can handle spills and tears until children get a bit older. Investments in stylistic expression may be thoughtfully postponed until the family gets farther along in the life cycle.

THE DECLINE OF OUTDOOR LEISURE

The home also exhibits clear material residues of busy families' vanishing leisure time. With so much of life focused on jobs and school activities, parents often convert areas such as bedrooms and corners of garages into home offices. Formal, dedicated office spaces and computer rooms (found in eighteen of the thirty-two households in our sample) are common, and almost every house has multiple computers and multiple desktops covered with work-related materials that take space from other home activities. And while families devote considerable money, effort, and sentiment to beautifying their front and back yards, they are rarely observed spending time in these leisure-oriented spaces. For example, Karita (mother) reported during her home tour:[22]

> I'm going to go outside now to the backyard. This is the outside patio. We sometimes eat here and things like that. We have a nice fireplace and barbecue, so we can, you know, use that. It's a big yard. We did get gardeners about two years ago because it took way too much time to do the yard. We were never home . . . doing baseball and softball every weekend. So we felt the yard started to kind of look kind of bad so . . . We have lots of side space, and again, it could be used better. It's more just putting stuff there that we don't use, I guess. I finally cleaned up a few days ago. We have this big pool, but we don't use it anymore, so I would like to get rid of it.

When we recorded how everyone spends time at home, we found that parents have moderate amounts of leisure—about 15 percent of their time at home. But virtually all their leisure moments happen inside, they occur in fragmented episodes, and they are most often associated with television watching (50 percent), followed by reading (21 percent) and playing games or playing with kids (18 percent).[23] Certain families prove to be exceptions to these trends, but even for them leisure at home is mainly devoted to sedentary indoor activities. Frequent interruptions arise from children, cell phones, and the need to attend to household chores.

Important gender differences exist as well. Mothers have less leisure time overall (roughly 13 percent of time at home), and the average duration of their leisure episodes is about ten to twenty minutes. Looking at all the mothers collectively, only 2 percent (one in fifty) of their leisure events lasted more than one hour. Fathers do better, enjoying an average of 21 percent of their time at home in leisure, and the episodes are slightly more likely to last longer: collectively, 5 percent (one in twenty) represents more than one hour. Leisure time experiences vary by gender across hours of the day as well. During busy meal preparation and cleanup time blocks, from 4:00 P.M. to 6:00 P.M., mothers have notably less leisure than their spouses. Mothers do chores or tasks on average 94 percent of the time between these hours (6 percent leisure), whereas fathers typically manage to enjoy leisure for about 18 percent of this time span.[24] The disparity lessens in the 6:00 to 8:00 P.M. block, but mothers are still investing more time in nonleisure tasks (mothers spend 86 percent of this time span doing chores; fathers, 81 percent).

One of the most striking discoveries of our study is the inability of busy L.A. parents to find time for outdoor leisure. Less than 3 percent of parents' hours at the house are enjoyed in leisure activities in their backyards. Fully three-fourths of parents have no outdoor leisure moments at all during a typical week (including weekends), and 58 percent of families—children included—spend *no time* in these spaces, for fun or even for yard work.[25] The children in just one-fourth of the families used their backyards for leisure activities one or more hours during the recording period. These minuscule usages of outdoor spaces occur despite the draws provided by southern California's famously good weather and the families' significant investments in their backyards in the form of swimming pools, slides, play sets, baseball cages, trampolines, skateboard ramps, large expanses of grass, brick fireplaces, barbecues, patios, decks, outdoor dining sets, lounge chairs, and hot tubs. Parents' and children's home tour narrations for a good number of the study households verify these minimal uses of outdoor spaces as the family norm.

CONCLUSION

This chapter describes the consequences of the sheer numbers of possessions American families have in their homes. We can see that many parents point with pride during their home tours to objects of special meaning and value in their homes, including art, heirloom furniture, and artifacts from their travels or their home countries. Attachments to material culture are a nearly universal fixture of our modern cultural heritage and can give us pleasure and a strong sense of our family's history. Most furnishings and decorations in the study sample appear newer and may be valued simply for their monetary value, whereas others may be largely sentimental and related to family connections (children's art, grandma's sewing machine, an old wedding dress). Regardless, their importance to most people makes it clear that possessions have a powerful impact on our general well-being. Behavioral archaeologists have long understood this deep connection between people and their material culture.[26]

But taken to an extreme, great mountains of things in our homes cost us considerable money, drain our labor and energy, and detract from the attractiveness of our homes. For some adults, women more than men, persistent clutter exacts a psychological toll and causes unhealthful stress. The mania to accumulate prized goods prompts us to work harder, take less vacation time, enjoy less leisure at home, and savor startlingly little leisure outdoors. Many families in Los Angeles, as well as across much of the United States, take part in an unremitting work-and-spend cycle, engaging in competitive purchasing and spending fragmented leisure time in sedentary indoor pursuits. Still, as other chapters in this book reveal, many of these families absorb or deflect experiences of time stress, material abundance, and other pressures in ways that allow them to enjoy happy, energetic daily lives. Ultimately, the tale of the middle-class family at the opening of the twenty-first century is a story of remarkable resiliency.

NOTES

1. *Consuming Kids: The Commercialization of Childhood.* DVD. Media Education Foundation, 2008.

2. The archaeology/material culture researchers are Jeanne Arnold, Anthony P. Graesch, Margaret Beck, and Angela Orlando. See Appendix for a more detailed description of methods.

3. Bianchi, Robinson, and Milkie 2006.

4. Beck and Arnold 2009.

5. Schor 2004; Whybrow 2005.

6. When we set out to document the material culture of modern middle-class Los Angeles, we designed procedures that allowed us to count and classify the visible objects in each room of each house. Because so many objects are present, this proved a monumental task. Undaunted, our trained coders spent more than a thousand hours carrying out this project using our large digital photo archive. Coders assign every photographed object to an overarching category (e.g., furniture, media electronic, decorative item, lighting, toy) and then directly count (for most categories) or estimate (for abundant or piled items) the number of such items present, room by room.

7. Saxbe and Repetti 2010.

8. Clark 1986, 179.

9. Arnold and Lang 2007.

10. Beck and Arnold 2009.

11. This study included five cities in the Midwest, one in the Northeast, one in the Southeast, and one on the West Coast. Suburban, urban, and rural localities are represented. The 500-family study was conducted by the Sloan Center at the University of Chicago, and the comparative analysis was done by members of the Chicago and UCLA Sloan Centers (Broege et al. 2007).

12. Thornton 1984.

13. Tolin, Frost, and Steketee 2007.

14. Objects affixed to refrigerator panels comprise these categories, in descending order of frequency: Magnets, Photos, Magnetic Photo Frames, Children's Artwork, Calendars, Assorted Papers, Children's Schoolwork, Achievement Awards, Emergency Contact Numbers, School Notices, School Menus, Schedules, Lists, Magnetic Bins, Coupons, Receipts, Save-The-Date,

Magazine/Newspaper Cutouts, Post-Its, Business Cards, Holiday Cards, Invitations, Postcards, Rosters, White Boards, and Charts.

15. Clark 1986.
16. Ibid., 102.
17. Ibid., 112.
18. Ibid., 120.
19. Belk 2001.
20. Veblen 1899.
21. The visual record of home lives of the 32 Los Angeles families is provided in the book *Life at Home in the Twenty-First Century: 32 Families Open Their Doors* (Arnold et al. 2012).
22. This family did not use its 3,600-square-foot backyard space (with pool, batting cage, brick BBQ, tiled patio, and dining set) at all during the study.
23. Beck and Arnold 2009.
24. Ibid.
25. Arnold and Lang 2007.
26. Schiffer and Miller 1999.

References

Adelson, Naomi. 2000. *Being Alive Well: Health and the Politics of Cree Well-Being.* Toronto: University of Toronto Press.

Aldort, Naomi. 2006. *Raising Our Children, Raising Ourselves.* Bothel: Publishers Network.

Alexander, Larry. 2003. "Family, Youth and Consumer News." Mississippi State University website, July 7. http://msucares.com/news/print/fce-news/fce03/030707activity.html.

Alwin, Duane F. 2001. "Parental Values, Beliefs, and Behavior: A Review and Promulga for Research into the New Century." In *Children at the Millennium: Where Have We Come from, Where Are We Going?*, ed. Sandra L. Hofferth and Timothy J. Owens, 97–140. Advances in Life Course Research, vol. 6. New York: JAI.

Amato, Paul R., Alan Booth, David R. Johnson, and Stacy F. Rogers. 2007. *Alone Together: How Marriage in America Is Changing.* Cambridge, MA: Harvard University Press.

Andersen, Ross E., Carlos J. Crespo, Susan J. Bartlett, Lawrence J. Cheskin, and Michael Pratt. 1998. "Relationship of Physical Activity and Television Watching with Body Weight and Level of Fatness among Children." *JAMA* 279: 938–42.

Anderson-Fye, Elaine. 2004. "A Coca-Cola Shape: Cultural Change, Body Image, and Eating Disorders in San Andrés, Belize." *Culture, Medicine, and Psychiatry* 28: 561–95.

Antill, John K., Jacqueline J. Goodnow, Graeme Russell, and Sandra Cotton. 1996. "The Influence of Parents and Family Context on Children's Involvement in Household Tasks." *Sex Roles* 34: 215–36.

Arendell, Teresa. 2000. "'Soccer Moms' and the New Care Work." Working Paper #16. Center for Working Families, University of California, Berkeley.

Ariès, Philippe. 1962. *Centuries of Childhood.* Trans. Robert Baldick. London: Jonathan Cape.

Arnold, Jeanne, Anthony Graesch, Vincenzo Raggazini, and Elinor Ochs.

2012. *Life at Home in the 21st Century: 32 Families Open Their Doors.* Los Angeles: Cotsen Institute Press.

Arnold, Jeanne E., and Ursula A. Lang. 2007. "Changing American Home Life: Trends in Domestic Leisure and Storage among Middle-Class Families." *Journal of Family and Economic Issues* 28: 23–48.

Aronsson, Karin, and Asta Cekaite. 2011. "Activity Contracts and Directives in Everyday Family Politics." *Discourse and Society* 22 (2): 1–18.

Aronsson, Karin, and Lucas Gottzén. 2011. "Generational Positions at Family Dinner: Food Morality and Social Order." *Language in Society* 40 (4): 405–26.

Backett, Kathryn. 1992. "Taboos and Excesses: Lay Health Moralities in Middle-Class Families." *Sociology of Health and Illness* 14: 255–74.

Balli, Sandra J., David H. Demo, and John F. Wedman. 1998. "Family Involvement with Children's Homework: An Intervention in the Middle Grades." *Family Relations* 47: 149–57.

Baumeister, Roy. 1991. *Meanings of Life.* New York: Guilford.

Bazelon, Emily. 2008. "The Mac-and-Cheese Effect: Why Family Dinner Makes Working Parents (Especially Moms) Feel Better." *Slate.* www.slate.com/id/2195143.

Beck, Margaret. 2007. "Dinner Preparation in the Modern United States." *British Food Journal* 109 (7): 531–47.

Beck, Margaret E., and Jeanne E. Arnold. 2009. "Gendered Time Use at Home: An Ethnographic Examination of Leisure Time in Middle-Class Families." *Leisure Studies* 28: 121–42.

Beeghley, Leonard. 2006. *Social Stratification in America: A Critical Analysis of Theory and Research.* 6th ed. Boston: Allyn and Bacon.

Before Sunset. 2004. Dir. Richard Linklater. 80 min. Warner Independent Pictures.

Belk, Russell W. 2001. *Collecting in a Consumer Society.* New York: Routledge.

Belkin, Lisa. 2007. "The Pangs of Family Mealtime Guilt." *New York Times,* June 14.

Bempechat, Janine. 2004. "The Motivational Benefits of Homework: A Social–Cognitive Perspective." *Theory into Practice* 43: 189–96.

Bernas, Karyn H., and Debra A. Major. 2000. "Contributors to Stress Resistance: Testing a Model of Women's Work-Family Conflict." *Psychology of Women Quarterly* 24 (2): 170–78.

Bianchi, Suzanne M. 2000. "Maternal Employment and Time with Children: Dramatic Change or Surprising Continuity?" *Demography* 37 (4): 401–14.

———. 2011. "Changing Families, Changing Workplaces." *Work and Family* 21 (2): 15–36.

Bianchi, Suzanne M., John P. Robinson, and Melissa Milkie. 2006. *Changing Rhythms of American Family Life.* New York: Russell Sage Foundation.

Black, Steven P. 2008. "Creativity and Learning Jazz: The Practice of 'Listening.'" *Mind, Culture, and Activity* 15 (4): 279–95.

Blair, Sampson. 1992a. "Children's Participation in Household Labor: Child

Socialization versus the Need for Household Labor." *Journal of Youth and Adolescence* 21: 241–58.

———. 1992b. "The Sex-Typing of Children's Household Labor: Parental Influence on Daughters' and Sons' Housework." *Youth and Society* 24: 178–203.

Blaxter, Mildred. 1990. *Health and Lifestyles.* London: Routledge.

———. 1997. "Whose Fault Is It? People's Own Conceptions of the Reasons for Health Inequalities." *Social Science and Medicine* 44: 747–56.

———. 2004. *Health.* Cambridge: Polity Press.

Bolin, Inge. 2006. *Growing up in a Culture of Respect: Child Rearing in Highland Peru.* Austin: University of Texas Press.

Bond, James T., Ellen Galinsky, and Jennifer E. Swanberg. 1998. *The 1997 National Study of the Changing Workforce.* New York: Families and Work Institute.

Bourdieu, Pierre. 1977. *Outline of a Theory of Practice.* Trans. Richard Nice. Cambridge: Cambridge University Press.

———. 1984. *Distinction: A Social Critique of the Judgment of Taste.* London: Routledge.

Bradbury, Thomas N., ed. 1998. *The Developmental Course of Marital Dysfunction.* New York: Cambridge University Press.

Bradbury, Thomas N., and Benjamin R. Karney. 2010. *Intimate Relationships.* New York: Norton.

Bradley, Robert H., and Robert F. Corwyn. 2004. "'Family Process' Investments That Matter for Child Well-Being." In *Family Investments in Children's Potential: Resources and Parenting Behaviors That Promote Success,* ed. Ariel Kalil and Thomas DeLeire, 1–32. Mahwah, NJ: Erlbaum.

Bradley, Robert H., Robert F. Corwyn, Harriette Pipes McAdoo, and Cynthia Garcia Coll. 2001. "The Home Environments of Children in the United States: Part I: Variations by Age, Ethnicity and Poverty Status." *Child Development* 72 (6): 1844–67.

Brannen, Julia. 2005. "Time and the Negotiation of Work-Family Boundaries: Autonomy or Illusion?" *Time & Society* 14: 113–31.

Breton, André. 2003. "Choose Life." In *André Breton Selections,* ed. Mark Polizzotti, 68–69. Berkeley: University of California Press, 2003.

Broege, Nora, Ann Owens, Anthony P. Graesch, Jeanne E. Arnold, and Barbara Schneider. 2007. "Librating Measures of Family Activities between Large- and Small-Scale Data Sets." *Sociological Methodology* 37 (1): 119–49.

Budig, Michelle J., and Nancy Folbre. 2004. "Child Care vs. Child-Minding: Measuring Activities, Responsibilities, and Time." In *Family Time: The Social Organization of Care,* ed. Nancy Folbre and Michael Bittman, 51–68. New York: Routledge.

Bumpus, Matthew F., Ann C. Crouter, and Susan M. McHale. 1999. "Work Demands of Dual-Earner Couples: Implications for Parents' Knowledge about Children's Daily Lives in Middle Childhood." *Journal of Marriage and Family* 61: 465–75.

Burman, Bonnie, R. Mangolin, and R. S. John. 1993. "America's Angriest

Home Video: Behavioral Contingencies Observed in Home Re-enactments of Marital Conflict." *Journal of Consulting and Clinical Psychology* 61: 28–39.

Burt, Sandra, and Linda Perlis. 2006. *Raising a Successful Child: Discover and Nurture Your Child's Talents.* Berkeley, CA: Ulysses Press.

Campos, Belinda, with Anthony Graesch, Rena L. Repetti, Thomas Bradbury, and Elinor Ochs. 2009. "Opportunity for Interaction? A Naturalistic Observation Study of Dual-Earner Families after Work and School." *Journal of Family Psychology* 23: 798–807.

Campos, Belinda, Shu-wen Wang, Tatyana Plaksina, Rena L. Repetti, Dominik Schoebi, Elinor Ochs, and Margaret E. Beck. n.d. "Positive and Negative Emotion in the Daily Life of Dual-Earner Couples with Children." Unpublished manuscript.

Capps, Lisa, and Elinor Ochs. 2001. *Living Narrative.* Cambridge, MA: Harvard University Press.

Chau, Amy. 2011. *Battle Hymn of the Tiger Mother.* New York: Penguin Press.

Cheal, David J. 2003. "Children's Home Responsibilities: Factors Predicting Children's Household Work." *Social Behavior and Personality* 31 (8): 789–94.

Cherlin, Andrew. 2004. "The Deinstitutionalization of American Marriage." *Journal of Marriage and Family* 66: 848–61.

———. 2005. "American Marriage in the Early Twenty-First Century." *Future of Children* 15 (2): 33–55.

Child Trends Data Bank Survey. 2003. www.childtrendsdatabank.org.

Chodorow, Nancy J. 1989. *Feminism and Psychoanalytic Theory.* New Haven: Yale University Press.

———. 2001. *The Power of Feelings: Personal Meaning in Psychoanalysis, Gender, and Culture.* New Haven: Yale University Press.

Christensen, Kathleen, and Barbara Schneider. 2010. "Introduction: Evidence of the Worker and Workplace Mismatch." In *Workplace Flexibility: Realigning 20th-Century Jobs for a 21st-Century Workforce,* ed. K. Christensen and B. Schneider, 1–14. Ithaca: Cornell University Press.

Christiansen, Shawn L., and Rob Palkovitz. 2001. "Why the 'Good Provider' Role Still Matters: Providing as a Form of Paternal Involvement." *Journal of Family Issues* 22 (1): 84–106.

Clark, Clifford E., Jr. 1986. *The American Family Home, 1800–1960.* Chapel Hill: University of North Carolina Press.

Clarke, Jean I., Connie Dawson, and David Bredehoft. 2004. *How Much Is Enough? Everything You Need to Know to Steer Clear of Overindulgence and Raise Likeable, Responsible, and Respectful Children.* New York: Marlowe & Company.

Clavan, Sylvia. 1978. "The Impact of Social Class and Social Trends on the Role of Grandparent." *Family Coordinator* 27 (4) : 351–35.

Coakley, Jay. 2006. "The Good Father: Parental Expectations and Youth Sports." *Leisure Studies* 25 (2): 153–63.

Coltrane, Scott. 2000."Research on Household Labor: Modeling and Measuring the Social Embeddedness of Routine Family Work." *Journal of Marriage and Family* 64 (4): 1208–33.

Coltrane, S., R. D. Parke, and M. Adams. 2004. "Complexity of Father Involvement in Low-Income Mexican American Families." *Family Relations* 53 (2): 179–89.

Conrad, Peter. 1994. "Wellness as Virtue: Morality and the Pursuit of Health." *Culture, Medicine, and Psychiatry* 18: 385–401.

Cooke, Lynn P. 2006. "'Doing' Gender in Context: Household Bargaining and Risk of Divorce in Germany and the United States." *American Journal of Sociology* 112 (2): 442–72.

Coontz, Stephanie. 2005. *Marriage, a History: How Love Conquered Marriage.* New York: Penguin.

Cooper, Harris. 1989. *Homework.* New York: Longman.

———. 1994. *The Battle over Homework: An Administrator's Guide to Setting Sound and Effective Policies.* Thousand Oaks, CA: Corwin Press.

Costa, Paul T., and Robert R. McCrae. 1992. *NEO PI-R.* [Professional manual.] Odessa, FL: Psychological Assessment Resources.

Costigan, Catherine L., Martha J. Cox, and Ana Mari Cauce. 2003. "Work-Parenting Linkages among Dual-Earner Couples at the Transition to Parenthood." *Journal of Family Psychology* 17: 397–408.

Craig, Lyn. 2007a. *Contemporary Motherhood: The Impact of Children on Adult Time.* Surrey: Ashgate.

———. 2007b. "Is There Really a Second Shift, and If So, Who Does It? A Time-Diary Investigation." *Feminist Review* 86: 149–70.

Crain, William. 2003. *Reclaiming Childhood: Letting Children Be Children in Our Achievement-Oriented Society.* New York: Henry Holt.

Crawford, Robert. 1984. "A Cultural Account of 'Health': Control, Release, and the Social Body." In *Issues in the Political Economy of Health Care,* ed. J. McKinlay, 60–101. London: Tavistock.

———. 2004. "Risk Ritual and the Management of Control and Anxiety in Medical Culture." *Health* 8: 505–27.

———. 2006. "Health as Meaningful Social Practice." *Health* 10: 401–20.

Crouter, Ann C., S. M. MacDermid, S. M. McHale, and M. Perry-Jenkins. 1990. "Parental Monitoring and Perceptions of Children's School Performance and Conduct in Dual- and Single-Earner Families." *Developmental Psychology* 26: 649–57.

Crouter, Ann C., and S. M. McHale. 2005. "Work Time, Family Time, and Children's Time: Implications for Child and Adolescent Relationships, Development, and Well-Being." In *Workforce/Workplace Mismatch: Work, Family, Health, and Well-Being,* ed. S. Bianchi, L. Casper, K. E. Christensen, and R. B. King, 49–66. Mahwah, NJ: Erlbaum.

Crowley, Kevin, and Melanie Jacobs. 2002. "Building Islands of Expertise in Everyday Family Activity." In *Learning Conversations in Museums,* ed. K. Crowley and K. Knutson, 333–56. Mahwah, NJ: Erlbaum.

Daly, Kerry J. 1996. *Families and Time: Keeping Pace in a Hurried Culture.* Thousand Oaks, CA: Sage.

———. 2001a. "Deconstructing Family Time: From Ideology to Lived Experience." *Journal of Marriage and Family* 63: 283–94.

———. 2001b. "Introduction." In *Minding the Time in Family Experience: Emerging Perspectives and Issues,* ed. Kerry Daly, 1–6. Oxford: Elsevier Science.

D'Andrade, Roy G., and Claudia Strauss. 1992. *Human Motives and Cultural Models.* New York: Cambridge University Press.

Darrah, Charles N. 2006. "Ethnography and Working Families." In *The Work and Family Handbook: Multi-Disciplinary Perspectives and Approaches,* ed. Marcie Pitt-Catsouphes, Ellen Ernst Kossek, and Stephen Sweet, 367–85. Mahwah, NJ: Erlbaum.

———. 2007. "The Anthropology of Busyness." *Human Organization* 66 (3): 261–69.

Darrah, Charles N., James M. Freeman, and J. A English-Lueck. 2007. *Busier than Ever: Why American Families Can't Slow Down.* Stanford: Stanford University Press.

David, Nicholas, and Carol Cramer. 2001. *Ethnoarchaeology in Action.* Cambridge: Cambridge University Press.

Davies, Gary, and Canan Madran. 1997. "Time, Food Shopping, and Food Preparation: Some Attitudinal Linkages." *British Food Journal* 99 (3): 80–88.

Dawkins, Richard. 1976. *The Selfish Gene.* Oxford: Oxford University Press.

De Carvalho, Maria E. P. 2001. *Rethinking Family-School Relations: A Critique of Parental Involvement.* Mahwah, NJ: Erlbaum.

de León, Lourdes. 2011. "'Calibrando' la atención: Directivos, adiestramiento y responsabilidad en el trabajo doméstico de los niños mayas zinacantecos." In *Aprendizaje, cultura y desarrollo: Una aproximación interdisciplinaria,* ed. S. Frisancho, M. T. Moreno, P. Ruiz Bravo. and V. Zavala, 81–110. Lima: Fondo Editorial de la Pontificia Universidad Católica del Perú.

Doane, Janice L., and Devon L. Hodges. 1992. *From Klein to Kristeva: Psychoanalytic Feminism and the Search for the "Good Enough Mother."* Ann Arbor: University of Michigan Press.

Dovey, Terence M., with Paul A. Staples, E. Leigh Gibson, and Jason C. G. Halford. 2007. "Food Neophobia and 'Picky/Fussy' Eating in Children: A Review." *Appetite* 50 (2–3): 181–93.

Dukes, Richard L., and Jay Coakley. 2002. "Parental Commitment to Competitive Swimming." *Free Inquiry in Creative Sociology* 30 (2): 185–97.

Dunn, Janet S., David A. Kinney, and Sandra L. Hofferth. 2003. "Parental Ideologies and Children's After-School Activities." *American Behavioral Scientist* 46 (10): 1359–86.

Duranti, Alessandro. 1997. "Universal and Culture-Specific Properties of Greetings." *Journal of Linguistic Anthropology* 7 (1): 63–97.

———. 2010. "Husserl, Intersubjectivity and Anthropology." *Anthropological Theory* 10 (1): 1–20.

Eagleton, Terry. 2009. *Trouble with Strangers: A Study of Ethics*. Malden, MA: Wiley-Blackwell.

Eccles, Jacquelynne S., B.L. Barber, M. Stone, and J. Hunt. 2003. "Extracurricular Activities and Adolescent Development." *Journal of Social Issues* 59 (4): 865–89.

Ehrenreich, Barbara. 1989. *Fear of Falling: The Inner Life of the Middle Class*. New York: Pantheon Books.

Eldridge, Kathleen A., and Andrew Christensen. 2002. "Demand-Withdraw Communication during Conflict: A Review and Analysis." In *Understanding Marriage: Developments in the Study of Couple Interaction*, ed. P. Noller and J.A. Feeney, 289–322. New York: Simon and Schuster.

Elkind, David. 2001. *The Hurried Child: Growing up Too Fast Too Soon*. Cambridge: Perseus.

Farkas, Steve, Jean Johnson, Ann Duffett, Claire Aulicino, and Joanna McHugh. 1999. "Playing Their Parts: Parents and Teachers Talk about Parental Involvement in Public Schools. A Report from Public Agenda." www.publicagenda.org/reports/playing-their-parts.

Fasulo, Alessandra, Vivian Liberati, and Clotilde Pontecorvo. 2002. "Language Games in the Strict Sense of the Term: Children's Poetics and Conversation." In *Talking to Adults: The Contribution of Multiparty Discourse to Language Acquisition*, ed. S. Blum-Kulka and C.E. Snow, 209–37. Mahwah, NJ: Erlbaum.

Fasulo, Alessandra, Heather Loyd, and Vincenzo Padiglione. 2007. "Children's Socialization into Cleaning Practices: A Cross-Cultural Perspective." *Discourse and Society* 18: 1.

Fatigante, Marilena, Tamar Kremer-Sadlik, and Alessandra Fasulo. 2007. "The Emergence of Moral Parenthood within the Ethnographic Relationship." Paper presented at the panel Doing the Right Thing: The Discursive Portrayal of Good Parents and Moral Families, International Pragmatics Association (IPrA) annual conference, Gothenburg, Sweden, July 10.

Fiese, B.H., T.J. Tomcho, M. Douglas, K. Josephs, S. Poltrock, and T. Baker. 2002. "A Review of 50 Years of Research on Naturally Occurring Family Routines and Rituals: Cause for Celebration?" *Journal of Family Psychology* 16: 381–90.

Finch, Janet. 1989. *Family Obligations and Social Change*. Cambridge: Polity Press.

Fisher, Kevin. 2009. "Elite Place-Making and Social Interaction in the Late Cypriot Bronze Age." *Journal of Mediterranean Archaeology* 22 (2): 183–209.

Folbre, Nancy. 2001. *The Invisible Heart: Economics and Family Values*. New York: New Press.

Forsberg, Lucas. 2007. "Homework as Serious Family Business: Power and

Subjectivity in Negotiations about School Assignments in Swedish Families." *British Journal of Sociology of Education* 28 (2): 209–22.

———. 2009. *Involved Parenthood: Everyday Lives of Swedish Middle-Class Families*. Linköping: Linköping University Press.

Foucault, Michel. 1977. *Discipline and Punish: The Birth of the Prison*. New York: Vintage Books.

———. 1979. *Discipline and Punish: The Birth of the Prison*. New York: Random House.

———. 1984. "Docile Bodies." In *The Foucault Reader,* ed. P. Rabinow, 179–87. New York: Pantheon.

———. 1988. *Technologies of the Self: A Seminar with Michel Foucault*. Ed. L. H. Martin, H. Gutmann, and P. H. Hutton. Amherst: University of Massachusetts Press.

Galinsky, Ellen. 1999. *Ask the Children: What America's Children Really Think about Working Parents*. New York: William Morrow.

Garro, Linda. 2010. "Beyond the Reproduction of Official Accounts: Parental Accounts Concerning Health and the Daily Life of a California Family." *Medical Anthropology Quarterly* 24: 472–99.

———. 2011. "Enacting Ethos, Enacting Health: Realizing Health in the Everyday Life of a California Family of Mexican Descent." *Ethos* 39 (3): 300–330.

Garro, Linda, and Kristin Yarris. 2009. "'A Massive Long Way': Interconnecting Histories, a 'Special Child,' ADHD, and Everyday Family Life." *Culture, Medicine, and Psychiatry* 33: 559–607.

Gergen, Kenneth J. 1991. *The Saturated Self: Dilemmas of Identity in Contemporary Life*. New York: Basic Books.

Gerson, Kathleen. 2004. "Understanding Work and Family through a Gender Lens." *Journal of Community, Work, and Family* 7 (2): 163–79.

Getzels, Jacob W., and Mihály Csikszentmihalyi. 1976. *The Creative Vision: A Longitudinal Study of Problem-Finding in Art*. New York: Wiley.

Giddens, Anthony. 1990. *The Consequences of Modernity*. Stanford: Stanford University Press.

Gillis, John R. 1996. *A World of Their Own Making: Myth, Ritual, and the Quest for Family Values*. Cambridge, MA: Harvard University Press.

———. 2001. "Never Enough Time: Some Paradoxes of Modern Family Time(s)." In *Minding the Time in Family Experience: Contemporary Perspectives in Family Research,* ed. Kerry J. Daly, 19–37. Contemporary Perspectives in Family Research, vol. 3. Thousand Oaks, CA: Sage.

———. 2003. "Childhood and Family Time: A Changing Historical Relationship." In *Children and the Changing Family: Between transformation and Negotiation,* ed. An-Magritt Jensen and Lorna McKee, 149–64. New York: Routedge Falmer.

———. 2006. "Never Enough Time: Some Paradoxes of Modern Family Time(s)." In *Minding the Time in Family Experience: Emerging Perspectives and Issues,* ed. Kerry J. Daly, 19–36. Contemporary Perspectives in Family Research, vol. 3. Thousand Oaks, CA: Sage.

Goffman, Erving. 1959. *Presentation of Self in Everyday Life*. New York: Doubleday.

———. 1961. *Encounters: Two Studies in the Sociology of Interaction*. Indianapolis: Bobbs-Merrill.

———. 1963. *Behavior in Public Places: Notes on the Social Organization of Gathering*. New York: Free Press.

———. 1967. *Interaction Ritual: Essays on Face-to-Face Behavior*. Garden City, NY: Doubleday.

———. 1981. *Forms of Talk*. Oxford: Blackwell.

Gonerko, Christina, Marjorie H. Goodwin, and Eve Tulbert. 2008. *Socializing Accountability: Relations between Parent-Child Interaction and Sibling Caretaking Stylistic Repertoire*. Working Paper #78. Center on Everyday Lives of Families, University of California, Los Angeles.

Good, Jeffrey. 2009. "Multitasking and Attention in Interaction: Negotiating Multiple Tasks in Everyday Family Life." Ph.D. diss., University of California, Los Angeles.

Goodnow, Jacqueline J. 1988. "Children's Household Work: Its Nature and Functions." *Psychological Bulletin* 103 (1): 5–26.

Goodwin, Charles. 1994. "Professional Vision." *American Anthropologist* 96 (3): 606–33.

———. 2006. "Retrospective and Prospective Orientation in the Construction of Argumentative Moves." *Text & Talk* 26 (4–5): 443–61.

———. 2007. "Environmentally Coupled Gestures." In *Gesture and the Dynamic Dimension of Language*, ed. S. Duncan, J. Cassell, and E. Levy, 195–212. Amsterdam: John Benjamins.

Goodwin, Marjorie Harness. 2005. "Interaction, Language Practice, and the Construction of the Social Universe." *Calidoscopio* 3 (3): 184–95.

———. 2006. "Participation, Affect, and Trajectory in Family Directive/Response Sequences." *Text & Talk* 26 (4–5): 513–42.

———. 2007. "Occasioned Knowledge Exploration in Family Interaction." *Discourse and Society* 18 (1): 93–110.

———. 2010. "From Task to Play: Shifting Frame in Sibling Interaction." Paper presented at session Children's Play and Multimodality, org. Ann-Carita Evaldsson and Amy Kyratzis, International Conference on Conversation Analysis ICCA10 "Multimodal Interaction," Mannheim, July 6.

Goodwin, Marjorie Harness, Asta Cekaite, and Charles Goodwin. Forthcoming. "Emotion as Stance." In *Emotion in Interaction,* ed. M.-L. Sorjonen and A. Perakyla. Oxford: Oxford University Press.

Goody, Esther. 1972. "'Greeting', 'Begging', and the Presentation of Respect." In *The Interpretation of Ritual*, ed. J.S. La Fontaine, 39–71. London: Tavistock.

Goran, Michael I., Kim D. Reynolds, and Christine H. Lindquist. 1999. "Role of Physical Activity in the Prevention of Obesity in Children." *International Journal of Obesity* 23: S18–S33.

Gornick, Janet C., and Marcia K. Meyers. 2003. *Families That Work: Poli-*

cies for Reconciling Parenthood and Employment. New York: Russell Sage Foundation.

Gosden, Chris. 2001. "Making Sense: Archaeology and Aesthetics." *World Archaeology* 33: 163–67.

Gottman, John M. 1994. *Why Marriages Succeed or Fail.* New York: Simon and Schuster.

Govier, Trudy. 1998. *Dilemmas of Trust.* Montreal: McGill-Queen's University Press.

Graesch, Anthony P. 2004. "Notions of Family Embedded in the House." *Anthropology News* 45 (5): 20.

———. 2006. "An Ethnoarchaeological Study of Contemporary U.S. Houses and Households." Working Paper #59. Center on Everyday Lives of Families, University of California, Los Angeles.

———. 2009. "Material Indicators of Family Busyness." *Social Indicators Research* 93 (1): 85–94.

Grolnick, Wendy S., Carrie E. Price, Krista L. Beiswenger, and Christine C. Sauck. 2007. "Evaluative Pressure in Mothers: Effects of Situation, Maternal, and Child Characteristics on Autonomy Supportive versus Controlling Behavior." *Developmental Psychology* 43 (4): 991–1002.

Grolnick, Wendy S., and Kathy Seal. 2007. *Pressured Parents, Stressed-Out Kids: Dealing with Competition while Raising a Successful Child.* Amherst, MA: Prometheus Books.

Gutiérrez, Kris, Carolina Izquierdo, and Tamar Kremer-Sadlik. 2010. "'Middle-Class Working Families' Ideologies and Engagement in Children's Extra Curricular Activities." *International Journal of Learning* 17 (3): 633–56.

Halldén, Gunilla. 1991. "The Child as Project and the Child as Being: Parents' Ideas as Frames of Reference." *Children and Society* 5 (4): 334–46.

Harkness, Sara, and Charles Super. 1996. *Parents' Cultural Belief Systems: Their Origins, Expressions, and Consequences.* New York: Guiford Press.

———. 2006. "Themes and Variations: Parental Ethnotheories in Western Cultures." In *Parental Beliefs, Behaviors, and Parent-Child Relations: A Cross-Cultural Perspective,* ed. Kenneth H. Rubin and Ock Boon Chung, 61–79. New York: Psychology Press.

Havel, Vaclav. 1990. Address to the Joint Session of the United States Congress. Washington, DC, February 21. http://vaclavhavel.cz/showtrans.php?cat=projevy&val=322_aj_projevy.html&typ=HTML.

Hays, Sharon. 1996. *The Cultural Contradictions of Motherhood.* New Haven: Yale University Press.

Hochschild, Arlie. 1997. *The Time Bind: When Work Becomes Home and Home Becomes Work.* New York: Metropolitan Books.

Hochschild, Arlie, and Anne Machung. [1989] 2003. *The Second Shift.* New York: Penguin.

Hofferth, Sandra L. 2009. "Changes in American Children's Time, 1997–2003." *International Journal of Time Use Research* 6 (1): 26–47.

Hofferth, Sandra L., and Sally C. Curtin. 2005. "Leisure Time Activities in Middle Childhood." In *What Do Children Need to Flourish? Conceptualizing and Measuring Indicators of Positive Development*, ed. L. Lippman and K. Moore, 95–110. New York: Springer Science & Business.

Hofferth, Sandra L., and John F. Sandberg. 2001a. "Changes in American Children's Time, 1981–1997." In *Children at the Millennium: Where Did We Come from, Where Are We Going?*, ed. Sandra L. Hofferth and Timothy J. Owens, 193–232. Advances in Life Course Research, vol. 6. New York: Elsevier Science.

———. 2001b. "Changes in Children's Time with Parents: United States, 1981–1997." *Demography* 38: 423–36.

Hollan, Douglas. 2009. "Selfscapes of Well-Being in a Rural Indonesian Village." In *Pursuits of Happiness: Well-Being in Anthropological Perspective*, ed. Gordon Mathews and Carolina Izquierdo, 211–27. New York: Berghahn Press.

Holloway, Wendy. 2006. *The Capacity to Care: Gender and Ethical Subjectivity*. London: Routledge.

Hook, Jennifer L. 2006. "Care in Context: Men's Unpaid Work in 20 Countries, 1965–2003." *American Sociological Review* 71 (4): 639–60.

Hoover-Dumpsey, Kathleen V., Otto C. Bassler, and Rebecca Burow. 1995. "Parents' Reported Involvement in Students' Homework: Strategies and Practices." *Elementary School Journal* 95: 435–50.

Hoover-Dumpsey, Kathleen V., Angela C. Battiato, Joan M. T. Walker, Richard P. Reed, Jennifer M. DeJong, and Kathleen P. Jones. 2001. "Parental Involvement in Homework." *Educational Psychologist* 36 (3): 195–209.

Husserl, Edmund. 1982. *Ideas Pertaining to a Pure Phenomenology and to a Phenomenological Philosophy*. The Hague: Martinus Nijhoff.

Ingold, Tim. 2000. *The Perception of the Environment: Essays in Livelihood, Dwelling and Skill*. London: Routledge.

Izquierdo, Carolina. 2005. "When 'Health' Is Not Enough: Societal, Individual and Biomedical Assessments among the Matsigenka of the Peruvian Amazon." *Social Science and Medicine* 61: 767–83.

Jackson, Michael. 1996. *Things as They Are: New Directions in Phenomenological Anthropology*. Bloomington: Indiana University Press.

Jacobs, Jerry A., and Kathleen Gerson. 2001. "Overworked Individuals or Overworked Families? Explaining Trends in Work, Leisure, and Family Time." *Work and Occupations* 28 (1): 40–63.

———. 2004. *The Time Divide: Work, Family, and Gender Inequality*. Cambridge, MA: Harvard University Press.

James, William. 1977. *The Writings of William James*. Chicago: University of Chicago Press.

Jeske, Diane. 2002. "Special Obligations." In *Stanford Encyclopedia of Philosophy*. Stanford, CA: Metaphysics Research Lab, CSLI, Stanford University.

Johnson, M. D., C. L. Cohan, J. Davilla, E. Lawrence, R. Rogge, and B. Karney. 2005. "Problem-Solving Skills and Affective Expression as Predictors of

Change in Marital Satisfaction." *Journal of Consulting and Clinical Psychology* 73: 15–27.

Keenan, Elinor Ochs. 1977. "Making It Last: Repetition in Children's Discourse." In *Child Discourse*, ed. S. Ervin-Tripp and C. Mitchell-Kernan, 125–38. New York: Academic Press.

Kendall, Shari. 2006. "'Honey, I'm home!': Framing in Family Dinnertime Homecomings." *Text & Talk* 26 (4–5): 411–41.

Kendon, Adam. 1990. "Spatial Organization in Social Encounters: The F-Formation System." In *Conducting Interaction: Patterns of Behavior in Focused Encounters*, ed. A. Kendon, 209–38. Cambridge: Cambridge University Press.

Kiecolt-Glaser, Janice K., and Tamara L. Newton. 2001. "Marriage and Health: His and Hers." *Psychological Bulletin* 127 (4): 472–503.

Kennedy, Tracy L. M., Aaron Smith, Amy Tracy Wells, and Barry Wellman. 2008. *Networked Families*. Pew Internet & American Life Project, October 19. www.pewinternet.org/pdfs/PIP_Networked_Family.pdf.

King, Edith W. 1999. *Looking into the Lives of Children: A Worldwide View*. Melbourne: James Nicholas.

Klein, Felix, and Arnold Sommerfeld. 2008. *The Theory of the Top*, vol. 1: *Introduction to Kinematics and Kinetics of the Top*. Trans. Raymond J. Nagem and Guido Sandri. New York: Birkhäuser; Boston: Springer Science+Business Media.

Klein, Wendy, Anthony P. Graesch, and Carolina Izquierdo. 2009. "Children and Chores: A Mixed-Methods Study of Children's Household Work in Los Angeles Families." *Anthropology of Work Review* 30 (3): 98–109.

Klein, Wendy, Carolina Izquierdo, and Thomas N. Bradbury. 2007. "Working Relationships: Communicative Patterns and Strategies among Couples in Everyday Life." *Qualitative Research in Psychology* 4: 29–47.

Klein, Wendy, Carolina Izquierdo, Thomas N. Bradbury, and Francesco Arcidiacono. 2005. *Collaboration and Conflict: Insights into the Division of Household Labor among Working Couples in the United States and Italy*. Working Paper #36. Center on Everyday Life of Families, University of California, Berkeley.

Klein, Wendy, and Tamar Kremer-Sadlik. 2009. "State of the Union: Gender Roles and Support among Couples in Los Angeles." Paper presented at the Annual Meeting of the American Anthropological Association, Philadelphia, December 5.

Kleinman, Arthur. 1988. *Rethinking Psychiatry: From Cultural Category to Personal Experience*. New York: Free Press.

Kleinman, Arthur, and Joan Kleinman. 1991. "Suffering and Its Professional Transformation: Toward an Ethnography of Interpersonal Experience." *Culture, Medicine, and Psychiatry* 15: 275–301.

Klinck, Betty. 2010. "Survey: 89% Will Eat Family Dinner on Thanksgiving." *USA Today*, November 30.

Kraehmer, Steffen. 1994. *Quality Time: Moving beyond the Quality Time Myth*. Minneapolis: Deaconess Press.

Kralovec, Etta, and John Buell. 2000. *The End of Homework: How Homework Disrupts Families, Overburdens Children, and Limits Learning*. Boston: Beacon Press.

Kremer-Sadlik, Tamar. 2008. "Work-Family Conflict: A Parent's Problem." Paper presented at the Workplace Flexibility Sloan Conference, Washington, DC, May 29.

Kremer-Sadlik, Tamar, Marilena Fatigante, and Allesandra Fasulo. 2008. "Discourses on Family Time: The Cultural Interpretation of Family Togetherness in Los Angeles and Rome." *Ethos* 36 (3): 283–309.

Kremer-Sadlik, Tamar, Carolina Izquierdo, and Marilena Fatigante. 2010. "Making Meaning of Everyday Practices: The Case of Children's Extra-Curricular Activities in the United States and in Italy." *Anthropology and Education Quarterly* 41 (1): 35–54.

Kremer-Sadlik, Tamar, and Jeemin L. Kim. 2007. "Lessons from Sports: Children's Socialization to Values through Family Interaction during Sports Activities." *Discourse and Society* 18 (1): 35–52.

Kremer-Sadlik, Tamar, and Amy L. Paugh. 2007. "Everyday Moments: Finding 'Quality Time' in American Working Families." *Time and Society* 16: 287–308.

Kusserow, Adrie. 2004. *American Individualisms: Childrearing and Social Class in Three Neighborhoods*. New York: Palgrave Macmillan.

Lacan, Jacques. 1968. *The Language of the Self: The Function of Language in Psychoanalysis*. Baltimore: Johns Hopkins University Press.

———. 2006. *Écrits: The First Complete Edition in English*. Trans. B. Fink. New York: Norton.

Lacroix, Alexandre, and Martin Legros. 2010. "Mon réveillon chez Platon." *Philosophie Magazine* 45: 54–58.

Lambek, Michael. 2010. "Introduction." In *Ordinary Ethics: Anthropology, Language, and Action*, ed. M. Lambek, 1–38. New York: Fordham University Press.

Lareau, Annette. 2003. *Unequal Childhoods: Class, Race, and Family Life*. Berkeley: University of California Press.

Larson, Reed W. 2001. "How U.S. Children and Adolescents Spend Time: What It Does (and Doesn't) Tell Us about Their Development." *Current Directions in Psychological Science* 10 (5): 160–64.

Larson, Reed, and Maryse H. Richards. 1994. *Divergent Realities: The Emotional Lives of Mothers, Fathers, and Adolescents*. New York: Basic Books.

Larson, Reed W., and Suman Verma. 1999. "How Children and Adolescents Spent Time across the World: Work, Play, and Developmental Outcomes." *Psychological Bulletin* 25 (6): 701–36.

Lee, Yun-Suk. 2005. "Measuring the Gender Gap in Household Labor: Accurately Estimating Wives' and Husbands' Contributions." In *Being Together*

Working Apart: Dual-Career Families and Work-Life Balance, ed. Barbara Schneider and Linda J. Waite, 229–51. Cambridge: Cambridge University Press.

Levey, Hilary. 2009. "Pageant Princesses and Math Whizzes: Understanding Children's Activities as a Form of Children's Work." *Childhood* 16 (2): 195–212.

Levine, Madeline. 2008. *The Price of Privilege: How Parental Pressure and Material Advantage Are Creating a Generation of Disconnected and Unhappy Kids.* New York: Harper.

Lévi-Strauss, Claude. 1969. *The Raw and the Cooked. Mythologiques.* Vol. 1. Chicago: University of Chicago Press.

Locke, Harvey J., and Karl Wallace. 1959. "Short Marital Adjustment Prediction Tests: Their Reliability and Validity." *Marriage and Family Living* 21: 251–55.

Luria, A. R. 1979. *The Making of Mind: A Personal Account of Soviet Psychology.* Ed. M. Cole and S. Cole. Cambridge, MA: Harvard University Press.

Maier, Kimberly S., Timothy G. Ford, and Barbara Schneider. 2007. "Are Middle Class Families Advantaging Their Children?" In *The Way Class Works: Readings on School, Family, and the Economy,* ed. L. Weis, 134–48. London: Routledge.

Mathews, Gordon. 2009. "Finding and Keeping a Purpose in Life: Well-Being and *Ikigai* in Japan and Elsewhere." In *Pursuits of Happiness: Well-Being in Anthropological Perspective,* ed. Gordon Mathews and Carolina Izquierdo, 167–85. New York: Berghahn Press.

Mathews, Gordon, and Carolina Izquierdo. 2009. "Introduction: Anthropology, Happiness, and Well-Being" and "Conclusion: Towards an Anthropology of Well-Being." In *Pursuits of Happiness: Well-Being in Anthropological Perspective,* ed. Gordon Mathews and Carolina Izquierdo, 1–19, 248–66. New York: Berghahn Press.

McCarthy, Jane Ribbens, Rosalind Edwards, and Val Gillies. 2000. "Moral Tales of the Child and the Adult: Narratives of Contemporary Family Lives under Changing Circumstances." *Sociology* 34 (4): 785–803.

Maynard, Ashley E. 2002. "Cultural Teaching: The Development of Teaching Skills in Maya Sibling Interactions." *Child Development* 73 (3): 969–82.

Mead, Margaret. [1950] 2001. "The School in American Culture." *Society* 39 (1): 54–62.

Meissner, M., E. Humphreys, S. Meis, and W. Scheu. 1975. "No Exit for Wives: Sexual Division of Labour and the Cumulation of Household Demands." *Canadian Review of Society and Anthropology* 12: 424–39.

Messner, Michael. 2009. *It's All for the Kids: Gender, Families, and Youth Sports.* Berkeley: University of California Press.

Miller, Pavla. 2005. "Useful and Priceless Children in Contemporary Welfare States." *Social Politics: International Studies in Gender, State, and Society* 12 (1): 3–41.

Mintz, Steven. 2004. *Huck's Raft: A History of American Childhood.* Cambridge, MA: Harvard University Press.

Mintz, Steven, and Susan Kellogg. 1988. *Domestic Revolutions: A Social History of American Family Life*. New York: Free Press.

Murphy, Keith M. 2005. "Collaborative Imagining: The Interactive Use of Gestures, Talk, and Graphic Representation in Architectural Practice." *Semiotica* 156 (1–4): 113–45.

Nash, Ogden. 1933. *Happy Days*. New York: Simon and Schuster.

National Center on Addiction and Substance Abuse at Columbia University. 2010. *The Importance of Family Dinners* VI. New York: National Center on Addiction and Substance Abuse.

Needleman, Robert. 2001. "Extra-Curricular Activities." *Dr. Spock*. www.drspock.com/article/0,1510,5922,00.html.

Neumark-Sztainer, Dianna, Peter J. Hannan, Mary Story, Jillian Croll, and Cheryl Perry. 2003. "Family Meal Patterns: Associations with Sociodemographic Characteristics and Improved Dietary Intake among Adolescents." *Journal of the American Dietary Association* 103: 317–22.

Newman, Denis, Peg Griffin, and Michael Cole. 1989. *The Construction Zone: Working for Cognitive Change in School*. Cambridge: Cambridge University Press.

Nocon, Honorine, and Michael Cole. 2006. "School's Invasion of 'After-School': Colonization, Rationalization, or Expansion of Access?" In *Learning in Places: The Informal Education Reader*, ed. Z. Bekerman, N. Burbules, and D. Keller, 99–122. New York: Peter Lang.

Ochs, Elinor. 1988. *Culture and Language Development: Language Acquisition and Language Socialization in a Samoan Village*. Cambridge: Cambridge University Press.

Ochs, Elinor, with Anthony Graesch, Angela Mittmann, Thomas Bradbury, and Rena L. Repetti. 2006. "Video Ethnography and Ethnoarcheological Tracking." In *Handbook of Work and Family*, ed. M. Pitt-Catsouphes, S. Sweet, et al., 387–410. Mahwah, NJ: Erlbaum.

Ochs, Elinor, and Carolina Izquierdo. 2009. "Responsibility in Childhood: Three Developmental Trajectories." *Ethos* 37 (4): 391–413.

Ochs, Elinor, Clotilde Pontecorvo, and Alessandra Fasulo. 1996. "Socializing Taste." *Ethnos* 6 (1): 7–46.

Ochs, Elinor, and Bambi Schieffelin. 1984. "Language Acquisition and Socialization: Three Developmental Stories and Their Implications." In *Linguistic Anthropology: A Reader*, ed. A. Duranti, 263–301. Malden, MA: Blackwell.

Ochs, Elinor, and Merav Shohet. 2006. "The Cultural Structuring of Mealtime Socialization." In *Family Mealtime as a Context of Development and Socialization*, ed. R. W. Larson, A. R. Wiley, and K. R. Branscomb, 35–50. San Francisco: Wiley Periodicals.

Ochs, Elinor, Merav Shohet, Belinda Campos, and Margaret Beck. 2010. "Coming Together at Dinner: A Study of Working Families." In *Workplace Flexibility: Realigning 20th-Century Jobs for a 21st-Century Workforce*, ed. K. Christensen and B. Schneider, 57–70. Ithaca: Cornell University Press.

Ochs, Elinor, Ruth Smith, and Carolyn Taylor. 1989. "Detective Stories at Dinnertime: Problem-Solving through Co-Narration." *Cultural Dynamics* 2 (2): 238–57.

Ochs, Elinor, and Carolyn Taylor. 1992. "Science at Dinner." In *Texts and Contexts: Cross-Disciplinary and Cross-Cultural Perspectives on Language Study*, ed. C. Kramsch, 29–45. Lexington, MA: D.C. Heath.

Odgen, Cynthia L., Katherine M. Flegal, Margaret D. Carroll, and Clifford L. Johnson. 2002. "Prevalence and Trends in Overweight among US Children and Adolescents, 1999–2000." *JAMA* 288: 1728–32.

Offer, Shira, and Barbara Schneider. 2010. "Multitasking among Working Families: A Strategy for Dealing with the Time Squeez.." In *Workplace Flexibility: Realigning 20th-Century Jobs for a 21st-Century Workforce*, ed. K. Christensen and B. Schneider, 43–56. Ithaca: Cornell University Press.

Orenstein, Peggy. 2009. "The Way We Live Now: Kindergarten Cram." *New York Times*, www.nytimes.com/2009/05/03/magazine/03wwln-lede-t.html?_r = 1&emc = eta1.

Ortner, Sherry B. 1998a. "Generation X: Anthropology in a Media-Saturated World." *Cultural Anthropology* 13 (3): 414–40.

———. 1998b. "Identities: The Hidden Life of Class." *Journal of Anthropological Research* 54 (1): 1–17.

———. 2003. *New Jersey Dreaming : Capital, Culture, and the Class of '58*. Durham: Duke University Press.

Osit, Michael. 2008. *Generation Text: How to Raise Kids in an Age of Instant Everything*. New York: Amacom.

Patrick, Heather, and Theresa A Nicklas. 2005. "A Review of Family and Social Determinants of Children's Eating Patterns and Diet Quality." *Journal of the American College of Nutrition* 24 (2): 83–92.

Patterson, Gerald R. 1982. *Coercive Family Process*. Eugene, OR: Castalia.

Patterson, Gerald R., and Lew Bank. 1986. "Bootstrapping Your Way in the Nomological Thicket." *Behavioral Assessment* 8: 49–73.

Paugh, Amy, and Carolina Izquierdo. 2009. "Why Is This a Battle Every Night? Negotiating Food and Eating in American Dinnertime Interaction." *Journal of Linguistic Anthropology* 19 (2): 185–204.

Perry-Jenkins, Maureen, Rena L. Repetti, and Ann C. Crouter. 2000. "Work and Family in the 1990s." *Journal of Marriage and the Family* 62: 981–98.

Peterson, R.R., and K. Gerson. 1992. "Determinants of Responsibility for Child Care Arrangements among Dual-Earner Couples." *Journal of Marriage and the Family* 54: 527–36.

Pew Research Center Publications. 2007. "As Marriage and Parenthood Drift Apart, Public Is Concerned about Social Impact." http://pewresearch.org/pubs/526/marriage-parenthood.

Philosophie Magazine. 2010. "La famille est-elle insupportable?" *Philosophie Magazine* 45: 38–57.

Pigeron, Elisa. 2008. "'Here's the Deal': Socialization into Morality through

Negotiations of Media Time Use." Working Paper #77. Center on Everyday Lives of Families, University of California, Los Angeles.

———. 2009. "The Technology-Mediated Worlds of American Families." Ph.D. diss., University of California, Los Angeles.

Pisarski, Alan E. 2006. *Commuting in America III: The Third National Report on Commuting Patterns and Trends*. Cooperative Research Program Report. Transportation Research Board of the National Academies. http://onlinepubs.trb.org/onlinepubs/nchrp/CIAIII.pdf.

Pleck, E. H., and J. H. Pleck. 1997. "Fatherhood Ideals in the United States." In *The Role of the Father in Child Development*, ed. M. E. Lamb, 33–48. New York: Wiley.

Plionis, E. M. 1990. "Parenting, Discipline, and the Concept of Quality Time." *Child and Adolescent Social Work* 7 (6): 513–23.

Pomerantz, Anita. 1984. "Agreeing and Disagreeing with Assessments: Some Features of Preferred/Dispreferred Turn Shapes." In *Structures of Social Action: Studies in Conversation Analysis*, ed. J. M. Atkinson and J. Heritage, 57–101. Cambridge: Cambridge University Press.

Press, Sarah. 2003. "Orders, Accounts, and the Culture of Control: Directives in Parent-Child Relationships." Honors thesis, University of California, Los Angeles.

Qvortrup, Jens. 2001. "School-Work, Paid Work and the Changing Obligations of Childhood." In *Hidden Hands: International Perspectives on Children's Work and Labour*, ed. Phillip Mizen, Christopher Pole, and Angela Bolton, 91–107. Future of Childhood. London: Routledge Falmer.

———. 2005. "Varieties of Childhood." In *Studies in Modern Childhood: Society, Agency, and Culture*, ed. Jens Qvortrup, 1–20. New York: Palgrave Macmillan.

Rabain-Jamin, Jacqueline, Ashley E. Maynard, and Patricia Greenfield. 2003. "Implications of Sibling Caregiving for Sibling Relations and Teaching Interactions in Two Cultures." *Ethos* 3 (2): 204–31.

Reay, Diane. 2004. "Education and Cultural Capital: The Implications of Changing Trends in Education Policies." *Cultural Trends* 13 (2): 1–14.

Redekop, Paul. 1984. "Sport and the Masculine Ethos: Some Implications for Family Interaction." *International Journal of Comparative Sociology* 25 (3–4): 262–69.

Repetti, Rena L. 1989. "Effects of Daily Workload on Subsequent Behavior during Marital Interaction: The Roles of Social Withdrawal and Spouse Support." *Journal of Personality and Social Psychology* 57 (4): 651–59.

———. 1994. "Short-Term and Long-Term Processes Linking Job Stressors to Father-Child Interaction." *Social Development* 3 (1): 1–15.

———. 2005. "A Psychological Perspective on the Health and Well-Being Consequences of Parental Employment." In Work, Family, Health, and Well-Being," ed. S. M. Bianchi, L. M. Casper, and R. B. King, 245–58. Mahwah, NJ: Erlbaum.

———. 2009. "Bringing It All Back Home: How Outside Stressors Shape Families' Everyday Lives." *Current Directions in Psychological Science* 18 (2): 106–11.

Repetti, Rena L., Shu-wen Wang, and Meredith S. Sears. 2012. "Using Direct Observational Methods to Study the Real Lives of Families: Advantages, Complexities, and Conceptual and Practical Considerations." In New Frontiers in Work and Family Research, ed. J. G. Grzywacz and E. Demerouti. New York: Psychology Press and Routledge.

Repetti, Rena. L., and Jennifer Wood. 1997. "Effects of Daily Stress at Work on Mothers' Interactions with Preschoolers." *Journal of Family Psychology* 11: 90–108.

RMC Research Corporation. 2005. *Healthy Youth Survey 2004*. Portland, OR: Washington State Department of Health, Maternal and Child Health Assessment Section.

Roberts, Linda J. 2000. "Fire and Ice in Marital Communication: Hostile and Distancing Behaviors as Predictors of Marital Distress." *Journal of Marriage and the Family* 62: 693–707.

Robinson, John P., and Geoffrey Godbey. [1997] 1999. *Time for Life: The Surprising Ways Americans Use Their Time*. 2nd ed. University Park: Pennsylvania State University Press.

Roxburgh, Susan. 2002. "Racing through Life: The Distribution of Time Pressures by Roles and Role Resources among Full-Time Workers." *Journal of Family and Economic Issues* 23 (2): 121–45.

———. 2006. "'I wish we had more time to spend together . . .': The Distribution and Predictors of Perceived Family Time Pressures among Married Men and Women in the Paid Labor Force." *Journal of Family Issues* 27 (4): 529–53.

Russell, Bertrand. 1932. *Education and the Social Order*. London: George Allen & Unwin.

Rybczinski, Witold. 1986. *Home: A Short History of an Idea*. New York: Viking.

Sacks, Harvey, Emanuel A. Schegloff, and Gail Jefferson. 1974. "A Simplest Systematics for the Organization of Turn-Taking for Conversation." *Language* 50: 696–735.

Saltonstall, Robin. 1993. "Healthy Bodies, Social Bodies: Men's and Women's Concepts and Practices of Health in Everyday Life." *Social Science and Medicine* 36: 7–14.

Saxbe, Darby E. 2009. "A Field (Researcher's) Guide to Cortisol: Tracking the HPA Axis in Everyday Life." *Health Psychology Review* 2 (2): 163–90.

Saxbe, Darby, and Rena L. Repetti. 2010a. "For Better or Worse? Correlation of Couples' Cortisol Levels and Mood States." *Journal of Personality and Social Psychology* 98 (1): 92–103.

———. 2010b. "No Place Like Home: Home Tours Predict Daily Patterns of Mood and Cortisol." *Personality and Social Psychology Bulletin* 36: 71–81.

Saxbe, Darby E., Rena L. Repetti, and Anthony P. Graesch. 2011. "Time Spent in Housework and Leisure: Links with Parents' Physiological Recovery from Work." *Journal of Family Psychology* 25 (2): 271–81.

Saxbe, Darby E., Rena L. Repetti, and Adrienne Nishina. 2008. "Marital Satisfaction, Recovery from Work, and Diurnal Cortisol among Men and Women." *Health Psychology* 27 (1): 15–25.

Schegloff, Emanuel A. 1968. "Sequencing in Conversational Openings." *American Anthropologist* 70: 1075–95.

———. 1987. "The Routine as Achievement." *Human Studies* 9: 111–51.

Schieffelin, Bambi B. 1983. "Talking Like Birds: Sound Play in a Cultural Perspective." In *Acquiring Conversational Competence*, ed. Elinor Ochs and Bambi B. Schieffelin, 177–84. Boston: Routledge & Kegan Paul.

———. 1990. *The Give and Take of Everyday Life: Language Socialization of Kaluli Children*. Cambridge: Cambridge University Press.

Schiffer, Michael B., with Andrea Miller. 1999. *The Material Life of Human Beings: Artifacts, Behavior and Communication*. New York: Routledge.

Schneider, Barbara, and David Stevenson. 1999. *The Ambitious Generation: America's Teenagers, Motivated but Directionless*. New Haven: Yale University Press.

Schneider, Barbara, and Linda Waite, eds. 2005. *Being Together, Working Apart: Dual-Career Families and the Work-Life Balance*. Cambridge: Cambridge University Press.

Schor, Juliet B. 1991. *The Overworked American: The Unexpected Decline of Leisure*. New York: Basic Books.

———. 2004. *Born to Buy: The Commercialized Child and the New Consumer Culture*. New York: Scribner.

Schwartz, Pepper. 1994. *Peer Marriage: How Love between Equals Really Works*. New York: Free Press.

Shweder, Richard. 2008. "The Cultural Psychology of Suffering: The Many Meanings of Health in Orissa, India (and Elsewhere)." *Ethos* 36: 60–77.

Sennett, Richard. 1974. *Fall of the Public Man*. New York: Knopf.

Sephton, Sandra E., Robert M. Sapolsky, Helena C. Kraemer, and David Spiegel. 2000. "Diurnal Cortisol Rhythm as a Predictor of Breast Cancer Survival." *Journal of the National Cancer Institute* 9: 994–1000.

Shohet, Merav. 2004. "Narrating Anorexia: Genres of Recovery." M.A. thesis, University of California, Los Angeles.

Sloan, A. Elizabeth. 2006. "What, When, and Where America Eats: A State-of-the-Industry Report." *Food Technology* 60 (1): 19–27.

Solomon, Yvette, J. O. Warin, and Charlie Lewis. 2002. "Helping with Homework: Homework as a Site of Tension for Parents and Teenagers." *British Educational Research Journal* 28 (4): 603–22.

Southerton, D. 2003. "Squeezing Time: Allocating Practices, Coordinating Networks, and Scheduling Society." *Time and Society* 12: 5–25.

Spiro, Melford E. 1993. "Is the Western Conception of the Self 'Peculiar' within the Context of the World Cultures?" *Ethos* 21 (2): 107–53.

Stearns, Peter N. 2003. *Anxious Parents: A History of Modern Childrearing in America*. New York: New York University Press.

———. 2006. *Consumerism in World History*. 2nd ed. New York: Routledge.

Stevens, Daphne Pedersen, Krista Lynn Minnotte, Susan E. Mannon, and Gary Kiger. 2007. "Examining the Neglected Side of the Work-Family Interface: Antecedents of Positive and Negative Family-to-Work Spillover." *Journal of Family Issues* 28 (2): 242–62.

Story, L.B., and Rena L. Repetti. 2006. "Daily Occupational Stressors and Marital Behavior." *Journal of Family Psychology* 20: 690–700.

Super, Charles M., and Sara Harkness. 1986. "The Developmental Niche: A Conceptualization at the Interface of Childand Culture." *International Journal of Behavioral* Development 9 (4): 545–69.

Taylor, Astra. 2005. *Zizek!* 70 min. Zeitgeist Films.

Thin, Neil. 2009. "Why Anthropology Can Ill Afford to Ignore Well-Being." In *Pursuits of Happiness: Well-Being in Anthropological Perspective*, ed. Gordon Mathews and Carolina Izquierdo, 23–44. New York: Berghahn Press.

Thornton, Peter. 1984. *Authentic Decor: The Domestic Interior*. Viking, New York.

Tolin, David F., Randy O. Frost, and Gail Steketee. 2007. *Buried in Treasures: Help for Compulsive Acquiring, Saving, and Hoarding*. New York: Oxford University Press.

Trudeau, Garry. 2004. *Doonesbury*. June 8.

Tulbert, Eve, and Marjorie Harness Goodwin. 2011. "Choreographies of Attention: Multimodality in a Routine Family Activity." In *Embodied Interaction: Language and Body in the Material World*, ed. J. Streeck, C. Goodwin, and C.D. LeBaron, 79–92. Cambridge: Cambridge University Press.

U.S. Department of Education. 2009a. "My Child's Academic Success: Homework Tips for Parents." www.ed.gov/parents/academic/involve/homework/index.html/.

———. 2009b. No Child Left Behind and Other Elementary/Secondary Policy Documents. www.ed.gov/policy/elsec/guid/states/index.html/.

———. 2009c. Partnership for Family Involvement in Education. www.ed.gov/pubs/PFIE/index.html/.

Van Hamersveld, Kristine A., and Marjorie H. Goodwin. 2007. "Temporality and Trajectory inn Parent-Child Assessment Interaction Concerning Extra-Curricular Activities." Working Paper #69. Center on Everyday Lives of Families, University of California, Los Angeles.

Veblen, Thorstein. 1899. *The Theory of the Leisure Class*. New York: Macmillan.

Voorpostel, Marieke, Tanja van der Lippe, and Jonathan Gershuny. 2009. "Trends in Free Time with a Partner: A Transformation of Intimacy?" *Social Indicators Research* 93 (1): 165–69.

Vygotsky, L. S. 1978. *Mind in Society: The Development of Higher Psychological Processes*. Cambridge, MA: Harvard University Press.

Wang, Shu-wen, Rena L. Repetti, and Belinda Campos. 2011a. "Job Stress and Family Social Behavior: The Moderating Role of Neuroticism." *Journal of Occupational Health Psychology* 16: 441–56.

——. 2011b. "Links between Observed Naturalistic Social Behavior and Hpa-Axis Activity in the Family." Unpublished manuscript.

Warner, W. Lloyd, Marchia Meeker, and Kenneth Eells. 1949. *Social Class in America: A Manual of Procedure for the Measurement of Social Status*. Chicago: Science Research Associates.

Warren, Elizabeth, and Amelia Warren Tyagi. 2003. *The Two-Income Trap: Why Middle-Class Mothers and Fathers Are Going Broke*. New York: Basic Books.

Watson-Gegeo, Karen Ann, and David W. Gegeo. 1989. "The Role of Sibling Interaction in Child Socialization." In *Sibling Interaction across Cultures: Theoretical and Methodological Issues*, ed. P. G. Zukow, 54–75. New York: Springer.

Weber, Max, C. Wright Mills, and Hans Heinrich Gerth. 1946. *From Max Weber: Essays in Sociology*. New York: Oxford University Press.

Weinstein, Miriam. 2005. *The Surprising Power of Family Meals: How Eating Together Makes Us Smarter, Stronger, Healthier and Happier*. Hanover, NH: Steerforth Press.

Weisner, Thomas. 1989. "Comparing Sibling Relationships across Cultures." In *Sibling Interaction across Cultures: Theoretical and Methodological Issues*, ed. P. G. Zukow, 11–25. New York: Springer.

——. 1998. "Human Development, Child Well-Being, and the Cultural Project of Development." In *Socioemotional Development across Cultures*, ed. S. Dinesh and Kurt W. Fischer, 69–85. San Francisco: Jossey-Bass.

——. 2001. "The American Dependency Conflict." *Ethos* 29 (3): 271–95.

——. 2002. "Ecocultural Understanding of Children's Development Pathways." *Human Development* 45: 275–81.

——. 2009. "Well-Being and Sustainability of Daily Routines: Families with Children with Disabilities in the United States." In *Pursuits of Happiness: Well-Being in Anthropological Perspective*, ed. Gordon Mathews and Carolina Izquierdo, 228–47. New York: Berghahn Press.

Weisner, T. S., and R. Gallimore. 1977. "My Brother's Keeper: Child and Sibling Caretaking." *Current Anthropology* 18 (2): 169–90.

Wetherell, Margaret. 2003. "Racism and the Analysis of Cultural Resources in Interviews." In *Analyzing Race Talk: Multidisciplinary Approaches to the Interview*, ed. Harry Van Den Berg, Margaret Wetherell, and Hanneke Houtkoop-Steenstra, 11–30. Cambridge: Cambridge University Press.

Whiting, Beatrice B., and John W. M. Whiting. 1975. *Children of Six Cultures*. Cambridge, MA: Harvard University Press.

Whybrow, Peter C. 2005. *American Mania: When More Is Not Enough*. New York: Norton.

Wikan, Unni. 1990. *Managing Turbulent Hearts: A Balinese Formula for Living.* Chicago: University of Chicago Press.

Wilk, Richard R. 1996. *Economies and Cultures: Foundations of Economic Anthropology.* Boulder, CO: Westview Press.

Willihnganz, Heather, and Wingard Leah. 2005. "Exploring Emotion Work in Interaction." Working Paper #29. Center on Everyday Lives of Families, University of California, Los Angeles.

Wingard, Leah. 2006a. "Mentioning Homework First in Parent-Child Interaction." *Text & Talk* 26 (4–5): 573–98.

———. 2006b. "Verbal Practices for Accomplishing Homework: Socializing Time and Activity in Parent-Child Interactions." Ph.D. diss., University of California, Los Angeles.

———. 2007. "Constructing Time and Prioritizing Activities in Parent-Child Interactions." *Discourse and Society* 18: 75–91.

Wingard, Leah, and Lucas Forsberg. 2008. "Parents' Involvement in Children's Homework in American and Swedish Dual-Earner Families." *Journal of Pragmatics* 41: 1576–95.

Winnicott, Donald W. 1953. "Transitional Objects and Transitional Phenomena." *International Journal of Psychoanalysis* 34: 89–97.

———. 1964. *The Child, the Family, and the Outside World.* Cambridge, MA: Perseus.

Witmer, Denise D. 2004. *The Everything Parents Guide to Raising a Successful Child: All You Need to Encourage Your Child to Excel at Home and School.* Avon: Adams Media.

Zaff, Jonathan F., Kristin A. Moore, Angela P. Papillo, and Stephanie Williams. 2003. "Implications of Extracurricular Activity Participation during Adolescence on Positive Outcomes." *Journal of Adolescent Research* 18 (6): 599–630.

Zeitlin, M., R. Megawangi, E. Kramer, N. Colletta, E. D. Babatunde, and D. Garman. 1995. *Strengthening the Family: Implications for International Development.* New York: United Nations University Press.

Zelizer, Viviana A. 1994. *Pricing the Priceless Child: The Changing Social Value of Children.* Princeton: Princeton University Press

———. 2005. "The Priceless Child Revisited." In *Studies in Modern Childhood: Society, Agency, and Culture,* ed. Jens Qvortrup, 184–200. New York: Palgrave Macmillan.

Zukow, Patricia Goldring. 1989. "Siblings as Effective Socializing Agents: Evidence from Central Mexico." In *Sibling Interaction across Cultures: Theoretical and Methodological Issues,* ed. P. G. Zukow, 79–105. New York: Springer.

Arnold's paper is an impressive piece of modern "ethnoarchaeology," that is, finding out from contemporary peoples what might produce the pattern of material culture we see in the archaeological record. A predecessor study in the 1970s and 1980s in Tucson, Arizona, led by Professor William Rathje, asked people about their garbage and then went and looked at it to compare what people say they throw out with what they actually threw out. Not surprisingly, the answers were different. In this study, Arnold and her colleagues try to document what people have in their houses (a useful thing to do because archaeologists analyze deposition patterns in houses from the past). The main take-away from the article is the degree of clutter that Americans have generated—possibly to our detriment.

CONCLUSION: WRAP-UP

Wrap-Up: *The Theory of the Leisure Class* was Thorsten Veblen's humorous way to highlight what he regarded as the moral bankruptcy of the elite class in turn of twentieth century America. Although one might argue that no one nowadays uses $100 bills as napkin holders, as the Robber Barons did in their parties in Newport, Rhode Island during the Gilded Age, one might ask if the uses of buildings such as Mar-a-Largo are not in some way comparable today.

Arnold shows us that, in our haste to establish our identities, we have piled up material objects in a manner that is totally unprecedented (it would be interesting to carry out a similar analysis in another country and culture to see if the same thing is happening elsewhere—it probably is, but maybe on a lesser scale). The main take-away is how much stress is generated by our "Mountains of Things." Is that a result that we should be comfortable with and continue to allow?

ACTIVITIES

Activity Reading 11: In small groups, brainstorm examples of conspicuous consumption; gather 3-6 examples and then see if there is a pattern in what the intention behind the consumption might be.

Activity Reading 12: split into small groups and come up with answers to the following questions: Start with your list of 10 items you cannot do without. Then, compare notes with your colleagues: what was your home refrigerator like while you were growing up?

- Do you think Arnold's correlation of refrigerator clutter and overall household clutter holds up?

- Do a quick and dirty analysis, even in rough terms, such as, "our refrigerator had 10s, or 100s of things on it," with the overall characterization of the house, "a little cluttered" or "very cluttered"?
- Do you agree with Arnold that "clutter fascinates"?
- Is her conclusion that women are more stressed than men about the clutter accurate?
- In light of Arnold, is Scott correct that Americans prefer good and services over free time?
- One anthropological response to Veblen is to assert that, anthropologically, humans have always used material culture to construct identities. Is the wealth display of elites understandable on that level, and thus, less an object of moral condemnation?

SOURCES

Thorsten Veblen, an Upper Midwestern Scandinavian-American educated at Carleton College, Minnesota, was an economist at the University of California, Berkeley. His *Theory of the Leisure Class* has been re-issued by Oxford University Press, 2007, originally published in 1899 by MacMillan in New York. William Rathje's *Rubbish! the archaeology of garbage* was published in 1993 by New York's Harper Perennial.

Chapter 5

Poverty and Hunger: A Place at the Table for 12 Billion?

OBJECTIVES

- Analyze how the change from foraging to agriculture affected human life in general.
- Determine what are the chief problems in getting food to the people that need it.
- Explain why, if enough food for everyone on the planet can be produced, there is hunger in the world.
- Suggest improvements to the distribution of food both in the United States and the rest of the world.

KEY TERMS

Foraging: getting food by means of hunting, killing, and consuming other live animals and gathering, processing and consuming edible plants foodstuffs; this way of life has characterized the human organism for at least two million years.

Agriculture: deliberate food production by growing of edible plants, chiefly grains (domesticated from wild grasses); simple agriculture is called horticulture, while the more complex form of agriculture carried on by state-level societies is called intensive agriculture, which means that there is a short fallow to planting ratio of fields. A common ratio worldwide is 2:1, meaning that a field is planted one year and left fallow the next so that two years are required to grow on one piece of land.

Malnutrition: the situation in which an individual human organism is consuming food in quantities insufficient to assure good health and protection from disease; that state can have long-term effects on the individual's health and in the worst cases can lead to death.

Famine: periods when the expected harvest of crops falls short and wide-spread hunger, malnutrition and starvation can occur.

Agri-business: the most intensive form of agricultural exploitation practiced in complex industrial societies of today, in which agricultural companies carry out the production of crops rather than being accomplished by independent, small or family famers.

SCHEMA ACTIVATION ACTIVITY

Based on either your own experiences growing up on a farm or visiting one, *describe the four or five leading features of farming life; reflect on and give an answer to the question: what factor is most responsible for farming success?*

(Save these to share later in your discussion sections.)

INTRODUCTION

In the two readings for this chapter, the main theme is food production. In the first reading. Diamond explains how humans have only been agriculturalists for a short time during their evolutionary history. The article also, perhaps controversially, makes the case that almost all of the contemporary world problems stem ultimately from the adoption of agriculture by the majority of humans on the planet. Fisher, in the second reading, zeroes in on hunger in America. He argues that the problem of feeding people in the United States is due to the failures of a sytem that is based on charitable giving.

The Worst Mistake in the History of the Human Race

By Jared Diamond

To science we owe dramatic changes in our smug self-image. Astronomy taught us that our earth isn't the center of the universe but merely one of billions of heavenly bodies. From biology we learned that we weren't specially created by God but evolved along with millions of other species. Now archaeology is demolishing another sacred belief: that human history over the past million years has been a long tale of progress. In particular, recent discoveries suggest that the adoption of agriculture, supposedly our most decisive step toward a better life, was in many ways a catastrophe from which we have never recovered. With agriculture came the gross social and sexual inequality, the disease and despotism, that curse our existence. At first, the evidence against this revisionist interpretation will strike twentieth century Americans as irrefutable. We're better off in almost every respect than people of the Middle Ages, who in turn had it easier than cavemen, who in turn were better off than apes. Just count our advantages. We enjoy the most abundant and varied foods, the best tools and material goods, some of the longest and healthiest lives, in history. Most of us are safe from starvation and predators. We get our energy from oil and machines, not from our sweat. What neo-Luddite among us would trade his life for that of a medieval peasant, a caveman, or an ape?

For most of our history we supported ourselves by hunting and gathering: we hunted wild animals and foraged for wild plants. It's a life that philosophers have traditionally regarded as nasty, brutish, and short. Since no food is grown and little is stored, there is (in this view) no respite from the struggle that starts anew each day to find wild foods and avoid starving. Our escape from this misery was facilitated only 10,000 years ago, when in different parts of the world people began to domesticate plants and animals. The agricultural revolution spread until today it's nearly universal and few tribes of hunter-gatherers survive.

From the progressivist perspective on which I was brought up, to ask "Why did almost all our hunter-gatherer ancestors adopt agriculture?" is silly. Of course they adopted it because agriculture is an efficient way to get more food for less work. Planted crops yield far more tons per acre than roots and berries. Just imagine a band of savages, exhausted from searching for nuts or chasing wild animals, suddenly grazing for the first time at a fruit-laden orchard or a pasture full of sheep. How many milliseconds do you think it would take them to appreciate the advantages of agriculture?

The progressivist party line sometimes even goes so far as to credit agriculture with the remarkable flowering of art that has taken place over the past few thousand years. Since crops can be stored, and since it takes less time to pick food from a garden than to find it in the wild, agriculture gave us free time that hunter-gatherers never had. Thus it was agriculture that enabled us to build the Parthenon and compose the B-minor Mass.

While the case for the progressivist view seems overwhelming, it's hard to prove. How do you show that the lives of people 10,000 years ago got better when they abandoned hunting and gathering for farming? Until recently, archaeologists had to resort to indirect tests, whose results (surprisingly) failed to support the progressivist view. Here's one example of an indirect test: Are twentieth century hunter-gatherers really worse off than farmers? Scattered throughout the world, several dozen groups of so-called primitive people, like the Kalahari bushmen, continue to support themselves that way. It turns out that these people have plenty of leisure time, sleep a good deal, and work less hard than their farming neighbors. For instance, the average time devoted each week to obtaining food is only 12 to 19 hours for one group of Bushmen, 14 hours or less for the Hadza nomads of Tanzania. One Bushman, when asked why he hadn't emulated neighboring tribes by adopting agriculture, replied, "Why should we, when there are so many mongongo nuts in the world?"

While farmers concentrate on high-carbohydrate crops like rice and potatoes, the mix of wild plants and animals in the diets of surviving hunter-gatherers provides more protein and a bettter balance of other nutrients. In one study, the Bushmen's average daily food intake (during a month when food was plentiful) was 2,140 calories and 93 grams of protein, considerably greater than the recommended daily allowance for people of their size. It's almost inconceivable that Bushmen, who eat 75 or so wild plants, could die of starvation the way hundreds of thousands of Irish farmers and their families did during the potato famine of the 1840s.

So the lives of at least the surviving hunter-gatherers aren't nasty and brutish, even though farmes have pushed them into some of the world's worst real estate. But modern hunter-gatherer societies that have rubbed shoulders with farming societies for thousands of years don't tell us about conditions before the agricultural revolution. The progressivist view is really making a claim about the distant past: that the lives of primitive people improved when they switched from gathering to farming. Archaeologists can date that switch by distinguishing remains of wild plants and animals from those of domesticated ones in prehistoric garbage dumps.

How can one deduce the health of the prehistoric garbage makers, and thereby directly test the progressivist view? That question has become answerable only in recent years, in part through the newly emerging techniques of paleopathology, the study of signs of disease in the remains of ancient peoples.

In some lucky situations, the paleopathologist has almost as much material to study as a pathologist today. For example, archaeologists in the Chilean deserts found well preserved mummies whose medical conditions at time of death could be determined by autopsy (Discover, October). And feces of long-dead Indians who lived in dry caves in Nevada remain sufficiently well preserved to be examined for hookworm and other parasites.

Usually the only human remains available for study are skeletons, but they permit a surprising number of deductions. To begin with, a skeleton reveals its owner's sex, weight, and approximate age. In the few cases where there are many skeletons, one can construct mortality tables like the ones life insurance companies use to calculate expected life span and risk of death at any given age. Paleopathologists can also calculate growth rates by measuring bones of people of different ages, examine teeth for enamel defects (signs of childhood malnutrition), and recognize scars left on bones by anemia, tuberculosis, leprosy, and other diseases.

One straight forward example of what paleopathologists have learned from skeletons concerns historical changes in height. Skeletons from Greece and Turkey show that the average height of hunger-gatherers toward the end of the ice ages was a generous 5' 9" for men, 5' 5" for women. With the adoption of agriculture, height crashed, and by 3000 B. C. had reached a low of only 5' 3" for men, 5' for women. By classical times heights were very slowly on the rise again, but modern Greeks and Turks have still not regained the average height of their distant ancestors.

Another example of paleopathology at work is the study of Indian skeletons from burial mounds in the Illinois and Ohio river valleys. At Dickson Mounds, located near the confluence of the Spoon and Illinois rivers, archaeologists have excavated some 800 skeletons that paint a picture of the health changes that occurred when a hunter-gatherer culture gave way to intensive maize farming around A. D. 1150. Studies by George Armelagos and his colleagues then at the University of Massachusetts show these early farmers paid a price for their new-found livelihood. Compared to the hunter-gatherers who preceded them, the farmers had a nearly 50 per cent increase in enamel defects indicative of malnutrition, a fourfold increase in iron-deficiency anemia (evidenced by a bone condition called porotic hyperostosis), a theefold rise in bone lesions reflecting infectious disease in general, and an increase in degenerative conditions of the spine, probably reflecting a lot of hard physical labor. "Life expectancy at birth in the pre-agricultural community was bout twenty-six years," says Armelagos, "but in the post-agricultural community it was nineteen years. So these episodes of nutritional stress and infectious disease were seriously affecting their ability to survive."

The evidence suggests that the Indians at Dickson Mounds, like many other primitive peoples, took up farming not by choice but from necessity in order to feed their constantly growing numbers. "I don't think most hunger-gatherers farmed until they had to, and when they switched to farming they traded quality for quantity," says Mark Cohen of the State University of New York at Plattsburgh, co-editor with Armelagos, of one of the seminal books in the field, Paleopathology at the Origins of Agriculture. "When I first started making that argument ten years ago, not many people agreed with me. Now it's become a respectable, albeit controversial, side of the debate."

There are at least three sets of reasons to explain the findings that agriculture was bad for health. First, hunter-gatherers enjoyed a varied diet, while early fanners obtained most of their food from one or a few starchy crops. The farmers gained cheap calories at the cost of poor nutrition, (today just three high-carbohydrate plants -- wheat, rice, and corn -- provide the bulk of the calories consumed by the human species, yet each one is deficient in certain vitamins or amino acids essential to life.) Second, because of dependence on a limited number of crops, farmers ran the risk of starvation if one crop failed. Finally, the mere fact that agriculture encouraged people to clump together in crowded societies, many of which then carried on trade with other crowded societies, led to the spread of parasites and infectious disease. (Some archaeologists think it was the crowding, rather than agriculture, that promoted disease, but this is a chicken-and-egg argument, because crowding encourages agriculture and vice versa.) Epidemics couldn't take hold when populations were scattered in small bands that constantly shifted camp. Tuberculosis and diarrheal disease had to await the rise of farming, measles and bubonic plague the appearnce of large cities.

Besides malnutrition, starvation, and epidemic diseases, farming helped bring another curse upon humanity: deep class divisions. Hunter-gatherers have little or no stored food, and no concentrated food sources, like an orchard or a herd of cows: they live off the wild plants and animals they obtain each day. Therefore, there can be no kings, no class of social parasites who grow fat on food seized from others. Only in a farming population could a healthy, non-producing elite set itself above the disease-ridden masses. Skeletons from Greek tombs at Mycenae c. 1500 B. C. suggest that royals enjoyed a better diet than commoners, since the royal skeletons were two or three inches taller and had better teeth (on the average, one instead of six cavities or missing teeth). Among Chilean mummies from c. A. D. 1000, the elite were distinguished not only by ornaments and gold hair clips but also by a fourfold lower rate of bone lesions caused by disease.

Similar contrasts in nutrition and health persist on a global scale today. To people in rich countries like the U. S., it sounds ridiculous to extol the virtues of hunting and gathering. But Americans are an elite, dependent on oil and minerals that must often be imported from countries with poorer health and nutrition. If one could choose between being a peasant farmer in Ethiopia or a bushman gatherer in the Kalahari, which do you think would be the better choice?

Farming may have encouraged inequality between the sexes, as well. Freed from the need to transport their babies during a nomadic existence, and under pressure to produce more hands to till the fields, farming women tended to have more frequent pregnancies than their hunter-gatherer counterparts -- with consequent drains on their health. Among the Chilean mummies for example, more women than men had bone lesions from infectious disease.

Women in agricultural societies were sometimes made beasts of burden. In New Guinea farming communities today I often see women staggering under loads of vegetables and firewood while the men walk empty-handed. Once while on a field trip there studying birds, I offered to pay some villagers to carry supplies from an airstrip to my mountain camp. The heaviest item was a 110-pound bag of rice, which I lashed to a pole and assigned to a team of four men to shoulder together. When I eventually caught up with the villagers, the men were carrying light loads, while one small woman weighing less than the bag of rice was bent under it, supporting its weight by a cord across her temples.

As for the claim that agriculture encouraged the flowering of art by providing us with leisure time, modern hunter-gatherers have at least as much free time as do farmers. The whole emphasis on leisure time as a critical factor seems to me misguided. Gorillas have had ample free time to build their own Parthenon, had they wanted to. While post-agricultural technological advances did make new art forms possible and preservation of art easier, great paintings and sculptures were already being produced by hunter-gatherers 15,000 years ago, and were still being produced as recently as the last century by such hunter-gatherers as some Eskimos and the Indians of the Pacific Northwest.

Thus with the advent of agriculture and elite became better off, but most people became worse off. Instead of swallowing the progressivist party line that we chose agriculture because it was good for us, we must ask how we got trapped by it despite its pitfalls.

One answer boils down to the adage "Might makes right." Farming could support many more people than hunting, albeit with a poorer quality of life. (Population densities of hunter-gatherers are rarely over on person per ten square miles, while farmers average 100 times that.) Partly, this is because a field planted entirely in edible crops lets one feed far more mouths than a forest with scattered edible plants. Partly, too, it's because nomadic hunter-gatherers have to keep their children spaced at four-year intervals by infanticide and other means, since a mother must carry her toddler until it's old enough to keep up with the adults. Because farm women don't have that burden, they can and often do bear a child every two years.

As population densities of hunter-gatherers slowly rose at the end of the ice ages, bands had to choose between feeding more mouths by taking the first steps toward agriculture, or else finding ways to limit growth. Some bands chose the former solution, unable to anticipate the evils of farming, and seduced by the transient abundance they enjoyed until population growth caught up with increased food production. Such bands outbred and then drove off or killed the bands that chose to remain hunter-gatherers, because a hundred malnourished farmers can still outfight one healthy hunter. It's not that hunter-gatherers abandoned their life style, but that those sensible enough not to abandon it were forced out of all areas except the ones farmers didn't want.

At this point it's instructive to recall the common complaint that archaeology is a luxury, concerned with the remote past, and offering no lessons for the present. Archaeologists studying the rise of farming have reconstructed a crucial stage at which we made the worst mistake in human history. Forced to choose between limiting population or trying to increase food production, we chose the latter and ended up with starvation, warfare, and tyranny.

Hunter-gatherers practiced the most successful and longest-lasting life style in human history. In contrast, we're still struggling with the mess into which agriculture has tumbled us, and it's unclear whether we can solve it. Suppose that an archaeologist who had visited from outer space were trying to explain human history to his fellow spacelings. He might illustrate the results of his digs by a 24-hour clock on which one hour represents 100,000 years of real past time. If the history of the human race began at midnight, then we would now be almost at the end of our first day. We lived as hunter-gatherers for nearly the whole of that day, from midnight through dawn, noon, and sunset. Finally, at 11:54 p. m. we adopted agriculture. As our second midnight approaches, will the plight of famine-stricken peasants gradually spread to engulf us all? Or will we somehow achieve those seductive blessings that we imagine behind agriculture's glittering facade, and that have so far eluded us?

Diamond starts with what he calls the progressivit perspective, the belief that the adoption of agriculture brought humanity all the benefits that we appreciate in the modern world. However, he then dismantles that perspective by suggesting that malnutritionm starvation, epidemics, class divisions and the inequality of the sexes are all due to agriculture. He concludes by suggesting that humanity faced the choice of limiting population or increasing the food supply. Which did humanity choose?

Getting Off the Anti-Hunger Treadmill

ANDY FISHER

FROM *A PLACE AT THE TABLE*

The '80s created the myth that (a) hungry people deserved it, and (b) well, we could fill in the gaps with charities.

—Joel Berg, executive director of the
New York City Coalition Against Hunger

Andy Fisher created and publicized the concept of community food security and played a key role in building the community food movement. From 1994 to 2011, he led the Community Food Security Coalition (CFSC), a national alliance of groups working on access to local food. Here he traces community food responses to hunger over the last three decades and examines the corporate influence on charities that dispense emergency food.

Last December, Orion, my third-grader, came home excited about his school's Christmas food drive. "There's a contest for which class can raise the most money and donate the most pounds of food for Oregon Food Bank. I want our class to win," he said as he started scouring the cupboard for the heaviest food items he could find. My wife stopped him from stripping our cupboard bare. A week later, as I was headed out the door on a shopping trip, he pleaded with me to buy some more heavy food, as his classroom's donation barrel wasn't very full. At the store, I looked for nutritious food that was heavy and inexpensive. Tempted by the cheapness and weight of half-gallon bottles of soda, I took the higher road of purchasing some cans of organic beans and whole wheat flour on sale.

As I was shopping, I realized that the food drive at Orion's school was a microcosm of one thing that really irritates me about food banks: they measure their success in the millions of pounds of food that they distribute. Here's a sample from the website of the Regional Food Bank of Oklahoma (a food bank that I admire for its food systems activity): "In Fiscal Year 2011, the Regional Food Bank of Oklahoma distributed a record-breaking 46.2 million pounds of food and product through a network of more than 825 partner agencies and schools throughout 53 central and western Oklahoma counties."[1]

I get it. On a very basic level, there are millions of people struggling to make ends meet, and the more food gets distributed, the better fed they are. But we're treating hunger like a sporting contest, a numbers game. It's not a game we can win by just pumping more food through the charitable food sector. Hunger is the result of both a failure of the political will to resolve an entrenched problem and a failure of the marketplace to meet the needs of the poor.

Every food banker worth his or her salt will tell you that they are trapped in a broken system, a Sisyphean challenge that cannot be resolved by more charitable food donations. Why can't we donate our way out of hunger?

First, the number of poor and hungry is too big for the charitable food sector to handle. Forty-nine million people are at risk of hunger, based on the fact that they qualify for food stamps. The charitable food sector would have to increase in size more than sixfold to even feed all of these persons for a week every month.[2] Second, even if we could manage this feat, the impacts on society and individuals are less than desirable. Charity, subject to the continued interest and ability of donors, is inherently unsustainable. For example, food banks have seen donations drop as manufacturers sell dented cans on the salvage market rather than donate them. As Sharon Thornberry points out in her essay (see Chapter 12), in some rural communities in Oregon struggling grocery stores lose crucial business when residents receive their free boxes of food.

Finally, food bank critics have long argued that distributing free food fosters dependence when in fact society should be encouraging self-reliance by creating jobs.

Every food bank annual report or website that heralds the millions of pounds the organization distributes each year leads us a step deeper into a labyrinth from which escape becomes an increasingly distant dream. The more we celebrate our charitable food achievements, the further we define these achievements as the solution to hunger rather than as an unfortunate activity we are morally obligated to undertake because of our societal failure to prevent hunger in the first place.

Yes, the millions of pounds that food banks gather and distribute are a testament to the generosity of our communities and should be celebrated as such. At the same time, however, these truckloads of free food are a reflection of our inability to create an economy and a safety net that meet Americans' basic food needs. Every increase in the amount that food banks distribute is a measure not of their success but of their—and our—collective dysfunction.

Going back twenty years or so, the unsustainability of the emergency food system was front and center in the minds of a small cadre of anti-hunger dissidents working on food and nutrition projects in low-income neighborhoods across the country. As a graduate student in urban planning at UCLA, I was part of a team that completed a comprehensive study of the food situation in inner-city Los Angeles in 1993. My colleagues and I saw that the food banks' "medical model" of solving hunger through providing doses of food, as if hunger were a disease carried by an individual, was a humane but inadequate way to address a more systemic problem. Instead, we believed that hunger could be prevented from happening in the first place by taking a public health approach that included public education, policy advocacy, and other interventions that addressed the root causes of hunger and poverty.

Hunger wasn't the only concern of this ragtag band of academics, policy advocates, and practitioners. We saw plenty of problems in the way food was produced and retailed: too few sources of healthy and affordable food in low-income neighborhoods; small farmers going out of business because they couldn't get a fair price for their crops; subdivisions replacing food as the primary "crop" on some of the nation's best farmland; rampant pollution from overuse of agrichemicals; and increasing concentration of the ownership of the nation's food supply into the hands of a few massive multinational companies. As a result, consumers were getting further and further alienated from the source of their food. Diet-related diseases among persons of color were on the rise, and they were higher than rates for whites. At the same time, we also saw the potential of alternative food production and distribution projects as tools for widespread social change. For example, we knew that urban farming could increase access to healthy food and provide economic opportunity.

Using the framework of a food system—the set of activities that lead to the production of food, its distribution, its consumption, and the handling of waste—we soon realized that the same food system that harmed low-income consumers also marginalized family farmers. We developed a conceptual framework that we called "community food security," which held that the transformation of the food system through reorienting food production and distribution around the needs and assets of communities and family farmers was a pathway to creating a healthier, more ecological, and more democratic society.

This idea morphed into a national alliance of groups from a wide range of sectors involved in food and farming, uniting them under an immediate goal of gaining passage of a community food security–oriented grants program in the 1996 Farm Bill and a longer-term agenda of building a community-based food movement. We won the inclusion of the Community Food Projects Competitive Grant Program (CFPCGP) in the Farm Bill, with mandatory funding. Although the CFP distributed only $2.5 million of federal funds per year to nonprofits, it was one of the few bright spots in an otherwise regressive piece of legislation.

Since 1996, the USDA has provided $66 million to nonprofit organizations for roughly four hundred grassroots projects aimed at meeting the food needs of low-income people while fostering self-reliance in communities to meet their own food needs.[3]

Following are a few examples of the diverse types of projects funded under this program:

- Along the Arizona-Mexico border, the Tohono O'odham tribe received funding to reintroduce traditional crops through farming and gardening projects. These traditional foods can help reduce the surging rates of diabetes among tribal members.
- In rural Missouri, Patchwork Family Farms received a grant to support a sustainable hog-farming operation that distributes pork through buying clubs. The project also brought together rural white farmers with African American church congregations.
- In western Massachusetts, Nuestras Raices supported Puerto Rican gardeners and farmers in local food production and created a regional food policy council.
- The National Farm to School Network received a training and technical assistance grant to support the development of farm-to-school projects across the nation.
- In Los Angeles, SEE-LA received a grant to establish a teaching and retail kitchen that emphasizes fresh produce consumption, job training, and food and nutrition education targeted to low-income residents.

Although community food projects often seek to improve the nutritional status of low-income households, they are not anti-hunger projects. They aim to improve the food security of their participants, but within a broader context of transforming an inequitable and unsustainable food system. They typically engage individuals at a more intensive level than food pantries, but the number of people they reach is much smaller.

CFPs cannot solve the massive and entrenched problem of hunger in the United States. They can, however, provide a glimpse of a very different approach to the same problem.

Community food projects are small investments in innovation in the context of the failure of the mainstream food system to meet the needs of marginalized communities and individuals. In other words, the Community Food Projects program would not have been born if the marketplace had been working as intended. Despite the diversity of programs funded, the CFPs are linked by the fact that they create methods of food production and distribution grounded in community needs and values. The only comprehensive analysis of these grants, conducted for a five-year period starting in 2005, indicates an astonishing impact for only $25 million in federal money:[4]

- The production of 19 million pounds of food, valued at $19.7 million
- The farming or gardening of over 56,000 acres of land, including 9,100 community garden plots
- Receipt of food by 2.5 million persons through a community food project
- Implementation of 183 policies in communities, affecting 33 million Americans
- Creation of 2,300 jobs
- Creation of 1,000 new businesses and support given to 2,600 existing businesses
- Preservation of 3,000 acres of land
- Formation of 40 food policy councils

Not only have these community food projects been highly effective in achieving their legislatively mandated goal of transforming the food system, but they have been transforming their communities and participants in unforeseen ways. The following is a brief description of some of these accidental benefits of community food projects.

At the neighborhood level, some CFPs have fostered a sense of community pride. The process of transforming a vacant lot in an underserved neighborhood into a thriving urban farm or community garden can imbue residents with an increased sense of ownership and foster their desire to care for their community. The City Farms Project in New York City provides a concrete example of the way in which residents of marginalized neighborhoods have reclaimed control over their space through collaborating in creating and caring for community gardens.

CFPs have helped to reinvigorate lost traditions, foster intergenerational communication, and rebuild connections between communities and their environments. Support to the Tohono O'odham nation in southern Arizona has helped them to re-create their traditional food system by increasing the cultivation of tribal lands for such crops as drought- and insulin-resistant tepary beans. The project has also engaged the elders to revive the long-lost custom of harvesting the fruit of the tree-size saguaro cactus, a ritual that includes the singing of songs that haven't been heard on the reservation for decades.

CFPs use food as a tool to bring together persons from different geographic areas, ethnicities, and socioeconomic standings. In doing so, these projects build increased social capital and a more nuanced understanding of the diverse cultures that make up our country. For example, the Food Project in Boston connects inner-city youth with suburban youth through food production, processing, and retailing. Youth gain not only valuable business and food production skills but also a greater understanding of each other's cultures. The project also helps to foster increased social capital—or personal connections—between communities that normally would be socially and geographically isolated from each other.

At the individual level, the intention of many CFPs has been to shape project participants' knowledge or behavior within the confines of the marketplace. For example, they have sought to improve small farmers' marketing expertise or to encourage individuals to become better consumers through increased knowledge of nutrition. Yet, interestingly, these projects are also fostering food citizenship by encouraging individuals to fully participate in their communities.

For example, the Watts Growing Project in Los Angeles, funded in 1996, largely failed to meet its goals of increasing incomes for Central American and Mexican immigrant community gardeners, but it yielded an unexpected crop: food democracy. Project staff had pushed hard to strengthen an existing but dysfunctional garden club as a tool for decision-making. Staff encouraged a democratic process with full participation by all gardeners, helping them develop written rules and hold regular elections for officers. By the end of the two-year project, the gardeners were much more engaged in the operation of the site. They were holding their leaders accountable to following the rules, such as no consumption of alcohol on the premises, and for the wise use of garden dues. Regular meetings were being held in an orderly fashion. The gender bias that had initially diminished the role of the women gardeners was substantially overcome by the end of the project. The garden did not turn into a model of democratic process, but it was clear that the project had helped the gardeners, many of whom were probably undocumented, become citizens, in the Athenian meaning of the word.

Sixteen years after the first Community Food Project grants were made, the importance of this seminal program as it relates to the mainstream corporate food system can be summed up in three primary ways.

First, as mentioned earlier, CFPs have filled in the cracks where the market has failed. They have provided services such as access to healthy food in underserved communities and helped small farmers stay on the land by providing them with new channels to market their products.

Second, CFPs play a research and development (R&D) function for the food movement to experiment with complex food systems programs for low-income communities. Increasingly, these grants are going to projects that seek to increase the scale of their impact by bringing in more powerful partners or shaping local policy. These policies tend to be less about defining the rules of the marketplace to constrain big agri-food interests and more about creating pathways for noncorporate, community-based players (such as farmers' markets) to thrive.

Third, CFPs challenge the basic premise of the mainstream food system: that food is a commodity. This premise holds that ten pounds of russet potatoes is ten pounds of russet potatoes, without regard to how those potatoes were grown, who grew them, and where they were produced. CFPs, like much of the local food movement, reject that notion, instead holding that the values embedded in food production, distribution, and retailing differentiate their products from those of the corporate-run marketplace. In other words, the process by which food is produced is of equal importance to the characteristics of the foodstuff itself. The utmost expression of this phenomenon is the Tohono O'odham and other Native American community food projects in which food is sacred, integral to the web that links environment, culture, and community.

So far, we have examined the work of nonprofit groups responding to the lack of political will and marketplace failures to produce healthy people, communities, and environments. Let's switch our focus to consider the role of those who have caused this situation and who benefit from it—large agri-food production, processing, and retailing multinational corporations. Supermarkets have increased their profits by focusing on middle-class customers and redlining low-income communities and communities of color.

Fast-food companies (among others) have made a fortune marketing super-sized, low-nutrient, high-profit foods. Companies such as Cargill, ConAgra, and Archer Daniels Midland have built vertical and horizontal monopolies of numerous key sectors of the food system across the globe. They have lobbied hard to keep their inputs, such as corn and soy, as cheap as possible so that they can maximize their profits on such products as beef and pork. By not paying employees a living wage, Wal-Mart saves billions of dollars annually, pushing the costs off onto taxpayers, who foot the bill for Wal-Mart employees' food stamps and other federal benefits.

As if this weren't bad enough, these companies are co-opting and managing civil society's responses to their harmful activities to minimize the impact of those responses to their bottom line. Food companies such as Dean Foods and Smucker's long ago co-opted the organic food movement's challenge to agribusiness by gaining a narrow definition of organic in USDA label standards. These standards now focus solely on production practices rather than on other integral aspects of the long-held definition of organic food, such as it coming from small community-oriented farms. The food industry is replicating this strategy with the new challenge of "local food."

In the anti-hunger movement, corporations have penetrated the food banking sector through and through. Food banks are dependent on large manufacturers and retailers for a significant percentage—if not a majority—of the food they distribute. (The actual totals vary by food bank.) Such multinationals as Wal-Mart, Tyson's, ConAgra, and Kraft have donated hundreds of millions of dollars in cash to food banks. There is scarcely a food bank website that is not plastered with the logos of its multinational corporate donors and partners.

More significantly, representatives from corporations make up roughly half of all board members of food banks affiliated with Feeding America, inevitably forging closer ties to corporations than to community activists. Similarly, the organizational culture of food banks is becoming more corporate as employees of the for-profit sector are hired into senior positions.

The close ties between the corporate world and the charitable food sector have diminished the participation of food bank clients and community activists on these boards and are an indicator of food banks' limited accountability to the clients they serve. Pittsburgh-based anti-hunger advocate Ken Regal points out that, "historically, food banks used to have a strong social justice orientation. Now they are mainstream community institutions, and the same people who serve on the boards of local museums also sit on their boards."[5]

Corporate participation on food bank boards is a double-edged sword. It reinforces the respectability of food banks, while providing access to corporations' excess food and philanthropic largesse. These resources are essential to help food banks meet the increasing demand from those affected by the latest recession. The more mainstream a food bank becomes, the more money it can raise to feed hungry people.

On the other hand, the policy changes needed to reduce or eliminate hunger are anathema to the wealthy and the corporations on food bank boards. Such policy changes might result in increased operational costs or federal taxes for businesses. Thus, the high degree of corporate participation on food bank boards deters advocacy for any redistributive policies that would provide a real solution for poverty reduction but go against the interests of the business sector.

As a nation, we have increasingly privatized our response to hunger over the past thirty years. Through this transfer of responsibility from the public sector to nonprofit-business partnerships, we have created a system that is effective in feeding hungry individuals but not in ending hunger. It is a system doomed to succeed in the short term—by lulling the public into the false belief that their charitable donations are fixing the problem—and doomed to fail in the long term as well.

Food bankers are like hamsters on a treadmill. They have been running faster and faster just to keep up with demand over the past thirty years. To get more food to feed more hungry people, they have had to compromise their values by partnering with corporations, some of which, such as Wal-Mart, are causing hunger through their labor practices.

These compromises have kept hunger at bay, but they do not advance us any further toward our goal. We need to stop the treadmill long enough to find another path to reach our vision of a hunger-free America.

The moment is ripe now. The attention on income inequalities in the 2012 elections provides the right moment to rethink our approaches to this persistent problem. To stop the treadmill we must rethink the way we address hunger as a nation; create new policies, programs, organizations, and partnerships for the long term; and revise our goals—perhaps even dropping the term "hunger" as the overarching metaphor. This new framework should focus on the root causes of hunger, such as ending poverty, and on health, since hunger and obesity are flip sides of the same malnutrition coin. Like the community food projects, the new framework must also embrace innovation and transformation at the community level. I look forward to the day when food banks measure their success not in pounds of food distributed to the poor but in the number of people they *don't* serve—those who are healthy and have enough food for their families.

P.S.: Orion's class did win the contest, not for poundage but for most money raised. Their prize was a party with the eighth-graders.

Andy Fisher led the Community Food Security Coalition, which he co-founded, from 1994 to 2011, and he led the Farm Bill campaign to gain passage of the Community Food Projects Program. He has written extensively on such topics as food from farm to school, farmers' markets in low-income communities, and local food policy. He lives in Portland, Oregon, with his wife and two children.

Notes

1. See Regional Food Bank of Oklahoma, "Our Mission Is Fighting Hunger . . . Feeding Hope," available at: http://www.regionalfoodbank.org/ (accessed January 28, 2012).
2. According to Feeding America, food banks distribute more than 3 billion pounds of food annually. Using the USDA estimate that the average American eats 4.7 pounds of food per day, I calculate 4.7×45 million $\times$ 7 days/month $\times$ 12 months = 17.7 billion pounds.
3. USDA, National Institute of Food and Agriculture, "Program Synopsis: Community Food Projects," available at: http://www.nifa.usda.gov/funding/cfp/cfp_synopsis.html (accessed February 14, 2012).
4. Jeanette Abi-Nader et al., "The Activities and Impacts of Community Food Projects, 2005–2009," Community Food Security Coalition, October 2010, available at: http://www.foodsecurity.org/pub/CPF_Activities_Impacts_2005–09.pdf (accessed February 14, 2012).
5. Ken Regal, personal communication, March 2010.

Fisher criticizes the practice of most Food Banks, suggesting that they have a medical model in providing "doses of food," as if hunger were a disease. Simply feeding the hungry will not end hunger. Privatization and corporate practices are blamed much for the situation, in which the problem of distributing food to those who need it is the challenge.

Privatized Response to Hunger

Archer-Daniels Midlands is a company mentioned in the article. That company once ran an advertisement acknowledging that soon the world could have 12 billion people, and that ADM would be providing "a place at the table" for each one of them. Putting aside the attempt to create a "feel good" moment about the company, one should reflect on the most important issue of all with regard to the industrial food production of today's agri-businesses: those entities are constituted to make a profit, they are not non-profit organizations.

Politics not Production

It is possible that ADM is correct: it IS possible to produce enough food to feed 12 billion people. However, the production is not the problem; it is the politics. Who will pay to feed the poor? Fisher's point is that the model of charitable giving to feed the hungry in America has not worked. Should we believe that it would work on a global scale?

CONCLUSION: WRAP-UP

Certainly, hunger, malnutrition, and death from starvation are major contemporary world problems. Even in the United States, college students can be food insecure. A surprisingly high percentage of students in the University of Wisconsin public university system are food insecure. If, as seems the case, enough food can be produced to feed every single individual on this planet, why do we have these problems? Food is like any other commodity: it must be produced, distributed, and consumed. All three steps cost energy which eventually means money. The main problem with distibution and consumption is that food degrades and spoils. Modern technology has made it possible to preserve food long enough to distribute it to hungy people almost anywhere, yet that still has not solved the problem. In the final analysis, it seems an inescapable conclusion that the real problem with food is a political one: who gets it depends on political power. Those without political power are the ones facing hunger, malnutrition, and starvation. That has been a problem ever since humans adopted agriculture. But, again, we ask, *must* it be so?

ACTIVITIES

General activity: class discussion on the Schema activation responses: *what is responsible for farming success?*

Activity Reading #13: Break into small groups and discuss whether each of the following: malnutrition, starvation, epidemics, class divisions, and inequality between the sexes, is present in either foraging societies or agricultural societies. Conclude by discussing whether people generally agree or disagree with Diamond that agriculture was the "worst mistake."

Activity Reading #14: A session in experimental archaeology to learn about decision making and hunting and gathering strategies. There will be three or four resource territories and each is supplied with four resources (pennies, jelly beans, pencils and paper clips).

- One by one, students take turns occupying a territory; each student must consume at least one resource to make it to the next round but can take as many as are available.
- Eventually, there will be more than one person per territory.
- Finally, territories will be at carrying capacity (four students).
- Each territory makes the choice to work (jump up and down ten times) to get double the amount of resources; the decision whether or not to do more work for more resources must be made by consensus.
- As supplies run out and there is not enough for everyone, the different groups must talk about potential strategies and options, such as war/raids, competitive feasting, further intensification, etc.
- A group can decide to remain hunters and gatherers and get their resources replenished without doing any work or letting any additional members in.
- Although the hunter-gatherer group live an easier life for much longer, eventually those who decided to intensify production turn hunter-gatherers into peripheral peoples.

SOURCES

Activity Reading #14 is adapted from John T. Omohundro *Thinking like an Anthropologist: A Practical Introduction to Cultural Anthropology* McGraw-Hill 2007; Jared Diamond's books have continually caused a stir: First there was *Guns and Germs and Steel: The Fates of Human Societies* W.W. Norton 1997; next came *Collapse: How Societies Choose to Fail or Succeed* Viking Penguin 2005, and then *The World Until Yesterday: What Can We Learn From Traditional Societies?* Viking Penguin 2012. Diamond is a professor of Geography at UCLA. His dabbling in other fields has raised the ire of anthropologists especially, but for a generalist, his work has achieved considerable respect.

Chapter 6
Population: People and Disease

OBJECTIVES

- Gain an awareness that arguments about population are often politically-motivated, but also come to appreciate that demographic realities have serious implications for the quality of human life.
- Understand the connection between population and disease; how a threshold of population size is required for epidemics and pandemics to propagate in human populations.
- Simulate the decision challenges facing government and health-care officials as they face the challenge of a new disease by playing a computer game about small pox.

KEY TERMS

Malthusian Checks: Referring to the work of Thomas Robert Malthus, who wrote an *Essay on Population* in 1798, arguing that human population grows geometrically while food supply grows arithmetically, so there is never enough food to support the total population, which is culled by famine, war, and disease.

Carrying Capacity: the term used by biologists to indicate the maximum number of organisms of one species that can live in a particular territory.

Demographic Transition: the world-wide change from the preindustrial demographic regime of high fertility and high mortality to low fertility and low mortality that took place as a result of the Industrial Revolution, modernization and modern medicine.

Fertility: the average number of live-born children a woman bears during her child-bearing years in a society (also called the **Total Fertility Rate** or **TFR**).

Mortality: the average number of deaths per one thousand people in a society.

Life Expectancy at Birth: From Life Table analysis, the average life span of all the people born in a particular society; because it counts and averages into the estimate babies who are stillborn or die at birth or early infancy. The statistic is really a measure of child mortality, not an informative measure of typical life span of those who have reached adulthood in that society.

Wealth Flow: the idea that in contexts where wealth is produced by children for the parents, families will be large; and where wealth is produced by parents for the children, families will be small.

Migration: the cultural universal that individual humans frequently move from place to place; one might hazard the judgment that it is a biological imperative because humans, as foragers, simply had to keep on the move in order to find fresh sources of food.

Urban Graveyard Effect: the demographically demonstrated effect that cities, throughout human history, have produced deaths at a greater rate than rural areas; in fact, most cities throughout history have required in-migration to maintain their populations.

SCHEMA ACTIVATION ACTIVITY

Think about what you know regarding population growth and *jot down four or five leading reasons for why human population grows; then give an answer to the question: is population growth a serious problem facing the world?*

(Save these to share later in your discussion sections.)

INTRODUCTION

You have probably heard or been taught in school that human population growth will reach 7-12 billion people in the next few decades, causing a serious challenge for the procurement of food resources to feed these extra mouths. Yes, population growth is commonly thought to be a serious world problem. One problem with the discussion of population growth is that it has always been a *politically-charged* issue. For example, the Roman Emperor Augustus, convinced that the Roman ruling class was not reproducing itself, tried to legislate marriage and child-rearing laws to force the Roman elites to respect and follow a more traditional Roman family morality. It is not clear that it was true, demographically. The Emperor Domitian, fearing that the peasantry of the Italian countryside were disappearing, started welfare schemes to provide funds for the children of Roman Italian farmers in order to revive rural agricultural life. He was mimicked loyally by rich Romans, but, once again, it is not at all clear whether it was a demographic necessity. In this chapter, you will read two articles out of a vast literature on population dynamics and one possible natural response to population growth—disease. The first article discusses how Paul Ehrlich's worrying 1968 book *The Population Bomb* (a book we read as undergraduates which made us agree that we shouldn't have children), presenting humanity with a modern Malthusian scenario, seems to have turned out spectacularly wrong, but brings little comfort. The second article discusses a computer game about vaccination for smallpox—a game which you will try out in your discussion sections.

The Global Baby Bust

Phillip Longman

THE WRONG READING

YOU AWAKEN to news of a morning traffic jam. Leaving home early for a doctor's appointment, you nonetheless arrive too late to find parking. After waiting two hours for a 15-minute consultation, you wait again to have your prescription filled. All the while, you worry about the work you've missed because so many other people would line up to take your job. Returning home to the evening news, you watch throngs of youths throwing stones somewhere in the Middle East, and a feature on disappearing farmland in the Midwest. A telemarketer calls for the third time, telling you, "We need your help to save the rain forest." As you set the alarm clock for the morning, one neighbor's car alarm goes off and another's air conditioner starts to whine.

So goes a day in the life of an average American. It is thus hardly surprising that many Americans think overpopulation is one of the world's most pressing problems. To be sure, the typical Westerner enjoys an unprecedented amount of private space. Compared to their parents, most now live in larger homes occupied by fewer children. They drive ever-larger automobiles, in which they can eat, smoke, or listen to the radio in splendid isolation. Food is so abundant that obesity has become a leading cause of death.

Still, both day-to-day experience and the media frequently suggest that the quality of life enjoyed in the United States and Europe is under threat by population growth. Sprawling suburban development is making traffic worse, driving taxes up, and reducing opportunities

---

PHILLIP LONGMAN is Senior Fellow at the New America Foundation and author of the forthcoming *The Empty Cradle* (Basic Books, 2004), from which this article is adapted.

to enjoy nature. Televised images of developing-world famine, war, and environmental degradation prompt some to wonder, "Why do these people have so many kids?" Immigrants and other people's children wind up competing for jobs, access to health care, parking spaces, favorite fishing holes, hiking paths, and spots at the beach. No wonder that, when asked how long it will take for world population to double, nearly half of all Americans say 20 years or less.

Yet a closer look at demographic trends shows that the rate of world population growth has fallen by more than 40 percent since the late 1960s. And forecasts by the UN and other organizations show that, even in the absence of major wars or pandemics, the number of human beings on the planet could well start to decline within the lifetime of today's children. Demographers at the International Institute for Applied Systems Analysis predict that human population will peak (at 9 billion) by 2070 and then start to contract. Long before then, many nations will shrink in absolute size, and the average age of the world's citizens will shoot up dramatically. Moreover, the populations that will age fastest are in the Middle East and other underdeveloped regions. During the remainder of this century, even sub-Saharan Africa will likely grow older than Europe is today.

FREE FALLING

THE ROOT CAUSE of these trends is falling birthrates. Today, the average woman in the world bears half as many children as did her counterpart in 1972. No industrialized country still produces enough children to sustain its population over time, or to prevent rapid population aging. Germany could easily lose the equivalent of the current population of what was once East Germany over the next half-century. Russia's population is already contracting by three-quarters of a million a year. Japan's population, meanwhile, is expected to peak as early as 2005, and then to fall by as much as one-third over the next 50 years—a decline equivalent, the demographer Hideo Ibe has noted, to that experienced in medieval Europe during the plague.

Although many factors are at work, the changing economics of family life is the prime factor in discouraging childbearing. In nations rich and poor, under all forms of government, as more and more of the world's population moves to urban areas in which children offer little or no economic reward to their parents, and as women acquire economic opportunities and reproductive control, the social and financial costs of childbearing continue to rise.

In the United States, the direct cost of raising a middle-class child born this year through age 18, according to the Department of Agriculture, exceeds $200,000—not including college. And the cost in forgone wages can easily exceed $1 million, even for families with modest earning power. Meanwhile, although Social Security and private pension plans depend critically on the human capital created by parents, they offer the same benefits, and often more, to those who avoid the burdens of raising a family.

Now the developing world, as it becomes more urban and industrialized, is experiencing the same demographic transition, but at a faster pace. Today, when Americans think of Mexico, for example, they think of televised images of desperate, unemployed youths swimming the Rio Grande or slipping through border fences. Yet because Mexican fertility rates have dropped so dramatically, the country is now aging five times faster than is the United States. It took 50 years for the American median age to rise just five years, from 30 to 35. By contrast, between 2000 and 2050, Mexico's median age, according to UN projections, will increase by 20 years, leaving half the population over 42. Meanwhile, the median American age in 2050 is expected to be 39.7.

Those televised images of desperate, unemployed youth broadcast from the Middle East create a similarly misleading impression. Fertility rates are falling faster in the Middle East than anywhere else on earth, and as a result, the region's population is aging at an unprecedented rate. For example, by mid-century, Algeria will see its median age increase from 21.7 to 40, according to UN projections. Postrevolutionary Iran has seen its fertility rate plummet by nearly two-thirds and will accordingly have more seniors than children by 2030.

Countries such as France and Japan at least got a chance to grow rich before they grew old. Today, most developing countries are growing old before they get rich. China's low fertility means that its labor force will start shrinking by 2020, and 30 percent of China's population could be over 60 by mid-century. More worrisome, China's social security system, which covers only a fraction of the population, already has debts exceeding 145 percent of its GDP. Making demographics there even worse, the spreading use of ultrasound and other techniques for determining the sex of fetuses is, as in India and many other parts of the world, leading to much higher abortion rates for females than for males. In China, the ratio of male to female births is now 117 to 100—which implies that roughly one out of six males in today's new generation will not succeed in reproducing.

All told, some 59 countries, comprising roughly 44 percent of the world's total population, are currently not producing enough children to avoid population decline, and the phenomenon continues to spread. By 2045, according to the latest UN projections, the world's fertility rate as a whole will have fallen below replacement levels.

REPAYING THE DEMOGRAPHIC DIVIDEND

WHAT IMPACT will these trends have on the global economy and balance of power? Consider first the positive possibilities. Slower world population growth offers many benefits, some of which have already been realized. Many economists believe, for example, that falling birthrates made possible the great economic boom that occurred in Japan and then in many other Asian nations beginning in the 1960s. As the relative number of children declined, so did the burden of their dependency, thereby freeing up more resources for investment and adult consumption. In East Asia, the working-age population grew nearly four times faster than its dependent population between 1965 and 1990, freeing up a huge reserve of female labor and other social resources that would otherwise have been committed to raising children. Similarly, China's rapid industrialization today is being aided by a dramatic decline in the relative number of dependent children.

Over the next decade, the Middle East could benefit from a similar "demographic dividend." Birthrates fell in every single Middle Eastern country during the 1990s, often dramatically. The resulting "middle aging" of the region will lower the overall dependency ratio over the next 10 to 20 years, freeing up more resources for infrastructure and industrial development. The appeal of radicalism could also diminish as young adults make up less of the population and Middle Eastern societies become increasingly dominated by middle-aged people concerned with such practical issues as health care and retirement savings. Just as population aging in the West during the 1980s was accompanied by the disappearance of youthful indigenous terrorist groups such as the Red Brigades and the Weather Underground, falling birthrates in the Middle East could well produce societies far less prone to political violence.

Declining fertility rates at first bring a "demographic dividend." That dividend has to be repaid, however, if the trend continues. Although at first the fact that there are fewer children to feed, clothe, and educate leaves more for adults to enjoy, soon enough, if fertility falls beneath replacement levels, the number of productive workers drops as well, and the number of dependent elderly increase. And these older citizens consume far more resources than children do. Even after considering the cost of education, a typical child in the United States consumes 28 percent less than the typical working-age adult, whereas elders consume 27 percent more, mostly in health-related expenses.

Largely because of this imbalance, population aging, once it begins creating more seniors than workers, puts severe strains on government budgets. In Germany, for example, public spending on pensions, even after accounting for a reduction in future benefits written into current law, is expected to swell from an already staggering 10.3 percent of GDP to 15.4 percent by 2040—even as the number of workers available to support each retiree shrinks from 2.6 to 1.4. Meanwhile, the cost of government health-care benefits for the elderly is expected to rise from today's 3.8 percent of GDP to 8.4 percent by 2040.

Population aging also depresses the growth of government revenues. Population growth is a major source of economic growth: more people create more demand for the products capitalists sell, and more supply of the labor capitalists buy. Economists may be able to construct models of how economies could grow amid a shrinking population, but in the real world, it has never happened. A nation's GDP is literally the sum of its labor force times average output per worker. Thus a decline in the number of workers implies a decline in an economy's growth potential. When the size of the work force falls, economic growth can occur only if productivity increases enough to compensate. And these increases would have to be substantial to offset the impact of aging. Italy, for example, expects its working-age population to plunge 41 percent by 2050—meaning that output per worker would have to increase by at least that amount just to keep Italy's economic growth rate from falling below zero. With a shrinking labor supply, Europe's future economic growth will therefore depend entirely on getting more out of each remaining worker (many of them unskilled, recently arrived immigrants), even as it has to tax them at higher and higher rates to pay for old-age pensions and health care.

Theoretically, raising the retirement age could help to ease the burden of unfunded old-age benefits. But declining fitness among the general population is making this tactic less feasible. In the United States, for example, the dramatic increases in obesity and sedentary lifestyles are already causing disability rates to rise among the population 59 and younger. Researchers estimate that this trend will cause a 10–20 percent increase in the demand for nursing homes over what would otherwise occur from mere population aging, and a 10–15 percent increase in Medicare expenditures on top of the program's already exploding costs. Meanwhile, despite the much ballyhooed "longevity revolution," life expectancy among the elderly in the United States is hardly improving. Indeed, due to changing lifestyle factors, life expectancy among American women aged 65 was actually lower in 2002 than it was in 1990, according to the Social Security Administration.

The same declines in population fitness can now be seen in many other nations and are likely to overwhelm any public health benefits achieved through medical technology. According to the International Association for the Study of Obesity, an "alarming rise in obesity presents a pan-European epidemic." A full 35 percent of Italian children are now overweight. In the case of European men, the percentage who are overweight or obese ranges from over 40 percent in France to 70 percent in Germany. And as Western lifestyles spread throughout the developing world so do Western ways of dying. According to the World Health Organization, half of all deaths in places such as Mexico, China, and the Middle East are now caused by noncommunicable diseases related to Western lifestyle, such as cancers and heart attacks induced by smoking and obesity.

GLOBAL AGING AND GLOBAL POWER

CURRENT POPULATION TRENDS are likely to have another major impact: they will make military actions increasingly difficult for most nations. One reason for this change will be psychological. In countries where parents generally have only one or two children, every soldier becomes a "Private Ryan"—a soldier whose loss would mean overwhelming devastation to his or her family. In the later years of the Soviet Union, for example, collapsing birthrates in the Russian core meant that by 1990, the number of Russians aged 15–24 had shrunk by 5.2 million from 25 years before. Given their few sons, it is hardly surprising that Russian mothers for the first time in the nation's history organized an antiwar movement, and that Soviet society decided that its casualties in Afghanistan were unacceptable.

Another reason for the shift will be financial. Today, Americans consider the United States as the world's sole remaining superpower, which it is. As the cost of pensions and health care consume more and more of the nation's wealth, however, and as the labor force stops growing, it will become more and more difficult for Washington to sustain current levels of military spending or the number of men and women in uniform. Even within the U.S. military budget, the competition between guns and canes is already intense. The Pentagon today spends 84 cents on pensions for every dollar it spends on basic pay. Indeed, except during wartime, pensions are already one of the Pentagon's largest budget categories. In 2000, the cost of military pensions amounted to 12 times what the military spent on ammunition, nearly 5 times what the Navy spent on new ships, and more than 5 times what the Air Force spent on new planes and missiles.

Of course, the U.S. military is also more technically sophisticated than ever before, meaning that national power today is much less dependent on the ability to raise large armies. But the technologies the United States currently uses to project its power—laser-guided bombs, stealth aircraft, navigation assisted by the space-based Global Positioning System, nuclear aircraft carriers—are all products of the sort of expensive research and development that the United States will have difficulty affording if the cost of old-age entitlements continues to rise.

The same point applies to the U.S. ability to sustain, or increase, its levels of foreign aid. Although the United States faces less population aging than any other industrialized nation, the extremely high cost of its health care system, combined with its underfunded pension system, means that it still faces staggering liabilities. According to the International Monetary Fund (IMF), the imbalance between what the U.S. federal government will collect in future taxes under current law and what it has promised to pay in future benefits now exceeds 500 percent of GDP. To close that gap, the IMF warns, "would require an immediate and permanent 60 percent hike in the federal income tax yield, or a 50 percent cut in Social Security and Medicare benefits." Neither is likely. Accordingly, in another 20 years, the United States will be no more able to afford the role of world policeman than Europe or Japan can today. Nor will China be able to assume the job, since it will soon start to suffer from the kind of hyper-aging that Japan is already experiencing.

EVEN IF there are fewer workers available to support each retiree in the future, won't technology be able to make up the difference? Perhaps. But there is also plenty of evidence to suggest that population aging itself works to depress the rate of technological and organizational innovation. Cross-country comparisons imply, for example, that after the proportion of elders increases in a society beyond a certain point, the level of entrepreneurship and inventiveness begins to drop. In 2002, Babson College and the London School of Business released their latest index of entrepreneurial activity. It shows that there is a distinct correlation between countries with a high ratio of workers to retirees and those with a high degree of entrepreneurship. Conversely, in countries in which a large share of the population is retired, the amount of new business formation is low. So, for example, two of the most entrepreneurial countries today are India and China, where there are currently roughly five people of working age for every person of retirement age. Meanwhile, Japan and France are among the least entrepreneurial countries on earth and have among the lowest ratios of workers to retirees.

This correlation could be explained by many different factors. Both common sense and a vast literature in finance and psychology support the claim that as one approaches retirement age, one usually becomes more reluctant to take career or financial risks. It is not surprising, therefore, that aging countries such as Italy, France, and Japan are marked by exceptionally low rates of job turnover and by exceptionally conservative use of capital. Because prudence requires that older investors take fewer risks with their investments, it also stands to reason that as populations age, investor preference shifts toward safe bonds and bank deposits and away from speculative stocks and venture funds. As populations age further, ever-higher shares of citizens begin cashing out their investments and spending down their savings.

Also to be considered are the huge public deficits projected to be run by major industrialized countries over the next several decades. Because of the mounting costs of pensions and health care, government spending on research and development, as well as on education, will likely drop. Moreover, massive government borrowing could easily crowd out financial capital that would otherwise be available to the private sector for investment in new technology. The Center for Strategic and International Studies has recently calculated that the cost of public benefits to the elderly will consume a dramatically rising share of GDP in industrialized countries. In the United States, such benefits currently consume 9.4 percent of GDP. But if current trends continue, this figure will top 20 percent by 2040. And in countries such as France, Germany, Italy, Japan, and Spain, somewhere between a quarter and a third of all national output will be consumed by old-age pensions and health care programs before today's 30-year-olds reach retirement age.

Theoretically, a highly efficient, global financial market could lend financial resources from rich, old countries that are short on labor to young, poor countries that are short on capital, and make the whole world better off. But for this to happen, old countries would have to contain their deficits and invest their savings in places that are themselves either on the threshold of hyper-aging (China, India, Mexico) or highly destabilized by religious fanaticism, disease, and war (most of the Middle East, sub-Saharan Africa, Indonesia), or both. And who exactly would buy the products produced by these investments? Japan, South Korea, and other recently industrialized countries relied on massive exports to the United States and Europe to develop. But if the population of Europe and Japan drops, while the population of the United States ages considerably, where will the demand come from to support development in places such as the Middle East and sub-Saharan Africa?

Population aging is also likely to create huge legacy costs for employers. This is particularly true in the United States, where health and pension benefits are largely provided by the private sector. General Motors (GM) now has 2.5 retirees on its pension rolls for every active worker and an unfunded pension debt of $19.2 billion. Honoring its legacy costs to retirees now adds $1,800 to the cost of every vehicle GM makes, according to a 2003 estimate by Morgan Stanley. Just between 2001 and 2002, the U.S. government's projected short-term liability for bailing out failing private pension plans increased from $11 billion to $35 billion, with huge defaults expected from the steel and airline industries.

An aging work force may also be less able or inclined to take advantage of new technology. This trend seems to be part of the cause for Japan's declining rates of productivity growth in the 1990s. Before that decade, the aging of Japan's highly educated work force was a weak but positive force in increasing the nation's productivity, according to studies. Older workers learned by doing, developing specialized knowledge and craft skills and the famous company spirit that made Japan an unrivaled manufacturing power. But by the 1990s, the continued aging of Japan's work force became a cause of the country's declining competitiveness.

Population aging works against innovation in another way as well. As population growth dwindles, so does the need to increase the supply of just about everything, save health care. That means there is less incentive to find ways of making a gallon of gas go farther, or of increasing the capacity of existing infrastructure. Population growth is the mother of necessity. Without it, why bother to innovate? An aging society may have an urgent need to gain more output from each remaining worker, but without growing markets, individual firms have little incentive to learn how to do more with less—and with a dwindling supply of human capital, they have fewer ideas to draw on.

IMPORTING HUMAN CAPITAL

If high-tech isn't the answer, what about immigration? It turns out that importing new, younger workers is at best only a partial solution. To be sure, the United States and other developed nations derive many benefits from their imported human capital. Immigration, however, does less than one might think to ease the challenges of population aging. One reason is that most immigrants arrive not as babies but with a third or so of their lives already behind them—and then go on to become elderly themselves. In the short term, therefore, immigrants can help to increase the ratio of workers to retirees, but in the long term, they add much less youth to the population than would newborn children.

Indeed, according to a study by the UN Population Division, if the United States hopes to maintain the current ratio of workers to retirees over time, it will have to absorb an average of 10.8 million immigrants annually through 2050. At that point, however, the U.S.

population would total 1.1 billion, 73 percent of whom would be immigrants who had arrived in this country since 1995 or their descendants.

Just housing such a massive influx would require the equivalent of building another New York City every 10 months. And even if the homes could be built, it is unclear how long the United States and other developed nations can sustain even current rates of immigration. One reason, of course, is heightened security concerns. Another is the prospect of a cultural backlash against immigrants, the chances of which increase as native birthrates decline. In the 1920s, when widespread apprehension about declining native fertility found voice in books such as Lothrop Stoddard's *The Rising Tide of Color Against White World-Supremacy*, the U.S. political system responded by shutting off immigration. Germany, Sweden, and France did the same in the 1970s as the reality of population decline among their native born started to set in.

Another constraint on immigration to the United States involves supply. Birthrates, having already fallen well below replacement levels in Europe and Asia, are now plummeting throughout Latin America as well, which suggests that the United States' last major source of imported labor will dry up. This could occur long before Latin nations actually stop growing—as the example of Puerto Rico shows. When most Americans think of Puerto Rico, they think of a sunny, overcrowded island that sends millions of immigrants to the West Side of New York City or to Florida. Yet with a fertility rate well below replacement level and a median age of 31.8 years, Puerto Rico no longer provides a net flow of immigrants to the mainland, despite an open border and a lower standard of living. Evidently, Puerto Rico now produces enough jobs to keep up with its slowing rate of population growth, and the allure of the mainland has thus largely vanished.

For its part, sub-Saharan Africa still produces many potential immigrants to the United States, as do the Middle East and parts of South Asia. But to attract immigrants from these regions, the United States will have to compete with Europe, which is closer geographically and currently has a more acute need for imported labor. Europe also offers higher wages for unskilled work, more generous social benefits, and large, already established populations of immigrants from these areas.

Even if the United States could compete with Europe for immigrants, it is by no means clear how many potential immigrants these regions will produce in the future. Birthrates are falling in sub-Saharan Africa as well as in the rest of the world, and war and disease have made mortality rates there extraordinarily high. UN projections for the continent as a whole show fertility declining to 2.4 children per woman by mid-century, which may well be below replacement levels if mortality does not dramatically improve. Although the course of the AIDS epidemic through sub-Saharan Africa remains uncertain, the CIA projects that AIDS and related diseases could kill as many as a quarter of the region's inhabitants by 2010.

A FUNDAMENTAL PROBLEM

SOME BIOLOGISTS now speculate that modern humans have created an environment in which the "fittest," or most successful, individuals are those who have few, if any, children. As more and more people find themselves living under urban conditions in which children no longer provide economic benefit to their parents, but rather are costly impediments to material success, people who are well adapted to this new environment will tend not to reproduce themselves. And many others who are not so successful will imitate them.

So where will the children of the future come from? The answer may be from people who are at odds with the modern environment—either those who don't understand the new rules of the game, which make large families an economic and social liability, or those who, out of religious or chauvinistic conviction, reject the game altogether.

Today there is a strong correlation between religious conviction and high fertility. In the United States, for example, fully 47 percent of people who attend church weekly say that the ideal family size is three or more children, as compared to only 27 percent of those who seldom attend church. In Utah, where 69 percent of all residents are registered members of the Church of Jesus Christ of Latter Day Saints, fertility rates are the highest in the nation. Utah annually produces 90 children for every 1,000 women of childbearing age. By comparison, Vermont—the only state to send a socialist to Congress and the first to embrace gay civil unions—produces only 49.

Does this mean that the future belongs to those who believe they are (or who are in fact) commanded by a higher power to procreate?

Based on current trends, the answer appears to be yes. Once, demographers believed that some law of human nature would prevent fertility rates from remaining below replacement level within any healthy population for more than brief periods. After all, don't we all carry the genes of our Neolithic ancestors, who one way or another managed to produce enough babies to sustain the race? Today, however, it has become clear that no law of nature ensures that human beings, living in free, developed societies, will create enough children to reproduce themselves. Japanese fertility rates have been below replacement levels since the mid-1950s, and the last time Europeans produced enough children to reproduce themselves was the mid-1970s. Yet modern institutions have yet to adapt to this new reality.

Current demographic trends work against modernity in another way as well. Not only is the spread of urbanization and industrialization itself a major cause of falling fertility, it is also a major cause of so-called diseases of affluence, such as overeating, lack of exercise, and substance abuse, which leave a higher and higher percentage of the population stricken by chronic medical conditions. Those who reject modernity would thus seem to have an evolutionary advantage, whether they are clean-living Mormons or Muslims, or members of emerging sects and national movements that emphasize high birthrates and anti-materialism.

SECULAR SOLUTIONS

How CAN secular societies avoid population loss and decline? The problem is not that most people in these societies have lost interest in children. Among childless Americans aged 41 years and older in 2003, for example, 76 percent say they wish they had had children, up from 70 percent in 1990. In 2000, 40-year-old women in the United States and in every European nation told surveys that they had produced fewer children than they intended. Indeed, if European women now in their 40s had been able to produce their ideal number of children, the continent would face no prospect of population loss.

The problem, then, is not one of desire. The problem is that even as modern societies demand more and more investment in human capital, this demand threatens its own supply. The clear tendency of economic development is toward a more knowledge-based, networked economy in which decision-making and responsibility are increasingly necessary at lower levels. In such economies, however, children often remain economically dependent on their parents well into their own childbearing years because it takes that long to acquire the panoply of technical skills, credentials, social understanding, and personal maturity that more and more jobs now require. For the same reason, many couples discover that by the time they feel they can afford children, they can no longer produce them, or must settle for just one or two.

Meanwhile, even as aging societies become more and more dependent on the human capital parents provide, parents themselves get to keep less and less of the wealth they create by investing in their children. Employers make use of the skills parents endow their children with but offer parents no compensation. Governments also depend on parents to provide the next generation of taxpayers, but, with rare exception, give parents no greater benefits in old age than non-parents.

To change this pattern, secular societies need to rethink how they go about educating young adults and integrating them into the work force, so that tensions between work and family are reduced. Education should be a lifetime pursuit, rather than crammed into one's prime reproductive years. There should also be many more opportunities for part-time and flex-time employment, and such work should offer full health and pension benefits, as well as meaningful career paths.

Governments must also relieve parents from having to pay into social security systems. By raising and educating their children, parents have already contributed hugely (in the form of human capital) to these systems. The cost of their contribution, in both direct expenses and forgone wages, is often measured in the millions. Requiring parents also then to contribute to payroll taxes is not only unfair, but imprudent for societies that are already consuming more human capital than they produce.

To cope with the diseases of affluence that make older workers less productive, rich societies must make greater efforts to promote public health. For example, why not offer reduced health care premiums to those who quit smoking, lose weight, or can demonstrate regular attendance in exercise programs? Why not do more to discourage sprawling, automobile-dependent patterns of development, which have adverse health effects including pollution, high rates of auto injuries and death, sedentary lifestyles, and social isolation? Modern, high-tech medicine, even for those who can afford it, does little to promote productive aging because by the time most people come to need it, their bodies have already been damaged by stress, indulgent habits, environmental dangers, and injuries. For all they spend on health care, Americans enjoy no greater life expectancy than the citizens of Costa Rica, where per capita health expenditure is less than $300.

In his 1968 bestseller *The Population Bomb*, Paul Ehrlich warned, "The battle to feed all of humanity is over. In the 1970s the world will undergo famines—hundreds of millions of people are going to starve to death in spite of any crash programs embarked upon now." Fortunately, Ehrlich's prediction proved wrong. But having averted the danger of overpopulation, the world now faces the opposite problem: an aging and declining population. We are, in one sense, lucky to have this problem and not its opposite. But that doesn't make the problem any less serious, or the solutions any less necessary.

So, that may not have been what you expected: no denunciation of the evils of population growth out of control. Precisely the opposite. The problem is the so-called Demographic Transition, which lets population grow if you have high fertility and low mortality, which may be the pattern in the developing world because there, wealth flow is from children (as agricultural laborers) to parents, whereas, in the developed world, wealth flows from parents to children (in the U.S., largely in the form of paying for college). Not everyone thinks that the Demographic Transition is a good concept. Feminist scholars have decried it for basically blaming women world-wide for there being too many people. Other scholars point out that it is an oversimplification (it is) because some areas of the world demonstrate it, others do not. Yet, overall, it appears to be reasonably accurate. All the archaeological study of human remains over the years has confirmed that, in the ancient world (up to the 1800s), life expectancy at birth was 25-35 years (meaning there was incredibly high infant mortality). With the advent of modern medicine, infant mortality has been brought to levels well-below what existed in the past, even in countries where modern medicine is a challnge to find. So, are there too many people or too few? In the article there is almost a call to arms every bit as loud as one worrying about too much population growth. Do you see how these opposing views are, at heart, about politics? Do Something! Malthus and Ehrlich predicted that millions of people would die because there were too many people. On the one hand, they were wrong; on the other hand, famine, war and disease HAVE killed millions; if you were one of them, it would be no comfort to know (if you even could!) that Malthusian Checks are not the scourge Malthus (called the "Dismal Priest") thought.

If population dynamics are a politically-charge issue, recall that the problem with food delivery from the last chapter is also a political problem. So, dealing with the politics appears to be key in trying to solve world problems of population dynamics, and that will require the give and take of debate and negotiation. As you will now see, individual decisions made in cases of human health and disease are also the issue, which you will cosnider with a chance for brief practice in the face of a pandemic.

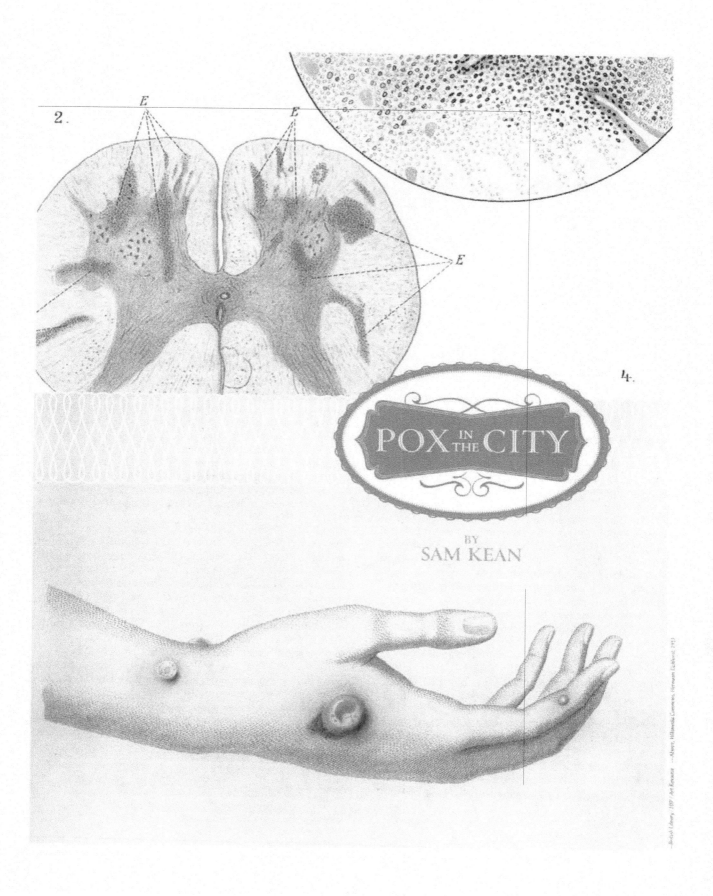

2.

4.

POX IN THE CITY

BY
SAM KEAN

—Istock.com

Not malaria. Not cholera. Not AIDS, influenza, measles, or tuberculosis. Not even bubonic plague. No disease in history has destroyed more lives than the "speckled monster," smallpox.

The pattern repeated itself in every empire: Egyptian, Hittite, Greek, Roman, Ottoman, and Chinese. Outbreaks always started subtly, with flu-like symptoms—fevers, headache, nausea. Days later came the speckles, the excruciating pustules that invaded every pore and orifice, including on the face. Victims were quarantined in pesthouses or on ships, and one-third died within weeks; survivors were left pockmarked and often blind. Smallpox invaded both palaces and slums, killing kings and peasants, czars and serfs, sultans and slaves throughout Europe, Asia, and Africa. And really, the Old World got off easy. Smallpox almost annihilated the New World, where some populations dropped by more than 90 percent in just decades.

There was one way to prevent smallpox, inoculation, a medieval Indian and Chinese practice imported to Europe in the early 1700s. Doctors collected pus or scabs from someone with a mild case, then scratched the inoculee's upper arm and introduced diseased matter. With luck, the patient got a mild case himself—some aches, a few pustules—and thereby acquired immunity. All too often, inoculation backfired, and a full-fledged case of smallpox flared up. For this reason, most people agonized over whether to inoculate their families. Ben Franklin, for instance, went round and round—and while he dithered, his four-year-old son Francis caught smallpox anyway and died. Even with inoculation, smallpox continued to kill with grim efficiency.

According to the standard history of smallpox, everything changed just before 1800. Edward Jenner—a doctor in rural England who had barely survived inoculation himself as a lad—had been hearing rumors for years that milkmaids never got smallpox, possibly because of exposure to cowpox, a mild infection that appeared on cows' udders. Jenner reasoned that cowpox might provide immunity. He tested this theory in May 1796, when a local milkmaid named Sarah Nelmes developed three pustules on her hand, infected by a cow named Blossom. Jenner lanced the boils and summoned his gardener's son, James Phipps. Phipps had never had smallpox or cowpox and was, at eight years old, the same age Jenner had been when inoculated. Jenner took the fluid from Nelmes and injected it into parallel half-inch scratches he made on Phipps's arm. Phipps soon fell ill, developing pustules and a mild fever. But he recovered quickly. That July, Jenner inoculated Phipps multiple times with live smallpox virus. Nothing happened: Phipps didn't even get a speckle.

Jenner soon "vaccinated"—from the Latin *vacca*, cow—twenty-two other patients with cowpox, and each one of them proved immune to smallpox, too. Jenner published these cases in a seventy-five-page treatise in 1798, and, according to the standard telling of the smallpox story, the world was never the same. Jenner set up clinics in England, and disciples began hauling dried cowpox matter from village to village on glass

ABOVE, EDWARD JENNER VACCINATES HIS SON AGAINST SMALLPOX.

LEFT TOP, SMALLPOX DEVASTATED THE HUMAN BODY, ENCROACHING EVEN TO THE SPINAL CORD, WHERE IT CAUSED LESIONS.

IN *AN INQUIRY INTO THE CAUSES AND EFFECTS OF THE VARIOLAE VACCINAE*, EDWARD JENNER INCLUDED AN IMAGE OF THE COWPOX-INFECTED ARM OF SARAH NELMES. BOTTOM LEFT, JENNER LANCED THE PUSTULES TO OBTAIN THE FLUID THAT MADE POSSIBLE VACCINATION AGAINST THE FAR DEADLIER SMALLPOX.

slides or dried twine, vaccinating everyone in sight. The vaccine soon spread worldwide, and it's often said then, probably truthfully, that Jenner saved more lives than any human in history.

But that standard history, while not wrong in outline, omits some crucial details. Jenner had originally hoped to publish his smallpox treatise through the famed Royal Society of London. (He was a fellow there, thanks to his groundbreaking studies of cuckoos.) But the Royal Society refused to print the initial version of it, saying that Jenner lacked enough data and urging him not to risk his reputation. He had to self-publish instead. Powerful doctors in the medical establishment also slandered vaccination as unsafe and unnatural, and Jenner found himself fighting their propaganda as much as smallpox itself.

And it wasn't just elites that resisted: Everyday folk also feared Jenner's methods, even as doctors throughout the British empire made heroic efforts to convince their patients to try vaccines. The standard telling of the smallpox story tends to skip this crucial struggle in the trenches. For this reason, NEH's Office of Digital Humanities is funding the development of a role-playing video game that will immerse biology students and students of medical history in this era. The smallpox campaigns of the time shaped every aspect of modern public health, and the game demonstrates firsthand how doctors had to fight corruption, drunkenness, apathy, and hostile newspapers—along with disease. In the end, it took a lot more than medical science to slay the speckled monster.

The leader of the anti-vaccination movement was Dr. Benjamin Moseley, a blueblood who had practiced medicine in Jamaica and had written pamphlets there urging people to eat more sugar. Upon returning to England,

Moseley joined the Royal College of Physicians and, like many doctors, made loads of money inoculating people against smallpox—income now threatened by vaccination.

Moseley and his ilk also had darker, more complex reasons to oppose vaccination. They focused especially on safety: Jenner had not proved the method safe, they argued, and no one knew the long-term consequences of introducing an animal disease into children, the target of most vaccination efforts. One political cartoon showed vaccinators heaving heaps of babies into the maw of a monstrous cow.

Moseley also feared that mingling cow and human matter violated natural law, and would lead to terrible and prodigious things. He fanned rumors that vaccinations would transform people into cows. In one article, he reproduced a drawing—worthy of a supermarket tabloid today—of the "ox-faced boy," with bovine eyes and a patch of hair on his face. Picking up on this meme, cartoonists portrayed vaccination clinics as scenes right out of Ovid: Hoofs and horns sprouted from patients' limbs and buttocks, while Jenner stood by coldly. In the background, people bowed down to worship a calf.

Moseley argued that vaccination would degrade people spiritually, making them near-brutes. Why, "owing to vaccination," he wrote, "British ladies might wander in the fields to receive the embraces of the bull." He even prophesied "a new Pasiphaë"—the mythological queen who had sex with a cow and gave birth to the Minotaur. Lisa Rosner, a historian at Stockton College helping develop the video game on vaccination, calls Moseley a talented demagogue: "He really had his finger on the pulse of what people are afraid of."

Vaccination also faced opposition in British colonies, especially India. Brahmans objected to receiving fluids from the arms of the low-caste children who caught cowpox.

Indians also equated vaccination with "consuming" cattle, which religious taboos forbid. If nothing else, vaccination left scars on the upper arm, a visible symbol of colonial oppression.

Jenner and his allies defended themselves, and counter-attacked, in various ways. They first cited statistical evidence that vaccination worked and was safe. Perhaps more power-fully, some doctors reportedly vaccinated their own babies and then exposed them to smallpox victims—seemingly risking their children.

Jenner sought help from other quarters, too. Nowadays, scientists who appeal directly to the press are often de-nounced as charlatans, but Jenner had no compunctions about courting writers—or flat out paying them—to pub-lish odes to vaccines in popular literary journals. Some of this was hackwork, but Robert Southey, while poet laureate, wrote a poem relating how "this hideous malady which lost its power / When Jenner's art the dire contagion stay'd." And Samuel Taylor Coleridge, who'd lost a son to inocula-tion, praised vaccines as a worthy subject for verse.

Just as important, Jenner cultivated political contacts. As early as 1800, the powerful Earl of Lonsdale vaccinated all the tenants in his village. This success opened doors, and Jenner soon met King George and Queen Charlotte, who sponsored the Royal Jennerian Society to promote vaccines. Jenner also met the king's sons, the Prince of Wales and Duke of York, who ordered vaccination for the entire army. Generals back then typically lost more troops to disease than enemy fire, and the military hailed Jenner as a patriot, England's greatest ally against Napoléon.

(Ironically, though, Napoléon would soon declare Jenner *his* ally, after vaccinating the French army in 1805. Later, l'Empereur even freed a relative of Jenner's, a captured British captain, saying, "I cannot refuse Jenner anything!")

Although rooted in lower-class folklore, vaccination quickly became a crusade of the upper classes. Moseley and company looked increasingly shrill and backward, and the majority of doctors joined Jenner's side. Having triumphed among the elites, now Jenner and his allies needed to con-vince the rest of society.

Even the imprimatur of the king couldn't allay every-one's fear, especially among the lower classes. And it's this struggle of everyday people that Rosner and a team of historians, designers, and programmers want to capture in their video game, "Pox and the City."

The game immerses players in early 1800s Edinburgh, a prestigious medical center and a major front in winning acceptance for vaccines. It offers the chance to play one of three roles: a doctor trying to open a vaccine clinic; an immigrant worker trying to avoid smallpox; or, unusually, a smallpox virus trying to infect the masses. To recreate classic Edinburgh neighborhoods, Rosner's team will draw on contemporary images from the archives of the College of Physicians in Philadelphia and from visits to Edinburgh. She hopes that players can someday even, say, duck into an eating hall and hear people singing Robert Burns's poems. For now, her team is concentrating on building the basic levels for the character of Doctor Alexander Robertson.

BEFORE VACCINATION WAS WIDELY AVAILABLE, THE ARRIVAL OF SMALLPOX WAS EQUALLY FEARED IN TOWNS, CITIES, AND THE COUNTRYSIDE. IN CREATING ART FOR "POX AND THE CITY," HANNAH UENO OF STOCKTON COLLEGE HIGHLIGHTS THE GRITTY SIDE OF LIFE IN EDINBURGH, ABOVE AND OPPOSITE. THE TIGHTLY PACKED CONDITIONS IN SOME PARTS OF THE CITY PROVIDED EXCELLENT CONDITIONS FOR SPREADING DISEASE.

The real Alexander Robertson wrote an outstanding thesis on vaccine science in 1799, says Rosner. After that, he disappears from the historical record, but "he's absolutely the kind of young physician who would have taken up vaccination in an entrepreneurial way," she adds, therefore making him an appropriate character. Rosner drew on diaries of Edinburgh doctors and other primary sources to flesh out the milieu in which a Robertson would have worked.

At its most basic level, the game requires Robertson to persuade people to try vaccines, and he has to tailor his pitch to whomever he encounters. With a young Irish washerwoman, Robertson might do well to drop her priest's name. For a striving merchant, Robertson could establish his scientific credentials, or mention that vaccination is all the rage in London. Other aspects of game play are more like quests, with multiple goals and subgoals along the way. For instance, one proposed subplot involving a corrupt doctor might require wheedling information from a drunken bar patron, haggling with journalists, and sneaking into the crooked doctor's office to gather evidence.

How Robertson actually wins the game—which, if everything goes according to plan, will first be play-tested in late spring and finished in 2017—is still up for debate. Robertson's ultimate goal is to set up a free vaccination clinic in Edinburgh for the poor. This will require him to impress wealthy patrons first and convince them to pay for everything. (Wealthy patrons might do this, Rosner says, because it was a reform-minded era, and many people saw medical charities as a good "investment." Or, if civic duty didn't convince them, naked self-interest might: Smallpox epidemics had a way of spilling over from the hovels of the poor into the parlors of the upper class.) Right now, Robertson wins the game by earning an official royal charter for his clinic, but Rosner says that goal might change after play-testing, depending on whether modern gamers find it satisfying enough.

Overall, "Pox and the City" explores the social side of medicine, and it's lessons ring true even today: People are no less stubborn now about taking preventive health measures, nor has the fear of vaccines ever quite dissipated. British laborers held massive protests against vaccines in 1885. In the twentieth century, Gandhi dismissed vaccinations as "filthy . . . harmful . . . little short of taking [eating] beef." And U.S. activists today continue to rail against vaccines as the cause of autism, even though the studies on which those claims are based have been retracted as fraudulent.

Jenner's own struggles to defend vaccination took a great deal out of him. Although he became famous worldwide, and although Parliament granted him huge bounties (first, £10,000; then, £20,000), he grew somewhat bitter and cantankerous in old age, and amassed debts he could never quite clear. Even the Royal Jennerian Society went bankrupt. When Jenner died in 1823, one of the few mourners at his funeral was James Phipps, the boy he'd vaccinated a quarter century earlier.

Nevertheless, Jenner's idea did triumph. Denmark, Russia, and Sweden all made vaccines mandatory for citizens in the early 1800s. The practice spread across the Atlantic as well: Thomas Jefferson personally vaccinated his children and staff at Monticello, and Ben Franklin, after studying the effectiveness of vaccination, eagerly promoted it. Great Britain outlawed inoculation in 1841. By 1853, it was

THE GREAT RISK EDWARD JENNER TOOK IN INTRODUCING A VACCINE AGAINST SMALLPOX PROVED TO BE A TURNING POINT IN THE HISTORY OF MEDICINE.

mandatory to vaccinate children against smallpox by their third month.

Eventually, the world achieved even Jenner's grandest hope: "to see Societies form'd throughout the Empire for the Extermination of the Smallpox." Smallpox still killed at least three hundred million people in the twentieth century, but year by year the number of victims dwindled, and the last natural case occurred in 1977, in a Somali hospital aide. (Armed guards stood at his door until the last pustule dried up.) Today, only a few frozen vials of the speckled monster still exist, in high-security labs in the United States and Russia. Smallpox remains the only human disease ever eradicated—a scourge destroyed by one brilliant man, and his equally brilliant powers of persuasion. Still, we cannot forget the everyday heroes like Dr. Robertson, either, who made Jenner's case day in and day out across the world. It can be hard to imagine nowadays why their patients required so much persuading—why they were equally afraid of the disease and its cure. But as Rosner reminds us, "scientific advances that we take for granted today were not obvious." "Pox and the City" shows how they came to be so.

Sam Kean is the author of the *New York Times* bestsellers *The Violinist's Thumb* and *The Disappearing Spoon*, two romps through science history.

The Richard Stockton College of New Jersey received $49,989 in NEH support to develop a digital role-playing game that explores the history of smallpox vaccine development.

So, the discovery of vaccination, and the battle to have the procedure accepted, was every bit as complicated as it is in the modern context of disease prevention. However, make no mistake: smallpox vaccination eradicated the disease (the one and only example of such a victory in human history). On the other hand, the victory may turn out to be a Pyrrhic one (named after the general from Epirus in Greece who defeated the Romans at such high cost that the victory proved hollow). As unforgettably stated by author Richard Preston: "one case of smallpox is a global emergency." The disease has been eradicated and no one is vaccinated against it anymore, so if the disease were to re-appear, it would be catastrophic. Fittingly, the article is titled Pox *in the City*. Major diseases such as smallpox can only thrive and propagate with a population on the order of 250,000 people in a reasonably circumscribed location. Such population concentrations have only become a reality since the beginning of the "Urban Revolution" about 6,000 years ago. And, it wasn't until the beginning of the Common Era that cities of that size have existed at all. You may have read somewhere that New Kingdom Egyptian pharaohs had small pox. That is very doubtful. The first smallpox epidemic is probably the pandemic known as the "Antonine Plague" which appeared in 165 CE, with several re-appearances later. The Emperor Marcus Aurelius may have died from it (and his physician, Galen, the most prolific writer from Mediterranean antiquity, may have abandoned his post to run away from it). The next big pandemic was the "Plague of Justinian" in 542 CE, which we now know from ancient DNA analysis to be bubonic plague (my archaeological site in Sicily, Gangivecchio, may have bodies of victims of this plague), the same disease that became known as the "Black Death" when it hit Europe in 1347 with recurrences thereafter and which decimated populations world-wide. Epidemic is Greek for ("upon the people") and describes a bad enough situation of disease heavily impacting a population. The city of Rome in antiquity may have experienced epidemics every 8-12 years. A pandemic (Greek for "all the people") is much worse because such a large proportion of the population is affected; virtually "all," even though it is probably closer to 50%-80% of the population.

Sanitation

One issue that ties the two articles and topics together is that of sanitation. One reason that cities are an ideal host for communicable disease (which does not affect foragers), is because cities bring humans together who produce waste: both in terms of the material culture people jettison, and the human waste that each human organism (more if they keep animals!) produces. Ancient cities, and even modern ones, were and are continuously challenged by trash. Trash, unless processed and removed safely, is unhealthy and promotes disease. So prevalent is the health challenge accorded by sanitation in cities that demographers long ago came up with the concept of the "Urban Graveyard Effect"—simply a way of stating the conclusion (reached after the study of skeletons from city cemeteries) that ancient cities were almost death traps: the mortality levels were much higher than in the countryside. Furthermore, many of the immigrants coming into the city were poor and food insecurity made them more vulnerable to malnutrition, disease and death.

If we reflect that the world's oceans now have huge, floating trash dumps, and that trash affects even the depths of the seas (a plastic bag was recently recovered from the Mariana Trench, the deepest point in the world's oceans, at 36,000 feet below sea level), we must admit that human production of waste must be one of the most serious challenges faced by humans today.

CONCLUSION: WRAP-UP

Population and disease. The scourge that did not affect our ancestors as they pursued their foraging lifestyle and did not gather in sufficient numbers to pass diseases came home to roost on humans when they adopted sedentary life and eventually lived in cities—partly blame our love of horses because the common cold comes from them. The majority of world population recently became urban. That does not mean that the world's population lives in big cities such as New York or Shanghai, but it does mean that more people live in an urban zone than live in rural communities now. How we will sort out the issue of human planetary population may well be one of the most important challenges humans face in the next century. However, it may also be that human population trends will defy easy characterization, as they have in the past. We really do not know what the population will do. However, that it is already straining the resources of the earth is not really in question. There is also the issue of disease, most of which are a result of human congregating. And some of the diseases are of an odd variety. The Center for Disease Control has routinely questioned the State of Iowa's driving age of 14, calling it an epidemic of teen death. As of this writing, the Santa Fe, Texas high school shooting has just occurred with the media pointing out that there has been at least one fatal school shooting in every week for the first 22 weeks of 2018. That is the equivalent of a disease. Those last two examples are diseases that are quite preventable, given the political (there it is again) will. Disease on human populations is likely to get worse because of another factor (the object of the next chapter) over which humans apparently have little control at this point: climate change.

ACTIVITIES

Activity Reading #15: break into small groups and discuss the following questions, using your Schema activation responses:

- Population: too much growth or too little growth?
- Which is the more challenging problem?
- Who is responsible for either too many people, or insufficient replacement numbers?
- Name the policies of some countries that has resulted in too many or too few people.

Activity Reading #16: The main activity in your discussion section is to try the game Pox and the City: http://poxandthecity.blogspot.com/2013/07/link-to-pox-and-city.html

SOURCES

Information on demography has been adapted from Richard H. Robbins *Global Problems and the Culture of Capitalism* (Fourth Edition) Pearson pp. 147-176. For Thomas Robert Malthus, a good edition is available to download from an online collection:
(http://www.esp.org/books/malthus/population/malthus.pdf)
An Essay on the Principle of Population, as it Affects the Future Improvement of Society with Remarks on the Speculations of Mr. Godwin, M. Condorcet, and Other Writers, originally published 1798, reprint 1998 Electronic Scholarly Publishing Project. Information on small pox is from Richard Preston *The Demon in the Freezer: A true story* 2002 New York Random House. For the Urban Graveyard Effect and sanitation in cities, see the introduction and several papers in Glenn R. Storey (editor) *Urbanism in the Preindustrial World: Cross-Cultural Approaches* 2006 University of Alabama Press. A good discussion of disease in the Roman Empire is in Kyle Harper *The Fate of Rome: Climate, Disease and the End of an Empire* 2017 Princeton University Press.

Chapter 7

Climate and Environment: Welcome to the Anthropocene

OBJECTIVES

- Review the evidence for the disappearance of ice worldwide and its implications for climate change.
- Determine how the politics of worldwide rising temperatures have played out in the arena of global responses to climate change.
- Explain the effects of various policies designed to address (or ignore) the challenge of a changing temperature and environmental regime.
- Come to understand how the approach of climate ethnography might be used to tell the local stories of climate change and help inspire collaboration to address the challenges posed by a changing climate.

KEY TERMS

Climate: the average weather in a region as measured over a long period of time.

Haber-Bosch Process: chemical process combining hydrogen and nitrogen gas to create ammonia from which synthetic fertilizer is easily produced thereby eliminating the need to gather bird dung fertilizer; the process was hailed as the ability to "make bread from air."

Anthropocene: awaiting final confirmation but recommended for recognition: the epoch which began in 1950, the Greek term meaning "the human recent," defined by the signature of atomic weapons, plastic pollution, soot from power plants, concrete, and the masses of domesticated chicken bones. It means that the trajectory of world evolution is now dominated by humanity.

Climate Forcing Mechanism: any force external to the climate itself, which affects the climate, including human-induced changes, also called "anthropogenic" (Greek for "caused by humans"). These includes orbital variations, solar variability, volcanic aerosols, tropospheric (lowest level of the atmosphere, 6-10 kms from the surface to 6-10 km up) aerosols, atmospheric trace gases and the carbon-dioxide and other chemicals released into the atmosphere on a large scale as a by-product of human activity.

Moulin: ice shaft at the bottom of an ice sheet that carries melt water down beneath the ice to the bedrock, which lubricates the base of the ice and speeds it movement into the ocean.

Little Ice Age: the period between roughly 1300 – 1800 CE when the worldwide temperature was cooler than it is today.

Dansgaard-Oeschger Event: wild swings of temperature, rising as much as 50 degrees in 50 years then falling back down again, which has happened 25 times in the last 15,000 years at irregular intervals and for unknown reasons.

Climatic tipping point or **threshold**: point at which a developing climate effect passes the "point of no return," when the new effects cannot be reversed.

Climate ethnography: a possible way for anthropology to help address climate change by focusing on the experiences and responses of individual communities to climate change, and combining them into a multi-sited ethnographic account directed towards finding ways to construct adaptation and resilience, by learning the language of science and developing effective forms of communication and collaboration.

SCHEMA ACTIVATION ACTIVITY

Think about your own experiences of weather in the last five years (or weather events you heard about elsewhere) and *describe three weather events that seemed unusual to you, and the effect the events had on the local community.*

(Save these to share later in your discussion sections.)

INTRODUCTION

The literature of climate change is huge, but the most dramatic demonstration that the earth's climate is indeed changing, is the story told by ice. In this chapter, you will read about the dramatic changes in inland and high-altitude glaciers. Then you will read a short piece about the politics of the climate change debate, which may be so confined to one particular moment (in

2015) that you need to do some research on to consider whether the argument of that article still holds true. What is not really at issue is that the academic and scientific communities as a whole strongly maintain that we have entered a new geologic epoch, the Anthropocene. The "-cene" part of this word and other words like it (Holocene, Pleistocene) is from the Greek work *kainos*, which means "new" or "recent." *Anthropos*, as you now recognize, means "human." The most recent geologic epochs are called "_____ recent"—the Holocene means "entirely recent" and the epoch before that, the Pleistocene, means "most recent." (The terms are distinctly odd but are now hallowed by common use.) So, the Anthropocene is the "human recent" and indicates that our effect on the planet is dominant. Your first reading talks about "forcing mechanisms"—the processes which are "forcing" the climate of the world to change.

Understanding Global Climate Change: Paleoclimate Perspective from the World's Highest Mountains[1]

LONNIE G. THOMPSON

Distinguished University Professor of Earth Sciences
The Ohio State University

ABSTRACT.   Glaciers are among the world's best recorders of, and first responders to, natural and anthropogenic climate change and provide a time perspective for current climatic and environmental variations. Over the last 50 years such records have been recovered from the polar regions as well as low-latitude, high-elevation ice fields. Analyses of these ice cores and of the glaciers from which they have been drilled have yielded three lines of evidence for past and present abrupt climate change: (1) the temperature and precipitation histories recorded in the glaciers as revealed by the climate records extracted from the ice cores; (2) the accelerating loss of the glaciers themselves; and (3) the uncovering of ancient fauna and flora from the margins of the glaciers as a result of their recent melting, thus illustrating the significance of the current ice loss. The current melting of high-altitude, low-latitude ice fields is consistent with model predictions for a vertical amplification of temperature in the tropics. The ongoing rapid retreat of the world's mountain glaciers, as well as the margins of the Greenland and Antarctic ice sheets, is not only contributing to global sea level rise, but also threatening fresh-water supplies in many of the most populous regions. More recently, strong evidence has appeared for the acceleration of the rate of ice loss in the tropics, which especially presents a clear and present danger to water supplies for at-risk populations in South America and Asia. The human response to this issue, however, is not so clear, for although the evidence from both data and models becomes more compelling, the rate of global CO_2 emissions continues to accelerate. Climatologically, we are in unfamiliar territory, and the world's ice cover is responding dramatically. The loss of glaciers, which can be viewed as the world's water towers, threatens water resources that are essential for hydroelectric power, crop irrigation, municipal water supplies, and even tourism. As these glaciers are disappearing, we are also losing very valuable paleoclimate archives.

---

[1] Read 14 November 2008, as part of the symposium "Action Not Words."

THE CLIMATE OF A REGION is defined as the average weather over an extended period, at least in reference to the average human lifespan. It is often measured with respect to variations in temperature and precipitation over interannual to millennial time scales. The world's climate is driven (or "forced") both internally by atmospheric, oceanic, cryospheric, and vegetative changes, and externally by changes in the amount of solar energy reaching the Earth. The variations in the Earth's orbit around the Sun, or orbital parameters, can affect the baseline climate of the entire planet over decades to hundreds of thousands of years. Incoming solar (or insolation) changes influence terrestrial temperatures and oceanic and atmospheric temperatures and circulations, which govern the expansion and retreat of ice sheets and glaciers, the rise and fall of sea levels, and vegetative cover. Recently imprinted on these natural variations are the climatic effects of a human population that has been increasing exponentially since the middle of the nineteenth century, along with the accompanying demands for energy, living space, and food.

Today the popular media refer to climate change primarily with respect to temperature, as demonstrated by the use of the term "global warming" to describe the average rise of 0.11°F per decade over the last century (NOAA State of the Climate Global Analysis 2009, http://www.ncdc.noaa.gov/sotc/?report=global&year=2009&month=13&submitted=Get+Report#trends). Since the late 1970s, this rate has more than doubled to 0.29°F per decade, and 11 of the warmest years on record have occurred in the last 12 years. Since these numbers are based on global averages, they do not reflect regional variations. For example, according to the National Climate Data Center, since 1970 the average annual temperature in the western United States has been rising more rapidly (0.46°F per decade) than in the southeastern part of the country (0.26°F per decade) (http://www.ncdc.noaa.gov/oa/climate/research/cag3/cag3.html). The recent changes are also seasonally inconsistent; for example, on average winters are warming faster than summers in the United States (Meehl et al. 2007). However, the most severe temperature increases appear to be concentrated in the polar regions as well as within the interiors of the large continents. In many of these cases the current changes are unique compared with those over the last several thousand years, in terms of both their rates and their geographic occurrences.

Paleoclimatologists not only strive to reconstruct past climate variations on regional to global scales, but also try to determine the forcing mechanisms, both natural and anthropogenic, that influence climate changes. This information is instrumental for placing the current climate into perspective, and for supplying data for computer models that project future scenarios. It is the role of paleoclimatologists to reconstruct records of temperature and precipitation variability over hundreds to thousands of years from geological and biological "media" that preserve evidence of these variations. Climate proxy data come from a variety of sources, such as written and historical records, corals, tree rings, glacial moraines, and cores. Cores are drilled from ocean and lake sediments and glaciers, and produce continuous climate records that vary from high (seasonal) to low (millennial) resolution.

It is climatic and environmental histories from ice cores that will be discussed in more detail here. A judiciously selected collection from all over the world has provided high-resolution archives of regional and global climate. In addition to the continuous, high-resolution records that glaciers and ice sheets produce, the rapid retreat of their margins also provides some of the most visible evidence for the recent changes.

MECHANISMS OF CLIMATE CHANGE

Natural forcing mechanisms

Since the dawn of human civilization, climate changes have been governed by both natural and anthropogenic processes; however, until the onset of the Industrial Revolution the natural causes were dominant. The most important natural forcing factor external to the Earth arises from variations in solar energy that reach the atmosphere and the surface. These variations occur in cycles, and the one most relevant to the human life span is the 11–12-year sunspot cycle. Much more influential on the Earth's long-term climate are the orbital variations of the Earth, which at 22,000 to 100,000 years in duration are orders of magnitude longer than the human lifespan and even human civilizations (Milankovitch 1930). These are in large part responsible for both the glacial periods during which large regions at high and middle latitudes are covered by thick ice sheets, and the warm interglacial periods such as the present Holocene epoch, which began about 10,000 years ago (Croll 1864; Milankovitch 1930; Hays et al. 1976).

Under natural conditions, the Earth's temperature is influenced internally by short- and long-term changes in the atmosphere and ocean. Short-term cooling can result from the injection of volcanic dust into the atmosphere following a massive eruption close to the equator, such as the 1991 Mt. Pinatubo event in the Philippines (Minnis et al. 1993). Other widespread but relatively short-lived variations in temperature and precipitation are associated with the linked oceanic/atmospheric system in the equatorial Pacific Ocean known as El Niño-Southern Oscillation. However, some regional climatic changes may last for decades or even centuries, such as the "Little Ice Age," which occurred between the sixteenth and nineteenth centuries (depending on location) and the preceding "Medieval Warming" between the tenth and twelfth centuries. The causes of these events are not completely understood, but they may be related to changes in oceanic circulation that may be triggered by solar intensity anomalies.

Anthropogenic forcing mechanisms

Records of atmospheric CO_2 and methane concentrations over the past several hundred thousand years have been recovered from ice cores drilled through the Antarctic ice sheet. These data show us that the levels of these so-called "greenhouse" gases have never been higher over the last 800,000 years than they are today (Loulergue et al. 2008; Lüthi et al. 2008). Numerous studies, beginning with Arrhenius (1896), have established linkages between atmospheric concentrations of CO_2 and CH_4 and temperature.

Human activity has also altered regional climate in other ways. For example, aerosols such as sulfates, which are the by-products of the burning of fossil fuels in power plants, may have a cooling effect, since they tend to block incoming short-wave solar radiation. Particles known as black carbon result from industrial activity and vegetation burning, which occurs in natural forest fires and during the process of forest clearing, particularly in the equatorial regions. Humans have also caused changes in the planet's reflectivity, or albedo, as darker forest regions are transformed into lighter cropland, grasslands are paved to facilitate transportation, and ice sheets and sea ice melt away to expose darker land and ocean water.

On the relationship between solar output and modern climate warming

When it comes to determining the validity of and causes for anthropogenic climate change, scientists look at the balance of evidence. Some have argued that the variations that we have experienced over recent decades are driven by changes in the Sun's energy output, which are governed by the 11-year sunspot cycle. However, these short-term solar variations are believed to have only minor influence on the Earth's climate, as the irradiance varied by 0.1% over the last two cycles (Fröhlich and Lean 2004). Models predict (and the data show) that in today's world the stratosphere is cooling as the planetary surface warms (Meehl et al. 2007). However, under natural conditions variations in the Sun's energy should cause similar temperature trends in both the troposphere and stratosphere, not the opposite trends that we currently see. In addition, nighttime and winter temperatures have increased at a greater rate than daytime and summer temperatures, which would not be expected if the Sun were driving those changes. High latitudes, which receive less sunlight than low latitudes, have nevertheless experienced greater warming, again the opposite of what would be expected if the Sun were the primary climate forcer.

EVIDENCE OF CLIMATE CHANGE FROM GLACIERS AND ICE SHEETS

Glacier ice is one of the most versatile and highly resolved recorders of the Earth's climate. Although they are restricted to regions where temperatures remain largely below freezing year-round, glaciers and ice sheets occur from the equatorial tropics to the polar regions (fig. 1). They can store anything that is found in the atmosphere, such as precipitation, gases, dust, salts, fallout from volcanic eruptions and above-ground thermonuclear emissions, emissions from biological activity, and even cosmic energy bombardment of chemical species in the atmosphere. Temperature records can be derived from isotopes (atoms of the same element but of different weights) of oxygen and hydrogen, the constituents of water and ice. The large variety of information available from the analysis of glacier ice is listed in figure 2.

Because the Earth is nearly spherical, 50% of the surface lies between 30°N and 30°S, which is the geographical definition of the tropics. It is also a region that contains immense thermal energy that is instrumental in driving the planet's weather systems. Many areas of the tropics are located in monsoon climates, which are characterized by distinct dry winters and wet summers. In glaciated mountain regions, the ice records these seasonal variations as thin dust laminae alternating with thick, cleaner layers (fig. 2). When an ice core is drilled through a tropical glacier, these alternating dark and light layers, constituting yearly cycles, can be counted back in time, so that they are analogous to tree rings. The ice can also record the seasonal variations in atmospheric dust content and variations in the ratio of heavy to light oxygen isotopes ($\delta^{18}O$), which are controlled by a variety of meteorological factors such as temperature and precipitation sources and amounts. Analysis of an ice core produces data showing these seasonal signals, which are useful for establishing a time scale, or chronology, for the climate record. One example of this type of ice core comes from the Dasuopu ice cap in the central Himalayas. A section of the record from this

Polar Regions

Huascarán, Peru

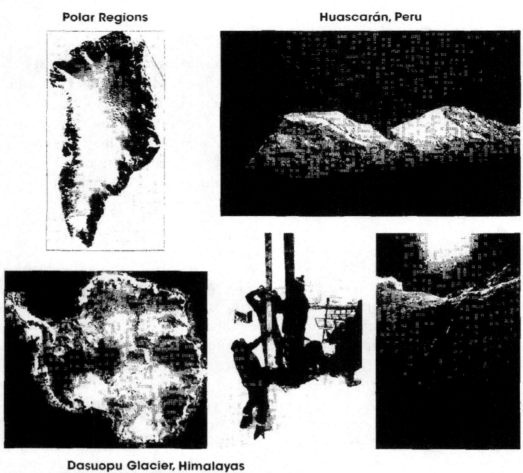

Dasuopu Glacier, Himalayas

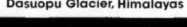

FIGURE 1. Ice cores provide unique climate histories from the polar to the tropical regions. Huascarán (6768 m) is the highest tropical mountain in the Andes of Peru, while Dasuopu (7,200 m) is the highest drill site drilled.

C

Environmental Data Include:

A Temperature ($\delta^{18}O$)
B Atmospheric Chemistry
C Net Accumulation
D Dustiness of Atmosphere
E Vegetation Changes
F Volcanic History
G Anthropogenic Emissions
H Entrapped Microorganisms

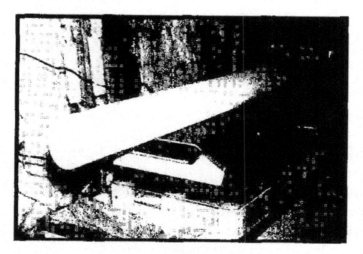

FIGURE 2.   Ice cores provide several lines on climatic and environmental data. The longitudinal view of a core (top) shows wet and dry seasons that are recorded as clear and dark layers, respectively. The variety of data that can be recovered from the analysis of the ice is listed. Center: An ice core is extracted from a drill barrel. Photo by Lonnie Thompson. Bottom: The mass of a core section is measured on a balance in a field laboratory. Photo by Ellen Mosley-Thompson.

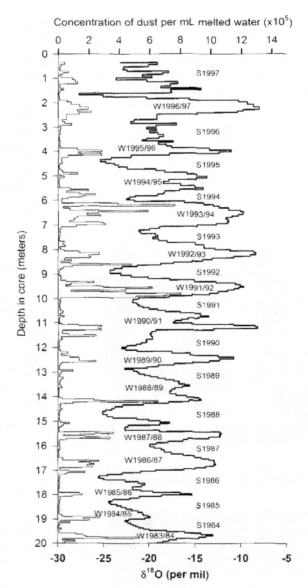

FIGURE 3. Data from the analysis of the top 20 meters of an ice core from the Dasuopu ice cap, Central Himalayas in Tibet, which was drilled in the summer of 1997. The diagram shows wet (summer) and dry (winter) seasonal variations in dust and oxygen isotopic ratios. Using these two measurements, this section of the ice core can be dated by counting the oscillations. Each year is marked on the figure, and the seasons are denoted by "S" (summer) and "W" (winter).

core, which illustrates the regular seasonality of the oxygen isotopic ratios and eolian (windblown) dust is shown in figure 3. The $\delta^{18}O$ shows summer and winter values that oscillate with the concentrations of dust. By counting these annual cycles an ice core can be dated at the top. Using these and other techniques, records can be extracted that document changes in climate and environment over hundreds to thousands of years. Because these records are long, continuous, and of high temporal resolution and contain information on numerous physical and chemical properties of the atmosphere, they are invaluable for providing relatively precise histories of climatic events that occurred during human development, but before humans had a significant influence over their environment.

Evidence from the Ice of Abrupt Climate Change in the Past

According to the National Research Council (2002), abrupt climate change is defined as the condition when "the climate system is forced to cross some threshold, triggering a transition to a new state at a rate determined by the climate system itself and faster than the cause." It "takes place so rapidly and unexpectedly that human or natural systems have trouble adapting to it." Because they produce high-resolution records of climate, ice cores have been valuable in the study of past abrupt climate change. One of the most remarkable examples was a sudden cold, wet event that occurred 5,200 years ago, and left its mark in many paleoclimate records around the world.[2] A record of this event comes from the ice fields atop Mt. Kilimanjaro in Tanzania, which shows a very intense and sudden decrease in the $\delta^{18}O$ levels (Thompson et al. 2002). Such a decrease is indicative of lower temperatures and/or more intense snowfall. This anomalously cold/wet climate lasted a relatively short time (at least in many places), perhaps a few decades, before the climate just as abruptly reverted to its previous state. A possible link to this anomalous cooling is observed in the methane records from the Greenland ice cores, which show that during the Holocene[3] epoch the lowest concentration of this gas occurred 5,200 years ago (Chappellaz et al. 1997; Raynaud et al. 2000). The cause of this methane decrease, and its implied link to the mid-Holocene cold event, are still not fully understood.

Several sudden recent appearances of long-buried fauna and flora resulting from rapidly melting alpine ice confirm the timing and severity of this abrupt climate reversal. Arguably the most famous is "Otzi" or the "Tyrolean ice man," whose remarkably preserved body was discovered in the Alps in 1991 when it was uncovered by a retreating glacier. When his remains were radiocarbon-dated, it was discovered that he died (the forensic evidence suggests he was murdered) and was quickly buried in permanent snow cover around ~5,200 years ago

---

[2] There are also numerous examples of this event that come from sources other than glaciers. Along the southern margin of Lake Tahoe in the Sierra Nevada Range there are trees preserved underwater. Examination of the trunks shows that the forest was immersed in rising water about 5,000 years ago. The preserved condition of the trees indicates that the water in the lake has remained high ever since (Lindstrom 1990). The Soreq Cave in Israel contains speleothems that have produced continuous climate records that cover several tens of thousands of years. As in the Kilimanjaro ice-core record, the Soreq Cave record shows that this abrupt cooling also occurred in the Middle East, and that it was the most extreme climatic event in the last 13,000 years (Bar-Mathews et al. 1999).

[3] The Holocene is the warm period since the end of the last ice age, or glacial stage. It is generally considered to cover the last 10,000 years.

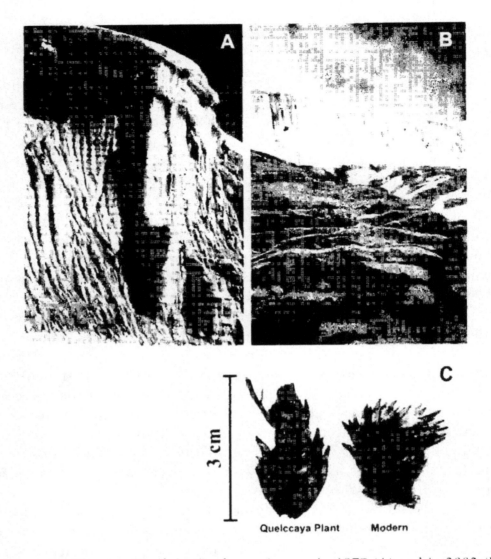

FIGURE 4. The margin of the Quelccaya ice cap in 1977 (A) and in 2002 (B). Photos by Lonnie G. Thompson. The retreat of this ice wall exposed several ancient plants (C, left) which were dated at 5,200 years ago and were identified as *Distichia muscoides*. A modern plant is shown (C, right) (Thompson et al. 2006).

(Baroni and Orombelli 1996). In other locations around the world, plants are being exposed for the first time in 5,200 years as glaciers are melting and shrinking in size. The margin of the Quelccaya ice cap in southern Peru is shown in figure 4A as it was in 1977; however, this margin has since melted back, and figure 4B shows that by 2002 a small lake had replaced the ice wall. At the base of the wall, a perfectly preserved wetland plant deposit, which contains no woody tissue, was discovered. It was identified as *Distichia muscoides* (fig. 4C), which today grows in the valleys below Quelccaya, and was radiocarbon-dated at ~5,200 years before present (Thompson et al. 2006). This is strong

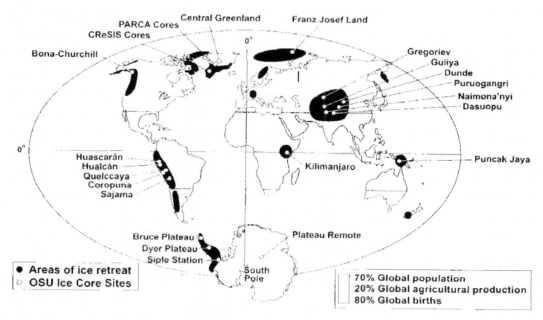

FIGURE 5. Global view of retreating ice over the twentieth to the twenty-first centuries, as shown by dark gray shading. The lighter shading depicts the geographical tropics. Sites where the Ohio State University has conducted ice-core drilling programs are shown.

evidence that this ice cap has not been smaller than its present size for more than five millennia. As the glacier continues to retreat, more plants have been collected and radiocarbon-dated, almost all of which confirm the original findings (Buffen et al. 2009).

LOSS OF GLACIERS IN TODAY'S WORLD

The world's cryosphere is in retreat as the tropospheric temperatures warm (fig. 5). Today glaciers cover about 10% of the Earth's surface area, compared with 30% coverage during the coldest part of the last ice age. Because this warming is amplified at high altitude (Bradley et al. 2006), the loss of ice is most drastic in mountainous areas such as the Andes and the Tibetan Plateau. The rising temperatures in the polar regions are especially troubling, as these are the locations of the largest ice sheets in the world.

Ice decline in the polar regions

Ninety-five percent of all the ice on the Earth is located in Antarctica and Greenland.[4] More than 30 years ago the late John Mercer, a professor

_____

[4] This comes to ~14.52 × 10⁶ km² of ice cover in Greenland and Antarctica.

at the Ohio State University, predicted that the first consequence of a warming climate linked to atmospheric CO_2 increase would be the breakup of the Antarctic ice shelves in a north to south direction (Mercer 1978). Average temperature on the Antarctic Peninsula has risen 2.5°C in the last 50 years, resulting in the breakup of the ice shelves in just the way Mercer foresaw. One of the most rapid of these deteriorations occurred in 2002, when the Larsen B collapsed in just 31 days. It is not the breakup of these ice shelves that contributes to sea level rise, since they are already floating and thus displacing sea water. However, because they serve as buttresses to land-based glaciers, their disappearance causes the ice flow to increase three to eight fold (Scambos et al. 2004). It is this effect that contributes to sea level rise.

Satellite documentation of the sea ice in the Arctic Ocean extends back three decades. Arctic sea ice cover (measured each September) decreased at a rate of about 8.6% per decade from 1979 to 2007, and in the year between September 2006 and September 2007, 24% of the ice disappeared, although in the last two years it has recovered ~13% (Perovich and Richter-Menge 2009). In 2006 the Northwest Passage was ice-free for the first time in recorded history. This presents advantages for ships, but it poses major problems for the indigenous people and animals of this region. Sea ice reflects solar radiation back to space; thus as sea-ice cover shrinks more dark ocean is exposed, which absorbs more incoming radiation. As this proceeds, a "feedback loop" develops in which the warming water melts more ice, which in turn increases the surface area of the ocean. Eventually one reaches the potential for a "tipping point" from which there may be little chance for recovery.[5]

The Greenland ice sheet has also experienced dramatic ice melt over the recent years, particularly in the Northern Hemisphere summer. There has been an increase in both the number and the size of lakes on the southern part of the ice sheet, and crevices often appear below the lakes. Water has been observed flowing through these crevices (moulins) down to the bottom of the ice sheet, where it acts as a lubricant that speeds the flow of basal ice (Zwally et al. 2002; Das et al. 2008). In the last decade, many glaciers draining Greenland and West Antarctica have accelerated their discharge to the ocean by 20% to 100%, but this has been highly variable over shorter time intervals.[6]

---

[5] The theory of climatic tipping points or thresholds is relatively new and is a very important line of research for paleoclimatologists and climate modelers to investigate.

[6] None of the most recent reports by the IPCC (2007) took into account these abrupt recent changes in ice flow, which have the potential to cause sea level to rise faster than predicted.

Tropical atmospheric temperatures tend to remain fairly uniform throughout the year. Alpine glaciers at these latitudes are located in the mid-troposphere (~15,000–20,000 feet above sea level), where persistent warming has been amplified over the last several decades. The smaller, thinner mountain glaciers of the world respond more quickly to changing climate than the massive polar ice sheets, since their surface area to volume ratio is much greater. Although alpine glaciers constitute only 3.6% of the world's ice cover, their rapid rate of melting in comparison with the large polar ice sheets may cause them to contribute more to sea level rise in the short term. Currently, 60% of the land-based ice loss is occurring on the small glaciers and ice caps. The ice loss from mountain glaciers may raise sea level ~0.25 meters by 2100 (Meier et al. 2007). Although global ice retreat at the beginning of the twenty-first century is driven mainly by increasing temperatures, regional factors such as deforestation and precipitation deficits can impact individual glaciers.

There are several documented examples of alpine glacier retreat throughout the world. A study of 67 glaciers in Alaska from the mid-1950s to the mid-1990s shows that all are thinning, and subsequent measurement on 28 of these in the following years shows that the thinning rate has been increasing (Arendt et al. 2002). In the Brooks Range of northern Alaska, 100% of the glaciers are in retreat, while in southeastern Alaska 98% are shrinking (Molnia 2007). When Glacier National Park in Montana was established in 1910, there were 150 glaciers within it. This number is currently down to 26, and it is estimated that by 2030, at the present rate of decrease, no glaciers will remain in the park (Hall and Fagre 2003).

Two of the most carefully documented case studies of alpine glacier retreat are on Kilimanjaro and on the Quelccaya ice cap in the Peruvian Andes. Using a combination of terrestrial photogrammetric maps, satellite images, and aerial photographs, it has been determined that the combined ice fields on Kibo, the highest crater on Kilimanjaro, have lost 85% of their surface area since 1912 (Thompson et al. 2009). At the current rate of retreat, it is estimated that Kibo will be ice-free in the next few decades for the first time in 11,700 years. Continued monitoring of these ice fields shows the extent to which their disappearance is accelerating. The deterioration of the Furtwängler Glacier, which lies in the center of Kibo, is shown in figure 6 as a series of aerial photographs from 2000 to 2007, when the glacier actually split into two sections. As it is shrinking in size, it is also thinning rapidly from 9.5 meters in 2000 to 4.7 meters in 2009.

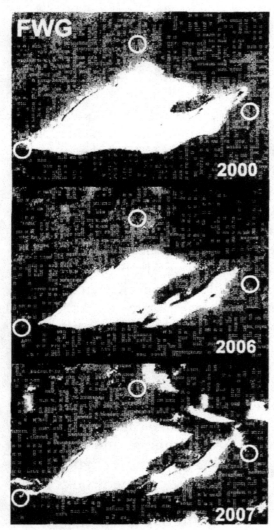

FIGURE 6. The Furtwängler glacier in the center of the Kibo crater on Mt. Kilimanjaro has been vanishing at a rapid rate over the last decade, as shown by the series of aerial photographs on the left. In 2007 the glacier divided into two sections. Qori Kalis, an outlet glacier on the Quelccaya ice cap, has been retreating at an accelerating pace as shown by the map (below) and the plot of ice terminus retreat over time. The melting of the Qori Kalis, and the growth of the forelake, are shown pictorially along the bottom. Photos by paleoclimate ice core team.

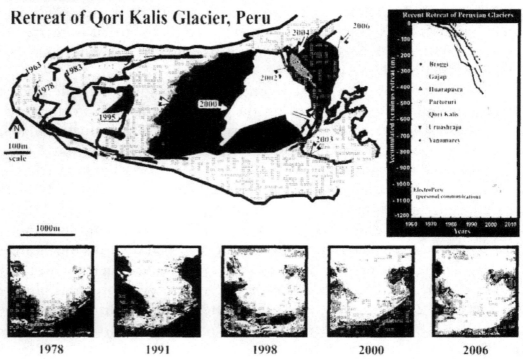

216

The Quelccaya ice cap, which is located in southern Peru adjacent to the Amazon Basin, is the largest tropical ice field on Earth. The Qori Kalis outlet glacier has been measured and photographed since 1963. At the beginning of the study the snout of the glacier extended 1,200 meters out from the ice cap, and there was no melt water at the terminus. By the summer of 2008 Qori Kalis had completely retreated to the edge of Quelccaya, and an 84-acre, 60 m deep lake had developed in its place (fig. 6). The work on this glacier has also documented an accelerating rate of ice loss: from 1963 to 1978 the retreat was calculated as a rate of about 6 m per year, but from 1991 to 2006 it was losing ice ten times faster on average than the initial rate (Thompson et al. 2006). This loss of ice from Quelccaya is not only occurring on the Qori Kalis glacier, but in fact is occurring on the margin of the ice cap itself, as shown in figure 4. Since 1978, 25% of this tropical ice cap has disappeared.

The amount of loss suffered by individual glaciers in many regions has been photographically documented through the twentieth century and into the twenty-first century. An example is the Qoyllur Rit'i glacier in Southern Peru, which is located at the site of an annually observed religious festival. Figure 7A is a photograph of the ice cover in 1935, and figure 7B is a photograph taken at approximately the same location in 2006. The overlap of these two pictures (fig. 7C) provides a view of the extent of the ice retreat over the 71-year interval. The glacier has retreated so much, in fact, that the participants in the religious rites are no longer permitted to carry away pieces of the ice that they regard as sacred (Kormann 2009).

The Himalaya Mountains are home to more than 15,000 glaciers that constitute a very important component of the dry season water supply for India, Nepal, and southern China via the major rivers of the region. Unfortunately, only a few of the glaciers have been monitored over an extended period, so reliable ground observations, which are crucial for determining ice retreat rates, do not yet exist. However, a recent study on an ice core from the Naimona'nyi Glacier in the southwestern Himalayas (Kehrwald et al. 2008) shows that ice is disappearing from the top of the glacier, as shown by the lack of the radioactive bomb horizons from the 1950s and early 1960s that appear in all Tibetan and Himalayan ice-core records (Thompson et al. 1990; 1997; 2000; 2006b).

The glaciologists at the Institute of Tibetan Plateau Research in Beijing have been monitoring 612 glaciers across the High Asian region since 1980. They have found that from 1980 to 1990, 90% of these glaciers were retreating, and from 1990 to 2005, this increased to 95% (Yao et al. 2007). Meteorological records from the Tibetan Plateau and

FIGURE 7. The Qoyllur Rit'i glacier in the Andes of Southern Peru photographed in (A) 1935 (photo by Martin Chambi) and in (B) 2006 (photo by Mary Davis). The extent of the ice retreat over 71 years is shown in the overlap of the two photos (C).

the Himalayas are scarce and of relatively short duration, most beginning in the mid-1950s to early 1960s; however, those that do exist show that surface temperatures are rising, and rising faster at higher elevations than at lower elevations (Liu and Chen 2000). The Tibetan Plateau has been warming at a rate of 0.16°C per decade, with winter temperatures rising 0.32°C per decade. A newly published paper by Matsuo and Heki (2010) shows that from 2003 to 2009 the average ice loss from the Asian high ice fields, as measured by GRACE (Gravity Recovery and Climate Experiment) satellite observations, had accelerated twice as fast as the rate four decades before, but the loss was not consistent over space and time. Ice retreat in the Himalayas slowed slightly, while loss in the mountains to the northwest increased markedly over the last few years.

Thus, taking into consideration the surface temperature measurements, the satellite studies, the ground studies on glaciers, and ice core results, a case can be made that glacier retreat at high elevations is indeed occurring concomitantly with increasing temperatures. This is consistent with the model results discussed in the IPCC report (Giorgi et al. 2001; IPCC 2007), which show not only low-latitude warming but an amplification of that warming at higher elevations where these glaciers are located. A projected planetary scale rise of 2 to 4.5°C between 1990–99 and 2090–99 translates to a 5 to more than 10°C increase over 18,000 feet above sea level (inferred from fig. 1 in Bradley et al. 2006), endangering even the highest alpine glaciers.

CLIMATOLOGICAL SIGNIFICANCE OF THE RECENT WARMING AND THE WORLD'S ICE LOSS

The loss of ice is accelerating throughout the tropics, and this has been directly observed in the Himalayas, on Kilimanjaro, and in the Andes. Rising temperatures are driven by water vapor feedback in the climate system, which has potential ramifications for the Earth's future climate, since it is linked to the circulation of the Hadley cell. This is the major atmospheric circulation between the equatorial latitudes, where annual precipitation is the highest, and the outer rims of the tropics at ~30°N and ~30°S, where the Earth's major deserts are located. The rising arm of the Hadley cell is located near the equator, and at the surface below this warm air lies the Intertropical Convergence Zone (ITCZ). As the warm, moist air rises and cools, the maximum latent heat release occurs at the 500 mbar level (Webster 2004), the altitude where tropical glaciers are located. There is evidence that over the last 20 years this cell has expanded north and south by about 2° of latitude, which may broaden the desert zones (Seidel et al. 2007; Seidel and Randel 2008) as the dry descending arms move poleward. Under this scenario droughts might become more persistent, not only in the American Southwest, but in the Mediterranean and in the Southern Hemisphere (Australia and parts of South America and Africa).

As recorded in a compilation of ice cores recovered from low-latitude glaciers, the twentieth century was the warmest in the past 2,000 years (fig. 8A) (Thompson et al. 2006a). This is in agreement with Northern Hemisphere temperature reconstructions (Jones and Mann 2004) and more modern meteorological observations (Jones and Moberg 2003) (fig. 8B). That a similar profile can be determined independently by so many different paleoclimate recorders gives us confidence that the warming trend at the end of the twentieth century and the beginning of the twenty-first century is unprecedented in at least the last two millennia. However, individual ice-core records indicate that in

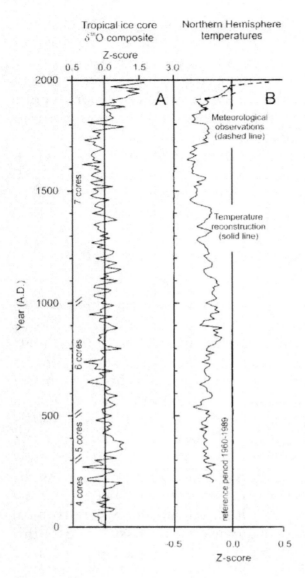

Tropical ice core
δ¹⁸O composite

Northern Hemisphere
temperatures

Z-score

FIGURE 8. (A) 2,000-year record of temperature variations reconstructed from an array of tropical ice cores from the Andes and the Tibetan Plateau (Thompson et al. 2000a). (B) Reconstructed temperature records (Jones and Mann 2004) from a variety of proxy data over a comparable time period, overlain by meteorological data (Jones and Moberg 2003) since the mid-nineteenth century.

some regions the twentieth century was the warmest in more than 5,000 years. The implications of the recent ice loss from Kilimanjaro in Africa and Naimona'nyi in the Himalayas are disturbing, given projections of warming in the twenty-first century at high elevations in these low-latitude regions. The observed rapid glacier flow in Greenland and Antarctica is not predicted by current climate models, which assume a slow, linear response to climate change. Glaciers in most parts of the world are melting within generational timescales, and the consequences could potentially affect billions of people.

Over most of the twentieth century, sea level has risen about 2.0 mm per year, and ~50% of the recorded rise has been caused by thermal expansion of the ocean water. Because they respond to climate change so quickly, the mountain glaciers have contributed about 27%

to global sea level rise between 1993 and 2003, while the more slowly reacting polar ice sheets account for only 15% (IPCC 2007, WGI, table 5.3). Since 1990, sea level has accelerated to a rate of about 3.1 ± 0.7 mm per year, and in the last decade many of the glaciers draining Greenland and Antarctica have accelerated their discharge rate into the world's oceans (IPCC 2007). Since these changes are highly variable, and long records of these variations are lacking, the paths of future trends are unpredictable.

SOCIETAL SIGNIFICANCE OF THE WORLD'S ICE LOSS

Within the geographic tropics reside 70% of the world's 6.8 billion people. For many countries, some of which are in economic peril, alpine glaciers are valuable water resources for hydroelectric power production, crop irrigation, and municipal water supplies. Peru relies on hydroelectric power for 80% of its energy (Vergara et al. 2007), and a significant portion of that comes from mountain streams that are fed by mountain glaciers and ice fields. In Tanzania, the loss of Kilimanjaro's fabled ice cover is already impacting tourism, which is the country's primary source of foreign currency. Even in California, one of the wealthiest regions in the world, the glaciers and snowpacks in the Rocky Mountain Range complex are essential for agriculture.

As discussed above, the rate of average sea level rise, as well as the contribution from melting of alpine glaciers and polar ice sheets, has accelerated over the last 20 years. It would *not require* the loss of much of the total ice cover before catastrophic consequences ensue. If the Earth lost only 8% of its ice, the effects on some coastal regions would be dramatic. Low-lying areas such as the southern part of the Florida peninsula and much of southern Louisiana would be submerged, and major coastal cities such as New York and Shanghai would be endangered (Overpeck and Weiss 2009). Low-lying continental countries such as the Netherlands and much of Bangladesh find themselves battling flooding at an ever-increasing frequency. Already many small island nations in the western Pacific such as Vanuatu are facing imminent destruction as they are gradually overrun by the rising ocean surface. Currently, Indonesia has more than 17,000 islands, and many of them are at sea level. At the 2007 United Nations Climate Change Conference in Bali, Indonesian environmental minister Rachmat Witoelar stated that 2,000 of his country's islands could be lost to sea level rise by 2030.

Society's options

Over the next twenty years the decisions that our societies make and the actions we take to address the crises of climate change and environmental degradation will be critical for determining the quality of life our descendants experience over the coming centuries. Human societies have three options for dealing with any crisis: mitigate, adapt, or suffer. Mitigation is proactive, and in the case of anthropogenic climate change it involves taking measures to reduce the pace and magnitude of the changes by altering the underlying causes. The obvious and most hotly debated remedies involve those that reduce the emissions of the radiative gases (especially CO_2 and methane) that are involved in trapping the Earth's outgoing longwave radiation, leading to lower atmosphere and surface warming. Another solution that has received recent widespread attention is to enhance the natural carbon sinks through expansion of forests, or by "burying" carbon in the ocean. This latter proposal is an example of several geo-engineering procedures (e.g., Govindasamy and Caldeira 2000; Wigley 2006); however, some of these solutions are considered to be radical and may lead to unintended consequences (Parkinson 2010).

Adaptation is reactive; it involves reducing the potential adverse impacts on societal well-being resulting from the by-products of climate change. This might include construction of sea barriers such as dikes and tidal barriers (similar to those in the Thames River near London), relocation of coastal towns and cities inland, changes in agricultural practices to counteract shifting weather patterns, and strengthening human and animal immunity to climate-related diseases.

The third option is suffering, in which humans are forced to endure the adverse impacts that cannot be staved off by either mitigation or adaptation. Those who are affected most by the environmental and climatic changes that are instigated by wealthy nations are the least likely to have the resources to adapt. It is a cruel irony that so many of these people also live in or near ecologically sensitive areas, such as grasslands (Outer Mongolia), drylands (Sudan and Ethiopia), mountain glaciers (the Quechua of the Peruvian Andes), and coastal lowlands (Bangladesh and the South Sea island region).

Carbon dioxide is a gas that has a very long residence time in the atmosphere. Even if all anthropogenic emissions were to cease immediately, it would take several decades for the tropospheric temperatures to respond. It is estimated that 20% of the CO_2 released today will be impacting the Earth's climate more than 1,000 years from now (Archer and Brovkin 2008). Considering the lack of will among the world's wealthiest and most populous nations (which are also the primary greenhouse gas emitters) to curb their carbon-based fuel consumption, as well as the rapid destruction of carbon sinks such as temperate and tropical forests to make more room for human activities, it would seem that adaptation is the most feasible option for the wealthy, while suffering is the main option left for the world's poor. As challenging as the understanding of climate change is, the human response to the changes can be even more challenging. Often when the subject of climate change arises, it is spoken of in reference to the effects on future generations. What is ignored or disputed is that detrimental effects of changing climate are visible today.

From the late 1980s until the middle of the current decade, the concepts of global-scale warming and climate change were accepted by much of the American media and the general public. This may have been a reaction to a series of extreme weather events, such as deadly summer heat waves affecting North America in 1988, 1995, 1998, 2001, and 2006 and the punishing hurricane seasons of 2005 and 2006. Average winter temperatures in the United States trended noticeably upward from 1980 to 2006. However, since the 2006 Hurricane Katrina disaster Americans have experienced relatively quiet hurricane seasons, and average annual temperatures over the U.S. have decreased over the last two years. This may have lulled many of us into a false sense of security in which we feel that the world's climate is recovering, and thus warnings about anthropogenic climate change can be dismissed as "alarmist hype." However, one glance at a diagram showing annual temperatures over the mainland United States since 1895 (fig. 9) shows that while temperatures have indeed oscillated up and down, the overall trend has been upward, and the next series of oscillations may peak at higher levels.

In the next 20 years the changing climate will become clear to most of us, not just to citizens of some of the less wealthy nations who are already experiencing some of the consequences. Since the concentrations of CO_2 and methane are the highest they have been in 800,000 years, climatologically we are in unfamiliar territory. One of the immediate casualties, the world's ice cover, is responding dramatically. Glaciers, especially tropical glaciers, are the "canaries in the coal mine" for our global climate system as they integrate and respond to most key climatological variables such as temperature, precipitation, cloudiness, humidity, and solar radiation. Many parts of the world will lose their mountain glaciers, which will have swift and adverse impacts on millions of people through seasonal depletion of agricultural and municipal water supplies, hydroelectric power production, and even tourism (e.g., the loss of the famed ice fields of Kilimanjaro). The potential shifting of position and intensity of atmospheric pressure systems, which may result from warming sea surface and lower atmospheric temperatures, could contribute to the migration of jet streams, fronts, and precipitation patterns. If the recently observed expansion of the tropical Hadley cell continues, we might expect droughts in the American

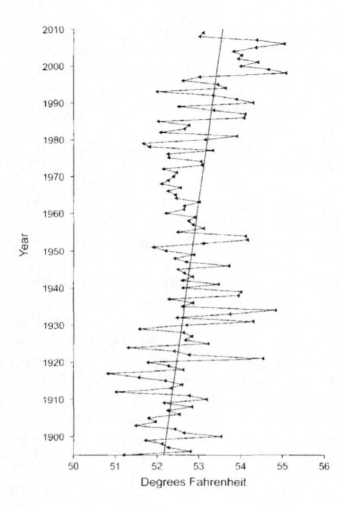

FIGURE 9. Annual average temperatures for the contiguous United States from 1895 to 2009. The straight line shows an upward trend of 0.12°F per decade. Data are from NOAA Satellite and Information Services Climate Monitoring Climate at a Glance Web site. (http://www.ncdc.noaa.gov/oa/climate/research/cag3/cag3.html).

Southwest, Mediterranean Sea region, and Australia to intensify. A hotly debated "wild card" in future climate scenarios is the relationship between Atlantic hurricane frequencies and sea surface temperatures (Vecchi et al. 2008). Considering the current data base and level of understanding of these linkages, we will probably require another 20 years before we are able to come to reliable conclusions about the nature of tropical storms in a changing climate.

REFERENCES

Archer, D., and V. Brovkin. 2008. Millennial atmospheric lifetime of anthropogenic CO_2. *Climatic Change* doi:10.1027/s10584-008-9413-1.

Arendt, A. A., K. A. Echelmeyer, W. D. Harrison, C. S. Lingle, and V. B. Valentine. 2002. Rapid wastage of Alaska glaciers and their contribution to rising sea level. *Science* 297:382–86.

Arrhenius, S. 1896. On the influence of carbonic acid in the air upon the temperature of the ground. *Philosophical Magazine* 41:237–76.

Bar-Matthews, M., A. Ayalon, A. Kaufman, and G. J. Wasserburg. 1999. The Eastern Mediterranean paleoclimate as a reflection of regional events: Soreq Cave, Israel. *Earth and Planetary Science Letters* 166:85–95.

Baroni, C., and G. Orombelli. 1996. The Alpine "Iceman" and Holocene climatic change. *Quaternary Research* 46:78–83.

Bradley, R. S., M. Vuille, H. F. Diaz, and W. Vergara. 2006. Threats to water supplies in the tropical Andes. *Science* 312:1755–56.

Buffen, A. M., L. G. Thompson, E. Mosley-Thompson, and K.-I. Huh. 2009. Recently exposed vegetation reveals Holocene changes in the extent of the Quelccaya ice cap, Peru. *Quaternary Research* 72:157–63.

Chappellaz, J., T. Blunier, S. Kints, A. Dällenbach, J.-M. Barnola, J. Schwander, D. Raynaud, and B. Stauffer. 1997. Changes in the atmospheric CH_4 gradient between Greenland and Antarctica during the Holocene. *Journal of Geophysical Research* 102:15,987–97.

Croll, J. 1864. On the physical cause of the change of climate during geological epochs. *Philosophical Magazine* 28:121–37.

Das, S. B., I. Joughin, M. D. Behn, I. M. Howat, M. A. King, D. Lizarralde, and M. P. Bhatia. 2008. Fracture propagation to the base of the Greenland ice sheet during supraglacial lake drainage. *Science* 320:778–81.

Fröhlich, C., and J. Lean. 2004. Solar radiative output and its variability: evidence and mechanisms. *Astronomy and Astrophysics Review* 12:273–320.

Giorgi, F., P. H. Whetton, R. G. Jones, J. H. Christensen, L. O. Mearns, B. Hewitson, H. vonStorch, R. Francisco, and C. Jack. 2001. Emerging patterns of simulated regional climatic changes for the 21st century due to anthropogenic forcings. *Geophysical Research Letters* 28:3317–20.

Govindasamy, B., and K. Caldeira. 2000. Geoengineering Earth's radiation balance to mitigate CO_2-induced climate change. *Geophysical Research Letters* 27:2141–44.

Hall, M.H.P., and D. B. Fagre. 2003. Modeled climate-induced glacier change in Glacier National Park, 1850–2100. *BioScience* 53:131–40.

Hays, J. D., J. Imbrie, and N. J. Shackleton. 1976. Variations in Earth's orbit—Pacemaker of ice ages. *Science* 194:1121–32.

Intergovernmental Panel on Climate Change. 2007. *Climate Change 2007: The Scientific Basis*. Cambridge: Cambridge University Press.

Jones, P. D., and M. E. Mann. 2004. Climate over past millennia. *Review of Geophysics* 42: doi:10.1029/2003RG000143.

Jones, P. D., and A. Moberg. 2003. Hemispheric and large-scale surface air temperature variations: An extensive revision and update to 2001. *Journal of Climate* 16:206–23.

Kehrwald, N. M., L. G. Thompson, T. Yao, E. Mosley-Thompson, U. Schotterer, V. Alfimov, J. Beer, J. Eikenberg, and M. E. Davis. 2008. Mass loss on Himalayan glacier endangers water resources. *Geophysical Research Letters* 35:L22503, doi:10/1029/2008GL035556.

Kormann, C. 2009. Last days of the glacier. *Virginia Quarterly Review*, 26–37, Spring.

Lindstrom, S. 1990. Submerged tree stumps as indicators of Mid-Holocene aridity in the Lake Tahoe basin. *Journal of California and Great Basin Anthropology* 12:146–57.

Loulergue, L., A. Schilt, R. Spahni, V. Masson-Delmotte, T. Blunier, B. Lemieux, J.-M. Barnola, D. Raynaud, T. F. Stocker, and J. Chappellaz. 2008. Orbital and millennial-scale features of atmospheric CH_4 over the past 800,000 years. *Nature* 453:383–86.

Liu, X., and B. Chen. 2000. Climatic warming in the Tibetan Plateau during recent decades. *International Journal of Climatology* 20:1729–42.

Lüthi, D., M. Le Floch, B. Bereiter, T. Blunier, J.-M. Barnola, U. Siegenthaler, D. Raynaud, J. Jouzel, H. Fischer, K. Kawamura, and T. F. Stocker. 2008. High-resolution carbon dioxide concentration record 650,000–800,000 years before present. *Nature* 453:379–82.

Matsuo, K., and K. Heki. 2010. Time-variable ice loss in Asian high mountains from satellite gravimetry. *Earth and Planetary Science Letters* 290:30–36.

Meehl, G. A., J. M. Arblaster, and C. Tebaldi. 2007. Contributions of natural and anthropogenic forcing to changes in temperature extremes over the United States. *Geophysical Research Letters* 34:L19709, doi:10.1029/2007GL030948.

Meier, M. F., M. B. Dyurgerov, U. K. Rick, S. O'Neel, W. T. Pfeffer, R. S. Anderson, S. P. Anderson, and A. F. Glazovsky. 2007. Glaciers dominate eustatic sea-level rise in the 21st century. *Science* 317:1064–67.

Mercer, J. H. 1978. West Antarctic ice sheet and CO2 greenhouse effect: a threat of disaster. *Nature* 271:321–25.

Milankovitch, M. 1930. *Mathematische Klimalehre und Astronomische Theorie der Klimaschwankungen. Handbuch der Klimalogie*, Band 1 Teil A. Berlin: Borntrager.

Minnis, P., E. F. Harrison, L. L. Stowe, G. G. Gibson, F. M. Denn, D. R. Doelling, and W. L. Smith. 1993. Radiative climate forcing by the Mount Pinatubo eruption. *Science* 259:1411–15.

Molnia, B. F. 2007. Late nineteenth to early twenty-first century behavior of Alaskan glaciers as indicators of changing regional climate. *Global and Planetary Change* 56:23–56.

National Research Council. 2002. *Abrupt Climate Change: Inevitable Surprises.* Washington, D.C.: National Academy Press.

Overpeck, J. T., and J. L. Weiss. 2009. Projections of future sea level becoming more dire. *Proceedings of the National Academy of Sciences* 106:21,461–62 doi:10/1073/pnas.0912878107.

Parkinson, C. L. 2010. *Coming Climate Crisis? Consider the Past, Beware the Big Fix.* Lanham, Md.: Rowland and Littlefield.

Perovich, D. K., and J. A. Richter-Menge. 2009. Loss of sea ice in the Arctic. *Annual Review of Marine Science* 1:417–41.

Raynaud, D., J.-M. Barnola, J. Chappellaz, T. Blunier, A. Indermühle, and B. Stauffer. 2000. The ice core record of greenhouse gases: A view in the context of future changes. *Quaternary Science Reviews* 19:9–17.

Scambos, T. A., J. A. Bohlander, C. A. Shuman, and P. Skvarca. 2004. Glacier acceleration and thinning after ice shelf collapse in the Larsen B embayment, Antarctica. *Geophysical Research Letters* 31:L18402, doi:10/1029/2004GL020670.

Seidel, D. J., Q. Fu, W. J. Randel, and T. J. Reichler. 2008. Widening of the tropical belt in a changing climate. *Nature Geoscience* 1:21–24.

Seidel, D. J., and W. J. Randel. 2007. Recent widening of the tropical belt: Evidence from tropopause observations. *Journal of Geophysical Research* 112:D20113, doi:10/1029/2007JD008861.

Thompson, L. G., H. H. Brecher, E. Mosley-Thompson, D. R. Hardy, and B. G. Mark. 2009. Glacier loss on Kilimanjaro continues unabated. *Proceedings of the National Academy of Sciences* 106:19,770–75.

Thompson, L. G., E. Mosley-Thompson, H. H. Brecher, M. E. Davis, B. Leon, D. Les, T. A. Mashiotta, P.-N. Lin, and K. Mountain. 2006a. Evidence of abrupt tropical climate change: past and present. *Proceedings of the National Academy of Sciences* 103:10,536–43.

Thompson, L. G., E. Mosley-Thompson, M. E. Davis, J. F. Bolzan, J. Dai, L. Klein, N. Gundestrup, T. Yao, X. Wu, and Z. Xie. 1990. Glacial stage ice-core records from the subtropical Dunde Ice Cap, China. *Annals of Glaciology* 14:288–97.

Thompson, L. G., E. Mosley-Thompson, M. E. Davis, K. A. Henderson, H. H. Brecher, V. S. Zagorodnov, T. A. Mashiotta, P.-N. Lin, V. N. Mikhalenko, D. R. Hardy, and J. Beer. 2002. Kilimanjaro ice core records: Evidence of Holocene climate change in tropical Africa. *Science* 289:589–93.

Thompson, L. G., T. Yao, M. E. Davis, K. A. Henderson, E. Mosley-Thompson, P.-N. Lin, J. Beer, H.-A. Synal, J. Cole-Dai, and J. F. Bolzan. 1997. Tropical climate instability: the last glacial cycle from a Qinghai-Tibetan ice core. *Science* 276:1821–25.

Thompson, L. G., T. Yao, M. E. Davis, E. Mosley-Thompson, T. A. Mashiotta, P.-N. Lin, V. N. Mikhalenko, and V. S. Zagorodnov. 2006b. Holocene climate variability archived in the Puruogangri ice cap in the central Tibetan Plateau. *Annals of Glaciology* 43:61–69.

Thompson, L. G., T. Yao, E. Mosley-Thompson, M. E. Davis, K. A. Henderson, and P.-N. Lin. 2000. A high-resolution millennial record of the South Asian Monsoon from Himalayan ice cores. *Science* 289:1916–19.

Vecchi, G. A., K. L. Swanson, and B. J. Soden. 2008. Climate Change: Whither Hurricane Activity? *Science* 322:687–89.

Vergara, W., A. M. Deeb, A. M. Valencia, R. S. Bradley, B. Francou, A. Zarzar, A. Grünwaldt, and S. M. Haeussling. 2007. Economic impacts of rapid glacier retreat in the Andes. *EOS* 88:261–68.

Webster, P. J. 2004. The Elementary Hadley Circulation. In *The Hadley Circulation: Past, Present and Future*, ed. H. Diaz and R. Bradley, 9–60. Cambridge: Cambridge University Press.

Wigley, T.M.L. 2006. A combined mitigation/geoengineering approach to climate stabilization. *Science* 314:452–54.

Yao, T., J. Pu, A. Lu, Y. Wang, and W. Yu. 2007. Recent glacial retreat and its impact on hydrological processes on the Tibetan Plateau, China and surrounding regions. *Arctic and Alpine Research* 39:642–50.

Zwally, H. J., W. Abdalati, T. Herring, K. Larson, J. Saba, and K. Steffen. 2002. Surface melt-induced acceleration of Greenland ice-sheet flow. *Science* 297:218–22.

The most important take-away from this article is the loss of ice which it documents. Most dramatically, Glacier National Park in Montana, when it was founded in 1910, had 150 glaciers. That number is now down to 26.

Looking at glaciers is an excellent way to appreciate climate change. It is completely anecdotal, but when flying back to the US from Iceland in 1996, my three-year old daughter suddenly said "Look at the mountains!" I thought that nonsense because we were over the North Atlantic. Of course, my daughter was looking at Greenland, a mass of snow-covered peaks and ice flowing into the ocean. Thirteen years later, flying from Amsterdam, I saw us over Greenland again. I was stunned. Instead of the snowy peaks and large masses of ice slowly sliding into the sea, I saw brown land mixed with white of snow and ice. Although it was August and the previous flight had been at the end of June, I could not believe that the difference was merely due to being more advanced into the summer.

Greenland

Needless to say, Greenland has been a focus of study for decades, inasmuch as it was understood early on that the character of Greenland's ice cover could be used as a barometer of the world's climate. (The ice cores there also recently have been studied to document industrial productivity in the Roman Empire, by determing times of greater lead production associated with the mining of silver.) The ice cover of Greenland is immense. The first measurements suggested that the ice cap was melting, but it did not seem dire at first. Scientists were taken by surprise by the phenomenon of the *moulin*, an ice shaft. No one could have predicted that these fissures take the melt-water from the surface of the ice and pour it down to the base of the ice where it acts as a lubricant between the ice and the rock and causes the ice to slide into the sea much faster than anticipated. The Jacobshavn Ice Stream was observed losing 6 feet per hour in 2012. On the other hand, the Dansgaard-Oeschger Events show wild swings of temperature, increasing by as much as 50 degrees in 50 years and then falling back down, happening at irregular intervals in Greeland over the last 15,000 years, with no apparent explanation. Could it be that we are in one of those events now? However, if that is the case and the temperature will go up 50 degrees, humanity will be brought to the brink of extinction.

Local Populations

Greenland and the mountain glaciers are a good example of how anthropology can document local effects on human populations to dramatically illustrate what is happening. For example, the town of Ilulissat in Greenland depends on its fishing industry. In the past, Disko Bay, on which the town sits, was inaccessible by sea in the winter. Now, it is ice free the entire year and the fisherman can ship their catches year-round, which is an economic boon to them. But really, isn't that a worry for the rest of us?

For example, many of the populations that live near the mountain glaciers depend on the melt from those glaciers for their water supply (and to attract tourists). With the disappearance of the ice, those populations are seriously at risk.

BY KATE ARONOFF

THE DEATH OF CLIMATE DENIALISM

Soon the Right will have to abandon its head-in-the-sand strategy—but its next tactic may be more dangerous

Lake Mead is now dry, cracked earth.

JUSTIN SULLIVAN/GETTY IMAGES

THE U.K.'S NEW SECRETARY OF ENERGY AND CLIMATE CHANGE, AMBER RUDD, HAS this to say about wind farms: "I personally quite enjoy seeing them." A Conservative Party MP, Rudd received a promotion last month when David Cameron's Tories beat out Labour. Less bland than her sentiments about wind farms are her policy proposals for them: They will receive no new federal subsidies, she says, and decisions on whether to build them will rest in the hands of local governments.

Therein lies the contradiction of Rudd, a former investment banker and self-professed "Thatcherite when it comes to climate change": She believes ardently in global warming and the necessity of mitigating it—so long as those efforts don't dip into public coffers.

To U.S. progressives, a Department of Climate Change like Rudd's might sound like a dream, let alone a conservative heading it who accepts the reality of anthropogenic global warming. This

winter, Sen. Jim Inhofe (R-Okla.), chair of the Committee on Environment and Public Works, threw a snowball on the Senate floor to disprove the 97 percent of "eggheads" in "science laboratories" who cite evidence of climate change. Not all U.S. conservative denialism is as quaint as Inhofe's: Oil barons Charles and David Koch have poured $79 million into talking heads, bogus scientific studies and front groups like Americans for Prosperity—all aimed at convincing the public that climate change is a bugaboo. A Drexel University study found

that between 2003 and 2010, conservative foundations invested $900 million in climate-change denial campaigns.

Despite all this, right-wing acknowledgement of climate change in the United States might not be far off. There are signs that conservative elites' opinions on global warming may head the way of their stance on gay marriage: Stalwart opposers will mysteriously "evolve" their views as it becomes politically expedient. The danger is that the shift will be accompanied by an American version of Rudd's "climate Thatcherism," in which deregulation and deep cuts to the public sphere go hand in hand with a move away from fossil fuels.

THE TEMPERATURE IN WASHINGTON

As Dana Milbank, a Beltway standard-bearer for the *Washington Post*, wrote in a recent op-ed, "Climate has become one of those issues where the gulf between the insular far right and the rest of American ... culture has become so vast that it is serving like a moat, keeping out the very demographic groups the GOP needs in coming years." Eighty-three percent of people in the United States believe climate change constitutes a "very" or "somewhat serious" threat, and institutions from the IMF to Goldman Sachs are sounding the alarm. A *New York Times* and Stanford University poll this year found that nearly half of Republicans nationwide support some type of government action to curb global warming.

Some influential Republicans are taking heed. Alex Lundry, vice president of the conservative polling firm Target Point Consulting, wrote in a January op-ed for The Daily Caller, "If Republicans insist on listening to those that believe we won't see the effects of climate change for decades, we are setting ourselves up for a political and a policy mistake that will damage the party and, *more importantly, the country.*" Tossing around the idea of a third presidential run, Mitt Romney said in January, "I'm one of those Republicans who thinks we are getting warmer and that we are contributing to that." Rand Paul, another 2016 hopeful, has taken a similar stance. Soon after Romney's pronouncement, 15 GOP senators, including Paul, voted for a resolution declaring that climate change is not a hoax and that human activity contributes to it.

CLIMATE REAGANISM

Climate Thatcherites are still Thatcherites, and Republicans who believe in climate change are still Republicans. Rudd remains a loyal member of Cameron's cabinet, from which Britain can expect, as British commentator Laurie Penny wrote, "More cuts to public services. More inequality. More lies." Similarly, even if American environmentalists could flip some magical switch to

eliminate climate denial outright, the reigning U.S. allergy to regulation and public spending would remain. While Rudd's use of catchy phrases like "local control" and "supporting innovation" may carry the rhetorical punch of bold governance proposals, in reality they shunt the onus to a private sector all too excited to step in.

Vox Media's David Roberts has done an impressive job mapping the Right's shift on climate science and predicting its trajectory. As climate denialism begins to falter as a political strategy, he writes, Republicans may move to "apocalyptic warnings about the high cost of government action. That is the GOP's native territory." Indeed, while there is bipartisan support among voters regarding the need for some type of action on climate change, a January Pew Research poll found that the question of what such action should look like is more divisive: 59 percent of Republicans responded that "stricter environmental laws and regulations have a negative economic impact."

Last month, Roberts interviewed libertarian Jerry Taylor, formerly of the "climate-skeptical" Cato Institute, about his idea for a carbon tax. "Taylor," Roberts writes, "has proposed a grand bargain of sorts: in exchange for the elimination of EPA carbon regulations and state renewable energy mandates, Congress would adopt a substantial and rising economy-wide carbon tax, made 'revenue-neutral' by reducing other taxes." Taylor went on to argue that this kind of governmental action is a win-win for libertarians, mainstream Republicans and even centrist Democrats: Emaciate the EPA and continue making high returns, all without a drop of federal spending.

In a March 2015 study, "The Conservative Case for a Carbon Tax," Taylor lays out a plan for "decision[s] about where, when, and how to reduce greenhouse gas emissions [to be left] to market actors (via price signals) rather than

to regulators (via administrative orders)." Republican heavyweights such as former Romney advisor Greg Mankiw and Reagan's secretary of state, George Schultz, have supported similar proposals, and the American Enterprise Institute, a conservative think tank, released its own proposal for a market-friendly carbon tax nearly identical to Taylor's.

Elon Musk, Tesla CEO and inventor wunderkind, is inclined to agree with such arguments. His development of electric cars was partially underwritten by a $465 million grant from the Department of Energy. After paying it off nine years early, in 2013, Musk went on to publicly denounce the very idea of government subsidies, clarifying on Twitter that he was, in fact, "arguing against subsidies & in favor of a tax on the end bad created. Market will then achieve the best solution."

Musk is among the free-market ideologues, Silicon Valley entrepreneurs and Wall Street tycoons who, sensing a change in the political, economic and actual weather, are dreaming up market-based climate solutions. By themselves, these measures are hardly nefarious; some are promising innovations. Musk's Tesla Energy has developed a relatively affordable household power source, the Powerwall. Costing just $3,000, the futuristic-looking white box could revolutionize global access to solar power by making it easier than ever to get off the grid. According to the Solar Energies Industry Association, the market for solar energy grew by 34 percent in 2014. Eager to cash in, Citibank will pour $100 billion into renewables by 2025, with Goldman Sachs pledging $40 billion by 2021.

THE LIMITS OF THE MARKET

Cast in the right light, these measures could be fodder for the argument that the free market is better suited than the state to take on the climate crisis.

Investors, however, cannot do a regulator's job. As Evergreen State College economist Peter Dorman points out, investment in clean energy is not the same as keeping fossil fuels in the ground. "If we generate more energy from renewables, that could just simply mean more energy," Dorman tells *In These Times*:

That in itself does not prevent energy being extracted from fossil fuels. ... From a climate sense, the only thing that ultimately matters is leaving the fossil fuels in the ground. I distrust the state in almost every way. ... I consider myself to have strong left-libertarian inclinations. But nobody but the state can do this. It's always going to be profitable for somebody ... to dig that stuff up, unless the state prevents that from happening and makes it unprofitable, either by taxing the hell out of it, or by requiring permits [for fossil fuel extraction] and putting people in jail if they dig it up without a permit.

Environmentalists in the United States have used confrontational showdowns over fossil-fuel divestment, Keystone XL and offshore drilling to wage a strong—and, arguably, winning—moral argument against the coal, oil and gas industries, but they have yet to issue a full-throated call for state action. Now that climate campaigners are convincing the public of what's wrong, they may be better positioned to start demanding what's right.

While private capital will inevitably play a part in the transition away from fossil fuels, mitigating and adapting to the climate crisis will require substantial public spending and robust federal enforcement agencies. Right now, those agencies are fighting for their lives: Between Mitch McConnell's war on the EPA and the fact that FEMA's National Flood Insurance Program is $24 billion in debt to the Treasury, the government bodies charged with preventing and responding to the climate crisis are struggling to stay afloat.

Taking on this crisis will require a movement able to defend regulators and engage the state with proposals for a livable planet and a vibrant public sector. "In some sense," Dorman says, "the money is already there and has already been there, and the environmental movement has been too politically weak to get it." Annually, the United States invests $37.5 billion in subsidies to the fossil fuel industry. That the government is too poor to pay out for infrastructure and job creation is a fable.

The grueling battle to convince the public and policymakers of the reality of climate change is ending, a victory that can be claimed by scientists and by organizers who have staged massive rallies, direct actions and long-running strategic campaigns. The far more complex challenge ahead for campaigners will be ensuring that the transition away from fossil fuels will have Margaret Thatcher turning in her grave.

In this short piece, the author argues that climate denialism is over and that even commentators and politicians on the right no longer deny climate change. What they do say, however, is that addressing it should not be a part of the public budget. Instead, they argue, the response to climate change should be privatized and left to "market forces."

The commentator is not very optimistic that such a strategy would be effective. Most climate change experts agree that changes in policies regarding fossil fuels have to be implemented now, in order to have the effect of reversing climate change.

Too late?

Reading #17 has one section where Thompson discusses the "tipping-point" or "threshold"—the point at which a certain climatic change cannot be reversed. Many climate experts feel that we are close to, or have even passed, that point. The increased speed of Greenland's ice cap loss, via the moulin phenomenon, is one reason for that concern.

Technology to the Rescue?

Combining Chapters 6 and 7, one should reflect on whether we should place our faith in technology to find a solution to the challenges of population, disease, and climate change. In the previous chapter, the Haber-Bosch discovery allowed bread to be made from air, thereby short-circuiting the Malthusian effects and allowing world population to grow dramatically.

However, one result of that population growth has been an increase in human activities that have spurred human-induced climate forcing—such as the increase in carbon dioxide from fossil fuels—and helped change the climate.

CONCLUSION: WRAP-UP

Climate change is mostly accepted as a reality today. However, even some who accept its reality try to argue that human activities have not been responsible for it. Even if that were true, in many ways, it would be irrelevant. No matter the cause, it is a contemporary world problem that needs to be addressed—if for no other reason than for the benefit of our children and grandchildren. We have also not touched very much on the issue that the effects of climate change are likely to fall heaviest on the poorer populations of the world who have not contributed to it to the same degree as the wealthiest nations have.

About 30 years ago, in the United States, there was reasonable bi-partisan support for the work that warned of the coming and worsening problems of climate change. That changed in the post-9/11 milieu, and many commentators started to deny that climate change was real. Recent events have shown us that the hardest way to address climate change is to try and argue with adversaries on a global scale. Anthropology is showing that the best way to address the problem is to document, through ethnographies, the way local populations are adapting and seeking solutions of resilience and sustainability to the effects of climate change that are literally in their own backyards. By documenting local experiences, perhaps we can build the collaboration necessary to effect necessary change—assuming that it is not already too late!

ACTIVITIES

General activity: in class, start with a sharing of the Schema activation responses.

Activity for Reading #17: in small groups, see if you can find the most recent photos of some of the glaciers mentioned in the article, and any commentary about the local populations and what they think and are doing about the loss of ice. Discuss and document at least two local responses.

Activity for Reading #18: in small groups, briefly research any comment on climate change by government officials or media commentators. Then, discuss and answer the following question: *Aronoff claims that "the grueling battle to convince the public and policymakers of the reality of climate change is ending, a victory that can be claimed by scientists and organizers. . ." Is that statement true in the debate as it is proceeding now?*

SOURCES

An excellent accessible source for comment on climate change is the body of work by the journalist Elizabeth Kolbert, who writes for *The New Yorker*. Her article on Greenland: Letter from Greenland: A Song of Ice: What happens when a country starts to melt? *The New Yorker* October 24, 2016 pp. 50-61 is an excellent read (she has many such articles in that magazine). Susan A. Crate Climate and Culture: Anthropology in the Era of Contemporary Climate Change *Annual Review of Anthropology* 40 (2011) pp. 175-194 is a recent review of the anthropology of climate change. For the effect of climate change on societies in the past, see Rebecca Storey and Glenn R. Storey *Rome and the Classic Maya: Comparing the Slow Collapse of Civilizations* 2017 Routledge, Chapter 7. For the ice core documentation of lead pollution in the Roman Empire see Joseph R. McConnell et al Lead pollution recorded in Greenland ice indicates European emissions tracked plagues, wars, and imperial expansion during antiquity *Proceedings of the National Academy of Sciences* 2018 www.pnas.org/cgi/doi/10.1073/pnas.1721818115.

Chapter 8
Women's Rights

OBJECTIVES

- Analyze the rationale for the equation of the quest for equal rights for women as a quest for human rights.
- Reveal how Western calls to "liberate" women from the oppressive practices of other cultures ultimately proves to be ethnocentric and in the past has justified imperialism.
- Determine how the cultural practice of the seclusion of women can be viewed favorably by women themselves and be used by them as a liberating principle.
- Develop an awareness of how women's work has continued to be undervalued and compensated at much lower rates than men.
- Explain how various forms of global feminist resistance to patriarchal institutions and cultural patterns contribute to the enhancement of the rights of all.

KEY TERMS

Gender: a cultural construct that assigns roles and statuses to individuals based on their adopted sexual identity (either male, female or various biological manifestations of mixed sex); most cultures recognize two sexes, male and female, but multiple genders are also often recognized.

Gender stratification: differential access to resources based on whether one is male or female; generally, it is the female gender, which is given lesser access to resources.

Gender equality: a context in which all genders have equal access to resources of wealth, status and power.

Veiling: the Islamic practice whereby women are covered when going out in public, which provides a form of "portable seclusion" enabling women to maintain the separation of the home while outside it and to provide protection from unrelated males. There are many forms of covering used by Islamic women, often denoted by the Arabic term *hijab*, which means "veil." The Indian *sari*, the Iraqi *abbayah*, and the Afghani *burqa* are all forms of veiling.

Purdah: a Persian word meaning "curtain" used to characterize the Islamic practice of secluding women in the home and via clothing that hides the body.

Feminization of poverty: the worldwide statics that show that two out of every three individuals in poverty is female, while women do two-thirds of the work in the world for 10% of world income, owning 1% of the means of production.

Feminist Resistance: women protests of relegation to the domestic and private sphere of life, provision of generally low-paying jobs, and the undermining of public policies that protect women and children from poverty.

Glass ceiling: the invisible but acknowledged barrier impeding mobility to enhanced status, especially for women and minorities.

SCHEMA ACTIVATION ACTIVITY

Several years ago, several European countries debated the move to outlaw face-covering by immigrant Muslim women: briefly research these events, think about them and answer the question: *were Europeans right to try and ban Islamic face-covering?*

(Save these to share later in your discussion sections.)

INTRODUCTION

In this chapter, you are introduced to the worldwide issue of women's rights. We start with an article that was referred to in Chapter 2: Abu-Lughod's passionate defense of the practice of veiling among Muslim women that has been the most popular introductory anthropology article for many years, with Miner's Nacirema article often second. You then read an article about women housekeepers at a Harvard University-owned hotel who had to undertake an epic fight for better working conditions. Both pieces illustrate how women, even in the progressive West, have faced situations that are a challenge for the maintenance of basic rights.

LILA ABU-LUGHOD

Do Muslim Women Really Need Saving? Anthropological Reflections on Cultural Relativism and Its Others

ABSTRACT This article explores the ethics of the current "War on Terrorism," asking whether anthropology, the discipline devoted to understanding and dealing with cultural difference, can provide us with critical purchase on the justifications made for American intervention in Afghanistan in terms of liberating, or saving, Afghan women. I look first at the dangers of reifying culture, apparent in the tendencies to plaster neat cultural icons like the Muslim woman over messy historical and political dynamics. Then, calling attention to the resonances of contemporary discourses on equality, freedom, and rights with earlier colonial and missionary rhetoric on Muslim women, I argue that we need to develop, instead, a serious appreciation of differences among women in the world—as products of different histories, expressions of different circumstances, and manifestations of differently structured desires. Further, I argue that rather than seeking to "save" others (with the superiority it implies and the violences it would entail) we might better think in terms of (1) working with them in situations that we recognize as always subject to historical transformation and (2) considering our own larger responsibilities to address the forms of global injustice that are powerful shapers of the worlds in which they find themselves. I develop many of these arguments about the limits of "cultural relativism" through a consideration of the burqa and the many meanings of veiling in the Muslim world. [Keywords: cultural relativism, Muslim women, Afghanistan war, freedom, global injustice, colonialism]

WHAT ARE THE ETHICS of the current "War on Terrorism," a war that justifies itself by purporting to liberate, or save, Afghan women? Does anthropology have anything to offer in our search for a viable position to take regarding this rationale for war?

I was led to pose the question of my title in part because of the way I personally experienced the response to the U.S. war in Afghanistan. Like many colleagues whose work has focused on women and gender in the Middle East, I was deluged with invitations to speak—not just on news programs but also to various departments at colleges and universities, especially women's studies programs. Why did this not please me, a scholar who has devoted more than 20 years of her life to this subject and who has some complicated personal connection to this identity? Here was an opportunity to spread the word, disseminate my knowledge, and correct misunderstandings. The urgent search for knowledge about our sister "women of cover" (as President George Bush so marvelously called them) is laudable and when it comes from women's

studies programs where "transnational feminism" is now being taken seriously, it has a certain integrity (see Safire 2001).

My discomfort led me to reflect on why, as feminists in or from the West, or simply as people who have concerns about women's lives, we need to be wary of this response to the events and aftermath of September 11, 2001. I want to point out the minefields—a metaphor that is sadly too apt for a country like Afghanistan, with the world's highest number of mines per capita—of this obsession with the plight of Muslim women. I hope to show some way through them using insights from anthropology, the discipline whose charge has been to understand and manage cultural difference. At the same time, I want to remain critical of anthropology's complicity in the reification of cultural difference.

CULTURAL EXPLANATIONS AND THE MOBILIZATION OF WOMEN

It is easier to see why one should be skeptical about the focus on the "Muslim woman" if one begins with the U.S.

public response. I will analyze two manifestations of this response: some conversations I had with a reporter from the PBS *NewsHour with Jim Lehrer* and First Lady Laura Bush's radio address to the nation on November 17, 2001. The presenter from the *NewsHour* show first contacted me in October to see if I was willing to give some background for a segment on Women and Islam. I mischievously asked whether she had done segments on the women of Guatemala, Ireland, Palestine, or Bosnia when the show covered wars in those regions; but I finally agreed to look at the questions she was going to pose to panelists. The questions were hopelessly general. Do Muslim women believe "x"? Are Muslim women "y"? Does Islam allow "z" for women? I asked her: If you were to substitute Christian or Jewish wherever you have Muslim, would these questions make sense? I did not imagine she would call me back. But she did, twice, once with an idea for a segment on the meaning of Ramadan and another time on Muslim women in politics. One was in response to the bombing and the other to the speeches by Laura Bush and Cherie Blair, wife of the British Prime Minister.

What is striking about these three ideas for news programs is that there was a consistent resort to the cultural, as if knowing something about women and Islam or the meaning of a religious ritual would help one understand the tragic attack on New York's World Trade Center and the U.S. Pentagon, or how Afghanistan had come to be ruled by the Taliban, or what interests might have fueled U.S. and other interventions in the region over the past 25 years, or what the history of American support for conservative groups funded to undermine the Soviets might have been, or why the caves and bunkers out of which Bin Laden was to be smoked "dead or alive, as President Bush announced on television, were paid for and built by the CIA.

In other words, the question is why knowing about the "culture" of the region, and particularly its religious beliefs and treatment of women, was more urgent than exploring the history of the development of repressive regimes in the region and the U.S. role in this history. Such cultural framing, it seemed to me, prevented the serious exploration of the roots and nature of human suffering in this part of the world. Instead of political and historical explanations, experts were being asked to give religio-cultural ones. Instead of questions that might lead to the exploration of global interconnections, we were offered ones that worked to artificially divide the world into separate spheres—recreating an imaginative geography of West versus East, us versus Muslims, cultures in which First Ladies give speeches versus others where women shuffle around silently in burqas.

Most pressing for me was why the Muslim woman in general, and the Afghan woman in particular, were so crucial to this cultural mode of explanation, which ignored the complex entanglements in which we are all implicated, in sometimes surprising alignments. Why were these female symbols being mobilized in this "War against Terror-

ism" in a way they were not in other conflicts? Laura Bush's radio address on November 17 reveals the political work such mobilization accomplishes. On the one hand, her address collapsed important distinctions that should have been maintained. There was a constant slippage between the Taliban and the terrorists, so that they became almost one word—a kind of hyphenated monster identity: the Taliban-and-the-terrorists. Then there was the blurring of the very separate causes in Afghanistan of women's continuing malnutrition, poverty, and ill health, and their more recent exclusion under the Taliban from employment, schooling, and the joys of wearing nail polish. On the other hand, her speech reinforced chasmic divides, primarily between the "civilized people throughout the world" whose hearts break for the women and children of Afghanistan and the Taliban-and-the-terrorists, the cultural monsters who want to, as she put it, "impose their world on the rest of us."

Most revealingly, the speech enlisted women to justify American bombing and intervention in Afghanistan and to make a case for the "War on Terrorism" of which it was allegedly a part. As Laura Bush said, "Because of our recent military gains in much of Afghanistan, women are no longer imprisoned in their homes. They can listen to music and teach their daughters without fear of punishment. The fight against terrorism is also a fight for the rights and dignity of women" (U.S. Government 2002).

These words have haunting resonances for anyone who has studied colonial history. Many who have worked on British colonialism in South Asia have noted the use of the woman question in colonial policies where intervention into sati (the practice of widows immolating themselves on their husbands' funeral pyres), child marriage, and other practices was used to justify rule. As Gayatri Chakravorty Spivak (1988) has cynically put it: white men saving brown women from brown men. The historical record is full of similar cases, including in the Middle East. In Turn of the Century Egypt, what Leila Ahmed (1992) has called "colonial feminism" was hard at work. This was a selective concern about the plight of Egyptian women that focused on the veil as a sign of oppression but gave no support to women's education and was professed loudly by the same Englishman, Lord Cromer, who opposed women's suffrage back home.

Sociologist Marnia Lazreg (1994) has offered some vivid examples of how French colonialism enlisted women to its cause in Algeria. She writes:

Perhaps the most spectacular example of the colonial appropriation of women's voices, and the silencing of those among them who had begun to take women revolutionaries ... as role models by not donning the veil, was the event of May 16, 1958 [just four years before Algeria finally gained its independence from France after a long bloody struggle and 130 years of French control—L.A.]. On that day a demonstration was organized by rebellious French generals in Algiers to show their determination to keep Algeria French. To give the government of France evidence that Algerians were in agreement with them, the generals had a few thousand native men bused in from nearby villages, along with a few women who were solemnly unveiled by French women. . . Rounding up Algerians and bringing them to demonstrations of loyalty to France was not in itself an unusual act during the colonial era. But to unveil women at a well-choreographed ceremony added to the event a symbolic dimension that dramatized the one constant feature of the Algerian occupation by France: its obsession with women. [Lazreg 1994:135]

Lazreg (1994) also gives memorable examples of the way in which the French had earlier sought to transform Arab women and girls. She describes skits at awards ceremonies at the Muslim Girls' School in Algiers in 1851 and 1852. In the first skit, written by "a French lady from Algiers," two Algerian Arab girls reminisced about their trip to France with words including the following:

Oh! Protective France: Oh! Hospitable France! . . .
Noble land, where I felt free
Under Christian skies to pray to our God: . . .
God bless you for the happiness you bring us!
And you, adoptive mother, who taught us
That we have a share of this world,
We will cherish you forever! [Lazreg 1994:68–69]

These girls are made to invoke the gift of a share of this world, a world where freedom reigns under Christian skies. This is not the world the Taliban-and-the-terrorists would "like to impose on the rest of us."

Just as I argued above that we need to be suspicious when neat cultural icons are plastered over messier historical and political narratives, so we need to be wary when Lord Cromer in British-ruled Egypt, French ladies in Algeria, and Laura Bush, all with military troops behind them, claim to be saving or liberating Muslim women.

POLITICS OF THE VEIL

I want now to look more closely at those Afghan women Laura Bush claimed were "rejoicing" at their liberation by the Americans. This necessitates a discussion of the veil, or the burqa, because it is so central to contemporary concerns about Muslim women. This will set the stage for a discussion of how anthropologists, feminist anthropologists in particular, contend with the problem of difference in a global world. In the conclusion, I will return to the rhetoric of saving Muslim women and offer an alternative.

It is common popular knowledge that the ultimate sign of the oppression of Afghan women under the Taliban-and-the-terrorists is that they were forced to wear the burqa. Liberals sometimes confess their surprise that even though Afghanistan has been liberated from the Taliban, women do not seem to be throwing off their burqas. Someone who has worked in Muslim regions must ask why this is so surprising. Did we expect that once "free" from the Taliban they would go "back" to belly shirts and blue jeans, or dust off their Chanel suits? We need to be more sensible about the clothing of "women of cover," and so there is perhaps a need to make some basic points about veiling.

First, it should be recalled that the Taliban did not invent the burqa. It was the local form of covering that Pashtun women in one region wore when they went out. The Pashtun are one of several ethnic groups in Afghanistan and the burqa was one of many forms of covering in the subcontinent and Southwest Asia that has developed as a convention for symbolizing women's modesty or respectability. The burqa, like some other forms of "cover" has, in many settings, marked the symbolic separation of men's and women's spheres, as part of the general association of women with family and home, not with public space where strangers mingled.

Twenty years ago the anthropologist Hanna Papanek (1982), who worked in Pakistan, described the burqa as "portable seclusion." She noted that many saw it as a liberating invention because it enabled women to move out of segregated living spaces while still observing the basic moral requirements of separating and protecting women from unrelated men. Ever since I came across her phrase "portable seclusion," I have thought of these enveloping robes as "mobile homes." Everywhere, such veiling signifies belonging to a particular community and participating in a moral way of life in which families are paramount in the organization of communities and the home is associated with the sanctity of women.

The obvious question that follows is this: If this were the case, why would women suddenly become immodest? Why would they suddenly throw off the markers of their respectability, markers, whether burqas or other forms of cover, which were supposed to assure their protection in the public sphere from the harassment of strange men by symbolically signaling to all that they were still in the inviolable space of their homes, even though moving in the public realm? Especially when these are forms of dress that had become so conventional that most women gave little thought to their meaning.

To draw some analogies, none of them perfect, why are we surprised that Afghan women do not throw off their burqas when we know perfectly well that it would not be appropriate to wear shorts to the opera? At the time these discussions of Afghan women's burqas were raging, a friend of mine was chided by her husband for suggesting she wanted to wear a pantsuit to a fancy wedding: "You know you don't wear pants to a WASP wedding," he reminded her. New Yorkers know that the beautifully coiffed Hasidic women, who look so fashionable next to their dour husbands in black coats and hats, are wearing wigs. This is because religious belief and community standards of propriety require the covering of the hair. They also alter boutique fashions to include high necks and long sleeves. As anthropologists know perfectly well, people wear the appropriate form of dress for their social communities and are guided by socially shared standards, religious beliefs, and moral ideals, unless they deliberately transgress to make a point or are unable to afford proper cover. If we think that U.S. women live in a world of

239

choice regarding clothing, all we need to do is remind ourselves of the expression, "the tyranny of fashion."

What had happened in Afghanistan under the Taliban is that one regional style of covering or veiling, associated with a certain respectable but not elite class, was imposed on everyone as "religiously" appropriate, even though previously there had been many different styles, popular or traditional with different groups and classes—different ways to mark women's propriety, or, in more recent times, religious piety. Although I am not an expert on Afghanistan, I imagine that the majority of women left in Afghanistan by the time the Taliban took control were the rural or less educated, from nonelite families, since they were the only ones who could not emigrate to escape the hardship and violence that has marked Afghanistan's recent history. If liberated from the enforced wearing of burqas, most of these women would choose some other form of modest headcovering, like all those living nearby who were not under the Taliban—their rural Hindu counterparts in the North of India (who cover their heads and veil their faces from affines) or their Muslim sisters in Pakistan.

Even *The New York Times* carried an article about Afghan women refugees in Pakistan that attempted to educate readers about this local variety (Fremson 2001). The article describes and pictures everything from the now-iconic burqa with the embroidered eyeholes, which a Pashtun woman explains is the proper dress for her community, to large scarves they call chadors, to the new Islamic modest dress that wearers refer to as *hijab*. Those in the new Islamic dress are characteristically students heading for professional careers, especially in medicine, just like their counterparts from Egypt to Malaysia. One wearing the large scarf was a school principal; the other was a poor street vendor. The telling quote from the young street vendor is, "If I did [wear the burqa] the refugees would tease me because the burqa is for 'good women' who stay inside the home" (Fremson 2001:14). Here you can see the local status associated with the burqa—it is for good respectable women from strong families who are not forced to make a living selling on the street.

The British newspaper *The Guardian* published an interview in January 2002 with Dr. Suheila Siddiqi, a respected surgeon in Afghanistan who holds the rank of lieutenant general in the Afghan medical corps (Goldenberg 2002). A woman in her sixties, she comes from an elite family and, like her sisters, was educated. Unlike most women of her class, she chose not to go into exile. She is presented in the article as "the woman who stood up to the Taliban" because she refused to wear the burqa. She had made it a condition of returning to her post as head of a major hospital when the Taliban came begging in 1996, just eight months after firing her along with other women. Siddiqi is described as thin, glamorous, and confident. But further into the article it is noted that her graying bouffant hair is covered in a gauzy veil. This is a reminder that though she refused the burqa, she had no question about wearing the chador or scarf.

Finally, I need to make a crucial point about veiling. Not only are there many forms of covering, which themselves have different meanings in the communities in which they are used, but also veiling itself must not be confused with, or made to stand for, lack of agency. As I have argued in my ethnography of a Bedouin community in Egypt in the late 1970s and 1980s (1986), pulling the black head cloth over the face in front of older respected men is considered a voluntary act by women who are deeply committed to being moral and have a sense of honor tied to family. One of the ways they show their standing is by covering their faces in certain contexts. They decide for whom they feel it is appropriate to veil.

To take a very different case, the modern Islamic modest dress that many educated women across the Muslim world have taken on since the mid-1970s now both publicly marks piety and can be read as a sign of educated urban sophistication, a sort of modernity (e.g., Abu-Lughod 1995, 1998; Brenner 1996; El Guindi 1999; MacLeod 1991; Ong 1990). As Saba Mahmood (2001) has so brilliantly shown in her ethnography of women in the mosque movement in Egypt, this new form of dress is also perceived by many of the women who adopt it as part of a bodily means to cultivate virtue, the outcome of their professed desire to be close to God.

Two points emerge from this fairly basic discussion of the meanings of veiling in the contemporary Muslim world. First, we need to work against the reductive interpretation of veiling as the quintessential sign of women's unfreedom, even if we object to state imposition of this form, as in Iran or with the Taliban. (It must be recalled that the modernizing states of Turkey and Iran had earlier in the century banned veiling and required men, except religious clerics, to adopt Western dress.) What does freedom mean if we accept the fundamental premise that humans are social beings, always raised in certain social and historical contexts and belonging to particular communities that shape their desires and understandings of the world? Is it not a gross violation of women's own understandings of what they are doing to simply denounce the burqa as a medieval imposition? Second, we must take care not to reduce the diverse situations and attitudes of millions of Muslim women to a single item of clothing. Perhaps it is time to give up the Western obsession with the veil and focus on some serious issues with which feminists and others should indeed be concerned.

Ultimately, the significant political–ethical problem the burqa raises is how to deal with cultural "others." How are we to deal with difference without accepting the passivity implied by the cultural relativism for which anthropologists are justly famous—a relativism that says it's their culture and it's not my business to judge or interfere, only to try to understand. Cultural relativism is certainly an improvement on ethnocentrism and the racism, cultural imperialism, and imperiousness that underlie it; the problem is that it is too late not to interfere. The forms of lives we

240

find around the world are already products of long histories of interactions.

I want to explore the issues of women, cultural relativism, and the problems of "difference" from three angles. First, I want to consider what feminist anthropologists (those stuck in that awkward relationship, as Strathern [1987] has claimed) are to do with strange political bedfellows. I used to feel torn when I received the e-mail petitions circulating for the last few years in defense of Afghan women under the Taliban. I was not sympathetic to the dogmatism of the Taliban; I do not support the oppression of women. But the provenance of the campaign worried me. I do not usually find myself in political company with the likes of Hollywood celebrities (see Hirschkind and Mahmood 2002). I had never received a petition from such women defending the right of Palestinian women to safety from Israeli bombing or daily harassment at checkpoints, asking the United States to reconsider its support for a government that had dispossessed them, closed them out from work and citizenship rights, refused them the most basic freedoms. Maybe some of these same people might be signing petitions to save African women from genital cutting, or Indian women from dowry deaths. However, I do not think that it would be as easy to mobilize so many of these American and European women if it were not a case of Muslim men oppressing Muslim women—women of cover for whom they can feel sorry and in relation to whom they can feel smugly superior. Would television diva Oprah Winfrey host the Women in Black, the women's peace group from Israel, as she did RAWA, the Revolutionary Association of Women of Afghanistan, who were also granted the *Glamour Magazine* Women of the Year Award? What are we to make of post-Taliban "Reality Tours" such as the one advertised on the internet by Global Exchange for March 2002 under the title "Courage and Tenacity: A Women's Delegation to Afghanistan"? The rationale for the $1,400 tour is that "with the removal of the Taliban government, Afghan women, for the first time in the past decade, have the opportunity to reclaim their basic human rights and establish their role as equal citizens by participating in the rebuilding of their nation." The tour's objective, to celebrate International Women's Week, is "to develop awareness of the concerns and issues the Afghan women are facing as well as to witness the changing political, economic, and social conditions which have created new opportunities for the women of Afghanistan" (Global Exchange 2002).

To be critical of this celebration of women's rights in Afghanistan is not to pass judgment on any local women's organizations, such as RAWA, whose members have courageously worked since 1977 for a democratic secular Afghanistan in which women's human rights are respected, against Soviet-backed regimes or U.S.-, Saudi-, and Pakistani-supported conservatives. Their documentation of abuse and their work through clinics and schools have been enormously important.

It is also not to fault the campaigns that exposed the dreadful conditions under which the Taliban placed women. The Feminist Majority campaign helped put a stop to a secret oil pipeline deal between the Taliban and the U.S. multinational Unocal that was going forward with U.S. administration support. Western feminist campaigns must not be confused with the hypocrisies of the new colonial feminism of a Republican president who was not elected for his progressive stance on feminist issues or of administrations that played down the terrible record of violations of women by the United State's allies in the Northern Alliance, as documented by Human Rights Watch and Amnesty International, among others. Rapes and assaults were widespread in the period of infighting that devastated Afghanistan before the Taliban came in to restore order.

It is, however, to suggest that we need to look closely at what we are supporting (and what we are not) and to think carefully about why. How should we manage the complicated politics and ethics of finding ourselves in agreement with those with whom we normally disagree? I do not know how many feminists who felt good about saving Afghan women from the Taliban are also asking for a global redistribution of wealth or contemplating sacrificing their own consumption radically so that African or Afghan women could have some chance of having what I do believe should be a universal human right—the right to freedom from the structural violence of global inequality and from the ravages of war, the everyday rights of having enough to eat, having homes for their families in which to live and thrive, having ways to make decent livings so their children can grow, and having the strength and security to work out, within their communities and with whatever alliances they want, how to live a good life, which might very well include changing the ways those communities are organized.

Suspicion about bedfellows is only a first step; it will not give us a way to think more positively about what to do or where to stand. For that, we need to confront two more big issues. First is the acceptance of the possibility of difference. Can we only free Afghan women to be like us or might we have to recognize that even after "liberation" from the Taliban, they might want different things than we would want for them? What do we do about that? Second, we need to be vigilant about the rhetoric of saving people because of what it implies about our attitudes.

Again, when I talk about accepting difference, I am not implying that we should resign ourselves to being cultural relativists who respect whatever goes on elsewhere as "just their culture." I have already discussed the dangers of "cultural" explanations; "their" cultures are just as much part of history and an interconnected world as ours are. What I am advocating is the hard work involved in recognizing and respecting differences—precisely as products of different histories, as expressions of different circumstances, and as manifestations of differently structured desires. We may want justice for women, but can we accept

241

that there might be different ideas about justice and that different women might want, or choose, different futures from what we envision as best (see Ong 1988)? We must consider that they might be called to personhood, so to speak, in a different language.

Reports from the Bonn peace conference held in late November to discuss the rebuilding of Afghanistan revealed significant differences among the few Afghan women feminists and activists present. RAWA's position was to reject any conciliatory approach to Islamic governance. According to one report I read, most women activists, especially those based in Afghanistan who are aware of the realities on the ground, agreed that Islam had to be the starting point for reform. Fatima Gailani, a U.S.-based advisor to one of the delegations, is quoted as saying, "If I go to Afghanistan today and ask women for votes on the promise to bring them secularism, they are going to tell me to go to hell.' Instead, according to one report, most of these women looked for inspiration on how to fight for equality to a place that might seem surprising. They looked to Iran as a country in which they saw women making significant gains within an Islamic framework—in part through an Islamically oriented feminist movement that is challenging injustices and reinterpreting the religious tradition.

The situation in Iran is itself the subject of heated debate within feminist circles, especially among Iranian feminists in the West (e.g., Mir-Hosseini 1999; Moghissi 1999; Najmabadi 1998, 2000). It is not clear whether and in what ways women have made gains and whether the great increases in literacy, decreases in birthrates, presence of women in the professions and government, and a feminist flourishing in cultural fields like writing and filmmaking are because of or despite the establishment of a so-called Islamic Republic. The concept of an Islamic feminism itself is also controversial. Is it an oxymoron or does it refer to a viable movement forged by brave women who want a third way?

One of the things we have to be most careful about in thinking about Third World feminisms, and feminism in different parts of the Muslim world, is how not to fall into polarizations that place feminism on the side of the West. I have written about the dilemmas faced by Arab feminists when Western feminists initiate campaigns that make them vulnerable to local denunciations by conservatives of various sorts, whether Islamist or nationalist, of being traitors (Abu-Lughod 2001). As some like Afsaneh Najmabadi are now arguing, not only is it wrong to see history simplistically in terms of a putative opposition between Islam and the West (as is happening in the United States now and has happened in parallel in the Muslim world), but it is also strategically dangerous to accept this cultural opposition between Islam and the West, between fundamentalism and feminism, because those many people within Muslim countries who are trying to find alternatives to present injustices, those who might want to refuse the divide and take from different histories and

cultures, who do not accept that being feminist means being Western, will be under pressure to choose, just as we are: Are you with us or against us?

My point is to remind us to be aware of differences, respectful of other paths toward social change that might give women better lives. Can there be a liberation that is Islamic? And, beyond this, is liberation even a goal for which all women or people strive? Are emancipation, equality, and rights part of a universal language we must use? To quote Saba Mahmood, writing about the women in Egypt who are seeking to become pious Muslims, "The desire for freedom and liberation is a historically situated desire whose motivational force cannot be assumed a priori, but needs to be reconsidered in light of other desires, aspirations, and capacities that inhere in a culturally and historically located subject" (2001:223). In other words, might other desires be more meaningful for different groups of people? Living in close families? Living in a godly way? Living without war? I have done fieldwork in Egypt over more than 20 years and I cannot think of a single woman I know, from the poorest rural to the most educated cosmopolitan, who has ever expressed envy of U.S. women, women they tend to perceive as bereft of community, vulnerable to sexual violence and social anomie, driven by individual success rather than morality, or strangely disrespectful of God.

Mahmood (2001) has pointed out a disturbing thing that happens when one argues for a respect for other traditions. She notes that there seems to be a difference in the political demands made on those who work on or are trying to understand Muslims and Islamists and those who work on secular–humanist projects. She, who studies the piety movement in Egypt, is consistently pressed to denounce all the harm done by Islamic movements around the world—otherwise she is accused of being an apologist. But there never seems to be a parallel demand for those who study secular humanism and its projects, despite the terrible violences that have been associated with it over the last couple of centuries, from world wars to colonialism, from genocides to slavery. We need to have as little dogmatic faith in secular humanism as in Islamism, and as open a mind to the complex possibilities of human projects undertaken in one tradition as the other.

BEYOND THE RHETORIC OF SALVATION

Let us return, finally, to my title, "Do Muslim Women Need Saving?" The discussion of culture, veiling, and how one can navigate the shoals of cultural difference should put Laura Bush's self-congratulation about the rejoicing of Afghan women liberated by American troops in a different light. It is deeply problematic to construct the Afghan woman as someone in need of saving. When you save someone, you imply that you are saving her from something. You are also saving her *to* something. What violences are entailed in this transformation, and what presumptions are being made about the superiority of that to which you are saving her? Projects of saving other women depend on and reinforce a sense of superiority by Westerners, a form of arrogance that deserves to be challenged. All one needs to do to appreciate the patronizing quality of the rhetoric of saving women is to imagine using it today in the United States about disadvantaged groups such as African American women or working-class women. We now understand them as suffering from structural violence. We have become politicized about race and class, but not culture.

As anthropologists, feminists, or concerned citizens, we should be wary of taking on the mantles of those 19th-century Christian missionary women who devoted their lives to saving their Muslim sisters. One of my favorite documents from that period is a collection called *Our Moslem Sisters*, the proceedings of a conference of women missionaries held in Cairo in 1906 (Van Sommer and Zwemmer 1907). The subtitle of the book is *A Cry of Need from the Lands of Darkness Interpreted by Those Who Heard It*. Speaking of the ignorance, seclusion, polygamy, and veiling that blighted women's lives across the Muslim world, the missionary women spoke of their responsibility to make these women's voices heard. As the introduction states, "They will never cry for themselves, for they are down under the yoke of centuries of oppression" (Van Sommer and Zwemer 1907:15). "This book,' it begins, "with its sad, reiterated story of wrong and oppression is an indictment and an appeal.   It is an appeal to Christian womanhood to right these wrongs and enlighten this darkness by sacrifice and service" (Van Sommer and Zwemer 1907:5).

One can hear uncanny echoes of their virtuous goals today, even though the language is secular, the appeals not to Jesus but to human rights or the liberal West. The continuing currency of such imagery and sentiments can be seen in their deployment for perfectly good humanitarian causes. In February 2002, I received an invitation to a reception honoring an international medical humanitarian network called Médecins du Monde/Doctors of the World (MdM). Under the sponsorship of the French Ambassador to the United States, the Head of the delegation of the European Commission to the United Nations, and a member of the European Parliament, the cocktail reception was to feature an exhibition of photographs under the clichéd title "Afghan Women: Behind the Veil."

The invitation was remarkable not just for the colorful photograph of women in flowing burqas walking across the barren mountains of Afghanistan but also for the text, a portion of which I quote:

For 20 years MdM has been ceaselessly struggling to help those who are most vulnerable. But increasingly, thick veils cover the victims of the war. When the Taliban came to power in 1996, Afghan Women became faceless. To unveil one's face while receiving medical care was to achieve a sort of intimacy, find a brief space for secret freedom and recover a little of one's dignity. In a country where women had no access to basic medical care because they did not have the right to appear in public, where women

had no right to practice medicine, MdM's program stood as a stubborn reminder of human rights. . . . Please join us in helping to lift the veil.

Although I cannot take up here the fantasies of intimacy associated with unveiling, fantasies reminiscent of the French colonial obsessions so brilliantly unmasked by Alloula in *The Colonial Harem* (1986), I can ask why humanitarian projects and human rights discourse in the 21st century need rely on such constructions of Muslim women.

Could we not leave veils and vocations of saving others behind and instead train our sights on ways to make the world a more just place? The reason respect for difference should not be confused with cultural relativism is that it does not preclude asking how we, living in this privileged and powerful part of the world, might examine our own responsibilities for the situations in which others in distant places have found themselves. We do not stand outside the world, looking out over this sea of poor benighted people, living under the shadow—or veil—of oppressive cultures; we are part of that world. Islamic movements themselves have arisen in a world shaped by the intense engagements of Western powers in Middle Eastern lives.

A more productive approach, it seems to me, is to ask how we might contribute to making the world a more just place. A world not organized around strategic military and economic demands; a place where certain kinds of forces and values that we may still consider important could have an appeal and where there is the peace necessary for discussions, debates, and transformations to occur within communities. We need to ask ourselves what kinds of world conditions we could contribute to making such that popular desires will not be overdetermined by an overwhelming sense of helplessness in the face of forms of global injustice. Where we seek to be active in the affairs of distant places, can we do so in the spirit of support for those within those communities whose goals are to make women's (and men's) lives better (as Walley has argued in relation to practices of genital cutting in Africa, [1997])? Can we use a more egalitarian language of alliances, coalitions, and solidarity, instead of salvation?

Even RAWA, the now celebrated Revolutionary Association of the Women of Afghanistan, which was so instrumental in bringing to U.S. women's attention the excesses of the Taliban, has opposed the U.S. bombing from the beginning. They do not see in it Afghan women's salvation but increased hardship and loss. They have long called for disarmament and for peacekeeping forces. Spokespersons point out the dangers of confusing governments with people, the Taliban with innocent Afghans who will be most harmed. They consistently remind audiences to take a close look at the ways policies are being organized around oil interests, the arms industry, and the international drug trade. They are not obsessed with the veil, even though they are the most radical feminists working for a secular democratic Afghanistan. Unfortunately,

243

only their messages about the excesses of the Taliban have been heard, even though their criticisms of those in power in Afghanistan have included previous regimes. A first step in hearing their wider message is to break with the language of alien cultures, whether to understand or eliminate them. Missionary work and colonial feminism belong in the past. Our task is to critically explore what we might do to help create a world in which those poor Afghan women, for whom "the hearts of those in the civilized world break," can have safety and decent lives.

LILA ABU-LUGHOD Department of Anthropology, Columbia University, New York, NY 10027

NOTES

Acknowledgments. I want to thank Page Jackson, Fran Mascia-Lees, Tim Mitchell, Rosalind Morris, Anupama Rao, and members of the audience at the symposium "Responding to War," sponsored by Columbia University's Institute for Research on Women and Gender (where I presented an earlier version), for helpful comments, references, clippings, and encouragement.

REFERENCES CITED

Abu-Lughod, Lila
   1986   Veiled Sentiments: Honor and Poetry in a Bedouin Society. Berkeley: University of California Press.
   1995   Movie Stars and Islamic Moralism in Egypt. Social Text 42:53–67.
   1998   Remaking Women: Feminism and Modernity in the Middle East. Princeton: Princeton University Press.
   2001   Orientalism and Middle East Feminist Studies. Feminist Studies 27(1):101–113.
Ahmed, Leila
   1992   Women and Gender in Islam. New Haven, CT: Yale University Press.
Alloula, Malek
   1986   The Colonial Harem. Minneapolis: University of Minnesota Press.
Brenner, Suzanne
   1996   Reconstructing Self and Society: Javanese Muslim Women and "the Veil." American Ethnologist 23(4):673–697.
El Guindi, Fadwa
   1999   Veil: Modesty, Privacy and Resistance. Oxford: Berg.
Fremson, Ruth
   2001   Allure Must Be Covered. Individuality Peeks Through. New York Times, November 4: 14.
Global Exchange
   2002   Courage and Tenacity: A Women's Delegation to Afghanistan. Electronic document, http://www.globalexchange.org/tours/auto/2002-03-05_CourageandTenacityAWomensDele.html. Accessed February 11.
Goldenberg, Suzanne
   2002   The Woman Who Stood Up to the Taliban. The Guardian, January 24. Electronic document, http://222.guardian.co.uk/afghanistan/story/0,1284,63840.
Hirschkind, Charles, and Saba Mahmood
   2002   Feminism, the Taliban, and the Politics of Counter-Insurgency. Anthropological Quarterly, Volume 75(2):107–122.
Lazreg, Marnia
   1994   The Eloquence of Silence: Algerian Women in Question. New York: Routledge.
MacLeod, Arlene
   1991   Accommodating Protest. New York: Columbia University Press.
Mahmood, Saba
   2001   Feminist Theory, Embodiment, and the Docile Agent: Some Reflections on the Egyptian Islamic Revival. Cultural Anthropology 16(2):202–235.
Mir-Hosseini, Ziba
   1999   Islam and Gender: The Religious Debate in Contemporary Iran. Princeton: Princeton University Press.
Moghissi, Haideh
   1999   Feminism and Islamic Fundamentalism. London: Zed Books.
Najmabadi, Afsaneh
   1998   Feminism in an Islamic Republic. *In* Islam, Gender and Social Change. Yvonne Haddad and John Esposito, eds. Pp. 59–84. New York: Oxford University Press.
   2000   (Un)Veiling Feminism. Social Text 64: 29–45.
Ong, Aihwa
   1988   Colonialism and Modernity: Feminist Re-Presentations of Women in Non-Western Societies. Inscriptions 3–4:79–93.
   1990   State Versus Islam: Malay Families, Women's Bodies, and the Body Politic in Malaysia. American Ethnologist 17(2):258–276.
Papanek, Hanna
   1982   Purdah in Pakistan: Seclusion and Modern Occupations for Women. *In* Separate Worlds. Hanna Papanek and Gail Minault, eds. Pp. 190–216. Columbus, MO: South Asia Books.
Safire, William
   2001   "On Language." New York Times Magazine, October 28: 22.
Spivak, Gayatri Chakravorty
   1988   Can the Subaltern Speak? *In* Marxism and the Interpretation of Culture. Cary Nelson and Lawrence Grossberg, eds. Pp. 271–313. Urbana: University of Illinois Press.
Strathern, Marilyn
   1987   An Awkward Relationship: The Case of Feminism and Anthropology. Signs 12:276–292.
U.S. Government
   1907   Our Moslem Sisters: A Cry of Need from Lands of Darkness Interpreted by Those Who Heard It. New York: Fleming H. Revell Co.
   2002   Electronic document, http://www.whitehouse.gov/news/releases/2001/11/20011117. Accessed January 10.
Walley, Christine
   1997   Searching for "Voices": Feminism, Anthropology, and the Global Debate over Female Genital Operations. Cultural Anthropology 12(3):405–438.

Abu-Lughod here caustically criticizes the West's justifications for military intervention in Islamic countries on the grounds of "liberating" women, as "white men saving brown women from brown men." To her, the chief evidence against the idea that women needed rescuing from the Taliban is that the wearing of the *burqa* (the full body covering that shields even the eyes of the wearer) did not stop in Afghanistan with the overthrow of the Taliban, and that the garment had a long history prior to the government of the Taliban. She righlty points out that, even if the *burqa* were outlawed, Afghani women would choose some other form of head covering.

Salvation

Perhaps the greatest critcism Abu-Lughod levels is her questioning of the "need to save," which by definition implies an attitude of superiority, and an "arrogance that deserves to be challenged." She insists that Muslim think Western women are "bereft of community;" after working for more than 20 years in Egypt. she never found a single Egyptian woman who expressed envy of U.S. women.

Egalitarian Language

Abu-Lughod eloquently argues that the real need of Muslim women is similar to that in many other parts of the world; if women were given the same advantages as men, especially the same access to education, their lives would improve and thereby also the lives of others would be improved. The issue is not how to liberate women, but how to make the world a more just place. Instead of salvation, the talk should be of alliances, coalitions and solidarity. The Malaysian Sisters in Islam, representing a kind of "feminist communitarianism," while maintaining their Islamic faith, work to improve the lives of women by insisting on the same access to religious education as the men. The main point is that women's rights must make sense in the context of each cultural community.

HOUSEKEEPERS VS. HARVARD

by SARAH LEONARD

How working-class immigrant women fought for a union and forged a feminism for the 99 percent.

EW PEOPLE KNOW THAT HARVARD OWNS A HOTEL—OR, IN the words of a half-dozen corrections issued by *The Harvard Crimson*, owns a building that houses a hotel. The building is a nondescript DoubleTree Suites by Hilton at 400 Soldiers Field Road in Boston. The suite windows overlook the ugly highway along the Charles River, facing the Harvard undergraduate campus in Cambridge. On the October day I stayed there, the Boston chill had just set in. The DoubleTree brand is represented by a much-touted DoubleTree by Hilton cookie, which I received in a lobby crowned with a jumble of shiny metal hanging from the ceiling and adjacent to a lounge with leather armchairs and art books. The rooms are arranged in a square around an open atrium 15 floors high. To ascend, you step into a glass elevator that shoots you up through the middle, past floor after floor filled with dozens of housekeeping carts, piled six feet high with cleaning supplies, sheets, and comforters, being pushed door-to-door by discreet women in gray uniforms.

Harvard bought 400 Soldiers Field Road in 2005, when Jack R. Meyer, the famously successful CEO of the Harvard Management Corporation, was at his peak, guiding the university's massive $37 billion endowment away from conservative stocks and bonds and into a diverse range of financial instruments. Harvard bought real estate, bet on commodities like timber (at one point, Meyer had three professional lumberjacks on hand to advise him), and snapped up foreign and emerging stocks. Harvard is unusual among universities in that it manages much of its endowment internally and has become a microcosm of capital itself, with high-paid fund managers—two of Meyer's deputies made $25 million a year—and a mission to return annual gains of a few billion dollars. The endowment dwarfs the actual school, financially; just the endowment's growth in 2014 was larger than the entire operating expenses of the university. Practically speaking, Harvard is a massive investment corporation with a relatively small amount of education attached.

This endowment is perpetually bolstered by its high-caliber graduates, who maintain Harvard's reputation as a training ground for the American elite. Influential people across the political spectrum have attended Harvard, from Steve Bannon on the populist right, to Jared Kushner on the country-club right, to Barack Obama on the centrist left—indeed, before Donald Trump, the last president to attend neither Harvard nor Yale was Ronald Reagan. Elizabeth Warren, the favorite candidate of progressive Democrats, didn't go to Harvard either, but she did teach at Harvard Law School before becoming a senator. Since integrating women in 1977, the university has produced not only many of America's most powerful men but also some powerful women, though it continues to face its share of controversy over sexism on campus and in the classroom.

In the early 2000s, Harvard accumulated land in nearby Allston for the development of a science and engineering complex. There was no reason for Harvard to think that purchasing the Hilton DoubleTree Suites, conveniently located near this campus-in-the-making, would be different from any of its other in-

What happens when working-class women decide to lean in?

On the line: Unite Here Local 26 leads a protest in support of the DoubleTree workers.

vestments. The hotel was profitable in 2006, and by 2014 it would be bringing in millions. Since Harvard has less experience running hotels than growing endowments or producing future presidents, the Harvard Management Corporation kept Hilton on to manage it (Hilton has hundreds of these owner-operator agreements worldwide). The hotel hosts innumerable Harvard events, mostly for the nearby Harvard Business School.

Which brings us back to all those *Harvard Crimson* corrections, appended in 2013 and 2014 to articles dating back to 2005. Each one reads: "An earlier version of the headline of this article and statements in the article stated that the DoubleTree Suites hotel is Harvard-owned. To clarify, the company is housed in a Harvard-owned building." Harvard's sudden reluctance to claim its property stemmed from a labor dispute that would last three years and, in the end, lay bare the tension between a feminism increasingly embraced by corporate and elite women and the rights of their working-class counterparts. Sixty housekeepers fighting for better conditions at the Boston-Cambridge DoubleTree Suites petitioned Harvard's first female president for her support, and asked one of Harvard's most famous graduates, Sheryl Sandberg (BA, 1991; MBA, 1995), to lean in with them. The unfolding of their struggle for a union offers a startling view into the perverse role that feminism can play in 21st-century capitalism.

" ONESTLY, WHEN I BEGAN MY JOB, I thought I wouldn't last long," said Delmy Lemus, speaking in Spanish. Lemus is a 34-year-old housekeeper at DoubleTree, born in El Salvador and a mother of two. We settled in to chat on the fourth floor of Harvard's redbrick Phillips Brooks House, home to the Student Labor Action Movement (SLAM), an important ally in the workers' campaign. Near us hung a portrait of two identical sandy-haired young Harvard men with a model sailing boat, a reminder in oil that at Harvard, Winklevii spring eternal.

Few things have a longer lineage in feminism than chronicles of cleaning—how much it hurts, how little it's respected. Dorothy Lee Bolden, founder of the National Domestic Workers Union of America in the 1960s, declared that housekeepers, nannies, and in-home caregivers had built the nation from "the sweat of their brow" as surely as their parents had by working in the fields. Nearly half a million people work as housekeepers in hotels nationwide, about 90 percent of them women. Boston's hotel industry thrives on university business—at Harvard, Boston University, Boston College, and others—providing accommodations for conference participants, parents of college kids, and visiting scholars.

Lemus described work as a hectic race: 30 minutes to clean a room, with no extra time allotted if some louche businessman smoked weed, left dirty condoms around, or puked in the bathtub. Such messes were common enough, but the detritus was less exceptional than the pace. Unionized hotels in Boston typically require housekeepers to clean 15 single rooms per day, while the nonunionized housekeepers at DoubleTree were doing roughly double that by cleaning 14 suites (which include a bedroom, living room, and kitchenette). As a result, according to a report released by Local 26, a Boston-based local of Unite Here representing hospitality workers, the rate for work-related injuries and illnesses at Harvard's DoubleTree in 2013 was 75 percent higher than the rate for hotel and other accommodation workers in Massachusetts in 2012. Workers complained of chronic back pain from lifting the sofa beds installed in the suites in 2008—to put them away, they had to bend down, hoist a heavy mattress, and fold it back into the sofa. When surveyed by Local 26, 100 percent of the workers said that they were in pain. Their injuries sound like those of construction workers.

The hotel was a serene, white dreamland on top, all warm chocolate-chip cookies and Harvard Business School guests resting under thick comforters—with a sort of Dickensian factory churning underneath. One day, as Lemus ran toward a bed, trying to beat the clock, "my foot got caught on the sheet, and it twisted badly and I hit the wall and broke my nose. I was bleeding through the mouth, through the nose. I thought I had broken my teeth as well, because I was choking on my own blood." The first thing her supervisor asked as she was rushed to an ambulance was how many rooms she'd finished.

Such managers were almost certainly under pressure from above. Most workers at the Harvard DoubleTree, when surveyed for a different union report, stated that the workload had gotten heavier in the last several years. Managers blamed the economic downturn, but Lemus argued that it was more about the change in management. When the university took over, she said, things got so tight that the women were often told to bring their own cleaning supplies. While housekeepers juggled their way through each increasingly untenable day, long-time workers were fired. Lemus thinks they were trying to fire better-paid people for minor errors in order to replace them with new, lower-paid people, "like a game." A friend "had worked there for about eight years as a housekeeper and was fired because they found a tiny piece of trash" in a room she'd cleaned.

The mostly female housekeepers suffered especially from cruelty around their pregnancies. Lemus's daughter Adriana is now a healthy 6-year-old, but when she was lifting heavy furniture while pregnant with Adriana, Lemus began to feel terrible pain in her sciatic nerve. "I began to have contractions at eight months," she said. "When the

> **Unionized hotels in Boston typically require housekeepers to clean 15 rooms per day, while DoubleTree workers were doing roughly double that.**

Keeping up the pressure: Sandra Hernández and her fellow housekeepers went on a 24-hour strike to push their bosses to the negotiating table.

doctor examined me, he ordered me to bed rest." She says her doctor sent notes to her bosses, to no avail. Lemus's back pain persisted, and continues to this day. "Every time I was working, I was crying because I felt my baby was in danger and might have birth defects," she said. "But thank God, my daughter was born healthy."

In 2012, union organizers from Local 26 began knocking on the doors of workers at the DoubleTree. The local already represented workers at nearly half of the hotels in Boston. Nonunionized workers were well aware of the benefits accorded their unionized brethren: affordable health insurance, a more reasonable workload, better wages. Many of the housekeepers didn't need to be asked twice. Lemus took on an organizing role, persuading hesitant colleagues to sign on to the union drive, coordinating with the union representatives, and holding secret meetings out of management's earshot. By March 2013, a critical mass of hotel employees—not just housekeepers, but also waiters, porters, and custodians—had privately affirmed their desire for a union.

O N MARCH 11, 2013, TWO THINGS HAPpened: The DoubleTree workers filed a petition declaring their intent to unionize, and Sheryl Sandberg published a declaration of her own called *Lean In: Women, Work, and the Will to Lead.* That book begins with a pregnancy story, too. After a bad experience rushing from the far end of Google's parking lot to a client meeting while pregnant, Sandberg writes, "I marched in—or more like waddled in—to see Google founders Larry Page and Sergey Brin in their office, which was really just a large room with toys and gadgets strewn all over the floor." Stepping into the playroom of the maverick man-children, Sandberg demanded pregnancy parking. Brin quickly agreed. Sandberg observes that there must have been other pregnant Google employees suffering all along, concluding: "Having one pregnant woman at the top—even one who looked like a whale—made the difference." In 2008, Sandberg jumped to Facebook, becoming its chief operating officer. In 2010, she gave the TED Talk that made her famous: "Why We Have Too Few Women Leaders," which addressed "what we [professional women] can do as individuals" to make it to the disproportionately male top of the professional world.

That talk was famously spun off into the book called *Lean In*, which, like the lecture, encourages women to overcome the obstacles to corporate success by doing things like "sitting at the table" and "making your partner a real partner." It encourages women to form supportive "lean in" circles at work, a sort of corporate echo of 1960s consciousness-raising groups, and the Lean In foundation says that "85 percent of members credit their Circle with a positive change in their life." Because *Lean In* aims to increase equality by changing women's behavior, the book offers little about systemic changes like paid leave or child-care initiatives.

Before Sandberg joined Facebook's

board and C-suite, the company had faced a barrage of criticism for its sexist work environment and 100 percent male corporate board. Nor was it alone—Silicon Valley was growing rapidly, but its culture hadn't caught up to the norms in other big industries, which mandate at least gestures toward gender and racial equity. Tech sites like *Mashable* had issued criticisms of the company (it didn't help that Facebook famously got its start as a "Hot or Not" website for ranking women at Harvard and was still powered primarily by people looking at photographs of women). Activists with UltraViolet, an online organization dedicated to combating sexism, had picketed the company's New York offices to demand female board members. Facebook soon added Sandberg to its board, where today she is one of only two women. With a blockbuster book launch—supported by corporate partners like American Express, JPMorgan Chase, and Walmart—Sandberg entered the stratosphere of best-selling authors. She was no longer just a tech heavyweight. Alan Murray, editor of *Fortune*, noted in an interview that "you have sort of achieved one-name status: You're now Sheryl." She talked women and work with Diane Sawyer and on *Oprah*. Facebook's COO became the new face of feminism. And with that, *Lean In* changed Facebook's public image from that of a New Economy boys' club to the home of tech's leading feminist. Facebook founder Mark Zuckerberg weighed in (on Facebook) to proclaim Sandberg's book "radically realistic."

In April 2013, Sandberg returned to Harvard Business School to attend the W50 summit celebrating 50 years of that institution's admitting women, just before graduation. The event also marked the conclusion of a two-year effort by the school to address its rampant sexism, its consistently lower grades for women, and its inability to retain female faculty. The school had also been tainted, like the rest of Harvard, by the scent of sexism that wafted from former university president Larry Summers wherever he went—in 2005, Summers had remarked that innate differences could be responsible for women's lagging success in the sciences. He resigned in 2006, after only five years as president. Drew Faust, Harvard's first female president, succeeded him. According to a lengthy report by *The New York Times*, Faust appointed a new dean of the business school in 2010 who had set about trying to remedy the problem by doing everything from placing stenographers in every classroom to study class participation (a crucial part of grading) to intervening in the campus social life.

Sandberg began her address by congratulating the women on graduating 50 years after the first woman entered the business school. She asked them to lean in to their future workplaces and tell their bosses what they needed, enlisting those (mostly) men in creating a more equitable workplace. She talked about her book and told a story about her brother, a surgeon who had told the women on his team that he would support their pregnancies. "I'm going to help you take a leave, I'm going to help you come back," he had said. Sandberg concluded that "that conversation needs to start happening in every workplace in America. Every. Single. One." In the evening, conference attendees retired to the DoubleTree, where just such a conversation was beginning.

Tech support: Following Trump's election, Sheryl Sandberg joins the president-elect and other Silicon Valley leaders, including Peter Thiel (right), at a meeting in Trump Tower.

> **Every time I was working, I was crying because I felt my baby was in danger.**
> —Delmy Lemus, DoubleTree housekeeper

ON MARCH 11, 2013, THE DOUBLETREE WORKers presented their unionization petition to their manager. They arrived in a group that included workers, union staff, Harvard students, and members of the City Council. Lemus described it as a positive day, "but with lots of fear and nerves." Her role was to present the petition. After she introduced herself and began to explain the petition, the manager turned on his heels, walked out of the room, and "left me talking to myself." It was clear from the beginning that DoubleTree's management was not interested in conversation.

A month and a half after declaring their intent to form a union, and a few weeks after cleaning the rooms of the very W50 attendees whom Sandberg had urged to stand up for themselves at work, the DoubleTree workers filed charges of unfair labor practices with the National Labor Relations Board, accusing Hilton of interfering in their unionization process. Instead of allowing for a card-check election, or what unions call a fair process, Hilton wanted a ballot-box election. Through card-check, an employer voluntarily recognizes a union once a majority of employees have demonstrated their support for it; in a ballot-box election, the NLRB administers the election, and a majority vote by workers obliges the employer to recognize the union. The problem with NLRB elections is that they can be held on the premises, and the employer can keep out supportive workers on the day of the election. Without a fair-process agreement, the employer can also show workers anti-union propaganda and engage in threatening behavior, such as speaking to them individually about the harm that a union will do to their jobs.

The workers began the public phase of their campaign and, with it, the endless meetings that define organizing. Every day, Lemus met with students, other workers, sympathetic clergy, and City Council members. Sometimes she brought her daughters. "The little one doesn't understand" why they had to be out picketing in the rain and snow, Lemus said. "But the oldest is a 12-year-old girl and understands what I am doing and says, '*Mami*, I am proud of you because you don't give up.'" At first, her husband warned her against putting her job in jeopardy. Not to mention another obstacle: "I had to leave my husband without dinner because I had to go to so many organizations and attend meetings, and he would be upset." Couldn't he cook? "He burns water."

The obvious strategy was to go after Harvard, the hotel's owner. According to Local 26 president Brian Lang, that strategy was "based on our experience in the hotel industry. Most hotels are not owned by the companies that operate them, so we have a lot of experience dealing with the owner-operator dynamic, and without exception at the end of the day, we've found that the owner calls that shot."

The seeming strangeness of a Harvard-owned hotel is less strange in the context of today's hotel market, in which most are owned by real-estate investment trusts and private-equity companies. "Dealing with Harvard was just like dealing with another financial institution," Lang explains. "They do a little education on the side. I don't say that to be derogatory; it's just useful for us to understand."

Going after Harvard meant enlisting the Student Labor Action Movement. SLAM has been involved in a number of prominent Harvard actions over the years, most recently as part of the struggle to help dining-hall workers win benefits. As paying Harvard customers, SLAM students have the ability to demand time with administrators, hold protests on campus, and generally freak out the administration a lot more than workers can alone.

K ARELY OSORIO IS A HARVARD JUNIOR (THOUGH still a sophomore when we spoke) and a first-generation college student whose parents came from Mexico to Texas before she was born. When she was a child, Osorio had never heard of Harvard, and when she got in, with the support of appreciative teachers at her private high school for low-income kids, she wasn't sure she wanted to go. "People just assumed I would say yes to Harvard," she recalled. We're across from the dining hall that workers fought to unionize 78 years ago, and where they went on strike this fall during contract negotiations. "I always had an image in my mind of Harvard as this school where rich white kids go. I didn't know if I would fit in there. My high school was 90 percent Latino. Many of us were English-language learners—we were all low-income kids." She feared that she would miss her family, and she does. One of the first DoubleTree stories she encountered was in Local 26's report "DoubleTree, Double Standard," in which Lemus describes her incapacitating back pain. Osorio's dad works installing carpets, and when he was involved in a car crash years ago, the damage to his back made the heavy work particularly hard. "He always would ask if I wouldn't mind giving him a massage or something, or ask, 'Would you please get me a glass of water or bring my food, because I'm just tired and I don't want to get up?' And hearing that this was happening in this hotel that my school owned was just horrifying."

Ignored and insulted by the managers, the workers decided to go straight to the top and, with the help of their student allies, attempted to meet with Drew Faust, who, before becoming Harvard's president, had made her academic reputation as a historian writing about plantation mistresses during the American Civil War. Sandra Hernández, one of Lemus's fellow housekeepers, told me that when workers visited the president's office, "they allowed three of us to enter. But the secretary dealt with us, because none of the higher-ups at Harvard would deal with us." Lemus reported that "many times we've come to protest and to be heard by the office of the president, and the police have been called, and they've removed us as if we were criminals that don't belong."

The students tried to get to Faust by signing up for her office hours. Four times a year, she sets aside two hours during which students or groups can sign up for 10-minute slots. Osorio had attended one of these sessions on behalf of

The price that women often pay for the honor of being first in the boys' club is cleaning up the club's misogyny.

At the top: Drew Faust, Harvard's first female president, refused to meet with activists involved in the DoubleTree unionization effort.

the dining-hall workers. She said Faust seemed fairly uninterested, telling the delegation that they were welcome to send a letter to her office. Osorio recalls Faust denying control over the situation and asking why the students were coming to her. "Our response to that is, even if you don't have ultimate control, you definitely have influence," Osorio said. Faust's office did not respond to *The Nation*'s request for comment.

Confronted with the housekeepers' demands, the university would not clarify to the students, workers, or union whom they should petition within the Harvard administration—and even now, no one on the outside knows who has the final say. The non-office-hour delegations that tried to meet with Faust were met by a firmly unhelpful secretary and campus security. Fellow women historians signed a letter to Faust, expressing their delight at seeing a female colleague leading Harvard and their "puzzlement" at the university's refusal to support a fair process for a 90 percent female workforce. Historian Amy Kesselman, who circulated the letter, received a response from Faust saying that she would forward the letter to the employee-relations department. So, said Kesselman, "our effort to invoke sisterhood and solidarity didn't work." The response made her "feel a little naive."

Meanwhile, the campaign for a fair unionization process took many forms. Along with distributing leaflets, DoubleTree housekeepers and SLAM members dragged beds onto campus and challenged Harvard students to make them up to the exacting standards of DoubleTree. The workers stood by and graded the students, and apparently had not gotten the memo about Ivy League grade inflation—no A's were awarded. Then, on March 27, 2014, workers called a boycott of the Harvard DoubleTree. Delegations to Harvard and to Hilton had failed; there weren't many tactics left to be tried. The boycott kicked off with a picket on a cold Thursday, with more than 100 workers and supporters in attendance. Lemus took turns on the picket line with her kid. Osorio served as a translator for the media.

On April 3, Harvard Business School showed its disdain for the boycott by lodging participants in the second annual Gender and Work Symposium at the DoubleTree for the duration of the conference. Dozens of women gathered to discuss how women could excel in business, giving talks like "Prescriptions for Female Solidarity and Women's Relationships" and "Branding Feminism: The Race to Recruit the 'Lean In' Generation." The union says it put fliers in the mailboxes at the business school and tried to meet with professors, but received no expressions of support.

One month later, with the boycott still ongoing, one of the union organizers heard that Sheryl Sandberg would be giving a speech at Harvard's Class Day on May 28. Lemus headed up a petition effort to persuade Sandberg to lead a lean-in circle with the DoubleTree workers—all women who hoped to better their working conditions with many of the benefits that Sandberg had demanded for herself, including maternity accommodations and wage increases. The DoubleTree housekeepers made a lo-fi video in front of the hotel: "Sheryl!" they said. "We are leaning in!" *The Boston Globe* covered their plea, as did the *Crimson*. The housekeepers figured that if Sandberg talked with Harvard administrators, they might listen to one of their most famous graduates. According to the union, Sandberg said she didn't have time. Or, in Lemus's blunter assessment: "Maybe she wasn't going to have a moment for those of us who are just workers in the lower classes. She had more important things with people from upper classes."

Sandberg did speak at Class Day, charmingly. She thanked the crowd for being there "given the weather, the one thing Harvard hasn't figured out how to control." Meanwhile, two City Council members boycotted the graduation, noting that they were "ashamed" of Harvard's resistance to a fair process for DoubleTree workers.

Nearly out of options, the housekeepers went on a one-day strike in November. It was the first hotel strike in Boston in 100 years. The workers woke up early. Some prayed together at an old Boston cathedral. Students strung signs across the campus listing the workers' complaints—of injuries, of the hotel's refusal to accommodate their pregnancies. The workers had cleared out their lockers the night before, in case they were fired. The strike went on all day. But the workers weren't fired; nor were they given a fair process. Nothing changed—and, exhausted, the workers settled in for a long wait.

ON APRIL 7, THE UNION SUMMONED THE workers and students to their headquarters. Hilton had agreed to a fair process. Three years of fighting were over. To this day, no one knows if Faust conceded the workers' point, or if some obscure Harvard office decided that the fight wasn't worth it. On April 11, the workers announced that they had officially voted to join Unite Here.

Today, the workers at DoubleTree have successfully negotiated their first contract, which brings their working conditions in line with those at the other hotels represented by Local 26. They also have one unique provision: Workers have the explicit right to negotiate for lighter loads during pregnancy. This may not be much—the contract doesn't mandate any particular outcome. But it's the first of its kind in Boston hotels, and a concession to women's needs that the union hopes to replicate and expand on when the contracts for all the hotel workers that it represents come up for simultaneous negotiation in 2018. The story, in short, has a happy ending. But, said Osorio, "It's easy to look back in hindsight and be like, 'Oh yeah, they stood up, that's great'—but that's because we won." Had they lost, the women likely would have been out of their jobs. Asked by *The Nation* to comment on DoubleTree today, Sandberg said through a spokesperson: "The workers at the Double-Tree Suites successfully unionized, and I support their rights to organize."

The courageous battle waged by the DoubleTree housekeepers shows how women have, against the odds, united since well before Trump's election, when the enemies were often people or institutions who purported to hold liberal values. Today, when we ask "How can we resist?," we might look to their example. As Magally A. Miranda Alcazar and Kate D. Griffiths have pointed out

" Our effort to invoke sisterhood and solidarity didn't work. "
—Amy Kesselman

in these pages ["Female Privilege," March 27], the most vulnerable women have been engaged in the most militant resistance this year—in prison strikes, in the Black Lives Matter movement, in the Standing Rock Sioux's fight against the Dakota Access Pipeline, and in the Day Without Immigrants protest. The struggle for union representation strikes at the heart of growing inequality.

This poses a challenge to powerful liberal feminists like Faust and Sandberg, both of whom have publicly taken issue with some of Trump's plans. Faust has signed a letter decrying Trump's Muslim ban, and Sandberg has published Facebook posts about her great-grandmother's immigration from Lithuania and about the harm that reinstituting the global gag rule against abortion would have on women who rely on US foreign aid. She has also, after the death of her husband, acknowledged the difficulty of single parenting and mothers' need for more resources. After receiving voluminous criticism for not acknowledging the Women's March, Sandberg donated $1 million to Planned Parenthood and met privately with the march's organizers. After all, to be a corporate feminist is still to be a feminist—Trump's agenda is appalling even to those who are safe from its most immediate effects. And Sandberg's brand is now so wrapped up with gender that failing to engage with recent feminist organizing stands to harm her reputation.

Engaging with the broader, resurgent feminist movement will not be so easy, though. The price that high-up women often pay for the honor of being first in the boys' club is that of cleaning up the club's misogyny and laundering capital's reputation. Sandberg spoke up for Summers when he embarrassed himself at Harvard, penning an op-ed about his concern for women, and helped Zuckerberg and Facebook by becoming their official feminist. Faust righted Harvard after Summers drove it into a ditch, and now she travels to girls' schools abroad to champion the importance of education for gender equity. On December 14, Trump hosted a meeting with tech leaders, in which he aimed to smooth their rocky relationship (97 percent of Silicon Valley donors' support went to Hillary Clinton during the campaign). Sandberg attended, looking appropriately unimpressed. She was seated front and center, two seats from Trump, and right next to Vice President Mike Pence, who voted

Facebook feminism: Sandberg speaks on "The Future of the Digital Economy" at the World Economic Forum in Davos in 2015.

three times against the Lily Ledbetter Fair Pay Act while in Congress. (A spokesperson for Sandberg says that she raised the issue of paid leave in the meeting.) Faced with a choice between protecting Facebook by playing ball with the new administration and rejecting an odious politician, there is only one way a responsible COO can go. Directly to Trump's left was Palantir chairman Peter Thiel, part of Trump's transition team and another member of the Facebook board.

Labor issues may continue to divide corporate and working-class feminists. Faust has continued to oppose labor-justice and unionization efforts on campus. When the dining-hall workers went on strike last fall, management was refusing to agree to a $35,000 minimum wage per year and better health-care benefits. Faust has also opposed efforts by graduate students to unionize, despite their precarious employment and low wages. Along with other Ivy League presidents, including famous liberals like Columbia University's Lee Bollinger, she has taken her opposition to the National Labor Relations Board, filing an amicus brief arguing that graduate students are not employees. Her chances of success are bolstered by Trump's election; as a passionate opponent of organized labor, his NLRB is likely to shoot down unionization efforts. Corporate feminists like Faust seem determined to demonstrate the reasons that working people have ceased to trust liberal authorities.

Sandberg seems to have done a better job of catching up with progressive politics. In 2015, she announced new standards for Facebook's contractors and vendors, including a $15-an-hour minimum wage. She offers paid leave to Facebook employees and has said she supports national paid-leave legislation. Through a spokesperson, she told *The Nation* that "women who are single mothers, people of color, and women who lack resources are especially vulnerable…and I believe that women who don't face those barriers have a responsibility to stand with women who do." She recognized the value of unions in protecting workers, noting that "it is important that workers continue to have the right to collectively bargain and do not face unfair barriers in their right to organize." Asked if she would support women in pursuit of a union in the future, Sandberg replied: "I am not sure that it is logistically or practically possible for me to make individual endorsement decisions on all the specific efforts women and men take across our country."

SLAM demonstrates a model for real solidarity that has antecedents in the earliest labor struggles. As described in Susan Faludi's article "Facebook Feminism, Like It or Not," during some of the first female-led labor struggles at the textile mills of Lowell, Massachusetts, in the 1830s, middle-class women were horrified by a deadly factory collapse. They "flocked to provide emergency relief and, radicalized by what they witnessed, went on to establish day nurseries, medical clinics and hospitals, and cooperative housing to serve the needs of working women." Or take the National Women's Trade Union League, established in the United States in 1903. According to historian Dorothy Sue Cobble (one of the historians who signed that letter to Faust), the organization benefited from the sponsorship of elites as it coordinated internationally with working women to demand international labor standards—but the leadership was required to be mostly working-class women, affiliated with trade unions. Appealing to an economically and racially diverse array of women through feminist celebrities and billionaires, as Hillary Clinton attempted to do in securing Sandberg's

How political is Sandberg willing to become to support women up and down the income scale?

Watch an accompanying video directed by Rebecca Rojer at TheNation.com.

endorsement in the 2016 presidential race, cannot help but highlight an elitist worldview that is alien to most women's lives.

WHAT THE MAJORITY OF WOMEN WANT has, in many ways, not changed in decades: economic security, good and accessible child care, freedom from violence, the pleasures of life with enough education and leisure time to allow us to flourish. But intractable problems remain. Pregnancy is penalized by a lack of time off, or by time off for women but not for men, which exacerbates the wage gap. The Department of Health and Human Services has found that child care is unaffordable in every single state. Ninety-eight percent of women in abusive relationships are subject to financial abuse, and a woman without an income has a hard time getting away—a topic that was the subject of Sandberg's own undergraduate thesis, "Economic Factors and Intimate Violence." Luckily, we actually know quite a bit about how to fix these things. In Sweden, women and men are motivated to take parental time off (if the man doesn't take his time, they both lose some), ensuring family time and a smaller wage gap. We know that universal child care, as organized in Norway, produces happy kids and greater gender equity. In fact, the United States almost had something comparable in 1971, when a bill for universal child care passed both houses of Congress, only to be vetoed by then-President Richard Nixon under the influence of a young Pat Buchanan.

Lobbying for universal child care, unionization, or any of the other measures we know help most women would mean making enemies in a way that advocating for "empowerment" or "banning bossy," as Sandberg has done, never would. It would mean a fight not just with Republicans (Sandberg gives money mostly to Democrats, but she has paid into Olympia's List and Facebook's PAC, both of which have supported several Republicans), but with Democrats, too, and maybe even some of Sandberg's pals on the Davos circuit. It would mean being political, and it would not serve her as PR. It would not help Facebook. But it would place her considerable resources in the service of women up and down the income scale. In the words of Osorio, without a feminism that emphasizes solidarity, "you haven't solved *the* problem. You've just solved *your* problem."

When I asked Lemus what she would have Sandberg do, she answered that Sandberg had enough money to make the government listen to the needs of women. Osorio noted that Sandberg could listen to women who are unlike her. The problem is not that women like Sandberg and Faust have failed to be saviors; as the DoubleTree workers have shown, working-class women are leading their own movements. It's that women like the DoubleTree housekeepers are doing the concrete work of pushing toward equality, and women like Faust and Sandberg are thwarting or, in the best case, ignoring them instead of helping them. They demonstrate that it is possible for women to sound like feminists but function as The Man. We don't need them to lead us, but if they aren't going to express solidarity, they can at least get out of the way.

Leonard documents the trials and tribulations of the women who cleaned the rooms in Harvard University's DoubleTree hotel. It is true that 90% of hotel room cleaners are women. The disparity between hotel workers who are unionized and those who are not can be notably wide. As observed in the article, most hotel room cleaners must do 15 rooms a day. At the DoubleTree, the women were doing about double that, cleaning 14 *suites* of rooms. The pressures on them to speedily complete the work were dibilitating.

First in the Boy's Club

What was notable about the women cleaners was the trouble they had in gaining support from the women corporate leaders. Drew Faust, the first woman president of Harvard, did not lend the women her support (even when petitioned to do so by female faculty). She also opposed the union for the women and for graduate students (the unioniziation of graduate students is now fairly common throughout United States universities). The author characterized Faust's attitude (and less so but also of Sheryl Sandberg, author of *Lean In*) as women, "first in the boy's club," who are required to do the dirty work of "cleaning up the club's misogyny." It has often been the case that women who have made it to the top are required to be as ruthless as the men. Witness Margaret Thatcher's reputation as the "Iron Lady," who led Britain through a largely useless war with Argentina over the Falkland Islands. As Leonard concluded: "it is possible for women to sound like feminists but function as The Man." The DoubleTree unionization movement resulted in some powerful women figures giving no help to the working women, with an accompanying lament on the lack of sisterhood and solidarity.

CONCLUSION: WRAP-UP

These two articles help illustrate how far women have to go to achieve equality. It is no wonder that in the developed world, many institutions pay lip service to the need to equal the playing field for women on so many fronts. The United Nations has made the issue of gender equality a leading concern, and yet, even progressive institutions, such as universities, struggle to make gender equality a reality. Just as an aside, it is now well-known that teaching evaluations are gender-biased to the detriment of female faculty; reading #20 also noted that Facebook started as a "Hot or Not" website for ranking Harvard women. It has recently been reported that, in the entire world, there is no place where men do more housework than women, which is not really surprising. There is a great hypocrisy at work in the treatment of women, especially as set out by Abu-Lughod, tying gender bias to imperialistic colonialism. When speaking of the U.S. conquest of the Philippines, President William McKinley claimed that the U.S. invasion was for the good of the "misguided Filipino": "Did we need their consent to perform a great act for humanity?. . . the United States never goes abroad in search of selfish advantage; it seeks only to help less fortunate peoples, even if they cannot understand that they are being helped; and it always acts in accordance with noble ideals." This statement beautifully illustrates Abu-Lughod's comment that such help implies a feeling of superiority. Unfortunately, McKinley's statement has resonated as a guiding principle in much U.S. foreign policy, and as we shall see in a later chapter, the principle he articulates is still held by many U.S. officials. But, as Abu-Lughod has demonstrated, and as a British journalist remarked on U.S. policy in that era: "That is what the unctious rectitude of the Anglo-Saxon always ends in. He always begins by calling Heaven to witness his unselfish desire to help his neighbor, but he always ends by stealing his spoons." No, Muslim women do not need saving, but justice bewteen nations is something that would benefit all, as we shall explore in Chapter 10.

ACTIVITIES

Activity for Reading #19: in small groups, compare your Schema Activation answers to the question posed there:

- were European governments right to ban face-veiling for Muslim women.
- In light of Abu-Lughod's article, what do you think now?
- Did Abu-Lughod change your mind or not?

Activity for Reading #20: in Iceland in the 1970s, a number of women's groups started a movement called "Wages for Housework." The movement shattered the notion that people, especially women, should just do housework "out of love." As women started to enter the workforce, and given that women still do more housework than men, having a full-time job climbing the corporate ladder meant that women had more work piled on them. On top of that, housework is always in a context of isolation, irregular hours, and exclusion from labor laws. In small groups, discuss the implications of this movement.

- Should people be paid for doing the housework?
- How would this work and if we were to look at this retrospectively, would it not require a reparations demand?
- Is this a revolutionary idea?

SOURCES

Some of the definitions are adapted from Shirley A. Fedorak *Anthropology Matters* (Third Edition) 2017 University of Toronto Press; other concepts are adapted from Richard H. Robbins *Global Problems and the Culture of Capitalism* (Fourth Edition) Pearson pp. 348-355; the quotes about the U.S. invasion of the Philippines are taken from Brenda Wineapple The Large Policy:

How the Spanish-American War laid the groundwork for American Empire *The Nation* February 26, 2018 pp. 31-34; the information about the Wages for Housework movement is from Sarah Jaffe The Factory in the Family: The radical vision of Wages for Housework *The Nation* April 9, 2018 pp. 27-31.

Chapter 9

Religious and Ethnic Conflict: The Power of Sacrifice

OBJECTIVES

- Analyze the history of ethnic conflict from the ancient Romans to the modern Middle East, in order to understand how such problems defy easy resolution.
- Determine for yourself how the dynamic of suicide terrorism appears directed towards ending the perceived occupation of one's country by foreign troops.
- Attribute correctly the origin and development of terrorism to many other cultural entities other than Islamist groups.
- Explain how the nature of terrorism functions as a strategy to achieve "political ends by other means."

KEY TERMS

Terrorism: violent acts against random members of the public at large or targeted power-holding individuals carried out by governments or resistance groups directed towards frightening people into submission to the government or into agitating for changes from the government.

Suicide Terrorism: violent acts committed in public against citizens at large in which the attacker is killed as part of the the violent attack itself.

SCHEMA ACTIVATION ACTIVITY

Briefly research one terrorist event of the past {you may use Reading #23 to identify one, but do not use 9/11}: consider the description of the event and answer the following question: *what were the apparent motivations of the attacker(s) and where they successful at all in bringing about some change?*

(Save these to share later in your discussion sections.)

INTRODUCTION

We tackle here the difficult and emotionally challenging issue of terrorism that has grown out of ethnic conflict. We start with a fascinating comparison of the mythical story of the foundation of Rome (by Trojan exiles taking over the territory of the Latins) with the displacment of Palestinians by Jews in the modern state of Israel. We then review the analysis of the Chicago Project on Security and Terrorism, which has concluded that suicide terrorism for the past couple of decades appears to be almost completely the result of protest against occupation by foreign military forces and not religious extremism. We then look at an article that powerfully sets out the argument that terrorism has only recently been associated with Islamist dissidence.

How the Israeli–Palestinian conflict makes sense of Virgil's Aeneid

by Michael Fontaine

What is wrong with the second half of the *Aeneid*? Why does nobody read or teach it?

Maybe it seems too much like a fairy tale. It's no surprise that the best modern retelling of *Aeneid* 7–12, Ursula Le Guin's 2009 novel *Lavinia*, was written by a master of fantasy fiction.

I suspect, however, the problem is how we translate its story into modern terms. Scholars tend to compare it to Italian fascism, Nazism, colonialism, or the Vietnam War. No wonder students' eyes glaze over. For many of them these political movements are as good as ancient history, and worse, none of the parallels provide all that close a fit.

I would like to suggest a better way of understanding what's at stake in the *Aeneid*. This parallel is a real-life scenario unfolding before our eyes, and it's one that generates such strong feelings—sometimes violent feelings—that it ought to carry a trigger warning.

Why is that? Recall the situation of Virgil's Trojans. After the Greeks destroyed their city and murdered all the inhabitants they could, there was nowhere to go. It was too dangerous for survivors to stay, so they banded together and set sail for another continent. Apollo has told them to head to Italy, and nowhere else, because Italy was their ancestral homeland of long ago. But they got there only to find that other people were already living in it, and these natives weren't about to surrender or quit their land just because a bunch of ragtag refugees have come along claiming divine title to it. War, terrorism, and atrocities follow, intractably and inevitably so.

That is the stuff of *Aeneid* 7–12, but the amazing thing is that it just as easily describes the Israel-Palestine conflict, one of the biggest hot-button issues today. Looking at the *Aeneid* through the lens of the ongoing violence in the Middle East might help bring the little-read second half of the *Aeneid* alive for our students. And, if we're lucky, Virgil may be able to teach us something about the modern conflict, too.

Why do I say the second half of the poem recapitulates what we are seeing in the modern Middle East? Because the Trojan experience in the *Aeneid* matches the harried Jewish experience since World War II, from the Holocaust in Europe to its struggle for statehood and acceptance in Palestine.

Jewish resettlement in Palestine precedes the foundation of Israel in 1948 by over fifty years, of course, but the Holocaust made plain a new justification for the Zionist dream. In the three years between the end of the war and Israel's declaration of statehood, Jewish immigration—which was illegal and risky under the then-ruling British authority— increased significantly. It is that desperate wave of immigration from 1945–1948—known as Aliyah Bet—as well as the moral justification that Zionism provided it, that parallels *Aeneid*7–12.

"MedinatHayehudim" by Unknown. The scene shows Haifa port, 1947. Licensed under Public Domain via Wikimedia Commons

Why? A foundational axiom of Zionism—and an axiom that makes Israel unique among the countries of the world—is that Jewish settlement in Palestine in modern times marks a *latter-day return* of Jews, and not an *immigration* or *colonization* (because there's no metropolis), to their *ancestral homeland*. Resettlement thus rests on a historical claim.

A second axiom holds that it is *God's will* that Jews resettle in Palestine—a belief so powerful it prompted early Zionists to reject offers for settlement in other lands, such as Uganda, where life might have proven easier. Resettlement thus rests also on a religious claim, a second claim that is without parallel in the modern world.

Amazingly, however, both axioms are matched exactly by the Trojans' stance in the *Aeneid*. As Ilioneus, the Trojan ambassador, explains to King Latinus, it is no accident that Trojans have come looking to make their homes in his realm (7.239–242, which here and throughout I cite in the translation of Frederick M. Ahl, occasionally modified):
God-declared destiny, though, drove us to come looking for your lands
By its commands. Here Dardanus started; he's calling us back here.
Powerful orders Apollo once gave force us on to the Tuscan
Tiber...

LIB. VII. ÆN. ꝟ. 192.
Tali intus templo divûm, patriaꝗ Latinus
Sede sedens, Teucros ad sese in tecta vocavit:

usꝗ 248.
30.

The background to this point, about "God-declared destiny" and Dardanus coming from Italy, is found in book 3—another book most readers skip. In it, according to Aeneas, the Trojans' Penates—relaying the will of Apollo—explain that Italy is their ancestral homeland (3.167–171):

That *is our proper home* (propriae sedes): *where Dardanus came from, and also*
Father Iasius. They are the ultimate source of our bloodlines (genus).
Come on, get up! And report what we've said to your elderly father
Joyfully. It's beyond doubt! Let him seek out Corythus, seek out
Lands in Ausonia...

Aeneas is sixth in descent from Dardanus, founder of the Trojan bloodline—which is to say, the Trojan "return" is long past living memory.

Of course, the Trojans didn't just come to Italy because they got sick of living in Troy. They've arrived because they are the last remnant of a holocaust perpetrated on their people—a holocaust cast in explicitly racial terms. When Juno spots the Trojans disembarking in Latium, she exclaims (7.293–6):

Oh! Damn this detestable race (stirpem invisam), *and damn the Phrygians' future,*
Blocking the future as I had it planned! Could they not die on Sigeum's
Plains (campis), *stayed captured when captured? Of course not! When Troy was a bonfire*
Didn't she cremate (cremavit) *her menfolk? Oh no! They discovered a pathway,*
Right through the thick of the front and the fires (ignis).

Juno sees the Trojan remnant not as individual humans perhaps worthy of compassion but as representatives of an evil collective. She hates the whole cunning race.
Replace *Phrygians*, *Sigeum's*, and *Troy* with *Jews*, *Europe's*, and *Auschwitz* and Juno starts to sound like an embittered S.S.-man witnessing the birth of Israel rising from the ashes of the Holocaust, three years after Germany's defeat. Her words even evoke—albeit coincidentally—the camps and the crematoria.

Aeneas, too, sees the Trojan destruction as genocide. In 3.1–2 he says:
After the powers on high had approved the destruction of Priam's
innocent race (evertere gentem)...

And he begins book 2 by telling Dido (2.3–5),
Words can't express, my queen, what you bid me relive, all the rueful
Pain: telling how the Danaans rooted out (eruerint) Troy's wealth and domains
Makes for a dirge of lament.

As before, swapping *Germans* and *the Jews'* for *Danaans* and *Troy's* puts the survivor's perspective into familiar terms.

It is from this background of extermination, survival, regrouping, and departure for a new homeland that we come to events in *Aeneid* 7–12 that echo the headlines we see daily from the Middle East. The Trojans' arrival in Latium is met with split sentiment among the native population, a population that played no part in the Trojans' misfortunes. Some welcome the newcomers but others are suspicious of their intentions, with one even declaring that—

despite there being no metropolis—the Trojans are really engaged in a *colonialist* project. In 7.421–2 Allecto, a fury disguised as an elderly maidservant, goads Turnus:
Turnus, will you let all of your labor's sweat run for nothing,
And let the scepter that's yours be signed over to colonist (colonis) *Dardans?*

It isn't logical but it works; in 11.484 Turnus himself calls Aeneas a bandit (*praedo*)—that is, one who has come not to settle and start a new life in peace but to plunder resources from hapless natives.

On the other hand, Turnus does have a point, because the first thing the Trojans do upon landing in Latium is to occupy territory and begin building illegal settlements on it. In 7.157–9,
Aeneas plows a shallow trench that will outline his city's
Bounds, starts work on the site, and encloses their first coastal dwellings,
Just like an army encampment, with crenellate walls and a rampart.

As Frederick Ahl comments (p. 385), "One usually consulted local peoples *before* setting up a colony—as the Phoenician settlers at Carthage had done. Aeneas seizes territory as an enemy invader would and forces the Latins either to accept him or fight him."

Jacopo Amigoni (1682–1752): Duel between Turnus and Aeneas (Schleißheim New Palace, Munich)

The Trojan-Latin conflict devolves into hardening politics, reciprocal provocations, mounting atrocities, and spiraling cycles of violence—just as in the Middle East. And the parallels don't end there. Some are downright eerie, such as the settlers' uprooting of an ancient olive tree (12.766–71):

Here, so it chanced, a wild olive had stood, consecrated to Faunus.
Sailors had honored it once (though its bitter leaves marked it for firewood).
They made a practice, when saved from the seas, of fixing upon it
Gifts for the Laurentine god, and of hanging up garments as offerings.
Teucrians, wanting to fight on a plain free of any obstruction
Made no exceptions and hacked this sacred plant to a low stump.

An Israeli bulldozer uproots an olive tree (source: http://ijsn.net/stopthejnf/fight-greenwashing-and-green-sunday/)

The equations I have been listing are obvious to me. They illustrate the aptness of a remark made in 1949 by Arthur Koestler (1905–1983), the Hungarian journalist who began his career in the service of Ze'ev Jabotinsky, father of Revisionist Zionism. "Whatever else the State of Israel may be," wrote Koestler, weeks after witnessing its violent birth firsthand, "it has come to signify to me a country more transparent than any other to the basic archetypes of human conflict and experience. For Israel is merely reproducing today a very old drama in modern costume...." (p. ix)

But the equations are lost on scholars and the conflicting parties alike. It is not surprising that average Israelis and Palestinians, Jews and Arabs are oblivious to them, but the similarities escaped even Shlomo Dykman (1917–1965), who published a Hebrew translation of the *Aeneid* in Jerusalem in 1962. To celebrate his translation Dykman included a dedication of his devising. The Latin is clumsy but the author's patriotism and pride come through clearly:

Hos tibi, posteritas, versus nunc pectore ab imo
quos legis ut noris laetusque in saecula sacro!
Percipe, sancta Sion, siquid mea carmina possunt,
auribus ipsa tuis, qualis fuit hostis acerbus,
olim qui magnis legionibus imperitarit!
Discite nunc, pueri, qualis fuit ille Romanus,
qui regere imperio populos terramque paternam
iussus erat—qualis fuerat Latina potestas!
Non eadem est aetas, non gens... Obadia noster
vicit Vergilium et voluntas omnipotentis
has evertit opes stravitque a culmine Idumen.
Posuit ecce Deus finem atque tempora Romae...
Sic placitum est: Sion, devicta—nunc reviviscis!
Salve, sancta parens frugum, carissima tellus,
sancta virum! Tibi res antiquae laudis et artem
ingredior versus ausus renovare Maronis,

Hebraeumque cano rediviva per oppida carmen!
(Hierosolymis. Anno XIII a patria recreata)
You must know, posterity, that it is to you that I dedicate the verses
you're reading. I do so eternally glad and with all my heart.
Lend an ear, o hallowed Zion! If my poem but can,
hear the manner of our bitter foe,
that foe who once wielded mighty legions!
Now, children, behold the manner of the Roman,
of him commanded to control the gentiles and the Land
of our ancestors — behold what Latium's power had once been!
Our age and race are not what they were; our prophet <u>*Obadiah*</u>
outdid Virgil: the Almighty's will did destroy
all that we had, and did annihilate Idumea.
But look! God did put an end, a limit, to Rome!
Such was His pleasure. Zion, you who lost—you are coming to life again!
Hail, blessed mother of earth's fruits, blessed mother of men,
our beloved Land! For you I am engaging the stuff and style of venerable praise,
as I presume to refashion Maro's verses anew,
and through towns that live once more, I am singing a Hebrew song.
(Jerusalem, in the 13th year since the restoration of my country)

It is easy to share Dykman's awe at the miraculous fulfillment of the Zionist dream. It is
hard to condone, however, his failure to identify the tensions and passions generated by that
dream in any way with the tensions on display in Virgil's epic. Much as Sigmund Freud
admired the Carthaginian general Hannibal as a "Semitic avenger" of the Romans (whom he

associated with the Catholic Church), so Dykman identifies the Zionist movement entirely with the Jews of antiquity. He sees Virgil's mythical pre-Romans as those historical Romans who, under Titus, destroyed Jerusalem's Second Temple in 70 C.E.

Contemporary authors fare no better. A review last year of Ari Shavit's *My Promised Land: The Triumph and Tragedy of Israel* is titled "Israel's Virgil." It is easy to agree in general with the reviewer that "The distinction between Homer's *Iliad* and Virgil's *Aeneid* sheds much light on the way that Ari Shavit's new, much discussed book aims to change our perceptions and discussions about Israel." Yet the obvious parallels elude him. "But war is so terrible," he writes, "causing enormous bloodshed and destruction, thousands to flee into exile, families to be sacrificed, that it should be contained and avoided wherever possible (in his [Virgil's] view, through a *Pax Romana*)." I doubt the reviewer meant to imply that Israel should impose a *Pax Israelitica*—a Rome-like empire without limit—across the Middle East. The Palestinian plight does not figure into the equation.

What a missed opportunity! If, as the cliché goes, literature is "good to think with," readers could benefit from pondering the *Aeneid* through the lens of the Israeli-Palestinian problem, beginning with why anyone came up with Zionism in the first place.

The goddess Juno's implacable hatred of the Trojans, for example, is one of the hardest elements of Virgil's story to translate into real-world concerns today. Her hatred is brooding, eternal, and it has a litany of causes. It seems mythical or artificial, and hence remote—yet for those same reasons, it is remarkably comparable to European anti-Semitism. Juno's hatred transcends space and history, and it readily makes enemies of neutrals, friends, and neighbors. On a whim it moves men to murder and—what is most relevant—it is rooted in race. Juno calls the Trojans a *stirps invisa*, a hated race, and, if she only could, she would *perdere gentem*—annihilate the race (7.304). Mirroring this language exactly—and later, becoming justification for anti-Semitism in Christian times, in *Histories* 5.3 Tacitus calls Jews "a race the gods hate" (*genus hominum...invisum deis*).

Or better, How does the rhetoric of the Israeli Proclamation of Independence mirror the rhetoric of Ilioneus's speech in *Aeneid* 7? I quoted a snippet above, but here is more of how the Trojan diplomat justifies to Latinus his people's presence in Latium (7.222–5, 228–30, 239–242):

How huge a hurricane rolled out of savage Mycenae all over
Ida's plains, what forces of destiny drove into conflict
Europe and Asia, two distinct spheres: there's a tale that the whole world's
Heard....
Out of that primal flood, men borne over so many vast seas
Ask, for our fathers' gods, just a tiny home, just a harmless
Haven, and water and air, which are nobody's private possessions....
God-declared destiny, though, drove us to come looking for your lands
By its commands. Here Dardanus started; he's calling us back here.
Powerful orders Apollo once gave force us on to the Tuscan
Tiber...

Just so, the 1948 State of Israel Proclamation of Independence justifies its need for statehood (translation from the Israeli government website):

ERETZ-ISRAEL [(Hebrew)—the Land of Israel, Palestine] was the birthplace of the Jewish people [sc. after the Second Temple Period, in antiquity]. ...

The catastrophe which recently befell the Jewish people—the massacre of millions of Jews in Europe—was another clear demonstration of the urgency of solving the problem of its homelessness by re-establishing in Eretz-Israel the Jewish State...
Survivors of the Nazi holocaust in Europe, as well as Jews from other parts of the world, continued to migrate to Eretz-Israel [sc. 1945–8, Aliyah Bet], undaunted by difficulties, restrictions and dangers, and never ceased to assert their right to a life of dignity, freedom and honest toil in their national homeland.

The parallels are startling—Holocaust, national homeland, a return.

But founding stories, true or otherwise, aren't the only reason for reading the *Aeneid* in the light of the Israeli-Palestinian conflict. There's another inescapable dimension to all this, and it's the biggest of all.

Homer's *Iliad* is a war between equals, but Virgil's conflict between Trojans and Latins is a *clash of civilizations*. At stake are not just land and resources but core values and ways of life. One value is *religious*, a dispute over details within the same basic theological system. The Latins worship Saturn. The Trojans worship His son, Jupiter. Just so Jews worship Yahweh, while Palestinians worship Allah or Yahweh's son, Jesus. And just as Jews came to bring their God into Palestine, but without *missionary* purposes, so too the Trojans have come to bring their gods—the Penates—into Latium, but without missionary purposes.

A more salient problem, however, is the disparity in *modes of life*. The Trojans are cosmopolitans, chased from their homes and now rootless but formerly urban, refined, and united in purpose. The indigenous Latins are primitive and pastoral, most of them peasants. Their land, Latium, is somnolescent and underdeveloped. It is semifeudal, ruled by clans and kept in check by strong men or wealthy landowners. Accordingly, it is a balkanized patchwork of baffling disputes among neighboring tribes.

Virgil presents Latium's masses as peaceful and politically passive, but easily and instantly fanaticized. When Ascanius accidentally shoots a deer, for example, the cry of the bugle that sets the Latin peasants rioting conjures up Hollywood portrayals of the *adhan*, or Islamic call to prayer, that blares from Arab minarets (7.519–521):
Off men speed for the source of the sound, where the grimly demonic
Bugle has signaled. These farmers who've never been tamed grab for weapons
Everywhere.

And inevitably, of course, when the indigenous population takes up arms it is made to seem like a replay of the original enemy. We hear regularly of a "second Hitler." Just so Turnus is called an *alius Achilles*, another Achilles (6.89). It is all so depressingly familiar.

Strife in the Middle East shows no sign of abating but at some point it will have to end. How so? Many are eager for two separate states, one for each party, but a growing minority is clamoring for a single, binational state to absorb both groups. Those of us who don't live there might be tempted to ask some powerful agency—the U.S., say, or the U.N.—to impose a solution, perhaps by dictating terms such as these:

· Palestine's people will keep both native language and culture.
· Further, their name will remain as it is. Intermarriage will thin out what's left of Israelis: namely, their blood. We shall add rituals and customs.
· *And* we shall ensure that they'll all be collectively known as "the Arabs."
· Out of this blend with Palestinian blood you will see a new nation
Rise, and surpass all men and the gods in its righteous devotion.

Of course, this solution would horrify the majority of Jews, Israelis, Arabs and Palestinians that prefer two states. Perhaps it horrifies you too. Either way, it does translate into familiar, real-world terms the resolution of the conflict announced in the *Aeneid*. As the poem nears its end, Jupiter imposes this very one-state solution upon the Trojan-Latin conflict (12.834–9):

Italy's people will keep both native language and culture.
Further, their name will remain as it is. Intermarriage will thin out
What's left of Teucrians: namely, their blood. I'll add rituals and customs,
And I'll ensure that they'll all be collectively known as "the Latins."
Out of this blend with Ausonian blood you will see a new nation
Rise, and surpass all men and the gods in its righteous devotion....

What is the point of comparing Rome and Israel, of comparing the Palatine with Palestine?

Of all modern mass movements—national, religious, cultural, colonial—and ancient literature about mass movements, only do Virgil's *Aeneid* and Zionism invoke a *latter-day return* to an *ancestral homeland*, a claim doubly premised on *history* and *religious revelation*. In both cases the claim is preceded by war, holocaust, and the survival of displaced persons who vow to live on, despite the existence of a transcendent racial animus that follows them everywhere, and in both cases it meets with native rejection, accusations of colonialism, terrorism, and reciprocal violence seemingly without end.

Some parallels between the ancient and modern worlds are superficial or procrustean. Not here. Virgil's *Aeneid* and the Israeli-Palestinian conflict mirror each other fundamentally. We can learn from both of them, and with a double benefit. The modern events illuminate Virgil's poem, and Virgil's poem helps us better understand the basic archetypes of human conflict and experience that fill the daily newscasts.

Roman scholar Michael Fontaine tells how, according to Virgil's *Aeneid*, Roman civilization in Italy was founded by survivors from the destruction of Troy in the Trojan War. The *Aeneid* is a deliberate evocation of Homer's *Iliad* and *Odyssey*, with Books 1-6 of the *Aeneid* being the Roman *Odyssey* of Aeneas, and Books 6-12 being the Roman *Iliad* with Aeneas leading his Trojans to victory over the Latins and taking over their territory (with the claim that it is their original homeland). However, in the end, the Trojans, although victorious, are absorbed into the Latin people and become the Romans, no longer thinking of themselves as Trojans, but as the Latins they conquered.

Fontaine convincingly compares that story with the modern Mideast, arguing that the Jews, after the Holocaust, "wandered" as Aeneas did until they came to their ancestral homeland and took it over from the inhabitant people, the Palestinians. To Fontaine, the ancient tale is a paradigm for understanding the modern conflict. As Virgil, in his artistic humanity, understood the claims of both sides and empathized with their sufferings, so too can we, in the modern world, recognize the competing claims, watch the sufferings on both sides with compassion, understand how intractable can be some dilemmas in the modern world, and work to bring about a just solution.

Fontaine also comes to a startling conclusion: in the Aeneid, the resolution of the conflict comes in the form of having the Trojans and Latins merge into one great people—the Romans—but the newcomers subordinate their identity into that of the indigenous inhabitants. He realistically acknowledges that such a result for the Israelis and Palestinians is not very likely. But, he is probably right to take the long view and point out that, someday, peoples at odds over the rights to a homeland can resolve the conflict and become one people and thrive.

Why Focus on *Suicide* Terrorism

by Robert A. Pape and James K. Feldman

The right kind of public debate on terrorism is finally beginning.

For years after 9/11, the national discussion about how to deal with terrorism seemed to be frozen with little true debate about the root causes of the threat we face. First, we lived through the fear and anger in the immediate aftermath of that terrible day. Next, we lived through a period of hastily constructed responses, which led not only to the necessary war in Afghanistan to eliminate Al Qaeda's sanctuary there, but also the poorly based threat assessments that led up to the invasion of Iraq. After that came years of dealing with the repercussions of these decisions made in anger, fear, and haste, including the rise of the largest anti-American suicide terrorist campaigns in history in Iraq, Afghanistan, and Pakistan; the losses of over 100,000 Iraqi civilians who died in the civil war resulting from the U.S. invasion; and the emergence of a new Al Qaeda sanctuary in the tribal regions of Pakistan from which numerous plots have been hatched to kill Americans and their allies.[1]

Throughout these years, many have presumed that the root cause of the terrorist threat confronting us is Islamic fundamentalism—a religiously motivated hatred of American and Western values among a tiny fringe of Muslims scattered across the globe, and not related to any foreign or military policies by the United States or its allies. The idea that terrorists were willing to kill themselves to achieve religious martyrdom independently of any political goal seemed to explain why Islamic fundamentalists would

---

1. Major contributors to this book were Jacob Homan and the contributors listed individually by chapter. Research assistants for this book were Mohammand Abdeljalil, Almad Baasiri, Vanessa Bernick, Julia Clemons, Osama Eledam, Alicia May, Dina Rashed, Dahlia Rizk, Dana Rovang, Nicolaj Zemesaraja, and Brenda Kay Zylstra and the assistants listed individually by chapter.

commit suicide attacks, a tactic that appeared to reinforce just how much "they hate us."

This presumption fueled the belief that future 9/11s can be avoided only by wholesale transformation of Muslim societies, which was a core reason for the invasion of Iraq.[2] Indeed, for those advocating transformation, Iraq appeared to be the perfect place to start, since its leader Saddam Hussein had already spent decades to diminish Islamic fundamentalism in the country, and so the United States could conquer Iraq without fear of much terrorism in response, establish a base of operations, and then move on to transform other Middle Eastern countries.[3] If the presumption was right—if religion independent of American and Western foreign policy was driving the threat—then the use of heavy military power to bring democratic institutions to Muslim countries should have reduced the frequency of anti-American inspired terrorist attacks, especially suicide terrorism, by eliminating the authoritarian regimes that were thought to be the breeding grounds for Islamic radicalism

Events, however, have not turned out as the presumption would have expected. Far from declining, anti-American–inspired terrorism—particularly suicide terrorism—is more frequent today than before 9/11 and even before the invasion of Iraq. In the 24-year period from 1980 to 2003, there were just under 350 suicide terrorist attacks around the world—of which fewer than 15% could reasonably be considered directed against Americans. By contrast, in the six years from 2004 to 2009, the world has witnessed 1,833 suicide attacks—of which 92% are anti-American in origin. America has made progress in bringing Western institutions to Iraq, but democracy has not proved to be a panacea for reducing terrorism directed toward Americans and American allies. As this book shows, the Madrid and London terrorist bombings of 2004 and 2005, respectively, and numerous plots against Americans were specifically inspired by the invasion of Iraq.

2. Not just among the public, but within the Bush administration as well. Long before President George W. Bush received high-level classified briefings on Iraq's weapons of mass destruction in December 2002, he was briefed in the days after the September 11 attacks about Bernard Lewis's famous explanation for why Islamic fundamentalism is the root of Muslim rage leading to anti-Western terrorism, and in the subsequent weeks Lewis himself advocated for "a military take-over of Iraq to avert still-worse terrorism" by "seeding democracy in the Mideast" to White House officials, including Condoleezza Rice and Vice President Richard Cheney. Peter Waldman, "A Historian's Take on Islam Steers U.S. in Terrorism Fight," *Wall Street Journal,* February 3, 2004.

3. David Frum and Richard Perle, *An End to Evil: How to Win the War on Terror* (New York: Random House, 2003).

The more we've gone over there, the more they've wanted to come over here—and the absence of another 9/11 is due more to extensive American domestic security measures, immigration controls, intelligence, and pure luck than to lack of intent or planning by our enemies.

As the facts have not fit our presumptions, public discussion on the root causes of terrorism has grown in recent years. During the 2008 presidential campaign, candidates, columnists, and commentators in the United States, Europe, and around the world critically examined the U.S. strategy in the "war on terror," and even whether the U.S. actions have inadvertently contributed to more terrorism. In recent years, news media have stopped running the endless stories about "why do only Muslims do it?" and more wide-ranging and informative debate on "who becomes a suicide terrorist" is occurring.

Why Suicide Terrorism Is Important

In the 1990s, any American watching the evening news or CNN, and even those closely following daily events in print and online, could be excused for not seeing an evolving terrorist threat to the United States.

To be sure, many violent problems consumed our attention. Crime in New York, Chicago, Los Angeles, and other major cities; ethnic cleaning in Bosnia, Rwanda, Kosovo, and other civil wars; and conventional military conflicts involving Iraq versus Kuwait and China versus Taiwan all attracted remarkable coverage in the national and international media and called for dedicated plans of action by leading policy makers in the United States, Europe, Asia, and other countries around the world.

What did not seem to matter much was terrorism. The main concern—some would say obsession—of publics and leaders in many major countries for years now was hardly a blip on our radar in the 1990s.

What changed? Today, many people might instinctively answer "9/11," meaning a terrorist attack in the heart of the United States against a leading symbol of America's freedom and prosperity—the World Trade Center. This instinctive answer is obviously true, as far as it goes. But it also masks an important, deeper reality about the new threat facing the United States after September 11, 2001.

The new threat was not "terrorism"—at least not the old-fashioned kind that has been with the world for centuries. Ordinary terrorism occurred in the United States for years before 9/11. Indeed, the first terrorist attack on the World Trade Center occurred on February 26, 1993, when Islamic terrorists detonated a car bomb in the parking garage of Tower One, seeking to knock it down. Although the tower did not fall that day, six people were killed—something few people now remember and something that did not turn the American government, our military, and much of the country upside down to prevent from happening again. No, the new threat was not simply "terrorism."

What made 9/11 different was the willingness of 19 individuals to give their lives to kill a large number of Americans. No doubt, the attack was evil—the 3,000 innocent people who died that day did nothing to deserve their horrible fate. No doubt, the attackers were terrorists, but what made 9/11 very different from the terrorism Americans had experienced in the 1990s was the element of *suicide* by the attackers. The element of suicide is what made it possible for 19 hijackers to kill thousands of people. Even though these 19 were surely dead, the thought of more *suicide terrorist attacks* propelled anxiety and fear to levels few Americans had experienced in their lifetimes.

More consequences followed. The element of suicide is what instantly persuaded millions of Americans that future attacks could not be deterred by the threat of retaliation against the attackers. Indeed, the element of suicide called into question all our standard ways of responding to violence and so opened the door to all manner of "out of the box" strategic thinking—from the idea of preventive war against countries not immediately attacking us to the concept of almost unlimited surveillance of virtually any person in the United States by agencies in the executive branch of the U.S. government without observing the normal (and constitutionally mandated) rules of congressional and judicial oversight.[4] Since suicide terrorists must be stopped before they strike, it seemed necessary to look for them almost everywhere, even if no evidence existed that "they" were "there" at all.

In the years since 9/11, these "out of the box" responses have come under increasing scrutiny. Even defenders of staying the course would hardly deny that many of the domestic and foreign policies associated with the "war on terrorism" have produced their own costs and risks—in lives, national debt, and America's standing in the world. As painful as side effects are, however, they do not really call into question the basic logic of the

4. For a riveting account, see Jack L. Goldsmith, *The Terror Presidency: Law and Judgment inside the Bush Administration* (New York: W. W. Norton, 2007).

threat we face and how we should respond to it. They are a bit like a doctor telling a patient to stop smoking to avoid the risk of lung cancer and the patient asking, "won't I gain weight?" The side effect is real, but far from clearly more worrisome than the main threat.

Suicide terrorism is like lung cancer in other ways too. Just as there are numerous forms of cancer, and some quite benign, there are a various forms of terrorism, not all of which are worth the dedicated attention of our national leaders for sustained periods of time. Lung cancer justifies inordinate resources and attention because it is the leading cause of death among all cancers (and many other diseases). So too suicide terrorism. It merits special attention, because this type of terrorism is responsible for more deaths than any other form of the phenomenon—from 1980 to 2001, over 70% of all deaths due to terrorism were the result of suicide terrorism even though this tactic amounted to only 3% of all terrorist attacks.

Lung cancer can also exist for years, hardly creating symptoms until its most virulent stage. So too suicide terrorism. Although it may sound surprising, the United States did not begin to keep statistics on suicide terrorism until the fall of 2000,[5] even though it had been tracking ordinary terrorism around the world for decades. This omission goes a long way toward explaining why 9/11 was so hard to see coming.

If one looks at the U.S. government data on the global patterns of ordinary terrorism from 1980 to 2001, there is an unmistakable decline in the threat. Indeed, the peak is 1988 when some 666 terrorist attacks occurred globally, and this number declined more or less steadily over the next 10 plus years to 348 in 2001. At the same time, what started out as a tiny number of suicide terrorist attacks around the world was climbing at an alarming rate, from an average of only 3 suicide attacks per year in the 1980s to 10 per year in the 1990s to 50 per year from 2000 to 2003 and to 300 per year from 2004 to 2009.

These facts help explain why there was such a broad failure of imagination before 9/11—not only among the public, not only among national policy makers, but even by "terrorism experts" at the time. Since all terrorism was dropping like a rock and we were not tracking suicide terrorism in anything like a comprehensive way, it was hard to see that the threat was growing.

---

5. This was confirmed by correspondence between Argonne National Laboratories and the data manager for the U.S. government's database on terrorism located at the Naval Post-Graduate School in Monterey California, in fall 2003.

To prevent future 9/11s, it is crucial to focus our attention on preventing anti-American suicide terrorism. True, other forms of terrorism also matter. Conventional truck bomb attacks against bridges, antiaircraft missile shots at civilian airliners, the proliferation of chemical, biological, or nuclear weapons that leads to their use by terrorists—every one of these other terrorist threats is nontrivial. Every one was with us in the 1990s. But, the crucial point is that every one is greatly magnified by the willingness of the terrorists to kill themselves in order to carry the attacks out. Although suicide terrorism is not the only kind of terrorism, it is the most virulent form of the phenomenon and makes every other form of terrorism far more deadly than before.

Consider the following thought experiment. Imagine for the moment that you are Osama bin Laden and you have finally achieved your heart's desire—possession of a working nuclear warhead. Its explosive power is about the size of the atomic bomb that destroyed most of Nagasaki in World War II, the likes of which could devastate Manhattan, Boston, or Los Angeles, surely killing tens of thousands, perhaps over a hundred thousand, of Americans if the bomb actually goes off in one of these cities. You, bin Laden, have hated America for years. You cannot wait to fulfill your dream of inflicting a sucking chest wound on the "far enemy." You want the world to know your power.

But you have a problem. What if you send this one nuclear warhead in a container on a merchant ship, unescorted by anyone, and something goes wrong? What if the port authorities—now so widely criticized in the media—come across the bomb either by accident or through unreported heightened security measures? What if the bomb gets through to the port, but then fails to explode either because the atomic triggers were faulty in the first place or became so during the 1,000-mile-plus voyage? What if tens of other problems occur that you cannot even now foresee? Will former Secretary of Defense Donald Rumsfeld's famous "unknown unknowns" make you look like a fool in front of the world and waste this precious asset?

Getting nuclear weapons for terrorists is hard, much harder than fearmongers in the Western media like to suggest.[6] You know this and know that you cannot count on getting more for years or may be ever. What do you, bin Laden, do?

6. John E. Mueller, *Atomic Obsession: Nuclear Alarmism from Hiroshima to Al Qaeda* (New York: Oxford University Press, 2009).

The answer should now be rushing to your mind. You look for individuals willing to escort the nuclear bomb all the way to its target, to protect the weapon from discovery and seizure along the way, to execute a suicide attack if the bomb works as advertised, and to bring the bomb back for repair if it does not. Just as finding 19 people willing to kill themselves was the key to killing thousands of Americans on 9/11, so too would relying on suicide attackers make all the difference in the likely success of killing 10 or more times as many Americans in a nuclear 9/11. Suicide attack is not the only way to strike the United States or any other country with a nuclear weapon. It is, however, the most reliable way to employ the one, or at most handful, of nuclear weapons likely to come your way.

This thought experiment could be multiplied many times over for truck bombs, chemical and biological attacks, and virtually any kind of terrorist strike plan that truly sought to kill large numbers of people. In all of these, adding the element of suicide to the attack drastically increases the odds of success. And this is the point of a suicide terrorist attack. From the perspective of the terrorist organization, the purpose of a suicide terrorist attack is not for the attacker to die—this is the easy part, once an attacker is willing to participate in such a mission at all. Rather, the purpose is to kill large numbers of people, which is true whether the suicide terrorist attack involves conventional explosives or weapons of mass destruction. Suicide terrorists are the ultimate smart bomb.

What We Know about Suicide Terrorism

Suicide terrorists are superpredators. They murder vast numbers of innocent people in each attack. They are the subject of seemingly endless "three-minute" discussions on Fox, CNN, and MSNBC. Yet, many people still wonder about the motives and dynamics that lead man after man, and increasingly woman after woman, to strap on bombs, load up their cars with explosives, or ram planes into buildings and kill themselves on missions to kill others.

To answer the question, we need to look at more than pictures of mangled bodies, blown out busses, and collapsed buildings. To know why suicide terrorist campaigns occur in some places and not others, why they start at some times and not others, and why they end, we need to look at more than the evil of suicide terrorism. It is all well and good to condemn suicide terrorists as murderers or "homicide terrorists." But when moral posturing comes to replace reasoned assessment of data and dispassionate consideration of the causes of a phenomenon, we may end up with a visceral response rather than an effective plan of action to protect those we care about. In the 1940s and 1950s, lung cancer was spreading, killing more and more people and causing more and more heartbreak, seeming more and more out of control each year. What helped was not simply more aggressive treatments after the fact, but new studies that explained the root causes of the phenomenon so that that lung cancer could be stopped before it started. In the decades since, this research probably did more than any treatment to save lives.[7]

We should learn from our experience with lung cancer. If collection of comprehensive data, reasoned assessment of the facts, and debate about how information we have fits or does not fit alternative explanations can help reduce suicide terrorism even modestly, this is all worth the effort.

Recently, academic research on the causes of terrorism has made significant progress, particularly on suicide terrorism. Although our understanding of the phenomenon is still growing, knowledge about the causes, conduct, and consequences of suicide terrorism has substantially improved since 9/11, much of which is embodied in the chapters in this volume. Important methodological advances and new data have helped to make this progress possible, as has the influx of new scholars.[8] In particular, we now have the first complete data set of all suicide terrorist attacks around the world from 1980 to 2009, which greatly improves our ability to assess possible causes of the phenomenon. As with lung cancer, we now know more clearly who is struck and who is not, and this significantly helps us understand why.

A central result has been the advent of a new theory to explain the phenomenon of suicide terrorism. Prior to 9/11, the expert debate on the causes of suicide terrorism was divided largely between two explanations, religious fanaticism and mental illness.[9] In the years after 9/11, new research on who becomes a suicide terrorist showed that virtually none could be diagnosed as mentally ill, while many were religious and, most striking, nearly all emerged from communities resisting foreign military occupation. *Dying*

7. Evelyn N. Powers and Jasmina B. Cabbot, *Smoking and Lung Cancer* (Hauppauge, NY: Nova Science Publishers, 2008).

8. For example, see the new research on terrorism in the special issue of *Security Studies,* December 2009.

9. For a good assortment of the 1990s literature, see Walter Reich, ed., *Origins of Terrorism* (Washington, DC: Woodrow Wilson Center Press, 1998).

to Win, published in 2005, was prominent in advancing this new explanation for the origins of suicide terrorism. From 1980 to 2003, there were 345 completed suicide terrorist attacks by 524 suicide terrorists who actually killed themselves on a mission to kill others, half of whom are secular. The world leader was the Tamil Tigers (a secular, Hindu group) who carried out more attacks than Hamas or Palestinian Islamic Jihad (PIJ) during this period. Further, at least a third of the suicide attacks in predominantly Muslim countries were carried out by secular terrorist groups, such as the Kurdistan Workers Party (PKK) in Turkey. Instead of religion, what over 95% of all suicide terrorist attacks before 2004 had in common was a strategic goal: to compel a democratic state to withdraw combat forces that are threatening territory that the terrorists' prize. From Lebanon to Sri Lanka to the West Bank to Chechnya, the central goal of every suicide terrorist campaign has been to resist military occupation by a democracy.[10]

What Is New in *Cutting the Fuse*

The years since 2004 have witnessed a substantial growth in the number of suicide terrorist attacks, nearly 500% more than all the years from 1980 to 2003 combined. This leads to three questions:

1. Do the global patterns of suicide terrorism since 2004 validate or invalidate the hypothesis that foreign military occupation, or the imminent threat of it, is the root cause of suicide terrorism?
1. Do the global patterns of suicide terrorism since 2004 indicate new factors that add to the causal logic of existing theories, telling us more about when and where suicide terrorism will occur?
2. Do the global patterns of suicide terrorism since 2004 suggest new solutions or major improvements to existing solutions to the threat we face?

The purpose of this book is to answer these questions, analyzing all suicide terrorist attacks around the world from 1980 to 2009, nearly 2,200 attacks in all. Each suicide terrorist attack is defined in the classic sense of an individual killing himself or herself on a mission to kill others and has been verified by two or more independent sources by a research team flu-

---

10. Robert A. Pape, *Dying to Win: The Strategic Logic of Suicide Terrorism* (New York: Random House, 2005).

ent in the key native languages associated with suicide terrorism (Arabic, Hebrew, Tamil, Russian, Urdu, etc.), and members of the team have also contributed to the analysis of individual suicide terrorist campaigns in this book.

In brief, the new research finds the following.

1) Strong confirmation for the hypothesis that military occupation is the main factor driving suicide terrorism. The stationing of foreign combat forces (ground and tactical air force units) on territory that terrorists prize accounts for 87% of the over 1,800 suicide terrorist attacks around the world since 2004. The occupation of Pakistan's western tribal regions by local combat forces allied to American military forces stationed across the border in Afghanistan accounts for another 12%. Further, the timing of the deployment of combat forces threatening territory the terrorists prize accounts for the onset of all eight major suicide terrorist campaigns[11] between 1980 and 2009, which together comprise 96% of the 2,188 attacks during that period. Simply put, military occupation accounts for nearly all suicide terrorism around the world since 1980. For this finding to be wrong, our research team would have had to miss hundreds of suicide attacks during this period, which is unlikely as readers can judge for themselves by reviewing the database of suicide attacks available online.[12]

Although each of the major suicide terrorist campaigns is important, perhaps the most urgent finding within specific campaigns concerns the recent abrupt spike of suicide terrorism in Afghanistan, where starting in early 2006 the number of suicide attacks suddenly rose from a handful to over 100 per year. The key reason was United States and NATO military deployments, which began to extend to the Pashtun southern and eastern regions of the country beginning in late 2005. In 2006, the United States pressured Pakistan to deploy large military forces in the Pashtun areas of western Pakistan, which also led to a large increase of suicide attacks in the country. In effect, the more the United States and its military allies have militarily occupied the Pashtun homeland, the more this has inspired suicide terrorism to end the occupation.

11. To be clear, a suicide terrorist campaign occurs when one or more suicide attacks are intended as part of a cluster organized by one or more groups to achieve a specific political goal. Suicide attacks that do not occur as part of campaigns are called "isolated" attacks.

12. For the specific sources for each attack, see the searchable database on suicide attacks by the Chicago Project on Security and Terrorism at http://cpost.uchicago.edu.

2) Strong evidence for new hypotheses about the causes of transnational suicide terrorism. Dying to Win explained that nationalism—the desire to perpetuate the local political, religious, and social institutions of a community independent of foreign interference—is the taproot explanation for why individuals from a community facing foreign military occupation would undertake costly measures to defend it, including, in extremis, suicide terrorism. This causal logic is important since the overwhelming number of suicide attackers do live in the occupied country or in immediately adjacent border regions that are also under spillover threat from the occupation. However, *Dying to Win* left unanswered the causal logic of transnational suicide attackers—individuals living in countries far removed from the occupied countries—who comprise about 10% of the over 2,600 suicide attackers from 1980 to 2009 and as much as a fifth to a third of some prominent suicide terrorist campaigns (Iraq and Al Qaeda).

Cutting the Fuse provides a new causal logic for the phenomenon of transnational suicide terrorism. Although existing theories contend that it is a product of religious fanaticism or economic alienation, this volume shows that the logic of military occupation should be extended to account for transnational suicide terrorism.

Transnational suicide terrorism is a classic instance of individuals with multiple national loyalties to different stable communities of people associated with a territory, distinctive culture, and common language, one loyalty for their kindred community and another for their current country of residence, in which the loyalty for their kindred community wins out. However, these dueling loyalties do not exist in a vacuum, but are powerfully influenced by external circumstances. Specifically, the hierarchy of competing national loyalties can be strongly influenced by which community, the kindred or local, is most under threat. The hierarchy of multiple loyalties is not an a priori weighting among demographic factors such as place of birth, current residence, ethnicity, or religion, but is often constructed by circumstances in the international environment that shape individuals' perceptions of the relative importance of their loyalties, most particularly the level of threat to the different communities valued by the individuals. Hence, the foreign military occupation of kindred communities can compel individuals with multiple loyalties to adopt a hierarchy that privileges the kindred community over the local one. Perhaps most important, for transnational suicide attackers, this hierarchy of loyalties is normally established among preexisting groups of individuals who become progressively more radical as a group over time. As *Cutting the Fuse* explains, only exceptionally rare social dynamics are likely to lead to this progressive radicalization of groups, which accounts for why transnational suicide terrorism is such a rare, Black Swan phenomenon.

3) Important evidence for the value of a new approach to more effectively combat suicide terrorism, likely to improve the effectiveness of already well-known solutions.   As *Dying to Win* explained, the key to stopping suicide terrorism campaigns, which by their nature necessarily involve a series of attacks by different individuals over time, is to prevent the rise of a new generation of suicide terrorists. Given the close association between foreign occupation and suicide terrorism, the goal of thwarting the rise of the next wave of suicide terrorism will likely require a major shift in military strategy by those target states with a military presence in foreign areas. This strategy is "offshore" balancing, which seeks to achieve foreign policy interests in key regions of the world by relying on military alliances and offshore air, naval, and rapidly deployable ground forces rather than heavy onshore combat power. In essence, this strategy would resemble America's military commitment to the Persian Gulf from the end of World War II in 1945 to the period before the first Iraq War up to 1990, when the United States successfully pursued its interests and obligations in the region despite local instabilities and wars without stationing tank, armor, or fighter aircraft units there—and without provoking terrorism against us or our allies. After the 1991 Iraq War, America left tens of thousands of heavy combat forces on the Arabian Peninsula as a residual force, which became the chief rallying cry for Osama bin Laden's terrorism against the United States and its allies. Conversely, as Israel withdrew combat forces from Gaza and large parts of the West Bank and relied on defensive measures such as the "wall" in 2004 and as the United States and its allies drew down the total number of combat forces from Iraq after January 2008, suicide terrorism in both conflicts substantially declined.

However, something else happened in Iraq. Starting in late 2006, the United States began to offer local political control and economic resources directly to large Sunni tribes in Anbar Province, which gave them significant wherewithal to provide for their own security. At the same time, the United States deployed ground forces to the most vulnerable Sunni neighborhoods in Baghdad, protecting them and allowing more vulnerable Sunnis to move to safe havens within the city and bordering Anbar Province, enabling the Sunni community as a whole to better secure itself in the future. This strategy of empowering a key local community to better provide for its security independently of the United States, the central government in the country, and the terrorists led to a decline of Iraqi suicide terrorism by over a third in the next year.

Most important, the strategy of "local empowerment" works by recognizing that suicide terrorism is driven by a strategic logic that seeks to remove foreign threats to local culture. A foreign state can remove a local population's primary reason for supporting suicide terrorist campaigns—safeguarding the local way of life—by providing the political, economic, and military wherewithal for the local community to detect and destroy terrorists, tasks that often require deep local knowledge to achieve success. Of course, the foreign occupier is often so powerful than it could still overwhelm newly empowered local groups, and so suicide terrorism may continue at a robust level so long as foreign ground forces remain in or near their community's area. However, the strategy of local empowerment is likely to moderate suicide terrorism over several years and serve as a useful transition strategy to offshore balancing, the grand strategy likely to work best over decades.

The Perspective of This Book

In the chapters that follow, *Cutting the Fuse* seeks to contribute to the growing public debate about the root causes of the threat we face by explaining the key findings about the new patterns of suicide terrorism since Iraq and by providing readers with the conceptual and empirical tools to assess these findings on their own. Chapters 1 and 2 explain what is driving the precipitous rise of suicide terrorism over the past five years and the special logic of transnational suicide terrorism. The body of this volume systematically assesses the causes, conduct, and consequences of the largest contemporary suicide terrorist campaigns: Iraq, Afghanistan, Pakistan, Al Qaeda, Palestine, Lebanon, Chechnya, and Sri Lanka. The conclusion offers policy recommendations, particularly why a strategy of local empowerment and offshore balancing is our best approach for safeguarding America and its allies from the threat of suicide terrorism.

This book is not written from a specific worldview, ideological orientation, or Democratic or Republican program. It is not authored by individuals who have voted consistently for one party (even in the past 10 years) or are committed to any political agenda. It is based fundamentally on a consideration of the facts of the matter and on the assumption that dispassionate consideration of the facts can create consensus and hope for a new future in American foreign policy.

To take a fresh look at the facts, it is helpful to keep a few basic ideas in mind:

First impressions can be faulty. After 9/11, it seemed easy to think that Islam, poverty, social alienation, or the more sinister-sounding "Islamo-fascism" were the root cause of our problems. Yet, these did not just suddenly emerge in recent decades and so are poor explanations for the rise of suicide terrorism during our lifetimes. The key to improving our security is to find out what has changed and how it is propelling suicide terrorism against us.

Spectacular problems can have hard to see causes. The ultimate cause of a deadly attack is not always the most obvious. Smokers often have no symptoms of the cancer growing in their bodies for decades until just before it becomes terminal. The root causes of suicide terrorism can also fester for years before producing spectacular harm.

"Patriots"—even the most well meaning—can let their emotions get the best of them. As Ronald Reagan used to say, "Going over a cliff, carrying flags, is still going over a cliff." Americans should take pride in our country. This should be our reason for wanting to improve our security even if this means developing new courses of action, not for staying the course with policies that actually reduce it.

Understanding what to track helps clarify a complex situation. In recent years, Americans have been inundated with an array of complicated concerns associated with the "war on terrorism"—the ebb and flow of potential proliferation of weapons of mass destruction in numerous countries, the rise and leveling off of the civil war in Iraq, and the capture of old and emergence of new Al Qaeda leaders and operatives—and these various and cross-cutting issues obscure the core question of whether the United States is winning or losing ground. Focusing on the trajectory of anti-American suicide terrorism helps to cut through the fog and provides a baseline for American security.

This book, then, seeks to demystify the terrorism threat we face. It recognizes that this threat has multiple causes and that solutions are not merely about "strong" versus "weak" policies. Being tough did not stop

Gary Cooper and Paul Newman from dying from lung cancer. Aggressive policy is sometimes the right and indispensable course of action, but aggression for aggression's sake, "getting two of them for one of us," and all other manner of blind fury can make matters worse.

Great victories often depend on a clear-eyed view of the merits of the case. Whether these facts help Democrats or Republicans in their domestic contests is far less important than whether they help improve the general welfare of the United States and our allies. The key is a willingness to consider information that may run against some of our first impressions, to see if the new data changes the overall picture in fundamental ways. Since there is no more common conventional wisdom than that the "war on terrorism" is making us safer, let us first ask: Why is anti-American suicide terrorism skyrocketing?

This work is the continuation of Robert Pape's analysis for the Chicago Project on Suicide Terrorism, a research center which has changed its name to the Chicago Project on Security and Terrorism (the acronym CPOST works for both). Pape and his colleagues, in their study of terrorism, started with the assumption that many people had after 9/11—that terrorism was a result of Islamist extremism. The project looked at terrorist attacks and found that the great majority of them in the last few decades were suicide attacks which killed the greatest number of people and the attacker died with the victims. The project then studied the lives of the individual attackers and found that few of them appear to have been motivated by religious extremism.

Foreign Occupation

Rather, Pape and his colleagues found that the great majority of attacks were motivated by groups wishing to achieve one major goal: have their governments expel the foreign troops (mostly U.S. military) from their homelands. The original study went up only to 2003. The study reported in this reading went up through 2009 and strongly confirmed the original conclusion.

Offshore Balancing and Local Empowerment

The authors recommended that one way to decrease the frequency of suicide terrorist attacks was to remove the external forces from the soil of the country in question. They point out that, before the Iraq-Kuwait War of 1991, the U.S. had a Persian Gulf military strategy that kept the U.S. fleet in the region—but offshore—able to engage with airpower and naval power. That changed when U.S. troops were based inside the region's nations. The authors also demonstrate how working with local constituencies, and truly empowering them to respond themselves to the violence taking place around them, also functioned to reduce suicide terrorist attacks.

The authors argue passionately that, based on scientific study of the patterns of terrorist attacks, proper responses to prevent them can be developed. Simply demonstrating "strength" and not appearing "weak" or "compromising credibility" (for credibility, see the nextt Chapter) did not stop the attacks, but removing the troops and empowering the locals can reduce them.

After al-Qaeda

Hijackings and suicide bombings didn't start, and won't end, with Islamists.

by PHILIP JENKINS

NEW PRESIDENT DECLARES VICTORY IN WAR ON TERROR—Patriot Act to be Repealed—Department of Homeland Security for Dissolution.

This will not be a headline in 2013, or anytime thereafter, because by its nature the War on Terror can have no end. If you are fighting a war, then you can envisage a victory in which the opposing force is destroyed. In the case of terrorism, particular movements might decline or vanish—and happily, al-Qaeda itself is on a downward trajectory—but terrorism as such is not going away.

Terrorism is a tactic, not a movement. As such, it can be deployed by states, movements, or small groups regardless of ideology. It is not synonymous with Islam, nor with Islamism. That runs contrary to the thinking of many supposed experts and media commentators, who see Islamic terrorism as the definitive form of the phenomenon. As Dennis Prager writes, "A very small percentage of Muslims are terrorists. But nearly every international terrorist is Muslim." In this view, Islamist organizations are the standard by which all terror groups must be measured, the model imitated by rivals. If terror has a history, it will be found in the Islamic past—shall we start with the medieval Assassins? Or better, just list the index entry: "Terrorism: *See* Jihad"?

In reality, terrorism in its modern form has a long history in the West—over a century—but not until the 1980s did Islamists play any role, and virtually never as innovators or leaders. The history of terrorism is strikingly diverse, with perpetrators of every race, creed, and color. The modern phenomenon probably begins in the 1880s with Irish bomb attacks against England and with Russian leftists and European anarchists of the 1890s pursuing their cult of the bomb.

More recently, the decade or so after World War II was an era of notable creativity, as Zionist extremists pioneered many new strategies—truck bombs direct-ed against hotels and embassies, attacks against buses and crowded public places. For a time, Zionist groups also led the way in international terrorism, with letter-bomb attacks on British soil, the bombing of the British embassy in Rome, and plots to assassinate foreign dignitaries such as German Chancellor Konrad Adenauer. The Algerian struggle of the 1950s popularized these innovations and spawned yet others.

But the golden age of terrorism occurred between 1968 and 1986. Then as now, Arab and Middle Eastern causes drove a wave of global violence, making the "Arab terrorist" as familiar a stereotype as today. Baby boomers recall the horrible regularity of waking up to hear of some new massacre of Western civilians, of kidnapping and hostage taking, and (with monotonous frequency) of attacks on airliners and transportation systems. They may remember the simultaneous hijacking and destruction of five airliners in Jordan in 1970—fortunately, without fatalities—or the massacre of Israeli athletes at the 1972 Munich Olympics.

Some attacks of this era stand out even today for their sadism and indiscriminate violence. In 1972, three Japanese tourists landed at Israel's Lod Airport, where their nationality prevented them from attracting suspicion. They proved to be members of the Japanese Red Army, working in alliance with the Arab Popular Front for the Liberation of Palestine, the PFLP. Producing automatic weapons, they slaughtered everyone they could see in the terminal—26 civilians, mainly Christian Puerto Rican pilgrims. The following year, Palestinian guerrillas attacked Rome's Fiumicino airport, throwing phosphorus grenades at an airliner and burning alive some 30 civilians. In 1974, Palestinian guerrillas killed 25 hostages in the

Philip Jenkins, Edwin Erle Sparks Professor of History and Religious Studies at Pennsylvania State University, is the author of Images of Terror *and* Jesus Wars.

Israeli town of Ma'alot. Horror was piled on horror.

The most notorious terrorist of the era was Palestinian mastermind Abu Nidal, as infamous in the 1970s and 1980s as Osama bin Laden has been in recent times. His career reached gruesome heights in the 1980s with a series of attacks that wrote the playbook for al-Qaeda. He specialized in simultaneous strikes against widely separated targets to keep security agencies off balance and win maximum publicity. Typical was the 1985 double-attack at the airports of Rome and Vienna in which 19 civilians were killed. Throughout the 1980s, the prospect of Abu Nidal obtaining a nuclear weapon alarmed intelligence services worldwide.

At this point, the identification of Islam with terrorism might appear to stand up well, with all these Arabs and Palestinians. Then as now, international terrorist actions tended to track back to the Middle East—but not to Islam. The militants of that era distanced themselves from any faith. Abu Nidal usually served Iraq's secularist Ba'ath regime, which persecuted Islamists.

Like Abu Nidal himself, most Palestinian activists in those years were secular socialist nationalists, and Christians played a prominent role in the movement's leadership. The most important Arab guerrilla leader of those years—a pioneer of modern international terrorism—was PFLP founder George Habash. He was an Eastern Orthodox Christian who eschewed religion after he became a strict Marxist-Leninist. He discarded his faith when Israeli forces expelled his family from their homes: "I was all the time imagining myself as a good Christian, serving the poor. When my land was occupied, I had no time to think about religion." Abandoning his church certainly did not mean adopting Islam: his inspiration was not some medieval Islamic warrior but rather Che Guevara.

Habash's story is emblematic. Also Orthodox was Wadie Haddad, who orchestrated the Dawson's Field attacks and the 1976 airliner seizure that provoked Israel's raid on Entebbe. Haddad, incidentally, recruited the once legendary Latin American playboy who earned notoriety as international terrorist Carlos "the Jackal."

Equally non-Islamist were the PFLP's several spinoffs, like the Maoist Democratic Front, DFLP, which murdered the hostages at Ma'alot. That faction's leader, Nayif Hawatmeh, was born Catholic. Several Palestinian attacks in these years sought to put pressure on Israel to release its most prestigious captive, Melkite Catholic Archbishop Hilarion Capucci, jailed for running guns to the guerrillas. Only in the late 1980s, after the rise of Hamas, did an Islamist group take the lead in armed assaults on Israel.

Earlier Middle Eastern movements had no notion of suicide terrorism, which was, moreover, unknown to the Islamist militant tradition before about 1980. The movement that used suicide attacks most frequently and effectively, the Tamil Tigers, is in fact Sri Lankan and mainly Hindu-Marxist. In other cases too, hideous terrorist actions we have come to associate with Islamic extremism have clearly non-Islamic roots. Think for instance of those unspeakable al-Qaeda videos depicting the ritualized execution of hostages in Iraq and elsewhere. To quote Olivier Roy, one of the most respected European scholars of Islamist terrorism, these videos are "a one-to-one re-enactment of the execution of Aldo Moro by the Red Brigades [in Italy in 1978], with the organization's banner and logo in the background, the hostage hand-cuffed and blind-folded, the mock trial with the reading of the sentence and the execution."

Through the 1970s and 1980s, terrorism was kaleidoscopic in its political coloring. White Europeans, on the left and the right, made their own contributions. During the 1970s, Italian far rightists and neo-Nazis tried many times to carry out a mega-terror attack on that nation's rail system. After several bloody attempts, they succeeded in killing 85 at Bologna's central station in 1980. The United States, meanwhile, had its own domestic terrorist violence, as Puerto Rican separatists carried out deadly bomb attacks in New York and Chicago. And after so many years, Irish terror groups, Protestant and Catholic alike, still pursued their age-old traditions of violence directed against rival civilians.

By no means was international terrorism the preserve of Arabs, let alone Muslims. In 1976, an anti-Castro rightist group based in Florida blew up a Cuban airliner flying from Barbados to Jamaica, killing 76. Prior to 9/11, the dubious record for the worst terror attack in history was held by the Sikh group that destroyed an Air India 747 in 1985, killing 329 innocent people. So commonplace were international attacks, and so diverse, that when a bomb killed 11 people at New York's La Guardia airport in 1975, the possible perpetrators were legion. (The current best guess points to Croatian opponents of Yugoslavia's Marshal Tito.)

Where, amidst all this bloodshed, were Islamist terror groups? They added little to the story prior to the rise of Hezbollah during the Lebanese civil war, with the bombing of the U.S. embassy in Beirut in 1983 and the subsequent attack on the Marine barracks. Only from the early 1990s do we find fanatical Sunni networks spreading mayhem around the world, including the early actions of al-Qaeda.

This chronology raises interesting questions for understanding the roots of terrorism. If Islam is so central to the phenomenon, we need to explain why Muslim terrorists should have been such latecomers. Why were they not the prophets and pioneers of terrorism? Why, moreover, did they have to draw all their tactics from the fighters of other religions and of none—from Western anarchists and nihilists, from the Catholic IRA and Latin American urban guerrillas, from Communists and fascists, from Zionist Jews and Sri Lankan Hindus?

Apart from the crucial element of suicide bombing, al-Qaeda brought little to the international terrorist repertoire. The Madrid rail station attack of 2004 neatly replayed the fascist strike at Bologna, while even 9/11 borrowed many elements straight from Abu Nidal, including the simultaneous targeting of multiple airliners. In its methods and strategies, the modern terrorist tradition owes much to the Marxist tradition—to Lenin, Guevara, and Mao—and next to nothing to Muslims.

None of these points should come as a surprise to anyone who remembers the 1970s and 1980s. In its day, the Dawson's Field affair of 1970 transfixed global media almost as much as the 9/11 enormity did a decade ago. So did the Munich Olympics attack of 1972, or the 1976 saga of the hostages at Entebbe. It's remarkable to see how readily modern audiences credit suggestions about the novelty of international terrorism or its association with Islamist groups. Particularly startling is how thoroughly Americans have forgotten their own terrorist crisis of the mid-1970s. How can something as horrendous as the La Guardia massacre have vanished from public memory? And is it really possible that the once satanic name of Abu Nidal carries next to no significance for anyone below the age of 50? There is no better illustration of how present-day concerns have eclipsed the older realities.

Terrorism can be used by groups of any ideological shade. The scale or intensity of terrorist violence depends on the opportunities available to militants and the potential opposition they face from law-enforcement agencies. By these criteria, Western nations will continue to be subject to attacks, and those events will follow precedents that we have witnessed over the past 40 years.

However hard we try, we cannot make our society invulnerable. The more we think about the gaps in our defenses, the more astonishing it is that incidents have occurred so rarely. If you fortify aircraft, terrorists attack airports; if you fortify airports, they can bring down aircraft with missiles; if you secure all aircraft, they attack ships; if you defend all public transportation, they undertake massacres in malls and sports stadiums.

Armed groups need only a handful of shooters and bombers to create havoc. The Provisional IRA probably never had more than 500 soldiers at any time, while the Basque ETA peaked around 200—supported, of course, by a larger penumbra of sympathizers. Both maintained campaigns spanning 30 or 40 years. A group of just ten or 20 militants can keep a devastating effort going for a year, and until they are hunted down they can convince a powerful Western nation that it is suffering a national a crisis.

No government can defend itself against terrorism solely by enhancing security. Ultimately, defense must always rely on effective intelligence, which means surveillance of militant groups and their sympathizers, infiltrating those groups, and winning over informants. The fact that attacks on U.S. soil have been so rare means that our intelligence agencies have been doing a pretty good job.

But there will always be vulnerabilities. However thoroughly agencies maintain surveillance on potential troublemakers, on occasion they will fail to mark those individuals who have made the transition from isolated blowhards to dedicated killers. By definition, they are most likely to err when confronting someone who does not fit the profile of the time—when, for instance, the suspect is a white Nazi rather than an Arab Muslim or vice versa. At some point a bomber or assassin—an Anders Breivik, a Timothy McVeigh, or a Mohamed Atta—will slip through, with catastrophic results.

We might call this the Apache Theory of terrorism. Of all the enemies the U.S. faced during its wars against Indian tribes in the 19th century, the Apaches were the most determined and resourceful. When nervous white residents of the Southwest asked, "How many Apaches are hiding in this room right now?" the answer was always, "As many as want to." Will there be terrorism in the U.S. or Europe? If enough people want to perpetrate it, some will get through.

And who are the new Apaches who might someday surpass the Islamist menace? While prophecy would be foolhardy, we know enough about the history of terrorism to suggest some areas of danger.

One peril is that old causes now quiescent will again spring to life. In the United States, that could mean the ultra-right groups that have such a lengthy record of activism. Presently they are close to inactive, and the menagerie of largely harmless militia groups serves mainly to provide bogeymen for leftist speculation. But that could change overnight: Oklahoma City was the work of one cell.

European groups could also revive, especially if the continent descends into economic anarchy. Imagine poorer nations like Ireland and Greece driven to ruin by what they see as exploitation by Europe's financial elite. Given the long experience of the Irish with direct militant action, do we think they will do nothing? Diehard IRA elements have for years threatened to renew their attacks on England, but their impact would be massively greater if they targeted European financial or political centers like Frankfurt or Strasbourg. Across the continent, economic collapse could reawaken ethnic hatreds we thought had perished with the Habsburg Empire.

Nor has Europe's neo-fascist tradition vanished. Although the media treated Breivik as a loner, he stands in a long and bloody tradition, one especially strong in those southern European nations most vulnerable to financial collapse. In the 1970s and 1980s, both left- and right-wing militants in Italy made bizarre deals to obtain weapons from Middle Eastern sources, including Iran and Libya. Who is to say those connections are extinct?

Terrorism also continues to be a weapon of state power, a covert means for achieving goals that cannot be obtained through the open exercise of force. In different forms, state-sponsorship has always been key to terror movements. Even in tsarist days, the Russians freely used terrorist proxies, and Mussolini's secret service, the OVRA, honed this tactic to a fine art. While the Soviet KGB was legendary for arming and funding extremist groups, it was absolutely not unique.

Some countries have even used the tactic as barefaced extortion. Through the 1980s, you could tell when an Arab Gulf state had fallen behind on money it owed Saddam Hussein because the mysterious "Abu Nidal Organization" would leap into action with an assassination or airliner bombing. When Mideast countries engaged in actual war—as Iran and Iraq did through the 1980s—they used their overseas proxies to promote clandestine goals. In retrospect, many of the terror attacks on European soil in the mid-1980s seem intended to persuade Western nations to supply arms to one or the other of the combatants in the Iran-Iraq conflict.

For some 40 years now, Libya, Syria, and Iran have

sponsored surrogate terrorist movements worldwide. Arguably, the weaker those regimes become, the more likely they will be to use those proxies to strike out at opponents, including the United States. Of course, attacks will not carry a brand identifying the country responsible; a strike would come under cover of some bogus front or Islamist cell. As long as unscrupulous states wish to exert pressure on others—to embarrass

Michael Hogue

them, to force them to take steps they do not want, to make their position in some region untenable—we can expect to see terrorism used as a form of proxy war.

That means terrorism will be with us as long as the world knows ethnic hatred and social division—which is to say, until the end of humanity. The phenomenon cannot be ended entirely, but individual movements certainly can be defeated and suppressed. And we should not imagine "terrorism" as a monolithic enemy that demands we militarize our whole society to meet the challenge.

Above all, we should not forget the lessons of the past. However appalling it might be to study individual groups or incidents, in the long term the story of terrorism contains a surprisingly positive lesson. Terrorism can inflict dreadful harm on a society, even claiming thousands of lives. But in the overwhelming majority of instances, these movements are not only beaten but annihilated—so thoroughly, in fact, that later generations forget they even existed.

In this article, Jenkins makes the case that, similarly to the conclusion of the CPOST, terrorism is not the sole preserve of Islamist extremism. Jenkins briefly traces the history of terrorism and reminds us of sad incidents of the past (it was amazing to acknowledge that those of us who lived through the incidents, including myself, had forgotten some of them). It is striking to note that Islamic particaption in terrorism is of relatively recent vintage. It thus behooves us more and more to combat the Islamaphobia that is current and widespread in the West. Jenkins may also well be right that "we can expect to see terrorism used as a form of proxy war." And, as we will review in the next chapter, war itself is another form of politics, so we can expect that terrorism will continue. It has always existed in the context of state-level societies, but, in this modern age of media immediacy, this form of politics is very much more visible than in the past.

CONCLUSION: WRAP-UP

Terrorism appears to be some modern form of disease. There was a time when getting on an airplane was as easy as getting on a bus. That has changed so much that the most notable scene in an airport is the Transport Safety Administration (TSA) apparatus. But terrorism is as old as the foundation of state-level society, and one should remember that the first use of the word was to describe the "State Terror" of the French Revolution descending into executions that were not part of the original motivation. How we respond to terrorism matters, and it is a contemporary world problem requiring our careful attention.

I will share a personal anecdote: when I lived in England, my best friend was a young man from Ulster, Northern Ireland, named Edgar S.D. Graham. Edgar was a moderate Unionist, favoring Northern Ireland to remain in the United Kingdom. Though a Protestant, he refused to join the Orange Order because it required its members to take an oath never to attend a Roman Catholic Mass. Edgar attended Mass frequently (because he liked the music) and so would have no truck with such a policy. As a member and spokesman of the largly powerless Northern Ireland Assembly, he abjured all forms of violence and insisted on the rule of law and the negotiating over redress of grievances, based on what to him was the "glory of English law," in its protection of the rights of the individual. Though proud to be British, he considered himself first and foremost, an Irishman. He said Belfast was not the true capital of his country, which was clearly Dublin. He proudly spoke of a relative who switched sides from the British-backed loyalist army of Michael Collins to the IRA because "he did what he thought was right, and that is good enough for me!" He was a lawyer on the faculty of the Queen's University of Belfast where, on December 7, 1983, an IRA gunman shot him dead outside the Faculty of Law building. Though the Good Friday Accord of 1998 largely spelled the end of "The Troubles" in Northern Ireland, Edgar's attacker has never been found.

How can we respond in such cases? When loved ones are victimized in violent conflicts, what is there to say or do? I am sure Edgar's attacker thought of himself as a soldier fighting British oppression; Edgar himself used the language of a soldier in once describing to me his refusal to leave off from his political career out of fear, even when threatened with the violence that took his life. To put it in best perspective, a quote from the Pape and Feldman excerpt is a fitting conclusion: "we need to look at more than the evil of suicide terrorism. It is all well and good to condemn suicide terrorists as murderers or 'homicide terrorists.' But when moral posturing comes to replace reasoned assessment of data and dispassionate consideration of the causes of a phenomenon, we may end up with a visceral response rather than an effective plan of action to protect those we care about."

ACTIVITIES

General activity: in class, share and discuss responses to Schema-activation question.

Activity for Reading #21: in small groups, do some quick online research about the Israeli-Palestinian conflict and the current state of "one" and two-state" solutions. Then, discuss whether or not Fontaine's one state solution inspired by Virgil is realistic, suggesting a possible path for its implementation.

Activity for Reading #22: The United States, twice before the Invasion of Iraq in 2003, experienced an insurgency resisting its occupation, in Mexico (during and after the Mexican War) and in the Philippines (during and after the Spanish-American War). The Mexican War is one of the most painful episodes to Mexicans because the U.S. invaded Mexico and captured Mexico City, However, what is often not realized is that after Winfield Scott's army occupied Mexico City, many Mexicans started an insurgency that bottled up the army in Mexico City by killing any soldiers who strayed too far from their billets. The insurgency was so effective that James Polk's envoy to Mexico, Nicholas Trist, desiring to extricate the U.S. Army from its difficult position cut-off in Mexico City, negotiated the Treaty of Guadalupe-Hidalgo on February 2, 1848, without President Polk's approval, even though the Treaty was very favorable to the United States and gained the country much of its territory from Texas to California. In small groups, discuss why there was an insurgency against the U.S. military in Mexico, the Philippines and Iraq, and come to some conclusion as to whether or not it supports the CPOST analysis.

Activity for Reading #23: in small groups, use your Schema activation responses to create a list of the 5 main motivations for historical acts of terrorism.

SOURCES

For Virgil's *Aeneid*, I recommend the Robert Fagles translations issued in Penguin Classics paperback 2010. Unlike the *Iliad* and *Odyssey*, the Aeneid has never had a good movie adaptation. For the Chicago Project on Suicide Terrorism, see Robert A. Pape *Dying to Win: The Strategic Logic of Suicide Terrorism* 2005 Random House. I recommend three *New Yorker* articles on issues addressed in this chapter: Ari Shavit "Lydda" 1948 *The New Yorker* October 21, 2013 pp. 40-46; Patrick Radden Keefe "Where the Bodies are Buried" *The New Yorker* March 16, 2015 pp. 42-61; and Jon Lee Anderson "Death of the Tiger" *The New Yorker* January 17, 2011 pp. 40-55. Pape's analysis was concurred in by Michael Scheuer 2007 *Imperial Hubris: Why the West Is Losing the War on Terror* Potomac Books (when the book was first issued the author's name was withheld because of his intelligence community identity). *Hubris* will be defined and featured in the next chapter.

Chapter 10

International Relations: The Thucydidean Paradox

OBJECTIVES

- Analyze the problem of international relations in terms of the sovereignty of nations.
- Determine what kinds of perspectives are valid approaches in international relations.
- Attribute to the Greek historian Thucydides a reasonable, more nuanced approach to international affairs and the proper conduct of wars, than with which he is usually credited.
- Explain why realism fails to address all the possible perspectives that international actors can adopt with all the anthropological contingencies that occur among nations.

KEY TERMS

Realism: the political philosophy that argues that only issues of power relations and national self-interest are valid motivations in the realm of international relations, and that the focus on self-interest is an expression of "rationality" that is part of human nature.

Neorealism: the same as realism except that it is not so much rationality and human nature so much as the anarchy at work in international relations (because sovereign nations need defer to no other polities) that is the key factor.

Credibility: in foreign policy, the argument that a nation must follow through on threatened actions in order to convince other nations that it will do the utmost to protect its interests and work to keep international order as it perceives it to be.

Hubris: excessive self-pride, directing actions amounting to arrogant violantions against common standards of decency and often leading to violent behavior and resistance to established norms.

SCHEMA ACTIVATION ACTIVITY

Briefly research what nations typically say when they are presenting action they wish to undertake. This will be obvious in just looking at the news for the day: pick one brief official statement from a national spokesperson and then consider the following: *what are the hidden motivations that the statement is trying to justify? What ethical or moral precept is the argument invoking to justify their action?*

(Save these to share later in your discussion sections.)

INTRODUCTION

In this chapter, you are introduced to the issue of international relations. Many people do not know that the ancient Greeks wrestled with this issue 2,500 years ago, as they looked at the wars and relations between their city-states, which never allied into one nation state called "Greece," as is the case today. We use the Athenian historian Thucydides as the heart of this discussion because the issues he defined are as freshly relevant today as they were then. We start with Thucydides' comments on how political crises can lead people to "change the ordinary meanings of words" to justify their questionable actions. We then look at the famous "Melian Dialogue," in which the Athenians negotiate with the small island of Melos to try and get them to surrender to the power of Athens. We then look at one paper on Thucydides and modern international relations, representative of a large literature wrestling with this most intractable of contemporary world problems.

READING #24: THUCYDIDES, TRANSLATIONS OF EXCERPTS FROM *THE PELOPONNESIAN WAR*

Book 3.82.4-8 Political Chaos and Language

The antagonists changed the accustomed meanings of words in relation to deeds via self-justification. <u>Audacity</u> without reason was deemed brave <u>party-loyalty</u>; <u>delay</u> based on foresight was deemed pretentious <u>cowardice</u>; <u>moderation</u> was thought to be a screen for <u>unmanliness</u>; <u>intelligence</u> in all matters became <u>inaction</u> in everything; <u>to deliberate</u> with an eye to security against failure was dismissed as a high-minded pretext for <u>avoiding action</u>. The angrily violent person was considered always trustworthy, while the one opposing that person was regarded as suspect. Anyone plotting against an adversary successfully was intelligent; and anyone suspecting someone was cleverer still; the person taking counsel in advance so as to not need any kind of plotting or counter-plotting was deemed a traitor to the party and panic-stricken in the face of enemies. Simply put, the one anticipating someone intending to do something evil and the one inciting someone who was not inclined to do so, both were praised. Blood relation was considered more alien than party affiliation on account of the party-member being readier for an audacious attack without excuse. . . Such loyalties were not for public benefit in conformity with statutory laws, but expressed in contravention of established laws. And their pledges to one another were not sanctioned by divine law, but only by their common breaking of the law. . .The cause of all these calamities was desire for power, motivated by greed and ambition. . .

The Melian Dialogue

84.3 The Athenian generals, Kleomedes, the son of Lykomedes, and Teisias, the son of Teisimachos, before laying waste to the island, first sent envoys, for the purpose of speaking to the Melians. The Melians did not lead the envoys before the popular assembly, but directed them to speak in the presence of the magistrates and the oligarchs only, about why they had come.

*85. **Athenians**: Our words are not for the assembly, so that the people should not be deceived hearing from us attractive and unquestioned arguments in one continuous speech—we know that is the reason for your leading us before you oligarchs; you who are sitting here have adopted a safer course. Make your judgment regarding each point, not in one speech, but replying immediately to anything not seeming to have been appropriately stated. But, first and foremost, speak up, if anything we say pleases you.*

*86. The Councilors of the **Melians** responded: The suitability of instructing each other calmly is not objectionable, but acts of war have already been committed by you, and that they are not contemplated for the future (you say), appears to be contradictory. We see that you have come treating yourselves as the judges of the things that will be said; in all likelihood, even were we to win the debate because of the justice of our cause and our not yielding to you, the outcome will be war for us. However, if we are persuaded by you, the outcome will be slavery.*

*87. **Athenians**: If, therefore, you have come here for the purpose of talking about your suspicions regarding the future, or the present circumstances, or what you see before you, rather than anything other than planning for your safety for your city, we might as well stop now. If you come for that purpose, we can speak.*

88. *Melians: It is reasonable and pardonable for those stuck in such a situation to be engaged in talking and thinking on many alternatives. However, this conference is here and now about our safety, and so let the discussion go according to your proposal, if that seems good to you.*

89. **Athenians**: *Nevertheless, we will not offer a long unconvincing speech with fine phrases to justify our empire, that we got it justly by defeating the Persians, or that we have made this expedition because we have been wronged by you. Nor do we think that you can possibly believe that you will persuade us, saying that either you did not ally with Sparta, although you are the descendants of a Spartan colony, or that you have not done Athens any harm. We think that you are trying to bring about possibilities (out of alternatives that we both truly understand), knowing full well what we also know full well, that justice is something reckoned in human discourse only from positions of equality, and that the more powerful do whatever they want, and the weak accede to them.*

90. **Melians**: *In the way we think about it all, it is useful for you (we have to emphasize that aspect, given that you insisted that we talk about what is advantageous as opposed to what is just) not to set aside the common good. But, for the one who is always in danger, reasonable things are just things—even for the person who has not been quite completely persuasive finds some benefit in reasonable justice. That is no less true in your case; so much so that if you were to fail in some endeavor or other, suffering great retribution in the process, you would become an example for others while gaining some credit were you to maintain a focus on the common good. [This sections reads very much like a prediction of the near future of what happens to Athens in the Sicilian Expedition.]*

91. **Athenians**: *We would not be upset at the fall of our empire, if that should happen. It is isn't the rulers of others (just as the Spartans rule others, but we have no quarrel with them) who are the ones ruthless with the defeated, but it is the subject peoples who are, when they somehow are able to go on the offensive and are able to overthrow their rulers. On that score, let us be the judge of whether it is worth it to run that risk. Make no mistake: it is for the advantage of our empire and the safety of your city that we are here present and we will make our arguments. We will make this clear above all: we wish, without trouble, to rule over you, and for you to be safe for both of our advantages.*

92. **Melians**: *Explain how it would be as useful for us to be slaves as it would be for you to rule over us.*

93. **Athenians**: *Because it would be useful for you to submit instead of suffering the most terrible consequences; we gain advantage by NOT having to destroy you.*

94. **Melians**: *So, you would not accept the result of having us stay out of the hostilities, becoming your friends instead of your enemies, by staying neutral and joining neither of the two sides?*

95. **Athenians**: *No, your enmity does not harm us as much as your friendship—the latter showing us weak in the eyes of our subjects, while the former—your hate—proves to be a sign of our power.*

96. **Melians**: *Do your subjects think about it and place in the same category those who are not part of your empire, and the mass of your colonists, some of whom have revolted from you, all indistinguishably as your conquests?*

97. **Athenians**: *Our subjects think that neither those unallied to our empire, nor our subdued colonists in revolt lack valid appeals to justice. However, they reckon to escape submission by having power so that we do not attack them out of fear of it. So that, apart from our coming to rule more subjects, you would also*

afford us safety by our conquering you, especially if, as islanders weaker than other islanders, you were not to get the best of us, master of the seas that we are.

98. **Melians**: *Do you not think there can be safety in an alternative course? It is necessary here and now to try to persuade you of its wisdom, informing you of what is useful for us that also happens to accord with your own interests, given that you have stopped us from all appeals to justice and your insistence that we act in accordance with your interests. Inasmuch as many polities are allying themselves with neither of the two sides, how will you not make enemies of them all, when, looking at our case, they think that someday you will also come against them? In your contemplated action, what do you accomplish other than strengthening existing enemies and bringing against you, not out of choice, those would were not about to become your enemies?*

99. **Athenians**: *We do not think those people are more difficult for us to deal with, inasmuch as many are free status mainlanders of diverse locations who will put off for a long time taking precautionary measures against us, than some of the islanders, such as yourselves, who are autonomous, and are already angered by the force represented by our empire. Those are the ones who would most likely, set upon a reckless course, put both themselves and us into foreseeable danger.*

100. **Melians**: *Surely, therefore, if you run so desperate a venture—you, so as to not to have to give up your empire, and those already slaves to it to have done with it—it would be a great evil and supreme cowardice for us, while still free, not to try everything before becoming your slaves.*

101. **Athenians**: *Not if you consider things realistically. It is not a question of a contest between you and us over courage from equal positions of power. It is not about bringing disgrace upon oneself, but rather the issue is about self-preservation and not standing up (futilely) against those by far more powerful than yourselves.*

102. **Melians**: *But we know that the fortunes of war sometimes take a more impartial turn than according to the disparate forces arrayed on each side. For us to yield right away is to leave us without hope, but by hazarding some great action, still there will be hope to end up in an upright position.*

103. **Athenians**: *Hope is an extravagance in danger; it may harm those resorting to it, but only as long as they have plenty of other resources to turn to, it will not destroy them. On the other hand, for those staking everything on one throw of the dice, hope is a luxury they cannot really afford. At the very moment that hope is recognized for what it is, when things have gone south, hope leaves behind no resources for the time when one is now on guard against it, now knowing what an empty thing it is. Which eventuality, weak as you are, dependent on one tip of the scale, you do not think that you will suffer from that, nor do you liken yourselves to the masses (when you still have the chance to be saved by rational action) who, whenever visible sources of hope fail and people begin to suffer greatly, turn themselves to unseen sources such as divination, oracles, and as many such things as bring ruin due to hopes raised in vain.*

104. **Melians**: *Know this well: we also think it difficult to contend against your power and fortune, unless from equal starting points. Nevertheless, we believe that we enjoy no deficiency in allotments of fortune from the divine, because, as religious people, we are taking a stand against the unjust, and there will be balanced for our benefit alliance with the Spartans against our deficiency of power. They will feel obliged*

to help us, if for no other reason, for the sake of our common Doric heritage, or simply out of a sense of shame. Thus we feel encouraged, not wholly without reason.

105. **Athenians**: We certainly do not think that we will be left behind in terms of divine favor. We think it right to call for or do nothing exceptional in regard to human notions in religious matters nor deliberations in regard to humans thinking itself. We hold the following opinion about the divine—regarding humans it is clearly so and always holds true because of the necessity imposed by nature: wherever the divine holds power, the divine rules. We neither enacted that "law" nor used it first once it was established. But taking it up once in existence, and leaving it as a legacy existing for all time—we follow that law. We do this in the full and confident knowledge that you and everyone else, should you come into the same power as we have, would be doing the exact same thing. So, regarding divine favor, reasonably, we do not fear to be so at a disadvantage as you suggest. As to your expectation towards the Spartans, which makes you believe that they will help you out of a sense of shame: well, while we indulge your simplicity, we do not envy your foolishness. The Spartans, when it is a question of themselves and the customs in their own land, are happy to employ virtue to the greatest extent. But when it is a question of how they behave towards others, one might have many things to say, but—in a word!—of all the people we are acquainted with, they make it very, very clear that they believe that things that are pleasant for them are honorable things and that what is in their interest is justice. Surely, such an attitude on their part is not conducive to your present unreasonable hope of salvation from them.

106. **Melians**: Well we too look chiefly at that very point. In terms of their intent, they would not betray us Melians (their colonists) because they would come to be regarded as untrustworthy in the eyes of the rest of the Greeks, who are well-disposed towards them, and they would thus be helping their enemies.

107. **Athenians**: Look at your own case: do you not think that the advantageous thing comes with safety and the just and honorable thing is fraught with danger? Following that path is the thing which the Spartans do least of all, for the most part.

108. **Melians**: We think that, for our sake, they would take in hand the dangers and consider them more secure than for they would be in the case of others, inasmuch as we are located close to the Peloponnese peninsula, where we could help with any operations to be carried out. We and they are like-minded; we are more trustworthy to them than other islanders.

109. **Athenians**: For those about to embark on a conflict, what appears most secure for them is not the goodwill of those who have called on them, but rather if one is far superior in the power of their actions. That is the consideration which the Spartans look at most of all in comparison to everyone else. Certainly, plagued by so much mistrust in their own preparations and resources, they only attack their neighbors when they have with themselves many allies. So, it is unlikely that they will cross over the sea to an island, while we hold mastery of the seas.

110. **Melians**: But they might even have in mind to send others, such as the Corinithians. The Cretan Sea is wide, on which capture at sea by a powerful navy is more difficult than safe passage by those who have planned carefully to get past a blockade. And, if they fail on the water, they might turn against your own territory and against the rest of your allies, as many as Spartan General Brasidas did not visit. Then you will have your hands full—not about territory that doesn't belong to you, but rather about your own empire—even your own homeland.

111. **Athenians**: *Something like this might come to pass; maybe you will even come to know it by experiencing it; but surely you are not ignorant of the fact that, not ever even once have the Athenians withdrawn from a siege out of fear of anyone else. We reflect on the fact that, having said you would make plans concerning your safety, you have said absolutely nothing in this long discussion which would give people confidence that things are going to turn out so as to provide them with safety. Your strongest hopes are hopes in the future, while your present straightened circumstances are up to surviving against forces already drawn up against you? You are presenting such incredibly illogical ways of thinking; you better think up something more sophisticated than your current conclusions, after allowing us to withdraw, while you deliberate. Surely, you are not going to turn yourselves to a false sense of shame—shame that above all destroys people caught in disgraceful and foreseeable dangers. The thing called "shame," by the power of its seductive name, is very tempting to many people who still face foreseeable situations into which they are being carried, yielding to the power of a word. By their action they fall into misfortunes, with "eyes wide shut," and take on a disgrace more disgraceful because of its being due to foolishness rather than bad luck. Against which outcome, if you plan well, you will guard against, and you will not think it unfitting to yield to the greatest city, which is making an offer of modest terms, inviting you to become allies, holding your own territory, subject to tribute only. And, having been given a choice between war and safety, don't be so obstinate as to choose the worse alternative. You will be just as people who do not yield to their equals, yet comport themselves well to those who are more powerful, while being moderate to those weaker than themselves—those are the sorts of people who are likely to be successful. And so, look to it, once we have withdrawn, and take it to heart constantly that you are taking counsel among yourselves regarding your homeland, concerning which single place it will be decided in a single decision, whether it will turn out well or not successfully.*

112. *And so, the Athenians withdrew from the conference. And the* **Melians**, *meeting among themselves, deciding, as it seemed best to them, very similar things they objected to before, said the following: No other course than the very things we said at the outset seem good to us, Athenians. Nor will we, in a short space of time, deprive our city of freedom, which has been inhabited now for 700 years. But, trusting in divine fortune that has preserved the city up to this time, and in help from other people, especially the Spartans, we will attempt to save ourselves. We invite you to be friends. We will be enemies to neither of the two sides. Please withdraw from our land, by treaty of the sort that seems sufficient to both sides.*

113. *The Melians answered in such a manner but the* **Athenians**, *now withdrawing from the conference said: As it seems to us from these counsels you have decided upon, you alone of all people judge things in the future more clearly than things in plain sight. You look for invisible results by wishing that they have already come to pass. And, having staked the greatest wager and put the greatest trust in the Spartans— and fortune—and hopes—you shall fail in your endeavor.*

114. *Thereupon, the Athenian ambassadors withdrew to their camp. The Athenian commanders, when the Melians did not submit, immediately made preparations for siege warfare. . .*

116.3 *And later, after all these events, another force was sent out from Athens, under the command of Philokrates, the son of Demeas. The Melians, already besieged with great force, and victimized by some treachery within, surrendered to the Athenians, under terms that the Athenians would decide their fate. The Athenians then killed as many adult males as they captured, and enslaved the children and women. The place they themselves occupied, later sending out 500 colonists. . .*

Imperial *Hubris*?

Hubris is the Greek term meaning "overly-puffed-up pride." It was a constant in Greek thought that nemesis (a Greek term meaning "vengeance") would overtake anyone acting with excessive boastfulness. It has been pointed out by generations of Thucydides scholars that the Dialogue you have just read ended Book 5 of Thucydides' book, which was followed by Book 6, introducing what has come to be called, the Sicilian Expedition. In 415 BCE, the Athenians decided to try and expand their empire into Sicily. So, the Athenians sent forces (and kept pouring troops and ships) into Sicily. In 413 BCE, after many ups and downs, the Athenians were hard-pressed by the Syracusans, who, as colonists of Corinth, sided with the Spartans. They won a great naval battle in the Great Harbor at Syracuse, destroyed the Athenian fleet, and then overtook the Athenian land troops, taking thousands prisoner and throwing them into a stone quarry as a POW camp, where thousands died like flies. Very few Athenians in the Sicilian Expedition ever made it home. The lesson was unmistakable, simply by juxtaposition. Thucydides, although he never explicitly said that the Athenians approached their imperial policy from a "might makes right" or "justice is the interest of the stronger" viewpoint, certainly implies that too much of their policy tended in that direction as the Melian Dialogue eloquently demonstrates. To Thucydides and his audience, Athens received her comeuppance for her "crime" against tiny Melos in the Sicilian disaster.

One recent study argues that the collapse of most complex civilizations of the ancient world was due to "social *hubris*" in that the powerholders of the culture in question acted with excessive arrogance in the face of social and environmental challenges, which failed to address the problems they faced and led to the collapse of the civilization. So, although an individual trait, the argument is that cultural groups, city-states and nation-states can act with *hubris* as a whole also. In the next reading, the author argues convincingly that Thucydides appreciated the difference in the political attitutudes of individuals as opposed to collectives—a factor which needs to be born in mind at all times. Anthropologists must continually sort out individual actions from collective ones, to see if some trait is personal or more characteristic of the culture as a whole.

Is "realism" still a theory of international relations?

Many global political science scholars of today seem to think that realism, said by some to be the brainchild of Thucydides {a theory with which I disagree}, is a dead letter in modern international relations. Yet, that does not seem to be the case: here are the words of President Donald J. Trump to the United Nations on September 19, 2017: *Our government's first duty is to its people, to our citizens, to serve their needs, to ensure their safety, to preserve their rights, and to defend their values. As president of the United States, I will always put America first. Just like you, as the leaders of your countries, will always and should always put your countries first. . . We have a policy of principled realism, rooted in shared goal, interests, and values. That realism forces us to confront the question facing every leader and nation. . .If we desire to lift up our citizens, if we aspire to the approval of history, then we must fulfill our sovereign duties to the people we faithfully represent. We must protect our nations, their interests, and their futures. We must reject threats to sovereignty. . .*

Here, the U.S. President bluntly states that our foreign policy is "realist," after claiming that "it has just been announced that we will be spending almost $700 billion on our military and defense. Our military will soon be the strongest it has ever been." To be fair, the President then insisted that the realism offered must be tempered by the fact that "making a better life for our people also requires us to with work together in close harmony and unity, to create a more safe and peaceful future for all people." However, the rest of his speech attacked other nations such as North Korea and Iran demanding common action against both which a majority of other nations in the UN almost certainly would not necessarily support. The whole episode reveals the greatest problem of all that is at the heart of the Thucydidean Paradox: what happens when the interests of sovereign nations conflict? Whose interests must prevail? The answer, despite the many Thucydides scholars who claim that he favored a hard-headed realism in international affairs, it seems to many others of us that what Thucydides thought of the Peloponnesian War is that "one shouldn't start a war; one never knows how it will turn out" is the message, summarized by the Spartan herald, as he was escorted out of Athenian territory when the last negotiation to stop the war failed: "Today is the beginning of great misfortune for all of Greece."

The use and abuse of Thucydides in international relations

Laurie M. Johnson Bagby

International relations scholars are prone to claiming that the ancient historian of the Peloponnesian War, Thucydides, is a realist of one kind or another. Paul Viotti and Mark Kauppi tell us that Thucydides "is usually credited with being the first writer in the realist tradition as well as the founding father of the international relations discipline."[1] Michael Doyle writes, "To most scholars in international politics, to think like a Realist is to think as the philosophical historian Thucydides first thought."[2] Kenneth Waltz found in Thucydides an expression of his "third image," in which the balance of power states find themselves in largely determines their actions.[3] Robert Keohane and Joseph Nye use Thucydides as a representative of their "overall power model" or the "traditional" international relations paradigm.[4] Both classical realists, who begin with an understanding of human nature, and neorealists, who emphasize the international structure, can find support for their theoretical viewpoint in Thucydides.[5]

This article contains revised material from the conclusion of my book, *Thucydides, Hobbes and the Interpretation of Realism,* © 1993 by Northern Illinois University Press used here with the permission of Northern Illinois University Press.

1. Paul R. Viotti and Mark V. Kauppi, *International Relations Theory: Realism, Pluralism, Globalism* (New York: Macmillan, 1987). These two scholars recently have made an earnest attempt to deal with Thucydides in more detail in *The Global Philosophers: World Politics in Western Thought* (New York: Macmillan, 1992). While emphasizing Thucydides as realist, they note other important "cautionary tales" in the *History of the Peloponnesian War* and some problems with identifying Thucydides totally with our notion of realism. They still claim, however, "One is hard pressed to find in Thucydides suggestions of alternatives to realism" (p. 50).

2. Michael Doyle, "Thucydidean Realism," *Review of International Studies* 16 (July 1990), p. 223.

3. Kenneth Waltz, *Man, the State, and War* (New York: Columbia University Press, 1959), p. 159.

4. Robert O. Keohane and Joseph Nye, *Power and Interdependence* (Boston: Little, Brown, 1977), p. 42.

5. See, for instance, Hans Morgenthau, *Politics Among Nations* (New York: Alfred A. Knopf, 1978), p. 38; Kenneth Waltz, *Theory of International Politics* (Reading, Mass.: Addison-Wesley, 1979), pp. 127 and 186–87; and Robert G. Gilpin, "The Richness of the Tradition of Political Realism," *International Organization* 38 (Spring 1984), pp. 287–304 and especially p. 290.

Keohane claims that Thucydides was among the first to set out these three basic assumptions of classical political realism:

> (1) states (or city-states) are the key units of action; (2) they seek power, either as an end in itself or as a means to other ends; and (3) they behave in ways that are, by and large, rational, and therefore comprehensible to outsiders in rational terms.[6]

Observations about human nature formed the philosophical basis of classical realism. But neorealism, Keohane writes, drops classical realism's use of human nature as an explanation for the inherently conflictual nature of international relations and instead focuses solely on international anarchy to explain the behavior of states. Within the neorealist framework, the analyst need not consider either individual nature or the nature of particular regimes, since the influence of international anarchy is expected to make states' behavior outwardly similar. "And in such systems," Keohane writes, "we need not be concerned with the functions performed by the units, since they are functionally alike. Thus the dimension of differentiation of the units 'drops out.'"[7]

Although there are some partial overlaps between classical realism and the Thucydidean perspective—especially in classical realism's pessimistic stance toward human nature, its consideration for the role of statesmanship, and its recognition of the moral tragedy of international politics—Thucydides would disagree with classical realists on the basic assumptions Keohane lists above.[8] That is, insofar as classical realists see states as "the key units of action" that always "seek power" and that are "by and large, rational, and therefore comprehensible to outsiders in rational terms," a close reading of Thucydides will show that he does not agree with some of the most important emphases and conclusions of classical realists.

Likewise, although there is some evidence to suggest that Thucydides understood the influence of international structure on the state behavior leading up to and during the Peloponnesian War, as we will see below he cannot be completely identified with neorealism either. Thucydides does not follow the neorealist method of disregarding, for purposes of theory, the differentiation among states within the system. On the contrary, Thucydides

6. Robert O. Keohane, "Realism, Neorealism and the Study of World Politics," in *Neorealism and Its Critics* (New York: Columbia University Press, 1986), p. 7.

7. Ibid., p. 14. See also David Dessler's discussion of this feature of Waltz's theory in "What's at Stake in the Agent-Structure Debate?" *International Organization* 43 (Summer 1989), pp. 441–73 and 450–54 in particular.

8. Loriaux rightly notes that Hans Morgenthau and other classical realists understood the limits of theory. Morgenthau, he writes, "argues that the rationalist, scientistic model of inquiry, based on monocausal, deterministic representation of things, provides very little purchase on social phenomena. Multiple causes, some of a nonmaterial nature, confer on social phenomena a good deal of contingency, making possible only a probabilistic understanding of them." See Michael Loriaux, "The Realists and Saint Augustine," *International Studies Quarterly* 36 (December 1992), pp. 401–20. The quotation is from p. 405.

thinks that an understanding of the political and cultural differences among city-states before and during the Peloponnesian War is crucial for understanding their behavior.

Therefore I hope to show not that realism or neorealism is entirely wrong, and that we should abandon them for the Thucydidean perspective, but to show that Thucydides may guide us in our studies beyond realism—and especially beyond neorealism. Indeed, Waltz seems to recognize the need for this kind of supplement to neorealism when he writes, "Clean and simple definitions of structure save us from the pernicious practice of summoning new systems into being in response to every salient change within a system. They direct our attention to the units and to unit-level forces when the particularity of outcomes leads us to search for more idiosyncratic causes than are found in structures."[9]

The Thucydidean perspective can be useful in explaining change and innovation that structure alone cannot explain. It can be useful as a guide for "layering" different theories and perspectives to obtain a fuller picture, one that may be of use to practitioners for obtaining wisdom about international politics from the work of international relations scholars.[10] It may also succeed in rattling the theoretical and moral assumptions of realism and neorealism enough to increase the depth of understanding of our own, more familiar theoretical and moral perspectives.

I will begin by turning to some recent attempts by international relations scholars to locate Thucydides within their field. I will suggest first that Thucydides has been misunderstood by these and other scholars and second, how he might be better understood. Then I will elaborate on how Thucydides provides an interesting alternative or supplementary approach to realism in the study of international politics. I will suggest that Thucydides departs from the realist position in both outlook and method by his methodology of (1) emphasizing the importance of what we might call "national character," (2) highlighting the influence of the moral and intellectual character of individual leaders, (3) showing the importance of political rhetoric for action and treating what we call realism as another argument in political rhetoric, not a theory that Thucydides thinks describes the whole truth about political things, and (4) showing that for him, moral judgments form an integral part of political

9. See p. 329 of Kenneth Waltz, "Reflections on *Theory of International Politics:* A Response to My Critics," in *Neorealism and Its Critics.*

10. Ferguson and Mansbach have noted that as things now stand, international relations literature, especially theoretical literature, is not palatable to the political practitioner. "The sad truth, of which there appears to be growing recognition and acknowledgement, is that international relations practitioners in governments, some of whom (perhaps mistakenly) in the 1950's and 1960's looked to the academic world for guidance in matters like deterrence, find very little of either interest or relevance in contemporary theory and therefore make little attempt to read it"; see Yale Ferguson and Richard Mansbach, *The Elusive Quest: Theory and International Politics* (Columbia: University of South Carolina Press, 1989), p. 212. It is my belief that a Thucydidean approach might serve to enlarge our readership outside of academic circles.

analysis. Finally, I will examine the merits of considering the method of Thucydides as an alternative or supplement to realism and put forth some possible examples of that alternative.

Thucydides in international relations scholarship

As we have seen, Keohane has identified Thucydides with three key assumptions of political realism. These assumptions claim that states should be considered the primary actors in international relations, that they should be assumed to consistently seek power, and that they should be assumed to act rationally. In this context acting rationally seems to mean acting to maximize self-preservation and security through the pursuit of power.

Keohane and others find the basis for the above claim in the statement of Thucydides that "the truest explanation [for the war], although it has been the least often advanced, I believe to have been the growth of the Athenians to greatness, which brought fear to the Lacedaemonians [Spartans] and forced them to war."[11] Keohane sees in this statement confirmation that the Spartans were acting rationally to protect themselves when they declared war on Athens in the way that realists and neorealists would both predict. He maintains that realist scholars will use the method of analysis the Spartans used, that is, "They will interpret the actions of [the states they are studying] not on the basis simply of their policies or on the assumption that they will behave morally, but rather on the premise that they are seeking rationally to increase their power."[12] The only problem with this analogy is that the Spartans did not react to the Athenian buildup of power in a way that would have been predicted by realist or neorealist assumptions. Indeed, the Athenian buildup was made possible by the lackadaisical and timid Spartan response to it, and the Spartans eventually reacted to it only with the goading of their allies.

Robert Gilpin interprets the above passage from the *History* in much the same way as Keohane.[13] For Gilpin, Thucydides' lesson is that the distribution of power within the international system largely determines states' actions within that system. Sparta responded in a rational manner to Athens' growth in power and was compelled to challenge Athens for hegemony. Hence the situation of Athens and Sparta is for Gilpin a good example of his "structural theory of war," inasmuch as Athens' growth in power caused Sparta's decision to go to war.

---

11. Thucydides, *History of the Peloponnesian War* (Cambridge, Mass.: Loeb Classical Library, Harvard University Press, 1980), Book 1, section 23, line 6 (hereafter cited as 1.23.6). Compare ibid., 1.88.
12. Keohane, "Realism, Neorealism and the Study of World Politics," p. 8.
13. Robert Gilpin, "The Theory of Hegemonic War," *Journal of Interdisciplinary History* 18 (Spring 1988), p. 591.

If Gilpin left his observations at the above reading of Thucydides, he would be as guilty as many of those already cited for distorting Thucydides for their own theoretical purposes. But Gilpin does acknowledge that Thucydides does not fit neatly into the mold of neorealism. He acknowledges for instance that Thucydides does retain a more classically realist emphasis on human nature as a cause of state behavior and conflict, and he notes that Thucydides at times makes much of the influence of the very different national characters of Athens and Sparta on their actions during the war.[14] Yet Gilpin does not find these deviations from the neorealist norm in Thucydides compelling enough to change his overall evaluation of Thucydides' theoretical position: "Underlying this analysis and the originality of Thucydides' thought was his novel conception of classical Greece as constituting a system, the basic components of which were the great powers—Sparta and Athens."[15] Hence, Gilpin goes a step toward a fuller understanding of Thucydides but does not fully comprehend the extent to which Thucydides' thinking differs from his own.

Gilpin is correct in thinking that Thucydides understands the effect of the distribution of power on the actions of the city-states he is examining. However, the influence of the distribution of power is neither Thucydides' most fundamental source of explanation nor his most original observation. Thucydides' explanation of the cause behind Athens' buildup and Sparta's fear is more fundamental and perhaps even more novel.

Daniel Garst presents an alternative to the determinism implied in Gilpin's reading of Thucydides. Garst's reading of Thucydides is that the actions of states have to be understood as grounded in the decisions of individuals.[16] Garst argues that neorealists ignore the speeches of the characters peopling Thucydides' history, seeing them as mere justifications for decisions made on calculations of power. Contrarily Garst believes that Thucydides takes the content of those speeches and their impact on the political process much more seriously. Garst writes that "though various sorts of 'laws' are invoked in the speeches put forward by individual actors, Thucydides makes no attempt to explain them in the course of his narration; indeed, he rarely puts forward explicit laws of his own."[17]

Hence, Garst would disagree with Gilpin that the distribution of power was what determined the response of Sparta to Athens' growth of power. Nevertheless, Garst does not take the next step in ascertaining what Thucydides' true teaching is by closely examining the political rhetoric surrounding the war. A closer examination of that rhetoric will show that Thucydides' characters, especially his Athenian characters, are responsible for the strongest and most deterministic statements about human nature and the affects of power

14. Gilpin, "The Theory of Hegemonic War," pp. 593, 599, and 605.
15. Ibid., p. 595.
16. Daniel Garst, "Thucydides and Neorealism," *International Studies Quarterly* 33 (March 1989), pp. 3–27 and especially pp. 3–7.
17. Ibid., p. 4.

calculations on themselves and other actors in the war. The Athenians utter the most convincing statements that could be considered realist or neorealist.

The Athenian rhetoric during the war was rife with realist-sounding phrases, much of them emphasizing what has become known as the "Athenian thesis." At the war conference Sparta held with its allies to discuss the possibility of going to war against Athens, some Athenian ambassadors attempted to frighten the Spartans into backing off with the following description of their motivations for taking and keeping their empire: "It was under the compulsion of circumstances that we were driven at first to advance our empire to its present state, influenced chiefly by fear, then by honour also, and lastly by self-interest as well."[18] The Athenians tell the Spartans that they have retained their empire because those whom they dominate are now hostile to them and therefore dangerous to let go. Also the Athenians fear that if they loosen their grip on their empire, disgruntled city-states will go over to the Spartan side.[19] Here the Athenians make a statement that many classical realists could agree with concerning the passions that move human nature. We should remember though that the Athenians are using this statement as a means both to justify their imperialism and to frighten the Spartans.

The Athenian thesis is repeated even more strongly later on to frighten the small island city of Melos to become a tribute-paying ally of Athens. The Athenians tell the much weaker Melians that they will be destroyed if they do not submit to Athenian rule and remind them of what seems to be a universal law of international politics:

> Of the gods we hold the belief, and of men we know, that by a necessity of their nature wherever they have power they always rule. And so in our case since we neither enacted this law nor when it was enacted were the first to use it, but found it in existence and expect to leave it in existence for all time, so we make use of it, well aware that both you and others, if clothed with the same power as we are, would do the same.[20]

While the Athenians sound very realistic, and we may be convinced at least somewhat of the validity of their argument, we must remember that it is they who speak these rather stark lines and not Thucydides.

The Thucydidean viewpoint

As indicated at the start of this article, several factors are important to Thucydides in explaining the events of the Peloponnesian War, including national character, the personalities and characters of various individual actors, the role of political rhetoric, and questions of morality. All of these

18. Thucydides, *History of the Peloponnesian War* 1.75.3–4.
19. Ibid., 1.75.5.
20. Ibid., 5.105.2–3.

layers add a depth and nuance to Thucydides' work that account for its usefulness throughout the centuries. These multiple perspectives allow the reader to develop political wisdom, knowledge about politics that cannot be entirely encompassed within any one theory.

As I have already noted, classical realists attempt to explain states' actions at least partly through a theory of human nature. As Hans Morgenthau puts it, man is characterized by egoism and *animus dominandi* (lust for power).[21] Human beings are driven by their passions and assumed to be interested primarily in self-preservation and enhancement of their power. Realist and the newer neorealist theories also emphasize the importance, sometimes even the determinative nature, of the international balance of power on how states will react in any given situation.[22]

The first evidence that Thucydides does not subscribe to such a view of human nature and balance-of-power politics is that Thucydides makes much of the difference, not sameness, in national character between the two great "superpowers" of the war, Sparta and Athens. These differences directly affect how the two superpowers react to one another's power or changes in power. Their reactions are not as predictable as the realist or neorealist might hope.

National character

Waltz has claimed that Thucydides represents the view that in the final analysis differences in national character should not be considered for purposes of neorealist theory—only a state's "placement" in the international system applies.[23] Throughout the *History*, the Athenians make the same theoretical assumption by claiming that human beings will react in the same manner concerning issues of power and dominance regardless of national origin or culture.[24] They insist that any state would engage in Athenian-style imperialism if only it had enough power. But if the Athenians are correct in their assumptions about human nature, why does Thucydides show Athens and

21. Hans Morgenthau, *Scientific Man versus Power Politics* (Chicago: University of Chicago Press, 1974), pp. 191–96.

22. Neorealists insist that they differ from classical realists because they have a theory that excludes all factors except the structure of the international system itself—how power is distributed within the system. They concentrate on questions of how different power distributions might affect or determine the actions of states. I make the argument that this distinction is at least partially invalid in Laurie M. Johnson, *Thucydides, Hobbes and the Interpretation of Realism* (De Kalb: Northern Illinois University Press, 1993). The literature on this question has quite a history. See, for instance, Ernst Haas, "On Systems and International Regimes," *World Politics* 27 (January 1975), pp. 147–74 and p. 149 in particular; Morton Kaplan, "The Great New Debate: Traditionalism vs. Science in International Relations," *World Politics* 19 (October 1966), pp. 1–20 and p. 2 in particular; Friedrich Kratochwil, "Errors Have Their Advantage," *International Organization* 38 (Spring 1984), pp. 305–20 and p. 309 in particular; Robert Gilpin, "The Richness of the Tradition of Political Realism," *International Organization* 38 (Spring 1984), pp. 287–304 and pp. 301–2 in particular.

23. Waltz, *Theory of International Politics,* p. 187n, which refers the reader back to p. 127.

24. Thucydides, *History of the Peloponnesian War* 1.76.2.

Sparta acting in such different ways concerning power and dominance? Contrary to Athenian claims, throughout the *History* Thucydides shows that the Athenians and their opponents reveal a complexity of character that cannot be captured by single explanations of what motivates human beings or states and that often has a great if not determinative impact on decisions and outcomes.

Thucydides describes the Spartans before the war as sometimes idly worrying about Athens' progress, sometimes ignoring their allies' reports of Athenian imperialism, and always tolerating the Athenian leader Themistocles' stalling for time until Athenian military might and fortifications were secure.[25] Thucydides makes it clear that Sparta was aware of Athens' growing military might and yet, like the proverbial ostrich, chose to stick its head in the sand until its allies became abusively insistent that Sparta defend itself and its allies. The speeches that make up the Spartan War conference show how ingrained was the famous Spartan reluctance. The Corinthians, for instance, say that the Spartans' old-fashioned, timid style will never be a match for Athenian boldness and innovation.[26]

On the other hand, the Corinthians say that the Athenians are courageous, creative risk-takers. They contrast Spartan timidity and lack of activity with the Athenians' restlessness. Indeed, they say that the Athenians act before they have to, whereas the Spartans act only when they are absolutely compelled by fear to do so.[27] King Archidamus of Sparta confirms these national differences when he proclaims to his fellow Spartans, "Be not ashamed of the slowness and dilatoriness for which they censure us most."[28]

At the last moment when they have all but created their own fate through lack of a response, the Spartans are indeed goaded into seeing the necessity for defending themselves and their allies. But Thucydides shows us that the Athenian growth in power, which was the cause of the eventual fear of Athens that led to war, was itself caused by two things: Spartan reticence and inwardness, and Athenian boldness and interest in glory.

To reinforce what is said of the Spartans, Thucydides gives plenty of examples throughout the *History* of their laconic nature. The Spartans cower in superstitious fear of earthquakes or tidal waves.[29] They hesitate when sacrifices prove unfavorable.[30] They are described by Thucydides as timid in battle in comparison with Athenians,[31] and they are depicted as slow to come to the aid of friends under attack.[32] The Spartans do not come to the aid of Melos, just as the Athenians predict.[33] Thucydides at one point comments that the Spartans

25. Ibid., 1.90.
26. Ibid., 1.71.
27. Ibid., 1.71.
28. Ibid., 1.84.
29. Compare ibid., 3.89; also see ibid., 6.95.
30. Ibid., 5.55.4 and 5.116.
31. Ibid., 4.55.
32. Ibid., 5.82.3.
33. Ibid., 5.112–113.

were "the most convenient people in the world for the Athenians to make war upon. . . . For being widely different in character—the one people being quick, the other slow; the one adventurous, the other timorous—it was especially in the case of a naval power that they were most helpful."[34] With this simple statement toward the *History*'s end Thucydides reiterates the judgment of the Corinthians he reported near its opening.[35]

Individual character

Just as national character plays a part in determining state policy, so do the personalities, intelligence, and moral characters of individual leaders. It was a "personality conflict" that led to Sparta's decision to abandon its leadership of the post–Persian War alliance in favor of Athens, leaving the door open for Athens' rise to power. Sparta's decision was due to the abrasive personality of the Spartan commander-in-chief, Pausanias, whose imperial style made Sparta unpopular with the allies and raised the level of support for Athens.[36] Athenian leaders like Themistocles and Pericles were crucial in molding the Athenian attitude toward building the empire and fighting the war. Athens, Sparta, and other city-states are not seen as undifferentiated "black boxes" in this process.[37]

According to Thucydides, Pericles' power came from the people's belief that Pericles was a man of rare unselfish character who cared about the common good. He was able to convince them to go to war and to wage that war in a rather conservative way for limited ends. But after Pericles, when there was no one great enough to unify the state, competition among rivals often ruined Athenian policy. Leaders' personalities and characters were instrumental in Athens' chances of winning or losing the war. Thucydides writes: "The successors of Pericles, being more on an equality with one another and yet each striving to be first, were ready to surrender to the people even the conduct of public affairs to suit their whims."[38]

The successors of Pericles are described as being ambitious and self-

34. Ibid., 8.96.5.

35. For the earlier passage, see ibid., 1.69–70. While at times Thucydides mentions that fear of a helot (slave) uprising made the Spartans less willing to extend themselves, much of the time he does not, and it is far from clear that Thucydides would attribute to this one factor the difference in the two nations' characters. For those passages mentioning the helots in this context see ibid., 1.101.2–3; 4.55.1–3; 4.80.2–5; and 5.14.4. For other passages depicting or commenting on Spartan character, see 3.29 and 3.31; 5.115.2–4; 6.93.1–3; and 8.24.5.

36. Ibid., 1.94–95.

37. Viotti and Kauppi note the effect this has on the realist assumption of the state as a unitary actor: "Thucydides' work differs from much of the behavioral literature of the 1960's and 1970's, which essentially black-boxed the state and focused on state interactions in order to uncover the causes of war. Similarly, current 'neorealists' who treat state actors as 'functionally similar units' differ somewhat from Thucydides on this point." See *The Global Philosophers*, p. 51.

38. Thucydides, *History of the Peloponnesian War* 2.65.10–11.

interested while Pericles had been patriotic and selfless.[39] It was the difference in character between Pericles and these future leaders that Thucydides said caused Athens' decline and eventual defeat.[40] After Pericles, competing leaders feared the judgment of the people and so competed for their favor in a sort of popularity contest—to the detriment of the common good.[41]

We see a successive decline in the quality of leadership in several persons or groups who tried to lead after Pericles. In the famous Mytilenaean debate Diodotus suggests that, unlike Pericles, he has to lie and attack his opponent's character to appear to be sincere.[42] Alcibiades abandoned Athens at Thurii when it truly needed his military know-how because he feared the people's retribution for his rather aristocratic lifestyle.[43] After being sent on the Sicilian expedition, the Athenian general Nicias seemed completely paralyzed by his fear of the people's judgment, to the ruin of his forces.[44] As understandable as these leaders' fear of the people might seem, Thucydides compares them unfavorably with Pericles because their self-interest impaired their ability to lead.[45]

Thucydides obviously believed that statesmanship or the lack thereof could change history. How can one reconcile this Thucydidean explanation for the course of the war with the realists' assumption of uniformity of motivation? It is precisely because they were not all motivated alike that Athens' chances for victory declined in Thucydides' judgment after Pericles died. Athens' military and economic resources, he wrote, were so great that even with all the conflict caused by ambitious politicians, Athens held out for an amazingly long time.[46] In the end, it was not Athens' capabilities or lack thereof that was to blame for its failure but its leadership. Yet leadership would not be so vitally important in Thucydides' explanation if he thought human motivation and hence the behavior of states was as predictable as the Athenians wanted it to appear at the Spartan War conference and at Melos.

39. Ibid., 2.65.7–8.

40. Ibid., 2.65.11–13.

41. Even Pericles tried to avoid suspicion by promising to donate his property to the state should Archidamus not destroy it when invading Attica. Generally, however, Pericles was more impervious to this hazard than any other Athenian leader.

42. For an analysis of this debate, see Laurie M. Johnson, "Rethinking the Diodotean Argument," *Interpretation: A Journal of Political Philosophy* 18 (Fall 1990), pp. 53–62.

43. Thucydides, *History of the Peloponnesian War* 6.61. For a thorough portrait of the character of Alcibiades see Steven Forde, *The Ambition to Rule: Alcibiades and the Politics of Imperialism in Thucydides* (Ithaca, N.Y.: Cornell University Press, 1989).

44. Thucydides, *History of the Peloponnesian War* 7.48.

45. One might be tempted to say that Thucydides blamed the ignorance and volatility of the Athenian people as a whole for creating such leaders, instead of the individual leaders themselves. But Thucydides shows that the Assembly, despite its handicaps, was capable of making informed, moderate decisions, not only under Pericles but also when listening to an orator like Diodotus, even though his rhetoric had to match the baseness of his opponent to be persuasive. The people could, in a crisis, realize the necessity to surrender their democracy in order to save the state. See ibid., 8.97.

46. Ibid., 2.65.13.

To sum up thus far, Thucydides does not explain the initiation and conduct of the war as being caused by the distribution of power between Athens and Sparta but more by the differences in national character and in the individual characters of leaders. Hence the fear that Sparta felt in response to Athens' power must be understood as describing the result of other underlying causes that involve national differences instead of sameness.[47] For Thucydides, the differences among states and their leaderships do matter. The growth of Athens to greatness could and was caused by human decision with the knowing acquiescence of Sparta until the point when Sparta's allies convinced it that Athens' actions were sufficiently threatening to declare war.

Thucydides' use of political rhetoric

Peter Pouncey notes that by the seventh and eighth books of the *History* there are no more long speeches.[48] Pouncey argues that this is deliberately done to show that the quality and thus the importance of political speech declined as the war took its toll on the political unity of many communities. Corcyra, as well as Athens, is shown as being torn apart by the conflict between democrats and oligarchs. Due to such political conflict, speech became more and more a tool of personal and partisan interest, and thus less important in Thucydides' eyes for understanding the conduct of the war.

The change in Thucydides' use of speeches indicates that he does not think that political speech is always mere justification for actions taken for more realistic reasons. Sometimes it does justify, sometimes it is used to frighten or inspire, and sometimes, to deliberate rather objectively on the pros and cons of a particular action or policy. Sometimes speech embodies very strongly felt moral beliefs and differences. Sometimes it accurately portrays the mind of the speaker or speakers. But in any case it must be seriously examined for its own content and relation to the deeds the speakers do. Further, even when it is mere cover, it is still important inasmuch as political actions must be effectively instigated through convincing speech.[49]

Another lesson Thucydides teaches us in the *History* is that theory itself can be a tool of rhetoric instead of a summation of reality. Thucydides uses the speech of Diodotus at Mytilene in this light, showing how pressing a theory to its ultimate conclusions can often yield impractical or unacceptable results. In the debate against Diodotus, the Athenian demagogue Cleon calls for a death sentence against the entire town of Mytilene because its oligarchs led a revolt against Athenian control. Cleon claims that even if it is unjust to kill all the

47. For a description of that fear, see ibid., 1.23.60.
48. Peter R. Pouncey, *The Necessities of War: A Study of Thucydides' Pessimism* (New York: Columbia University Press, 1980).
49. Cogan points this out in Marc Cogan, *The Human Thing: The Speeches and Principles of Thucydides' History* (Chicago: University of Chicago Press, 1981).

Mytilenaeans, it is nevertheless expedient.[50] If the Athenians do not punish the Mytilenaeans severely, other cities will revolt. Cleon argues that in this case the Athenians would be acting both with expedience and with justice because the Mytilenaeans as a people have revolted. Since the common people went along with their leaders, at least in the initial revolt, all should be punished.[51]

Diodotus, who appears only this once in the *History* and who is otherwise unknown, responds to this very tough-sounding argument with an argument that sounds even tougher but that culminates in a recommendation for a more restricted punishment of the Mytilenaeans. Diodotus says that he too will examine only what is expedient.[52] Using the by-now-familiar Athenian thesis, he claims that the Mytilenaeans were compelled to revolt since it is human nature to try to obtain as much power as possible and to always be hopeful of success. Therefore, sentencing the Mytilenaeans to death will not deter anyone.[53] Diodotus recommends a moderate sentence for the Mytilenaeans, in which only the leading oligarchs will be put to death.[54] This will encourage those who do revolt to give up when faced with an Athenian siege, instead of forcing Athens to spend precious resources while waiting them out.

In this way Diodotus uses the Athenian thesis to show that, given its assumptions, the only way that Athens can control its allies is to exercise an ever-present vigilance and terror over them so that they will not think of revolting in the first place.[55] Diodotus' recommendation for the punishment of the Mytilenaeans is much more moderate than that, however. It seems more just than Cleon's recommendation, since the people of Mytilene not only had not instigated the rebellion but had returned the city to the Athenians at the earliest opportunity. Diodotus used the Athenian thesis rhetorically, this time not to frighten an enemy or to get a small state to back down but to convince his fellow Athenians of the advantages of a more moderate and more just course of action. At the same time, however, he manages to show the extremism inherent in the thesis itself.[56]

According to the thesis, only constant forceful repression, not good respectable leadership, would keep states from rising up. Yet it was good respectable leadership that originally earned Athens the loyalty and respect of its allies, and it was the deterioration of this leadership into imperialistic repression that caused the allies to resent Athens and revolt in greater and greater numbers as the war went on.[57] In the speech the Athenians give at the Spartan War

---

50. Thucydides, *History of the Peloponnesian War* 3.40.4–5.
51. Ibid., 3.40.1–2.
52. Ibid., 3.44.4.
53. Ibid., 3.45.5–7.
54. Ibid., 3.47.4–5.
55. Ibid., 3.46.6.
56. Again, for the development of this argument see Johnson, "Rethinking the Diodotean Argument."
57. Garst, "Thucydides and Neorealism," especially pp. 10 and 13. Garst, however, seems to say that Athens got its empire, as opposed to simply leadership of the alliance, by persuasion and

conference before the war begins, the Athenians admit that they "have been more observant of justice than they might have been, considering their power."[58] They have allowed their allies access to their law courts to settle disputes and have treated them as near equals before the law, even though they did not have to. This generous disposition toward the allies is what has made the allies ever more demanding and dissatisfied.[59]

Thucydides' *History* teaches that as the Athenians came to believe and act on their theory of human nature and state action, their legitimacy declined among their allies and empire and their domestic political order became corrupt and disintegrated amid politicians who each followed his own self-interest. It seemed too much belief in and adherence to this theory proved unhealthy for Athens and her empire. Short of acting on the extreme implications of the Athenian doctrine or of excusing one's baser actions by using the doctrine, Thucydides finds the thesis useful for describing a particularly popular way of thinking, quite identifiable as sophistic, as one strain in a moral discourse. It is the one that when it is acted upon usually wins, at least in the short run. For him it is proof that, for better or worse, human beings can create their own world instead of being created by it. In that sense he sees the thesis in a very different light from most modern international relations scholars, for whom the thesis is, if anything, more like a determinative law of nature and not an ideology.

Thucydides' moral teaching

Thucydides provides us with standards of justice in his own words. Witness his description of the Thracian massacre at Mycallessus:

> For the Thracian race, like the worst barbarians, is most bloodthirsty whenever it has nothing to fear. And so on this occasion: in addition to the general confusion, which was great, every form of destruction ensued, and in particular, they fell upon a boys' school, the largest in the town, which the children had just entered, and cut down all of them. And this was a calamity inferior to none that had ever fallen upon a whole city, and beyond any other unexpected and terrible.[60]

The content of Thucydides' justice can be seen even more clearly in his account of the Corcyraean revolution.[61] Thucydides writes that during this time men abrogated "in advance the common principles observed in such cases— those principles upon which depends every man's own hope of salvation should

---

voluntary consent. Actually the *empire* commenced when the Athenians began to change their tactics into the international equivalent of a protection racket. One could, however, surmise that Athens' decline began as soon as its tactics changed.

58. Thucydides, *History of the Peloponnesian War* 1.76.3–4.
59. Ibid., 1.77.
60. Ibid., 7.29.4–5.
61. See Lowell Edmunds, "Thucydides' Ethics as Reflected in the Description of Stasis (3.82–83)," *Harvard Studies in Classical Philology* 79 (Winter 1975), pp. 73–92.

he himself be overtaken by misfortune—thus failing to leave them in force against the time when perchance a man in peril shall have need of some one of them."[62] Thucydides does write that "human nature, now triumphant over the laws," delighted in giving the passions free reign. But he treats this as an inversion of the normal, with the result of producing inverted values: noble simplicity was laughed at, while sophistication was admired. Intelligence lost out to force. Prudence was considered cowardice, and impulsiveness was seen as manliness.[63] Thucydides places the blame for this inversion of values on "the desire to rule which greed and ambition inspire, and also, springing from them, that ardour which belongs to men who once have become engaged in factious rivalry."[64] In the process of criticizing this moral deterioration, Thucydides must assume that these beliefs, attitudes, and behaviors are not the norm for human beings but are instead measurable against the norm.[65] Even in war, that "rough schoolmaster," Thucydides must expect that human beings are capable of being better, of not being led by their passions but capable of self-control.[66] Hence, even though such behavior will recur "while human nature is the same," it is not an adequate representation of human nature, even in war.

Besides the rather stark differences between Athens and Sparta described above, we find that Thucydides is very keen to show that some states operate according to different moral codes. His attention to the episodes concerning the smaller states of Plataea and Melos shows that he does not think resistance to overwhelming power is so futile and meaningless as not to be worth mentioning. It is not at all obvious that Thucydides condemns either small state for not giving in, even though it was clear that to do so would mean their destruction. Indeed, it seems that an understanding of the nobility of Plataea's and Melos's alternative motivations is crucial to gain a full understanding of those episodes.

In the first case, the Plataeans were up against the overwhelming might of the Spartans in alliance with the Thebans. The Thebans claim that the Plataeans should be destroyed because they have allied themselves with Athens, although in this war Plataea has been neutral. The Plataeans argue that they have done the Spartans no harm and that they have always behaved with virtue, especially in the Persian War, when they were recognized by the Spartans for their heroism.

What is interesting about the Plataean episode is not so much the outcome: the Plataeans are eventually destroyed. Instead, it is Thucydides' detailed and favorable treatment of the Plataeans that suggests that he thinks (1) understand-

62. Thucydides, *History of the Peloponnesian War* 3.84.3. This passage, however, has been deemed spurious by many scholars.

63. Ibid., 3.82.4–8.

64. Ibid., 3.82.8.

65. The distortions of self-interest, as Connor observes, are the "drive for dominance, self-aggrandizement, and ambition." See Robert W. Connor, *Thucydides* (Princeton, N.J.: Princeton University Press, 1984), p. 102.

66. Thucydides, *History of the Peloponnesian War* 3.82.2–3.

ing their particular character is crucial to understanding the confrontation's outcome and (2) who is morally right or wrong should matter to the analyst or historian regardless of the final outcome.

Thucydides emphasizes the Plataeans' courage and intelligence in standing against the Spartan siege.[67] Nature even comes to the Plataeans' rescue when the Theban attempt to burn their city is stopped by rain and again when a storm covers an escape attempt. Thucydides' description confirms that the Plataeans' character really is what they claim it is, both in the past and now. They remain heroic against great odds. Then again, Thucydides provides us with the history of the dispute between Plataea and Thebes so that we can judge the content of their speeches against their deeds. Thucydides uses the content of the Theban speech itself, juxtaposed against the Plataeans' speech and past and recent events, to discredit the Thebans' argument. He does this by having the Thebans speak in a contradictory and revealing manner. Thucydides does not have to say one word in his own voice to lead his readers to certain conclusions: the Plataeans are clearly on the side of justice, even though they do not prevail. Pouncey writes that "apart from the single comment at the end about the 'profitable' alliance with Thebes, Thucydides will not make the connections for us by any explicit moralization. His own device is to envelop the reader almost claustrophobically in details about the siege and its progress."[68]

Thucydides' depiction of the siege, trial, and execution of the Plataeans can be taken as a classic illustration of power politics and proof of the foolishness of appealing to notions of justice in relations among states. According to this view, the Plataeans' fate provides proof for the thesis first put forward by the Athenians at the Spartan War conference. The thesis assumes that justice in itself does not exist but is a product of power relationships, and then only when both sides' power is equal.[69] If instead Thucydides is sympathetic to the Plataeans' notion of justice, then he must think that justice and injustice are more than derivatives of power relations, and his view of justice must differ markedly from that of the Athenians.[70]

The Plataean debate helps us to understand exactly what Thucydides thought of justice. Here Thucydides seems to admire courage, intelligence, integrity, patriotism, and loyalty. Although the Plataeans do utter a few words about the gods, most of what makes them appear just are their past and present deeds and the loyal conviction of their speech. So it is neither traditional piety that Thucydides so admires nor mere keeping of agreements, since both the

67. Ibid., 3.21–23.
68. Pouncey, *The Necessities of War*, p. 18.
69. Thucydides, *History of the Peloponnesian War* 5.89.
70. Proctor writes, "Their [the Plataeans'] speech . . . and the Thebans' reply constitute, in fact, the only debate in the *History* which is conducted throughout on a purely moral plane. The fact that it is also the longest of the debates consisting of only two speeches may betoken Thucydides' recognition of its special character." See Dennis Proctor, *The Experience of Thucydides* (London: Aris and Phillips, 1980), p. 92.

Thebans and Plataeans are shown breaking their promises. The Plataeans are depicted as truly patriotic and loyal to the Athenians.

The Thebans are depicted as being more interested in party loyalty (the ideology of the current conflict) than in being true to themselves or to their ethnic brethren, of whom the Plataeans form a part. They insist that the Spartans not listen to the Plataeans' speech because it will contain nothing but justifications. The Thebans are obviously using Sparta to wreak their long-awaited revenge.

In the case of Melos, the Athenians confront a small nation that wishes to remain neutral in the war. In the Melian dialogue, the Athenians try to convince the Melians that they should be worried only about their safety, not justice or pride. The Athenians tell the Melians they should not have recourse to such resources as hope, the gods, justice, or help from their ancestors (the Spartans). Nevertheless, the Melians mention all of those in their speech. They refuse to give up their independence despite the Athenians' threat of destruction. In the end the Athenians besiege Melos until it surrenders. They then kill all the adult males and sell the women and children into slavery. Later they colonize the island themselves.

In the debate with the Melians before their destruction, the Athenians insist that all the traditional trappings of Greek oratory be done away with, that they have nothing to do with the "real thoughts" of human beings, and that the real thoughts of human beings do not dwell on justice, past virtue, or deeds but on present safety and power.[71] But if all talk of justice and honor is a mere trapping, why are the Athenians so eager to see such talk eliminated? It seems the Athenians understand that political rhetoric concerning justice is fundamentally opposed and presents an alternative to their own thesis. Indeed, the Athenians at Melos are shown as acting on the thesis that Diodotus put forth in the Mytilenaean debate, which, as described above, was used as a rhetorical tactic to win a moderate sentence for the Mytilenaeans. The purpose of destroying Melos would be to spread terror throughout the allied cities and stop them from ever thinking about revolt.[72]

For the Athenians at Melos, pursuit of honor as well as justice is only reasonable among equals, a position that makes honor and justice depend on power relationships.[73] This is a view the Athenians insist is held by all people, even though they might publicly deny it. However, as noted above, it is not a view that they themselves held in Pericles' time when they allowed the allies equal treatment in their own courts. They complained, but they treated this equality as the price that a great power paid for honor.[74] But toward the end of the Melian dialogue, when we hear the Athenians repeat the old formula, a

71. Thucydides, *History of the Peloponnesian War* 5.85, 5.87, and 5.89.
72. Ibid., 5.97.
73. Ibid., 5.101.
74. Ibid., 1.76–77.

part of which is that the stronger should treat the weaker with moderation, it has taken on a hollow ring.[75]

An act like the Athenians eventually perpetrated on the Melians also would have been considered unjust by the standards eventually arrived at in the Mytilenaean debate. Then the Athenians repented of their initial decision to execute all male Mytilenaeans and sell the women and children into slavery because they felt that the sentence was cruel and excessive as well as unwise. Yet they did pass this sentence against the Melians—and for less reason. The Athenians could make a sound argument that the Mytilenaeans had done them an injustice. They could not and did not make any such argument about Melos.

Thucydides does not openly praise the Melians' bravery in facing death rather than giving up their independence. He simply reports their fates. The very fact that he records the dialogue and the eventual destruction of the Melians, however, does make something valuable of the Melians' deaths. As recorded by Thucydides, the Melian episode is an enduring black stain on Athenian history, a reminder of the ugliness of injustice as well as a warning of what comes of such excess. The Melian dialogue is followed by the Sicilian expedition, in which the Athenians, in their hubris, go too far and begin their own eventual destruction. In the context of the *History* as a whole, the Melians' deaths illustrate the failure of the Athenian thesis when that thesis is taken to its ultimate conclusions.

The Thucydidean scholar

The Thucydidean perspective is a challenge to some aspects of both realist and neorealist thought. As we have seen, it does not consistently corroborate Keohane's three assumptions of political realism. It does not always treat states as the primary actors in international relations, since individual leaders and political groupings are also shown as key actors. It does not show that states consistently seek to maximize their power: a major actor, Sparta, is shown allowing by its very timidity Athens' rise to greatness and only reluctantly entering into war. It also shows lesser states like Plataea and Melos acting on principles other than maximization of power and security. In Thucydides' view, then, states do not always act rationally, if by "rationally" we mean in a way that maximizes self-preservation, since neither Plataea nor Melos (nor Sparta, consistently) does this. Athens, due to internal political chaos, does not appear to act rationally toward the end of the *History,* and inasmuch as Athenians are motivated not just by fear and interest but also by glory, we must doubt whether they ever acted rationally, as realists would define the term. Similarly I have shown that Thucydides does not rely on the neorealists' emphasis on the distribution of power to explain the actions of states but goes behind the

75. Ibid., 5.111.4–5.

distribution of power to explanations that involve individual and national character, political rhetoric, and moral distinctions.

Thucydidean scholars, while not necessarily abjuring the realist or neorealist framework, will be able to go beyond or supplement that framework with these additional considerations. They will be able to examine the sometimes crucial role played by extremely successful or dismally failed leadership. Great or infamous leaders sometimes have a determinative impact on state behavior, as illustrated by the roles of Pausanias, Pericles, and Alcibiades, among others, in the *History*. Although deemed a rather old-fashioned concept by today's standards, the Thucydidean analyst would need to consider national character as a possible factor in the actions of states. To get away from the possibility of stereotyping, a modern scholar would have to do as Thucydides does, backing up assessments of particular national attributes with historical analysis, current examples, and observations of political actors both inside and outside of the state in question.

A scholar taking the Thucydidean perspective would need to include an analysis of the important political rhetoric surrounding the state action being considered. He or she will not automatically assume that it is a mere by-product or justification of power politics, economic interests, or any other impersonal force. Neither will the Thucydidean scholar always take political rhetoric at face value. Rather he or she will judge the rhetoric against the deeds of political actors, just as Thucydides does, to assess its sincerity. The scholar will realize that while theory may be useful in analyzing international relations, it may also become an object of analysis when it is found to appear in the speech of politicians and statesmen. As we know, theory of any kind, including that of realism and neorealism, often promotes certain political or moral agendas. The Thucydidean scholar should not only watch for this use of theory in political rhetoric but also be careful to be as objective as possible in his or her own use of theory and/or make clear his or her political or moral agenda in espousing a particular theory. The Thucydidean method reduces the chances of unreasoned subjectivity by requiring the analyst to consider many factors, including the moral and ethical aspects of the subject matter. If the scholar feels free to explore these questions openly, there will be no need to pursue them under the cover of feigned objectivity. This should lead to sounder moral arguments because the author will feel compelled to back them up with reason and fact.

The Thucydidean scholar will avoid any explanation that is of a deterministic nature. That is, the analyst will not ascribe to the international structure of neorealists or to the human nature of realists or to any other uncontrolled force a determinative power over human actions. This must be so insofar as the analyst seriously considers the decisions of individuals and their political rhetoric to have a real impact on the actions of states. Only if it is assumed that individuals can and do exercise the freedom to choose will it be possible to analyze the decisions and actions of particular statesmen as being right or wrong, good or bad.

The Thucydidean scholar will do all these things and still be able to take into account the influence of the distribution of power in the international system, and that approach will allow the scholar to explain changes within the system as the results of human decision. Indeed, one of Thucydides' most powerful messages is that change is always taking place, the fortunes of states are always rising and falling, due at least partly to the character and intelligence of leaders and those they lead. The tragic tone of Thucydides' work is due to the impression he leaves that so much of what takes place in human relations relies on such impermanent factors that no state can stay forever at the center of the world stage.

As outlined, this Thucydidean approach seems a tall order for any one scholar. Here I will offer only a brief description of a few works that seem to at least partially fill that order. Much in the same way we might criticize the Athenians and their thesis, Richard Ashley has criticized neorealism on the grounds that it is not a passive scientific theory but an active ideological program that

> treats the given order as the natural order, limits rather than expands political discourse, negates or trivializes the significance of variety across time and place, subordinates all practice to an interest in control, bows to the ideal of a social power beyond responsibility, and thereby deprives political interaction of those practical capacities which make social learning possible. What emerges is an ideology that anticipates, legitimizes, and orients a totalitarian project of global proportions: the rationalization of global politics.[76]

Alan Gilbert recently attacked realism in a similar vein, criticizing what he perceives as its unethical implications. According to Gilbert, realism's emphasis on the national interest jettisons our responsibility toward those beyond our borders. Gilbert sees realism not so much as an objective theory as a rhetorical tool for propping up the legitimacy of the state and its national security efforts. Its stress on power and security reinforces an unethical way of thinking that can lead to neglect, imperialism, and oppression.

Gilbert wrongly identifies Thucydides as the first such realist: "As a view harking back to Thucydides and capable of endorsing *any* pursuit of a purported national interest, including fascist ones, realism has difficulty *explaining* as opposed to debunking" the trend toward social demands for democracy, rights, and peace.[77]

Although Gilbert is correct in his claim that realists and neorealists cannot account for the impact on the international system of recent trends toward

---

76. The quotation is from p. 288 of Richard K. Ashley, "The Poverty of Neorealism," *International Organization* 38 (Spring 1984) pp. 225–86.

77. See p. 31 of Alan Gilbert, "Must Global Politics Constrain Democracy? Realism, Regimes, and Democratic Internationalism," *Political Theory* 20 (February 1992), pp. 8–37, emphasis original.

democracy around the globe, I wonder along with Stephen Krasner whether Gilbert is misrepresenting the moral intentions of realism.[78] Nevertheless I find both Ashley's and Gilbert's criticisms of realism as an ideology with active political and moral repercussions intriguing. Realists, neorealists, and other theorists of international relations should be aware of the moral and political arguments their theories raise. The more their theories are heeded by practitioners, the more they should be prepared to welcome inquiries like those of Ashley and Gilbert and attempt to respond seriously to them. It is certainly in line with the Thucydidean perspective to address such questions.

Jack Snyder's *Myths of Empire* combines some of the elements of Thucydidean scholarship. A chief theme of his book is that political rhetoric is important insofar as it propelled "myths of empire" forward throughout history and across cultures. Chief among these myths is "the idea that the state's security can be safeguarded only through expansion."[79] Thus Snyder employs the Thucydidean idea that political theory—in this case a theory akin to realpolitik—can be used as a rhetorical device to justify imperialistic actions that actually are motivated by more narrowly defined interests. Snyder views these interests as economic and bureaucratic. Through coalition-building, interested parties move states to act in otherwise self-defeating ways by convincing the public (and sometimes themselves) of the importance of the imperial enterprise for the national interest. In this context Snyder recognizes the role of individual leaders in international relations.

Snyder attributes to Thucydides, Machiavelli, and Morgenthau a knowledge about international relations that neorealists lack:

> Theoretically, Realism must be recaptured from those who look only at politics between societies, ignoring what goes on within societies. Realists are right in stressing power, interests and coalition-making as the central elements in a theory of politics, but recent exponents of Realism in international relations have been wrong in looking exclusively to states as the irreducible atoms whose power and interests are to be assessed. These truncated realists have also been wrong in ignoring the role ideology plays in enhancing the power and shaping the perceived interests of political groups.[80]

Thus Snyder follows Thucydides in recognizing the motive power of rhetoric, and especially of theory or ideology-bearing rhetoric, but he departs from Thucydides when he assumes that all imperial rhetoric is nothing more than "strategic justifications." Such justifications include the domino theory and the Munich analogy, both of which were undoubtedly believed by some of their

---

78. See Stephen D. Krasner, "Realism, Imperialism, and Democracy," *Political Theory* 20 (February 1992), pp. 38–52.

79. Jack Snyder, *Myths of Empire: Domestic Politics and International Ambition* (Ithaca, N.Y.: Cornell University Press, 1991), p. 1.

80. Ibid., p. 19.

proponents, and can at least arguably reflect political reality.[81] Snyder's explanation for why some advocates of these strategies or policies believed what they said is that they are suffering from "blowback" or self-delusion, having convinced themselves or having been convinced by the previous generation of the truth of what was a consciously created justification.[82]

Snyder's error is not in thinking that rhetoric sometimes justifies other unspoken interests but that it always does. He squeezes all political rhetoric into the same mold and attributes to it a fixed underlying motivation in a way Thucydides does not. Therefore, he feels no need to examine thoroughly the content of the rhetoric itself for internal consistency or a match with policy or action. Trying to fit all speech into his theory, Snyder's account of the development of empire becomes less plausible. Yet for recognizing the effect of rhetoric and ideology on the actions of states, for examining the somewhat mitigating effect democratic regimes may have or the pernicious influence of this type of strategic justification, Snyder deserves much credit. He does all these things while addressing in a rather even-handed manner the explanatory claims of realism and neorealism.

Another book on empires, this one by Doyle, comes closer to the Thucydidean model. Doyle deals with the Athenian empire, the Spartan "hegemony," and the Roman, Ottoman, Spanish, English, French, and German empires, among others. He allows for multiple causes in the development of empires: "The forces and institutions that drive and shape imperialism ... are neither primarily economic nor primarily military; they are both economic and military, and also political, social, and cultural."[83] He contests the views of realists and neorealists that the distribution of power in the anarchic international system is what determines whether a state seeks empire. In doing this, Doyle explicitly addresses the views of Waltz, Benjamin Cohen, and other structuralist scholars.[84]

It is interesting to note how Doyle differs from realist and especially neorealist readings of Thucydides' History.[85] Doyle notes not only the influence of Athenian military might in sustaining the empire but also the influence of its popular democratic institutions, which appealed to the common people in many Greek city-states.[86] The political ideologies of both Athens and Sparta, and the different sectors of society they appealed to, were an important part of the conflict between the two. In this regard Doyle takes into account the ideological rhetoric with which both sides addressed each other.[87] Doyle also picks up on Thucydides' emphasis on the national character of Athens, both in

---

81. On the domino theory, see ibid., p. 273; on the Munich analogy, see p. 277.
82. Ibid., pp. 41–42; compare pp. 257 and 299.
83. Michael W. Doyle, *Empires* (Ithaca, N.Y.: Cornell University Press, 1986), p. 19.
84. Ibid., pp. 26–30.
85. Doyle does bring in other sources in his account of the Peloponnesian War, most notably Plutarch and Polybius, but he relies most heavily on the *History* as his classical text.
86. Ibid., pp. 57 and 59.
87. Ibid., pp. 60–62.

its restless culture and its democratic institutions, as well as the character of Sparta, with its "slow and cautious" character and the conservatism of its oligarchic institutions.[88] Similarly, Doyle notes the unifying effect of religious beliefs on the Ottomans that helped them obtain and hold their empire.[89] He notes the cultural differences between the Romans, who accepted other nationalities taken into their empires as a part of their own civilization, and the Spaniards, who treated all non-Spaniards as unassimilable.[90]

Doyle's thesis, which he recognizes does not fit equally as well in every case he examines but which nevertheless is quite convincing, is that political unity is the essential ingredient in the getting and especially the keeping of empire. The fact that the unity of the Athenian regime crumbled is largely what led to Athens' defeat. A great source of strength, Athenian democracy, became a source of weakness under the protracted pressures of war. This corresponds quite well to Thucydides' own account.

Doyle finds three main deficiencies of what he calls systemic theory for explaining the emergence, growth, and decline of empires: (1) "Its conception of the motives that animate the foreign relations of states is much too narrow"; (2) it is "too general" and thus cannot explain the particular circumstances that lead to any single case of imperialism; and (3) attributing imperialism to a disparity in power does not answer the questions of how much disparity is necessary and what caused the disparity in the first case.[91] Doyle takes into account the contributions of systemic theory in understanding empire but then sees the need to move beyond those insights in a way that is very reminiscent of the Thucydidean approach.

Finally much of John Stoessinger's work is an example of analysis that leans toward the Thucydidean approach, especially in its analysis of individual leaders. Stoessinger's treatment of Woodrow Wilson is reminiscent of Thucydides' method: "Wilson's personality collided with the conditions of the time. . . . In his dream was his greatness, in his rigid personality his tragedy."[92] Stoessinger assumes that individuals are responsible for great events in international relations and that they are therefore to be praised or blamed for their decisions. His studies of World War I, the United States' conduct in the Korean War, and the statecraft of Henry Kissinger are examples of his Thucydidean worldview. Kaiser Wilhelm made a crucial mistake in guaranteeing Serbia's security and allowed himself to be overtaken by war paranoia; Douglas MacArthur was a great general who tragically became a victim of his

88. Ibid., pp. 68–69.
89. Ibid., p. 107.
90. Ibid., pp. 121–22.
91. Ibid., p. 126.
92. John G. Stoessinger, *Crusaders and Pragmatists: Movers of Modern American Foreign Policy* (New York: Norton, 1985), p. 21.

own hubris; Kissinger made the world safer because of his ability to apply his intellect to politics without being obsessively uncompromising.[93]

Conclusion

The Thucydidean approach emphasizes the importance of the chance attainment of good political deliberation and judgment. To obtain and inculcate true political wisdom we may have to abjure the notion that any one theory or formula will accurately predict human behavior or solve human problems. In a sense this only is accepting what we already know: the price of celebrating our free will is lamenting the inability to easily explain and solve the problems of the human condition. Thucydides teaches us that even though internal passions and external forces may exert much force, humans are in control of themselves and morally aware; they can blame only themselves for their failures. Thucydides' *History* presents us with a very difficult challenge. It dares us to take ourselves and our leaders seriously. We take ourselves seriously when we openly and cogently evaluate the rhetoric, decisions, and actions of those who would lead us. In the process we honor even those whose actions we eventually criticize or condemn because we attribute to them—and not to some uncontrollable force—responsibility for what they do.

93. See John G. Stoessinger's works *Crusaders and Pragmatists, Nations in Darkness: China, Russia and America,* 4th ed. (New York: Random House, 1985), and *Why Nations Go to War,* 4th ed. (New York: St. Martin's Press, 1986).

The literature on Thucydides and realism is huge. However, Bagby is a typical example of attempts in the last couple of decades to shows that, although Thucydides at times writes as if he accepted realist assumptions, in truth, his thought is much more nuanced and he did in fact accept the role of appeals to morality in the international relations of his time. And above all, as pointed out previously, the Athenian disaster of the Sicilian Expedition is the ultimate punishment for the brutality—the social *hubris*—of Athens against Melos.

CONCLUSION: WRAP-UP

One commentator argues that Thomas Hobbes, in his book *Leviathan,* and not Thucydides, is the founder of realism. I support this idea because I do not think that Thucydides was an adherent of what we call realism in international affairs. One can online to see some famous quotes fo Thucydides. Some sites choose short passages, taken out of context, words in speeches that clearly do not necessarily reflect Thucydides' viewpoint, or are moments of clearly-expressed pessimism. Thucydides was very informed for his time and one problem with his work is that there are many speeches that he probably made up, regarding what he wrote as representative of what the protagonists *should* have been thinking (he virtually says as much). That does suggest a methodology that is at least pretty self-confident, if not such a good methology for our culture, committed as it is to accurate honesty in reporting. Many have pointed out that the Melian Dialogue is completed artificial. Politicians, the argument goes, almost never speak as bluntly as this. That is probably correct, but then it is astounding to reflect that the words of President Trump to the United Nations read somewhat close to the tone of the blunt words of the Athenian envoys to Melos. Some would say that is to the President's credit, because he does not speak like a politician. However, generally, other nations roundly condemned the President's address to the UN—it sounded to many as if the United States was bullying other nations into accepting our interests as those to be followed, and isn't that what the Athenians were doing at Melos? One of the most important lessons of Thucydides is that international relations are messy, precisely because there is no way to force a sovereign nation from action that it does not want to take. Hence, the frustration felt about the powerlessness of the United Nations—if one of the great powers vetoes an action, there is nothing the body as a whole can do, no matter how many other nations wish to do something. That would have made perfect sense to Thucydides, who, by no means thought that justice and morality had no place in international discourse. He just worried about the real motivations that underlay publicly-expressed policy and subsequent world history has borne him out. To Thucydides, war is a tragedy, and he must have grieved deeply the defeat of his beloved Athens, while he mourned the selfish and morally questionable policies that contributed to her downfall.

ACTIVITIES

General activity: the whole class can share, compare and discuss their responses to the Schema Activation activity.

Activity for Reading #24: in small groups, consider Thucydides' comments on changing the meaning of words. Identify in political rhetoric from a statement made in the media today where you can identify use of a term that is meant to signify something else.

Activity for Reading #25: in small groups, choose one of the four factors that author Bagby argues are alternative viewpoints that Thucydides invokes: 1) national character, 2) personalities and characters of individuals, 3) the role of political rhetoric, and 4) questions of morality. Have each group find an example of the factor your group chooses in the Melian Dialogue, and compare it to current political rhetoric, even possibly of the day of class.

General Activity: hold a debate in the class attempting to address the following question: what happens when the interests of sovereign nations do not align? How is that to be resolved?

SOURCES

The text for the translations are from the Loeb Classical Library's edition of Thucydides in four volumes, reprinted in 1956 by the Harvard University Press. I also used A.W. Gomme, A. Andrewes and K.J. Dover *A Historical Commentary on Thucydides* Volume IV Book V25-VII, 1970 Oxford University Press, as well as the commentary of C.E. Graves *The Fifth Book of Thucydides* 1891 MacMillan and Co. New York. An article by Peter J. Ahrensdorf Thucydides' Realistic Critique of Realism *Polity* 30(2) 1997 pp. 231-265 was also helpful. *Leviathan or The Matter, Forme and Power of a Common-Wealth Ecclesiasticall and Civil* was written by Thomas Hobbes and published in 1651. Numerous editions, including free online pdfs, are available. The book on social hubris is by Scott A. Johnson *Why Did Ancient Civilizations Fail?* published by Routledge in 2017. An important book on Thucydides by an anthropologist is Marshall Sahlins *Apologies to Thucydides: Understanding History as Culture and Vice-Versa* 2004 University of Chicago Press.

Chapter 11
War: Politics by Other Means

OBJECTIVES

- Analyze the role of anthropology in colonialism and in the making of war.
- Determine whether anthropologists can serve the military without breaking their code of ethics.
- Attribute the methodology of anthropology to its possible military use.
- Explain how anthropologists have assisted with war efforts in the past and what they could do in future wars.

KEY TERMS

Anthropology-at-a-Distance: the kind of anthropology carried out by scholar during World War II; they could not go into the field and live with people who were now enemies. Instead, they studied the ethnographies and written histories of the peoples in question to try and understand cultural patterns.

Colonialist Anthropology: because the discipline emerged as part of the colonial expansion of Europe, how anthropology was conducted was a by-product of the colonial context in which anthropologists interacted with the people they studied, which in turn affected the methodological and conceptual approaches of the discipline.

Warrior Society: a society in which there is great emphasis on the training for, and carrying out of, armed conflict with another group of people. In such societies, males especially (but females also in some cases) are socialized into formal military roles based on the aspiration of becoming a warrior, willing to kill as sanctioned by the society in question. In those warrior societies which are military states, upward social mobility (enhanced social and economic prestige due to military valor—achieved status) is characteristic of the existing warrior ethos.

SCHEMA ACTIVATION ACTIVITY

Think about how Americans react to warfare, today, in terms of some of our holidays and in terms of American history as you have learned it. Consider the treatment of war veterans and how any relatives, who might have served during wartime, talk about their service, and then consider the following question: *Are Americans a "warrior people?" Why or why not?*

(Save these to share later in your discussion sections.)

INTRODUCTION

We have just explored (in Chapter 10) how much of a problem it has been to sort out international relations in a world of sovereign states. One form of international relations is warfare. In this chapter, it will become clear that different cultures are kind of like different nations; cultures, too, have a form of sovereignty in that most members of one culture regard its influence as supreme. States and cultures are not co-terminous, but they are sufficiently closely connected that when conflict involves a state, the culture is often part of it. The two articles in this chapter feature the issue of culture during warfare. In the first, an anthropologist tries to draw the lessons for anthropology from the experience of anthropologists participating in the United States war effort during World War II. In the second, a military commentator argues for the importance of anthropology in coming to "know thy enemy." How anthropologists should respond to warfare—always a major world problem—is the burning question of the chapter.

Lessons from Second World War anthropology

Peripheral, persuasive and ignored contributions

DAVID PRICE

David Price is Associate Professor of Anthropology, St. Martin's College, Lacey, Washington, USA. A forthcoming essay examines some of the ways in which anthropological interactions with military and intelligence agencies in the Cold War became increasingly complicated and ignored. His email is dprice@stmartin.edu.

I am grateful for comments from numerous anonymous AT referees.

1 For more on anthropology and warfare see: Berreman 1981, Goldschmidt 1979, Leighton 1949, Mabee 1987, Nader 1997a and 1997b, Ross 1999, Stocking 1976, Wakin 1992.

2 Boas was censured in 1919 not because the facts of his accusation were inaccurate – indeed contemporary research indicates the accuracy of his claim – but because the AAA disapproved of his position that there was something inherently wrong with anthropologists using their professional positions as a front for espionage (Price 2000, 2001).

3 During World War I Durkheim wrote propaganda pamphlets, Weber served as an officer in the German Army Reserve Corps, Westermark considered and then declined espionage work, Veblen was a government analyst until he was fired for his support of the IWW. Others were affected in other ways, for example W.H.R. Rivers spent the war treating shell-shocked soldiers in British hospitals, Fritz Graebner was interned in Australia, while the war experiences of anthropologists such as Ralph Linton and Leslie White influenced their theoretical views of culture and the field of anthropology.

4 In analysing German anthropology during the war, Alfred Métraux referred to such strategies of passive resistance as 'playing possum' (Metraux 1948:717).

5 Proctor in fact establishes that 'The number of faculty in the fields of anthropology and prehistory at German universities increased from 150 in 1931 to 177 in 1940-41 – which contrasts, for example with the case of physics, which declined from 454 to 380, or medicine, which dropped from 3,303 to 2,362 over the same period' (Proctor 1988:166) For a list of German anthropologist members of the Nazi Party see

Anthropologists were largely called upon to contribute their specialized knowledge to the war effort. The nature of the contacts they had established with native peoples the world over and the methods they had developed for understanding varied modes of life permitted them to give realistic aid to intelligence units, or to those carrying on economic and psychological warfare and to advise concerning many types of postwar programs of rehabilitation.

> 'Anthropology 1944'
> *Britannica Book of the Year 1944*

The well established links between anthropologists and colonialism documented in the work of scholars like Talal Asad, Kathleen Gough, Dell Hymes, Adam Kuper and George Stocking stand in marked contrast with the sparse analysis of anthropological contributions to the wars of the 20th century. The latter reflects certain professional concerns of ethics, historically inevitable blind spots associated with the analysis of recent events, and the problems arising from critical evaluation of the actions of living and recently deceased anthropological elders.

While some anthropologists and historians have discussed various aspects of anthropological contributions to warfare, these periodic examinations tend to focus more on the specifics of particular military or intelligence campaigns, while the larger issues embedded in anthropological contributions to warfare are often downplayed.[1] But downplayed or not, these contributions raise serious questions concerning the ethical implications of using cultural knowledge and anthropological knowledge in the waging of war, and reveal fundamental symbiotic links between scholars and state.

Twentieth-century anthropologists applied their knowledge and ethnographic skills to warfare on many occasions, fighting with both books and guns. Such uses of anthropology in the past have been problematic, and the possibility of similar actions today raises a number of complex ethical and practical issues – issues that cannot be properly addressed until anthropologists confront the nature and scope of past anthropological contributions to warfare. America's sudden declaration of 'war on terror' finds most anthropologists with little understanding of the ways that anthropologists opposed or contributed to the wars of the last century. This article briefly describes the nature and scope of anthropological contributions to the Second World War in order to provide some critical historical basis for evaluating the meaning and dangers of current and future military-intelligence uses of anthropology. The applications of anthropology in Asia, Europe and the Americas during World War II raised fundamental ethical issues and led to a variety of intended and unintended outcomes. The discussion below describes some of the ways that anthropological analysis was used and ignored by the military, and how some of the most effective anthropological contributions to the war were directed not against foreign foes, but at the practices of military policy makers.

The decisions and actions of anthropologists during

World War II and other past wars must be viewed in the historical context of their times. The international anthropological community needs to be aware of past anthropological contributions to war, and we need to critically evaluate these past activities not in order to criticize past anthropologists, but to help provide a framework for coping with present and future pressures for anthropologists to contribute to military and intelligence operations. While past wartime anthropological decisions may be seen as appropriate for their times, the context of contemporary wars raises many more complex and problematic issues.

WWII: Anthropological warfare comes of age

The First World War brought a significant anthropological showdown, with implications for the wars that followed. This was the American Anthropological Association's (AAA) censure of Franz Boas after he criticized four anthropologists who had used their professional positions

IT'S A REAL WAR JOB!

as covers for espionage in Central America (Stocking 1968). To this day a general discomfort and ambivalence remains among AAA policy bodies concerning the merging of anthropology, espionage, covert research and warfare.[2] While a number of anthropologists and sociologists applied their skills in support of the First World War,[3] it was the Second World War that brought the widespread application of anthropology to the practice of warfare.

As the Second World War engulfed the world in a state of total war, motivations of nationalism, internationalism, racial supremacy and anti-totalitarianism led a variety of anthropologists into battle both as citizens and citizen-as-anthropologist-soldiers. In this war social scientists were harnessed at new levels as analysts, propagandists, foot soldiers, officers and spies. They directed their efforts at populations both within and outside the boundaries of their nations.

The links between German anthropologists and the Nazi regime remain contested. After the war, some German anthropologists maintained that they had resisted contributing to Nazi goals. For example, in 1946 Franz Termer argued that during the war many German anthropologists had recognized that German anthropology

> ...was in danger of becoming a servant of colonial propaganda. The wisest among us saw the danger and protected themselves against it. They did their best to have museums and research overlooked as otherwise might not have been the case. (Termer, quoted in Métraux 1948:717)[4]

Robert Proctor's work on Nazi anthropology finds that 'anthropology as a profession fared rather well under the Nazis', and points out that there were few German anthropologists who opposed the officially sanctioned views of racial science (Proctor 1988:166).[5] With the exception of isolated individuals such as Karl Saller, few wartime German anthropologists opposed Nazi views of race and anthropology, and Proctor found 'disturbingly little evidence that anthropologists resisted the expulsion of Jews

Earnest A. Hooton (1887-1945)

Proctor 1988:158

6. Hooton's FBI file records
an interesting internal FBI
memo in which FBI agent L B
Nichols ridiculed Hooton for
stating in a *Washington Daily
News* interview dated 21 July
1943 that the US government
should establish a centralized
human breeding bureau that
would determine which
Americans should be allowed to
breed and which should be
sterilized (FBI WFO 62-
73410).

7. Anthropologists serving in
the OSS included: E. Wyllys
Andrews IV, William Bascom,
Gregory Bateson, Lloyd Cabot
Briggs, Carleton Coon, Cora
DuBois, Anne Fuller, Nelson
Glueck, Gordon Hewes,
Frederick Hulse, Felix Keesing,
Alexander Lesser, Edwin Loeb,
Alfred Métraux, George
Murdock, David Rodrick,
Morris Siegel, Richard Starr,
David Stout and Morris
Swadesh.

8. Taylor was hand-picked
by Paul Linebarger to direct all
operations in Asia. Paul
Linebarger was a Johns
Hopkins-trained political
scientists who, at war's end,
drew upon his experiences at
OWI to write *the* book on what
he termed 'psychological
warfare' and to work covertly
with the CIA (see
Linebarger's1948
Psychological warfare,
Washington, DC: Infantry
Press). Later Linebarger,
publishing under the pen-name
of Cordwainer Smith, became
one of the most influential
writers of science fiction's
golden age.

9. David Price interview
with George Taylor conducted
17 July 1996, Seattle,
Washington.

10. The analysis of some
contemporary scholars,
however, suggests that the
impact of American
anthropologists on wartime and
post-war Japan have been
somewhat overstated (see
Janssens 1995 and 1999,
Neiburg and Goldman 1998).

Franz Boas (1858-1942)

from Germany' (Proctor 1988:164). As Michael
Burleigh's study of the German Ostforscher's contributions to the Nazi campaigns established,

> No one asked these scholars to put their knowledge at the
> service of the government: they did so willingly and enthusias-
> tically... Deportations, resettlements, repatriations and mass
> murder were not sudden visitations from on high, requiring the
> adoption of some commensurate inscrutable, quasi-religious
> meta-language, but the result of the exact, modern, 'scientific'
> encompassing of persons with card indexes, card-sorting
> machines, charts, graphs, maps and diagrams. (Burleigh
> 1988:8)

In post-war Germany there was a rethinking of such science in the service of war. In 1950 W.E. Muhlmann 'cau-
tioned against the use of anthropology by "the total state"
for political purposes' – a concern that reaches beyond the
circumstances of WWII Germany to all states engaged in
struggles of total war (Proctor 1988:169).

There were also non-German anthropologists promoting racial hierarchies or eugenics that were aligned
with Nazi views. Some continental and American anthropologists' support of eugenics and resistance to adapting a
Boasian view of race can be seen within this continuum.
E.A. Hooton went so far as to suggest that a national
breeding bureau be established to determine who should
reproduce with whom.[6] George H.L.F. Pitt-Rivers
(grandson of General A.H.L.F.
Pitt-Rivers) espoused pro-Nazi
racial views and was 'held as a
political prisoner by the [British]
Home Office' during the war
(Barkan 1988:193).

Numerous European scholars
sought refuge from the war in the
United States and elsewhere. In
New York, the New School in
Exile (founded by Columbia
University professors who
resigned in WWI after being censured by Columbia University's
president for their pacifist opposition to America's entry into World
War I) provided a haven for
scholars such as Claude Lévi-
Strauss and Karl Wittfogel. Some
anthropologists were identified by
name by the Nazis for apprehension and execution. Because of his
Communist links and his explicit denunciations of Nazi
Aryan racial myths, V. Gordon Childe was listed on Nazi
apprehension manifests (Peace 1995).

Some European anthropologists applied their field skills
in foreign lands to the needs of the war. In 1940 Evans-
Pritchard joined the British Army's campaigns in Ethiopia,
Sudan and Libya (Cyrenacia), where he combined military
service with ethnography among the Sanusi. S.F. Nadel
joined the Sudan Defence Force, then served in the British
Army's East African Command in Eritrea and ended the
war as a 'senior staff officer to the military government of
Tripolitania' (Feilich 1968:2). Though there are many
examples of such wartime applications of anthropology by
Europeans, the United States saw an even more extensive
application of anthropology as a weapon during the
Second World War.

American anthropology enters the war

Because American anthropology's most significant scientific and political contribution during the first half of the
20th century was the development of the Boasian critique
of the concept of race, many American anthropologists
found the Nazis to be an enemy of the core principles of

anthropology. For many anthropologists, any second
thoughts concerning the ethics of using anthropology as
cover for espionage were fleeting. Some anthropologists
had experiences similar to those of Jack Harris, who went
to West Africa with William Bascom under the cover of
conducting anthropological research while actually gathering intelligence for the CIA's institutional predecessor,
the Office of Strategic Services (OSS). As Harris later
noted, he did this with some reservations,

> because during my days at Columbia I was told by associates
> of Boas that he violently opposed using our scientific reputa-
> tion as a cover for intelligence activities in war. He based this
> on an incident in which a student of his had been involved in
> World War One.
> However, our feelings were so strong, I felt that whatever
> capabilities I could lend to the war effort in this war against
> infamy, I was pleased to do so. (Edelman 1997:10)

This passage articulates the motivations of a heroic
individual during a wartime crisis. Harris realized that the
Nazis needed to be stopped. He also had some understanding that Boas had opposed using science as a cover
for espionage. But the specifics of Boas' complaint, and
the penalties resulting from his objections, do not seem to
have been well understood or considered, especially in the
face of the Nazis' overbearing threat to humanity.
American anthropology's 1919 avoidance of confronting
the inherent problems of espionage
in wartime eased the way for
anthropologists to use fieldwork as
cover for spying during this 'good
war' that enjoyed widespread
public support. American anthropology later revisited these issues
during the 'bad wars' of Southeast
Asia in the 1960s and 70s, but it has
avoided more general considerations of the advisability or propriety
of anthropological contributions to
warfare. In any case, such considerations were pushed aside as new
wartime military and intelligence
agencies came into existence during
the latter half of 1942. American
anthropologists joined these agencies in increasing numbers, though
initially there was some discussion
concerning the propriety of committing the field and its organizations to the war effort (Patterson 2001).

"OF COURSE I CAN!"

I'm patriotic as can be—
And ration points won't worry me!"

American wartime anthropology applications

Like other citizens, many American anthropologists
enlisted in military and intelligence work out of a sense of
patriotic duty combined with a belief that military action
was the only way to stop the spread of Nazism, fascism
and colonial militarism in Asia. That anthropology should
be used to fight such a total war was a natural response for
most anthropologists of this period.

Some American anthropologists were reluctant to use
anthropology, or their professional associations, as instru-
ments of war. Fred Eggan reported that in late 1941 some
members of the AAA had unsuccessfully tried to use the
Association to organize support for the war effort.

> During this meeting, however, the council declined to set up a
> national committee on the use of anthropologists in World War
> II, which four members in Seattle had recommended, saying
> that centralization and government backing might lead many
> members to think the Association was an agent for propaganda
> (US National Anthropological Archives, Eggan to Ray, 25
> January 1942).

But such reservations were easily overcome. Despite

to relate that Dr. MEAD is very highly educated, bears a most excellent reputation, is very well thought of by her associates, and bears an enviable reputation as an anthropologist. Dr. MEAD is very much alert and interested in everything that goes on but is not politically minded in connection with political parties and has never expressed any political views to her knowledge. ▓▓▓▓▓▓▓▓ highly recommends Dr. MEAD as being a fine anthropologist and would not hesitate to say that she is a loyal and patriotic American and would do well at any task she undertook to accomplish. ▓▓▓▓▓▓▓▓ volunteered the information that she is sure that Dr. MEAD belongs to no subversive organizations.

▓▓▓▓▓▓▓▓▓▓▓▓▓▓▓▓▓▓▓▓▓▓▓▓ Division of Anthropology and Psychology, National Research Council, 2101 Constitution Avenue, with which division Dr. MEAD is associated, stated that Dr. MEAD has been employed by the National Research Council since February, 1942 as an anthropologist at a salary of $6,000.00 per annum and that at the present time she is in England lecturing under the auspices of the Office of War Information, her expenses being paid by that organization. She states that Dr. MEAD is of good character, bears an excellent reputation as a scientist, is a splendid speaker and lecturer, well-educated, and makes a good impression. She is well-liked, loyal, and patriotic. Dr. MEAD spent some time in Samoa making first-hand comparative observations of the food situation there. Her book "Coming of Age in Samoa" is widely read. She further added that Dr. MEAD is a prolific writer, having written many books and articles which are widely published and read, one of her more recent books being "And Keep Your Powder Dry," dealing with American culture and background. ▓▓▓▓▓▓ went on to say that Dr. MEAD is executive secretary of the Committee on Food Habits of the National Research Council and as such has been called upon frequently in connection with food problems in this country. She describes Dr. MEAD as a very capable and brilliant scientist with a well-established reputation as an anthropologist, and recommends Dr. MEAD very highly.

▓▓▓▓▓▓▓▓▓▓ advised that she has known Dr. MEAD since 1920, ▓▓▓▓▓▓▓▓ who was acquainted with Dr. MEAD and that she has known her personally since Dr. MEAD came to Washington ▓▓▓▓▓▓▓▓▓▓▓▓. She advised that Dr. MEAD is a very brilliant woman, having written many books, some of which she herself has read. She stated that Dr. MEAD is always very busy and sometimes is gone two and three weeks at a time in connection with her work. Her reputation and character are beyond question and she is very glad to have a person of Dr. MEAD'S calibre living in the apartment house. ▓▓▓▓▓▓▓▓ stated that Dr. MEAD does not associate with anyone else in the building except her roommate, Miss BESSIE McGREECH, due to the fact that she is so busy and is only at the apartment long enough to rest. She recommends Dr. MEAD very highly as a loyal and patriotic American.

A portion of Margaret Mead's WWII-era loyalty background investigation conducted by the FBI. Mead's FBI file spans the years from 1941 until her death in 1978 and is 992 pages in length.

In 1998 the United States Postal Service issued a stamp commemorating Margaret Mead as part of the Celebrate the Century Collection for the 1920 series. Below: Ruth Benedict.

Asad, T. (ed.) 1973. *Anthropology and the colonial encounter.* London: Ithaca Press

Barkan, E. 1988. Mobilizing scientists against Nazi racism, 1933-1939. In G.W. Stocking (ed.) *History of Anthropology*, Vol. 5, p. 193. University of Wisconsin Press

Benedict, R. 1946. *The chrysanthemum and the sword.* New York: C.E. Tuttle, Co.

Berreman, G.D. 1981. *The politics of truth.* New Delhi: South Asian Publishers

Burleigh, M. 1988. *Germany turns eastwards.* Cambridge

some members' reservations, the Association later passed a resolution placing 'itself and its resources and the specialized skills and knowledge of its members at the disposal of the country for the successful prosecution of the war' (Patterson 2001:96).

The war led to the cancellation of the 1942 annual meeting of the AAA, but a cluster of some 50 anthropologists conducting military and intelligence work near Washington, DC, met as a less-than-official representation of the Association and discussed developments and anthropological contributions to the war. AAA Secretary Fred Eggan reported to the American Association for the Advancement of Science that by 1943:

> Over one half of the professional anthropologists in this country are directly concerned in the war effort, and most of the rest are doing part-time war work. The comprehensive knowledge of the peoples and cultures of the world which anthropologists have gathered through field research has proved of great value to both the Army and the Navy, and to the various war agencies. The Association has cooperated in setting up the Ethnogeographic Board, the Committees on the Anthropology of Oceania and Africa and the Committee for Latin American Studies. (Eggan 1943)

Later that year the AAA created a 'Committee on Anthropology and the War Effort', with anthropologists Ralph Beals (chairman), Margaret Mead and David Mandelbaum leading the coordination of anthropological warfare at home and abroad (Frantz 1973).

As the majority of American anthropologists joined the war effort, a minority – some vocal, some silent – were troubled by the implications of these applications of anthropological methods and the use of bogus research fronts for warfare. The records of these dissenting views run counter to the common misconception that 'it was only after World War II that a few anthropologists seemed to become conscious of their real [ethical] responsibilities and this led gradually to a more general change of attitude' (Condominas 1979:189). In fact, before and during the

war some American anthropologists were extremely critical of anthropology's neo-colonialist role in the domination of the underdeveloped world, and questioned the ethical propriety of employing anthropology as a weapon against other cultures. Before the war Melville Herskovits recognized that when anthropologists used knowledge gained from fieldwork *against* peoples studied, unique ethical issues were raised. He wrote:

> Though as any other scientist, [the anthropologist] must repay his debt to his own society, he can not forget what he owes to the primitive peoples who give him the information without which his discipline could not exist. And in this, his situation is unique. The subject matter of the ethnologist is the human being; to obtain his data he must make friends of the primitives he studies, and only to the extent that he does gain their confidence will his research be of value. Yet often he belongs to a political entity which has taken away the right of self-direction from the very people he is studying. (Herskovits 1936:217)

While the Second World War found American anthropologists working to oppose these rights 'of self-direction' and working against the proclaimed interests of cultures that had hosted them and their research, these issues were rarely framed in this way. Some anthropologists, like Laura Thompson, raised questions regarding the legitimacy of wartime anthropology for the 'highest bidder', while John Embree and others questioned the methods and reliability of military anthropology (see Embree 1945, Stocking 1976). But during the war, these objections were mostly ignored.

American anthropology brings the war back home

In 1942 United States military social scientists determined that most American soldiers didn't even seem to know who they were fighting, much less why – though this seemed to matter little as most American soldiers were willing to fight without specific clarifications. New techniques of quantitative social sciences were devoted to studying the knowledge and attitudes of the American military and public.

> When soldiers were surveyed with open-ended questions about the war's aim, an astonishing 36 percent chose not to answer at all and only a handful ever mentioned fighting fascism or defending democracy. According to the Research Branch studies, the number of men who viewed the war 'from a consistent and favorable intellectual position' was somewhere between 10 and 20 percent. 'Why we are fighting the war' was typically on the bottom of the list of things that soldiers wanted the Army to teach them. In dismay, [Samuel] Stouffer concluded that 'the war was without a context... simply a vast detour made from the main course of life... It may be said that except for a very limited number of men, little feeling of personal commitment to the war emerged.' (Herman 1995:69-70).

W. Lloyd Warner studied the impact of World War II on a Midwestern conservative town, where he discovered that small American communities were frightened by the war, yet were invigorated by the intense social solidarity that

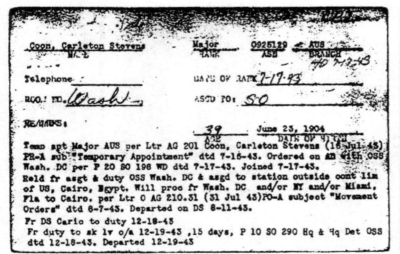

Coon, Carleton Stevens Major 0925129 AUS
NO. 2 RANK ASN BRANCH
Telephone : DATE OF RANK 7-19-43
RCO. NO. Wash. ASGD TO: SO
REMARKS:
39 June 23, 1904
Temp apt Major AUS per Ltr AG 201 Coon, Carleton Stevens (18 Jul 43)
PR-A sub "Temporary Appointment" dtd 7-16-43. Ordered on AD with OSS
Wash. DC per P 20 SO 198 WD dtd 7-17-43. Joined 7-17-43.
Reld fr asgt & duty OSS Wash. DC & asgd to station outside cont lim
of US, Cairo, Egypt. Will proc fr Wash. DC and/or NY and/or Miami.
Fla to Cairo. per Ltr O AG 210.31 (31 Jul 43)PO-A subject "Movement
Orders" dtd 8-7-43. Departed on DS 8-11-43.
Fr DS Cario to duty 12-18-43
Fr duty to sk lv o/a 12-19-43 ,15 days, P 10 SO 290 Hq & Hq Det OSS
dtd 12-18-43. Departed 12-19-43

Left: *Carleton Coon's OSS duty assignment card.*
Right: *OSS Director William 'Wild Bill' Donovan's letter requesting the assistance of the State Department in establishing a front for Carleton Coon's espionage work in North Africa.*

University Press.
Condominas, G. 1979. Notes on the present-day state of anthropology in the Third World. In G. Huizer and B. Mannheim (eds) *The politics of anthropology*, p. 189. The Hague: Mouton.
Coon, C. 1980. *A North Africa story: The anthropologist as OSS agent, 1941-1943*. Ipswich, MA: Gambit.
Edelman, M. 1997. Anthropologist, secret agent, witch-hunt victim, entrepreneur: An interview with Jack Harris ('40). *Anthropwatch* 5.8-14.
Eggan, F. 1943. '[Report on] The American Anthropological Association' *American Association for the Advancement of Science Bulletin* 2(5):38.
Embree, J.F. 1945. Applied anthropology and its relationship to anthropology. *American Anthropologist* 47:635-637.
Feilich, M. 1968. S.F. Nadel. In *International Encyclopedia of the Social Sciences*, pp. 1-3. New York: Crowell-Collier.
Fluehr-Lobban, C. 1994. Informed consent in anthropological research. *Human Organization* 53(1):1-10.
Frantz, C. 1974. 'Structuring and restructuring of the American Anthropological Association'. Paper read at Annual Meeting of the AAA, 22 November 1974.
Goldschmidt, W. (ed.) 1979. *The uses of anthropology*. Washington, DC: American Anthropological Association.
Gough, K. 1968. Anthropology and imperialism. *Monthly Review* April: 12-27.
Herman, E. 1995. *The romance of American psychology*. Berkeley: University of

accompanied the prospect of war (Warner 1949).

American anthropologists contributed to domestic propaganda programmes that kept the populace on a steady war footing. The inability of Americans to state why they were at war led to the creation of a variety of propaganda agencies to indoctrinate soldiers and the public about the evils of totalitarian governments. In fact,

> Congress was rather touchy about making it widely known that the army was engaged in such explicit propaganda during a war directed against exactly such efforts, and only one of Frank Capra's [propaganda] films was ever shown to civilians, who also knew nothing of the military's other experiments in direct indoctrination. (Herman 1995:69-70)

Margaret Mead helped reshape American dietary habits for the wartime national Research Council's Committee on Food Habits (Mabee 1987). In 1943 Ruth Benedict and Gene Weltfish combated prevailing racist attitudes among US troops by drafting a pamphlet on race originally intended to be distributed by the US Army to officers and enlisted men. However, because the pamphlet clearly stated the scientific case against claims of racial superiority it was seen as too controversial, and the Army and the United Service Organization banned its distribution (see Price forthcoming).

While some American anthropologists aimed their war efforts at the American people, most applied their skills to fighting the war abroad, working for agencies like the Office of Strategic Services, the Office of Naval Intelligence, the Ethnogeographic Board, the Office of War Information and the War Relocation Authority.

American anthropology fighting the war abroad

Dozens of anthropologists worked for the Office of Strategic Services (OSS) during the War.[3] These anthropologists undertook a variety of tasks ranging from policy analysis to covert missions in which they used their anthropological credentials as cover for clandestine operations.

In the early 1940s OSS agent Carleton Coon 'smuggled firearms and explosives to French resistance groups' and 'collected vital intelligence' in Morocco (Coon 1980:137-138). Coon brought his anthropological training to this task. When the OSS assigned him the task of compiling a 40-page text on Moroccan propaganda, he simply borrowed from his textbook '*Principles of anthropology* and padded it with enough technical terms to make it ponderous and mysterious, since [he] had found out in the academic world that people will express much more awe and admiration for something complicated which they do not quite understand than for something simple and clear' (Coon 1980:12).

Other anthropologists were recruited by the

April 10, 1942

Honorable G. Howland Shaw
Assistant Secretary of State
State Department
Washington, D. C.

Dear Mr. Shaw:

In connection with the work of this office, we should appreciate the appointment of Dr. Carleton S. Coon of Sudbury, Massachusetts, as Special Assistant at the American Legation at Tangier.

In order to facilitate Dr. Coon's activities, it is requested that arrangements be made which will authorize the proper officials of the Legation to honor all salary, travel and other expense vouchers submitted by Dr. Coon.

His salary will be $4800 and his per diem allowance is to be $6 a day. This office will reimburse the State Department in accordance with Section V-45 of Foreign Service Regulations of the Department for all payments made by the Legation in his behalf.

We should appreciate it if you will notify the American Legation at Tangier about Dr. Coon's status and the approximate date of his arrival.

Very truly yours,

William J. Donovan

FC:mc

cc: Colonel Donovan
     Mr. Stroh (State)
     Mr. Rehm

APPROVED
DATE: JUL 7

APPROVED FOR RELEASE
DATE: JUL 2000
RETIRED FILE
JOB NO. 93-01068 P
BOX 7 FOL. 456

Ethnogeographic Board, a wartime think tank that pooled anthropologists, linguists, and cultural geographers to generate cultural information of relevance to anticipated theatres of war. As director, William Duncan Strong helped collect its braintrust of such diverse anthropologists as Elizabeth Bacon, Homer Barnett, Ralph Beals, Wendell Bennett, Henry Collins, William Fenton, Robert Hall, Melville Herskovits, Ray Kennedy, George Murdock, Frank Roberts and Douglas Whitaker.

There are dozens of other agencies that used anthropology in the war. These included the Office of Naval Intelligence, where some anthropologists like Richard Francis Strong Starr used their experiences as a stepping-stone for a post-war career transition to the newly created Central Intelligence Agency (*Anthropology News*, May 1994:45). At the Office of Economic Warfare anthropologists like Clellan Ford worked under the directorship of future CIA Assistant DCI Max Millikan (see Price 1998b). Others applied anthropology at agencies such as the Army Intelligence Division (Wesley Bliss), the Army Special Training Program (Mortimer Graves), Air Force Intelligence (Hallam Movius), or worked as presidential advisers on issues of racism and warfare (Philleo Nash).

The Office of War Information: Fighting foreign and domestic foes

There are about two dozen World War II-era military and intelligence agencies that could be used to examine American anthropological applications during the war. This brief summary of some of the key dynamics and undertakings by anthropologists at the Office of War Information (OWI) is but one of many examples that sheds light on the uses and conflicts of anthropological wartime service.

My views on these issues have been textured by an ongoing examination of military and intelligence documents recording the actions of anthropologists working with various military agencies. Anthropological contributions to warfare have revealed repressed connections to our colonial and neocolonial roots, and these actions have also betrayed the very cultures studied by anthropologists.

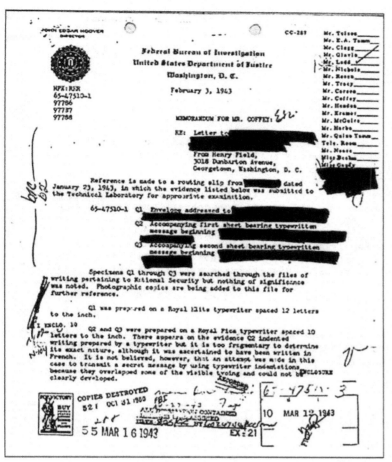

A 1943 FBI memo detailing the FBI's investigation into anthropologist Henry Field's personal correspondence during WWII.

California Press.

Herskovits, M.J. 1936 'Applied anthropology and the American anthropologist' *Science* 83:215-222

Hymes, D 1972 *Reinventing anthropology* New York Pantheon

Janssens, R.V.A. 1995 'What future for Japan?' *U.S. wartime planning for the postwar era, 1942-1945* University of Amsterdam Monographs in American Studies No. 5.

Janssens, R.V.A. 1999 'Toilet training, shame, and the influence of alien cultures'. In J. van Bremen and A. Shimizu (eds), *Anthropology and colonialism in Asia and Oceania*, pp. 285-304 London Curzon

Kuper, A 1973 'Anthropology and colonialism' In *Anthropology and anthropologists* London Allen Lane

Leighton, A 1949 *Human relations in a changing world.*

Left: *Chiang Kai-Shek and General Joseph Stilwell.*

Right: *General Joseph Stilwell commemorative postage stamp.*

But anthropological applications during World War II also found anthropologists fighting against their own government's policies, attitudes and strategies in support of principles of justice and peaceful stability that reached beyond nationalism. One of the most striking instances of this can be seen in the actions of anthropologists at OWI, where their most important work consisted of fighting attitudes of racial reductionism within the US War Department.

When I began studying the work of Ruth Benedict and other anthropologists at the OWI, my own views reflected the strong statements made by John Embree when he observed in 1945 that these culture and personality studies were largely comprised of 'The writings of the national character structure group [that had] been largely in the form of 'confidential' mimeographed pamphlets and so not subject to scientific criticisms; nonetheless their conclusions are presented to government agencies as the findings and methods of "anthropology"' (Embree 1945:635). While I remain critical of the validity of these culture and personality studies, I have come to see the efforts of anthropologists at OWI in a much more complex and sympathetic light.

Once America entered the war, the British historian of China George Taylor was appointed Deputy Director for the Far East at the OWI.[8] Because Taylor believed that an understanding of culture was vital to the success of his OWI team he recruited over a dozen anthropologists to work on his Japanese analysis and propaganda campaigns. He hired some thirty top-notch social scientists, including anthropologists Clyde and Florence Kluckhohn, Alexander Leighton, Dorothea C. Leighton, Alexander Lesser, Geoffrey Gorer, Ruth Benedict, Morris Opler, John Embree, Royal Hassrick, Fred Hulse and Kathrine Spencer (Leighton 1949).

Taylor directed his staff anthropologists to answer basic questions concerning the nature of Japanese national character, and to analyse the likely impact of various military strategies against the Japanese. In a 1996 interview Taylor recounted how he had initially viewed his psychological warfare programmes as a means of ending the war and helping the Japanese to overcome all the obstacles preventing their surrender. However, with time he came to see his job as being to convince the US military that they did not have to engage in acts of genocidal annihilation to end the war.[9] Early on, he was shocked by the crudeness of the military's propaganda leaflets which were dropped on Japanese troops and villages. Taylor recognized that an understanding of cultural nuance could change the effectiveness of such pamphlets, and using anthropologists and Nisei (second-generation Japanese American citizens) members of his staff he redesigned these pamphlets, leading to increased Japanese solider surrender rates.

Taylor recognized that his OWI team had a drastically different comprehension of Japanese culture from that of military and White House decision-makers. He saw a danger in this knowledge gap. In an effort to educate the military in the complexities of the situation, he moved his entire operation over to the Pentagon so that his staff would be closer to the military decision-makers.

Taylor said military leaders and President Roosevelt and his advisers were convinced that the Japanese were 'culturally incapable of surrender' and that they would have to fight to the very last Japanese citizen. As the war progressed, Taylor and his staff found themselves fighting this mindset more than they were fighting the Japanese.

When I interviewed Taylor he called General Joseph Stilwell a 'maniac', and recounted a disturbing story of how he (Taylor) had flown to China to meet with Stilwell and discuss what he and his team of anthropologists at OWI had learned about the Japanese and the uses of psychological warfare. Stilwell would listen to none of this, scoffing at the claim that academicians were needed to tell him how to fight his enemy or how to engage in effective psychological warfare. Stilwell then instructed one of his

New York: E.P. Dutton.

Mabee, C. 1987. Margaret Mead and behavioral scientists in World War II. *Journal of the History of the Behavioral Sciences* 23:3-12.

Métraux, A. 1948. Anthropology in Germany. *American Anthropologist* 50:717.

Nader, L. 1997a. The phantom factor: Impact of the Cold War on anthropology. In N. Chomsky (ed.) *The Cold War and the university*, pp. 107-146. New York: New Press.
― 1997b. Postscript on the phantom factor: More ethnography of anthropology. *General Anthropology* 4(1):1-8.

Neiburg, F. and Goldman, M. 1998. Anthropology and politics in studies of national character. *Cultural Anthropology* 13(1):56-81.

Patterson, T.C. 2001. *A social history of anthropology in the United States*. Oxford: Berg.

Peace, W. 1995. Vere Gordon Childe and the Cold War. In P. Gathercole *et al.* (eds), *Childe and Australia: Archaeology, politics and ideas*, pp. 135-151. Brisbane: University of Queensland Press.

Petersen, G. 1999. Politics in postwar Micronesia. In R. Kiste *et al.* (eds) *American anthropology in Micronesia,*

Far East Division

Dr. W. L. Langer   30 May 1944

Charles B. Fahs

Appointment of Dr. Edwin M. Loeb

It is recommended that Dr. Edwin M. Loeb be appointed for a period of three months as a temporary research analyst in the Pacific Islands Section, at a P-4 ($3800) classification.

Dr. Loeb, an American citizen by birth, is the author of a work, Sumatra, its History and its People. He did field research in Sumatra and the Mentawei Islands in 1926-1927, and has good knowledge of the Dutch and Malay languages which enables him to consult all important source materials. In addition, he knows German, French, and Spanish. He has a Ph.B. from Yale, and a Ph.D. from Yale Graduate School, and is now lecturing on anthropology for the University of California. His graduate work in ethnology, sociology, and economics, together with his regional specialization in islands of the Netherlands East Indies, provides excellent qualifications for research on peoples in that region.

It is intended that Dr. Loeb take charge of background studies and reports relating to Sumatra and its adjacent islands. These reports are needed for current R & A projects and for projects undertaken jointly with MO and SO. Dr. Loeb's services are also needed for the organisation of current information for situation reports.

---

soldiers to take the next five captured Japanese soldiers; right in front of Professor Taylor he was to take his sidearm and make one of the soldiers shoot the other four in their heads. The fifth prisoner was then to be flown behind enemy lines and set loose so that he could tell his countrymen what his enemy had made him do. Stilwell reportedly ended his display of disdain for Taylor by exclaiming, 'Now *that* is what I call psychological warfare!' While Taylor left before any such act could be carried out, he had no doubt Stilwell was capable of such deeds. Taylor gave up on trying to change Stilwell's limited way of thinking, and focused instead on changing the mentality of others in the War Department and White House. As part of this effort, Taylor asked Ruth Benedict and other OWI anthropologists to study the importance of the Emperor in Japanese society, and the position papers that came from this work eventually allowed Taylor to convince President Roosevelt to leave the Emperor out of any conditions of surrender at the inevitable end of the war – a point that Taylor said he did not have to reargue with Harry Truman once he became President.[10]

At the end of the war Taylor and many of his staff viewed their efforts as having accomplished mixed results. They had brought about some desired changes in military decision-making, yet they found their advice to be frequently ignored. In the spring of 1945 Taylor sent a memo to President Truman stating that he and his staff were convinced that the Japanese were ready to surrender, and the pressures coming from Russian forces on the Asian front made it obvious to the Japanese that the war could not continue. But even as these arguments were made, American military and political leaders were developing plans to employ not one, but two nuclear weapons against Japanese civilian targets, actions that were seen as politically and militarily unnecessary by anthropologists and other staff members at OWI.

Implications

Wars raise the stakes for anthropologists, exposing the nature of our commitments and principles, and as past wars and colonial campaigns have shown, anthropologists as a group have served both the oppressed and the oppressors. Many aspects of our field's relationship with power remain unresolved, but even if anthropologists were to somehow agree upon shared goals of serving the oppressed of the

Left: *A 1944 Secret OSS memo declassified and released by the CIA. This memo reports on some of Carleton Coon's actions for the OSS in North Africa.*

Right: *FBI Assistant Director Nichols, writing to Clyde Tolson (Hoover's right-hand man and reputed lover) derides Hooton's federal eugenics plan as that of 'a first rate fool'.*

pp.145-195 Honolulu University of Hawai'i Press

Price, D H. 1998a. Cold War anthropology: Collaborators and victims of the national security state. *Identities* 4(3-4): 389-430.

– 1998b 'CIA pillow talk: The uses of populations, undeclared agendas and development anthropology.' Paper presented at the Annual Meeting of the American Anthropological Association, Philadelphia, PA, December, 1998.

– 2000 Anthropologists as spies. *The Nation* 271(16): 24-27, 20 November 2000 (http://www.thenation.com/doc mhtml?i=20001120&s=price)

– 2001 'The shameful business': Leslie Spier on the censure of Franz Boas. *History of Anthropology Newsletter* 28(2) 9-12. (http://homepages.stmartin.edu/fac_staff/dprice/HAN-Spier.htm)

– (forthcoming) *Cold War witch hunts.* Durham, NC: Duke University Press

Proctor, R. 1988. From Anthropologie to Rassenkunde. In G W Stocking (ed.) *History of Anthropology*, Vol. 5, p. 166 University of Wisconsin Press

Ross, E. 1999 'Axel Wenner-Gren and the Nazi connection: An ethical dilemma for anthropology.' Paper presented at the Annual Meeting of the AAA, Chicago 18 November 1999.

Stocking, G W. 1968. The scientific reaction against cultural anthropology, 1917-1920. In G W. Stocking (ed.) *Race, culture, and evolution: Essays in the history of anthropology*, pp 270-307 University of Chicago Press

– 1976 Ideas and institutions in American anthropology: Toward a history of the interwar period. In G W Stocking (ed.) *Selected papers from the American Anthropologist*, pp 1-54 Washington, DC: AAA.

Wakin, E. 1992. *Anthropology goes to war: Professional ethics and counterinsurgency in Thailand.* Madison University of Wisconsin Center for Asian Studies, Monograph Number 7

Warner, W. L. 1949. *Democracy in Jonesville.* New York: Harper

Wolf, E R. and Jorgensen, J G. 1970. Anthropology on the warpath in Thailand. *New York Review of Books*, 19 November 27

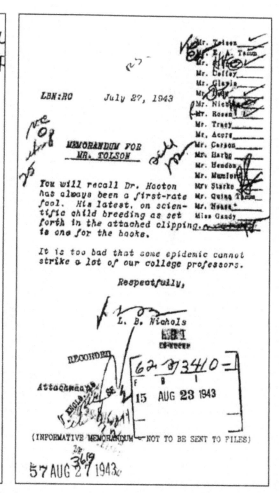

world, the question of how such goals were to be achieved would still be unresolved, and issues of anthropology as an instrument of warfare would remain to be settled. However, unsettled or not, the use of anthropology in World War II and other wars is a fertile field of study, raising many questions with implications for our current predicament.

The use of anthropology and anthropologists in Nazi Germany was neither unusual nor exotic, though Muhlmann's warning concerning the political uses of anthropology by 'total states' tends to be interpreted as applying primarily to such obviously depraved policies as those implemented by the Nazi administration. Yet less totalitarian state-managed anthropological research programmes in other hot and cold wars have impacted indigenous cultures in other devastating ways (see Petersen 1999, Price 1998a). As social scientists are now being recruited to assist in ethnic and racial 'terrorist profiling' campaigns, the stakes of ignoring such warnings intensifies. It is not enough to resist these developments; we have a professional duty to speak out against the futility and bigotry of such abuses of the social sciences.

The unresolved problems faced by George Taylor and his staff at OWI in World War II still have a fundamental importance in our present situation *vis-à-vis* policy makers' (mis)understanding of 'terrorism'. Today many military and governmental officials have limited conceptual frameworks for approaching the relativistic concept of terrorism, but the lessons of Taylor and others at OWI are less than clear. As with any applied anthropological venture, there is no guarantee that our recommendations will be heard, much less adopted, but in times of war we have a fundamental duty as scholars and citizens to counter the limited views of American and allied policy makers. We

have our own Stilwells to educate, and if they prove uneducable, to circumvent – though there is ample evidence to suggest that efforts in this direction would be most effective if we operate as citizen-scholars outside of governmental agencies.

Some of the decisions to be made by anthropologists in times of war are personal, while others are professional. Decisions to join or not join a war in any capacity are in the end always personal decisions, but decisions concerning the use of anthropology in the waging of war are fundamentally professional decisions. While it is not for me or anyone else to demand that others join or resist a particular military campaign, national and international professional anthropological associations have a duty to monitor and evaluate the uses to which anthropology is put in times of war. This duty springs from the basic responsibility of anthropologists to serve, rather than fight or oppress, those we study. If anthropologists will not take action to limit the wartime applications of their discipline, then we do not deserve the trust of those we study in the field.

Using cultural knowledge to fight other cultures raises serious questions involving conflict of interest, protecting the welfare of research subjects and basic issues of consent (Fluehr-Lobban 1994). While interpretation of past interactions during wartime is problematic, consideration of the ethical implications can help prevent future misapplications of anthropology in times of war. As the American President seems intent on committing his nation to a prolonged war against the ill-defined concept of terrorism – and many of his citizens seem suddenly frightened into supporting this quest – anthropologists have new reasons to focus on the issues embedded in their discipline's militaristically mobilized past. ●

The history of anthropology is touched on in this article, when Price notes that the issue of anthropologists in wartime overlaps with the whole question of the role of anthropology in Western colonialism of the 19th and 20th centuries. Some of the earliest anthropological writings come from individuals (many of whom were missionaries) who were present in the imperial colonies of European countries and assisted colonial administrators. Some then took their expertise to academia and were the first academic anthropologists. The whole enterprise of going among a "primitive people" to study them was only made possible (and of interest) because European states forcibly took over other parts of the world. Of course, some of these people were motivated not by colonialism, but by a genuine interest in "the Other." Two exemplars of this would be two 19th c. British men who tried to trace the Nile River back to its source: John Hanning Speke (who correctly identified Lake Victoria as the source) and Richard Burton (not the actor) who did not find the source of the Nile, but became so enamored of the indigenous peoples of East Africa that he kind of "went native," and admired (and assimilated to) the peoples with whom he came into contact. (Sadly, his extensive anthropological writings were destroyed by his wife on his death.) Speke was an imperalist (note that he named the Lake after the British queen) who (typically for his time) thought that the British were meant to civilize the world—it was the "White Man's Burden."

The author lists all the anthropologists, who, in one way or another, tried to help with the U.S. war effort in World War II. The most well-known example of this was Ruth Benedict, whose book *The Chrysanthemum and the Sword* (1946), summarized her wartime researches on the Japanese, aimed at attempting to understand a warrior people who were also devoted to flower arrangments and tea ceremonies. (I read this in graduate school and a Japanese women student colleague read it and found parts of it offensive, as unfairly unrepresentative.) Another anthropologist who worked on the Japanese was John Embree, who came to question the whole enterprise of anthropologists working for the military.

To Price, the major question representing THE lesson for anthropology from World War II? Is it even advisable or appropriate for anthropologist to contribute to their govenments during wars?

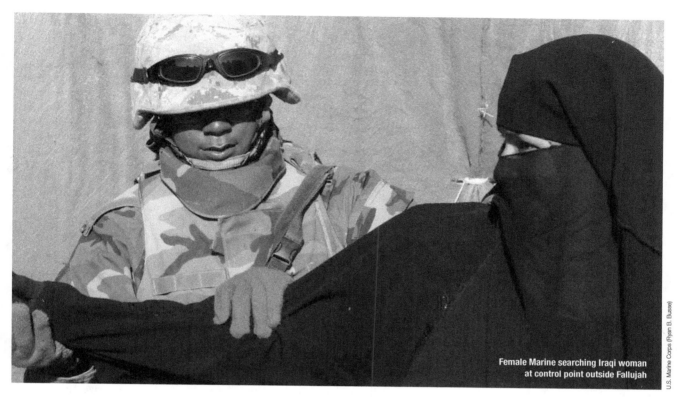

Female Marine searching Iraqi woman
at control point outside Fallujah

And when people are entering upon a war they do things the wrong way around. Action comes first, and it is only when they have already suffered that they begin to think.

—Thucydides, *The Peloponnesian War*

The Military Utility of Understanding Adversary Culture

By MONTGOMERY McFATE

Cultural knowledge and warfare are inextricably bound. Knowledge of one's adversary as a means to improve military prowess has been sought since Herodotus studied his opponents' conduct during the Persian Wars (490–479 BC). T.E. Lawrence (Lawrence of Arabia) embarked on a similar quest after the 1916 Arab rebellion against the Ottoman Empire, immersing himself deeply in local culture: "Geography, tribal structure, religion, social customs, language, appetites, standards were at my finger-ends. The enemy I knew almost like my own side. I risked myself among them many times, to learn."[1] Since then, countless soldiers have memorized Sun Tzu's dictum: "If you know the enemy and know yourself, you need not fear the result of a hundred battles."

Although "know thy enemy" is one of the first principles of warfare, our military operations and national security decisionmaking have consistently suffered due to lack of knowledge of foreign cultures. As former Secretary of Defense Robert McNamara noted, "I had never visited Indochina, nor did I understand or appreciate its history, language, culture, or values. When it came to Vietnam, we found ourselves setting policy for a region that was terra incognita."[2] Our ethnocentrism, biased assumptions, and mirror-imaging have had negative outcomes

Montgomery McFate is a cultural anthropologist and a defense policy fellow at the Office of Naval Research working on an initiative to promote social science research in the national security area.

during the North Vietnamese offensives of 1968 and 1975, the Soviet-Afghan war (1979–1989), India's nuclear tests (1998), the Iraqi invasion of Kuwait (1990), and the Shi'ite transformation of Iran (1979).

Despite the fact that cultural knowledge has not traditionally been a priority within the Department of Defense (DOD), the ongoing insurgency in Iraq has served as a wake-up call to the military that adversary culture matters. Soldiers and Marines on the ground thoroughly understand that. As a returning commander from

the ongoing insurgency in Iraq has served as a wake-up call to the military that adversary culture matters

3d Infantry Division observed: "I had perfect situational awareness. What I lacked was cultural awareness. I knew where every enemy tank was dug in on the outskirts of Tallil. Only problem was, my soldiers had to fight fanatics charging on foot or in pickups and firing AK–47s and RPGs [rocket-propelled grenades]. Great technical intelligence. Wrong enemy."[3] As this commander's observation indicates, understanding one's enemy requires more than a satellite photo of an arms dump. Rather, it requires an understanding of their interests, habits, intentions, beliefs, social organizations, and political symbols—in other words, their culture.[4]

This article argues that new adversaries and operational environments necessitate a sharper focus on cultural knowledge of the enemy. A lack of this knowledge can have grave consequences. Conversely, understanding adversary culture can make a positive difference strategically, operationally, and tactically. Although success in future operations will depend on cultural knowledge, the Department of Defense currently lacks the programs, systems, models, personnel, and organizations to deal with either the existing threat or the changing environment. A Federal initiative is urgently needed to

incorporate cultural and social knowledge of adversaries into training, education, planning, intelligence, and operations. Across the board, the national security structure needs to be infused with anthropology, a discipline invented to support warfighting in the tribal zone.

Changing Adversaries and Operational Environments

Cultural knowledge of adversaries should be considered a national security priority. An immediate transformation in the military conceptual paradigm is necessary for two reasons: first, the nature of the enemy has changed since the end of the Cold War, and second, the current operational environment has evolved fundamentally within the past 20 years as a result of globalization, failed states, and the proliferation of both complex and light weapons.

Although the United States armed and trained for 50 years to defeat a Cold War adversary, Soviet tanks will never roll through the Fulda Gap. The foe the United States faces today—and is likely to face for years to come—is non-Western in orientation, transnational in scope, non-hierarchical in structure, and clandestine in approach; and it operates outside of the context of the nation-state. Neither al Qaeda nor insurgents in Iraq are fighting a Clausewitzian war, where armed conflict is a rational extension of politics by other means. These adversaries neither think nor act like nation-states. Rather, their form of warfare, organizational structure, and motivations are determined by the society and the culture from which they come.

Attacks on coalition troops in the Sunni triangle, for example, follow predictable patterns of tribal warfare: avenging the blood of a relative (*al tha'r*); demonstrating manly courage in battle (*al-muruwwah*); and upholding manly honor (*al-sharaf*).[5] Similarly, al Qaeda and its affiliated groups are

replicating the Prophet Mohammed's 7th-century process of political consolidation through jihad, including opportunistic use of territories lacking political rulers as a base, formation of a corps of believers as a precursor to mass recruiting, and an evolution in targeting from specific, local targets (such as pagan caravans) to distant powerful adversaries (for instance, the Byzantine Empire). To confront an enemy so deeply moored in history and theology, the U.S. Armed Forces must adopt an ethnographer's view of the world: it is not nation-states but cultures that provide the underlying structures of political life.

Not only our adversaries have changed. The 2001 *Quadrennial Defense Review* predicted that smaller-scale contingencies—military operations of smaller scale and intensity than major theater or regional wars, such as humanitarian, peacekeeping, peace enforcement, noncombatant evacuation operations, and combating terrorism—will characterize the future operational environment. The use of the military for humanitarian disaster relief, peacekeeping, and counterterrorism operations means that the military will be increasingly forward-deployed in hostile, non-Western environments "disconnected from the global economy."[6] According to Andy Hoehn, former Deputy Assistant Secretary of Defense for Strategy, "The unprecedented destructive power of terrorists—and the recognition that you will have to deal with them before they deal with you—means that we will have to be out acting in the world in places that are very unfamiliar to us. We will have to make them familiar."[7]

Culture Matters Operationally and Strategically

Culture has become something of a DOD buzzword, but does it really matter? The examples below demonstrate three points: misunderstanding culture at a strategic level can produce policies that exacerbate an insurgency; a lack of cultural knowledge at an operational

Navy admiral discussing school construction in Najaf, Iraq, with tribal Sheik

U.S. Marine Corps (Robert K. Blankenship)

level can lead to negative public opinion; and ignorance of the culture at a tactical level endangers both civilians and troops. There is no doubt that the lack of adversary cultural knowledge can have grave consequences strategically, operationally, and tactically.

At a strategic level, certain policymakers within the Bush administration apparently misunderstood the tribal nature of Iraqi culture and society. They assumed that the civilian apparatus of the government would remain intact after the regime was decapitated by an aerial strike, an in-

when the United States cut off the hydra's Ba'thist head, power reverted to its most basic and stable form—the tribe

ternal coup, or a military defeat. In fact, when the United States cut off the hydra's Ba'thist head, power reverted to its most basic and stable form—the tribe. As a tribal leader observed, "We follow the central government. . . . But of course if communications are cut between us and the center, all authority will revert to our sheik."[8] Tribes are the basic organizing social fact of life in

Iraq, and the inner circle of the Ba'th Party itself was the purview of one tribe, the Al Bu Nasir. Once the Sunni Ba'thists lost their prestigious jobs, were humiliated in the conflict, and got frozen out through de-Ba'thification, the tribal network became the backbone of the insurgency.[9] The tribal insurgency is a direct result of our misunderstanding the Iraqi culture.

At the operational level, the military misunderstood the system of information transmission in Iraqi society and consequently lost opportunities to influence public opinion. One Marine back from Iraq noted, "We were focused on broadcast media and metrics. But this had no impact because Iraqis spread information through rumor. Instead of tapping into their networks, we should have visited their coffee shops." Unfortunately, the emphasis on force protection prevented Soldiers from visiting coffee shops and buying items on the economy. Soldiers and Marines were unable to establish one-to-one relationships with Iraqis, which are key to both intelligence collection and winning

hearts and minds. A related issue is our squelching of Iraqi freedom of speech. Many members of the Coalition Provisional Authority (CPA) and Combined Joint Task Force 7 felt that anticoalition and anti-American rhetoric was a threat to security and sought to stop its spread.[10] Closing Muqtada al Sadr's *Al Hawza* newspaper contributed to an Iraqi perception that Americans do not really support freedom of speech despite their claims to the contrary, reinforcing their view of Americans as hypocrites.

Failure to understand adversary culture can endanger both troops and civilians at a tactical level. Although it may not seem like a priority when bullets are flying, cultural ignorance can kill. Earlier this year, the Office of Naval Research conducted a number of focus groups with Marines returning from Iraq. The Marines were quick to acknowledge their misunderstanding of Iraqi culture, particularly pertaining to physical culture and local symbols, and to point out the consequences of inadequate training. Most alarming were the Iraqis' use of vehement hand gestures, their tendency to move in one's peripheral vision, and their tolerance for physical closeness. One Marine noted, "We had to train ourselves that this was not threatening. But we had our fingers on the trigger all the time because they were yelling." A lack of familiarity with local cultural symbols also created problems. For example, in the Western European tradition, a white flag means surrender. Many Marines assumed a black flag was the opposite of surrender—"a big sign that said shoot here!" as one officer pointed out. As a result, many Shia who traditionally fly black flags from their homes as a religious symbol were identified as the enemy and shot at unnecessarily. There were also problems at roadblocks. The American gesture for *stop* (arm straight, palm out) means *welcome* in Iraq, while the gesture for *go* means *stop* to Iraqis (arm straight, palm down). This and similar misunderstandings have had deadly consequences.

On the other hand, understanding adversary culture can make a positive difference strategically, operationally, and tactically. The examples below illuminate three key points: using preexisting indigenous systems creates legitimacy for the actions of the occupying power, indigenous social organization

postconflict reconstruction is most effective when the rebuilt institutions do not impose external concepts of social organization

(including tribal and kinship relationships) determines the structure of the insurgency, and avoiding the imposition of foreign norms will generate public cooperation.

Recognizing and utilizing preexisting social structures are the key to political stabilization in Iraq. While U.S. policymakers often seemed perplexed by the sub rosa tribal structure in Iraq, the British understood the indigenous system and used it to their advantage. Brigadier Andrew Kennett, commander of the British battlegroup

based in Basra, identified a core lesson learned during their history of empire: the importance of adjusting to local cultures and of not imposing alien solutions.[11] In Iraq, the most important element of local culture is the tribe and the associated patronage system. The majority of the population belong to one of the 150 major tribes, the largest containing more than a million members and the smallest a few thousand.[12] Tribes are invariably patronage systems in which powerful sheiks dispense riches and rewards to sub-sheiks, who in turn distribute resources to the tribal community. Sheiks always need money to generate loyalty from sub-sheiks. There is a saying in Iraq: you cannot buy a tribe, but you can certainly hire one.[13] In Amara, the British did just that. They appointed tribal leaders to local councils and gave the councils large sums to distribute, reinforcing the sheiks' political standing. As one officer noted, "We deal with

General Tommy Franks meeting with Ismail Khan, leader of the Tajiks ethnic group, in western Afghanistan, May 2002

U.S. Air Force (Joe Springfield)

what exists. In the five months we've been here, we're not going to change the culture of Iraq. We have to work with what there is."[14]

The structure of any insurgency will reflect the indigenous social organization of the geographical region. Thus, charting the Iraqi tribal and kinship system allowed 4th Infantry Division to capture Saddam Hussein. Although most U.S. forces were preoccupied with locating the 55 high-value targets on the Bush administration's list, Major General Raymond Odierno, USA, understood that relationships of blood and tribe were the key to finding Saddam Hussein.[15] Two total novices, Lieutenant Angela Santana and Corporal Harold Engstrom of 104th Military Intelligence Battalion, were assigned to build a chart to help 4th Infantry Division figure out who was hiding Saddam. According to Santana, a former executive secretary, their first thought was "Is he joking? This is impossible. We can't even pronounce these names." Despite the challenges, they created a huge chart called "Mongo Link" depicting key figures with their interrelationships, social status, and last-known locations. Eventually, patterns emerged showing the extensive tribal and family ties to the six main tribes of the Sunni triangle: the Husseins, al-Douris, Hadouthis, Masliyats, Hassans, and Harimyths, which led directly to Saddam Hussein.[16]

Postconflict reconstruction is most effective when the rebuilt institutions reflect local interests and do not impose external concepts of social organization. For example, Iraqis tend to think of the central government as the enemy. The longstanding disconnect between the center and the periphery meant that Baghdad did not communicate down and city councils could not communicate up. The CPA misunderstood the relationship between Baghdad and the rest of the country and imposed a U.S. model based on central government control. Yet many Marine Corps units intuitively had the right approach and began political development at the local level. A Marine captain was assigned to build a judicial system from the ground up. He refurbished the courthouse, appointed judges, and found the 1950 Iraqi constitution on the Internet. Because he used their system and their law, the Iraqis perceived the court as legitimate. Unfortunately, he was instructed to stop employing Ba'thists. It appears that we are often our own worst enemy.

An Inadequate System

Countering insurgency and combating terrorism in the current operational environment demand timely cultural and social knowledge of the adversary. As Andy Marshall, Director of the Office of Net Assessment, has noted, future operations will require an "anthropology-level knowledge of a wide range of cultures." Currently, however, DOD lacks the right programs, systems, models, personnel, and organizations to deal with either the existing threat or the changing environment.

Socio-cultural analysis shops, such as the Strategic Studies Detachment of 4th Psychological Operations Group and the Behavioral Influences Analysis Division of the National Air and Space Intelligence Center, are underfunded, marginalized, and dispersed. Because they lack resources, their information base is often out of date. Task Force 121, for example, was using 19th-century British anthropology to prepare for Afghanistan. With no central resource for cultural analysis, military and policy players who need the information most are left to their own devices. According to a Special Forces colonel assigned to the Under Secretary of Defense for Intelligence, "We literally don't know where to go for information on what makes other societies tick, so we use Google to make policy."

Although the Army Intelligence Center at Fort Huachuca, 82d Airborne Division, Joint Readiness Training Center, Naval Postgraduate School, and John F. Kennedy Special Warfare School

Religious leaders talk to military chaplain regarding male soldiers searching Iraqi women at checkpoint

55th Signal Company (Olga Steiert)

all offer some form of predeployment cultural training, their programs are generally rushed, oversimplified, or unavailable to all Soldiers and Marines who need them. Much so-called cultural awareness training focuses on do's and don'ts and language basics and tends to be geared toward Baghdad. As one Army colonel noted, "In Western Iraq, it's like it was six centuries ago with the Bedouins in their goat hair tents. It's useless to get cultural briefings on Baghdad." Troops rely on personal reading to make up for the lack of formal training. Inadequate training leads to misperceptions that can complicate operations. For example, Marines who were instructed that Muslims were highly pious and prayed five times a day lost respect for Iraqis when they found a brewery in Baghdad and men with mistresses. In actuality, Iraq has been a secular society for six

decades, and there were relatively few pious Muslims.

Even though all services now have a foreign area officer (FAO) program, the military still lacks advisers who can provide local knowledge to commanders on the ground. The FAO program is intended to develop officers with a combination of regional expertise, political-military awareness, and language qualification to act as a cross-cultural linkage among foreign and U.S. political and military organizations. Because few FAOs are ever subjected to deep cultural immersion totally outside the military structure, most do not develop real cultural and social expertise. Furthermore, most do not work as cultural advisers to commanders on the ground but serve as military attachés, security assistance officers, or instructors. The result is that commanders must fend for themselves. One Marine general explained that his unit had no local experts when it deployed to Afghanistan. The Pastoo-speaking cook on the ship, who happened to be born in Afghanistan, became the "most valuable player" of the mission.

The current intelligence system is also not up to the task of providing the required level of cultural intelligence. Retired Admiral Arthur Cebrowski, USN,

during the Vietnam era, anthropologists excelled at bridging the gap between the military and tribes

Director of the Office of Force Transformation, noted that "the value of military intelligence is exceeded by that of social and cultural intelligence. We need the ability to look, understand, and operate deeply into the fault lines of societies where, increasingly, we find the frontiers of national security."[17] Rather than a geopolitical perspective, threat analysis must be much more concrete and specific. According to Lieutenant General James Clapper, Jr., USAF, the former director of the Defense Intelligence Agency, "Of course we still provide in-depth orders of battle, targeting data, and traditional military capabilities analysis. But we must also provide the commanders on the ground with detailed information regarding local customs, ethnicity, biographic data, military geography, and infectious diseases." Producing intelligence on these factors can be challenging. As Clapper noted, "We provided detailed analysis on more than 40 clans and subclans operating in Somalia—far more difficult than counting tanks and planes."[18]

Back to the Future

A Federal effort is needed to infuse the national security structure with anthropology across the board. While this idea may seem novel, anthropology was developed largely to support the military enterprise.

Frequently called "the handmaiden of colonialism," anthropological knowledge contributed to the expansion and consolidation of British power during the era of empire. In the United States, the Department of Defense and its predecessors first recognized culture as a factor in warfare during the Indian Wars of 1865–1885, resulting in the formation of the Bureau of American Ethnology under Major John Wesley Powell. During World War II, anthropologists such as Gregory Bateson served the war effort directly, first conducting intelligence operations in Burma for the Office of Strategic Services, and later advising on how to generate political instability in target countries through a process known as *schizmogenesis*. American anthropologists produced ethnographies on the Axis powers that facilitated behavioral prediction based on national character. While Ruth Benedict's 1946 study of Japanese national character, *The Chrysanthemum and the Sword*, is the best known, studies such as Ladislas Farago's *German Psychological Warfare* (1942) collect dust on library shelves. Their predictions were often highly accurate: following recommendations from anthropologists at the Office of War Information, President Franklin Roosevelt left the Japanese emperor out of conditions of surrender.[19]

The legacy of World War II anthropology survives in the form of the Human Relation Area Files at Yale University. Established by the Carnegie Foundation, the Office of Naval Research, and the Rockefeller Foundation, this database provided information on Japanese-occupied former German territories of Micronesia. Although the database was maintained for decades after the war with Army, Navy, Air Force, and Central Intelligence Agency funds, U.S. Government agencies seeking "an anthropological-level of knowledge" have sadly now forgotten its existence.

During the Vietnam era, the defense community recognized that familiarity with indigenous, non-Western cultures was vital for counterinsurgency operations. The Director of the Defense Department's Advanced Research Projects Agency, R.L. Sproul, testified before Congress in 1965 that "remote area warfare is controlled in a major way by the environment in which the warfare occurs, by the sociological and anthropological characteristics of the people involved in the war, and by the nature of the conflict itself." To win hearts and minds, counterinsurgency forces must understand and employ local culture as part of a larger political solution. As General Sir Gerald Templer explained during the Malayan Emergency, "The answer lies not with putting more boots into the jungle, but in winning the hearts and minds of the Malayan people." Thus, the U.S. defense community determined that it must recruit cultural and social experts. Seymour Deitchman, DOD Special Assistant for Counterinsurgency, explained to a congressional subcommittee in 1965:

The Defense Department has . . . recognized that part of its research and development efforts to support counterinsurgency operations must be oriented toward the people . . . involved in this type of war; and the DOD has called on the types of scientists—anthropologists, psychologists, sociologists, political scientists, economists—whose professional orientation to human behavior would enable them to make useful contributions in this area.[20]

During the Vietnam era, the special warfare community understood that success in unconventional warfare depended on understanding indigenous, non-Western societies, and they turned to anthropologists. U.S. Special Operations Command's *Special Operations in Peace and War* defines *unconventional warfare* as "military and paramilitary operations conducted by indigenous or surrogate forces who are organized, trained, equipped, and directed by an external source." To conduct operations "by, with, and through," Special Forces units must have the support of the local population, which can be decidedly difficult to secure. While he was acting as an adviser to U.S. troops in Vietnam in 1965, British expert Sir Robert Thompson suggested that anthropologists be used to recruit aboriginal tribesmen as partisans. Indeed, anthropologists excelled at bridging the gap between the military and tribes. Special Forces in Vietnam, for example, were assisted by Gerald Hickey in working with the Montagnards.

So where are the anthropologists now that the Government needs them? Although the discipline's roots are deeply entwined with the military, few anthropologists are interested in national security. Their suspicion of military activity stems from a question of ethics: if professional anthropologists are morally obliged to protect those they study, does their cooperation with military and intelligence operations violate the prime directive? They believe it does. This conclusion was based on a number of defense projects that sought to use anthropological tools in potentially harmful ways. In 1964, the Army launched Project *Camelot*, a multinational social science research project, to predict and influence politically significant aspects of social change that would either stabilize or destabilize developing countries. The effort was canceled in July 1965 after international protests erupted in target countries. Critics called *Camelot* an egregious case of "sociological snooping."[21]

While anthropological knowledge is now necessary to national security, the ethics of anthropologists must be taken into account. In addition to direct discussion and debate on using ethnographic information, policymakers and military personnel must be trained to apply anthropological and social knowledge effectively, appropriately, and ethically.

The changing nature of warfare requires a deeper understanding of adversary culture. The more unconventional the adversary, and the further from Western cultural norms, the more we need to understand the society and underlying cultural dynamics. To defeat non-Western opponents who are transnational in scope, nonhierarchical in structure, clandestine in approach, and who operate outside the context of nation-states, we need to improve our capacity to understand foreign cultures.

The danger is that we assume that technical solutions are sufficient and that we therefore fail to delve deeply enough into the complexity of other societies. As Robert Tilman pointed out in a seminal article in *Military Review* in 1966, British counterinsurgency in Malaya succeeded because it took account of tribal and ethnic distinctions, while similar U.S. efforts in Vietnam were bound to fail because they lacked anthropological finesse.[22]

NOTES

[1] T.E. Lawrence, quoted in B.H. Liddell Hart, *Lawrence of Arabia* (New York: DeCapo, 1989), 399.

[2] Robert S. McNamara, *In Retrospect* (New York: Random House, 1995), 32.

[3] Steve Israel and Robert Scales, "Iraq Proves It: Military Needs Better Intel," *New York Daily News*, January 7, 2004.

[4] *Culture* is "those norms, values, institutions and modes of thinking in a given society that survive change and remain meaningful to successive generations." Adda Bozeman, *Strategic Intelligence and Statecraft* (New York: Brassey's, 1992), 57.

[5] Amatzia Baram, "Victory in Iraq, One Tribe at a Time," *The New York Times*, October 28, 2003.

[6] Greg Jaffe, "Pentagon Prepares to Scatter Soldiers in Remote Corners," *The Wall Street Journal*, May 27, 2003, 1.

[7] Ibid., 1.

[8] Baram.

[9] Ibid.

[10] Christopher Varhola, "The U.S. Military in Iraq: Are We Our Own Worst Enemy?" *Practicing Anthropology* 26, no. 4 (2004), 40.

[11] John F. Burns, "The Reach of War: The Occupation," *The New York Times*, October 17, 2004.

[12] Neil MacFarquhar, "In Iraq's Tribes, U.S. Faces a Wild Card," *The New York Times*, January 7, 2003.

[13] Baram.

[14] Charles Clover, "Amid Tribal Feuds, Fear of Ambush and the Traces of the Colonial Past, UK Troops Face up to Basra's Frustrations," *Financial Times* (UK), September 6, 2004, 11.

[15] Vernon Loeb, "Clan, Family Ties Called Key to Army's Capture of Hussein," *The Washington Post*, December 16, 2003.

[16] Farnaz Fassihi, "Charting the Capture of Saddam," *The Wall Street Journal*, December 23, 2003.

[17] Arthur K. Cebrowski, Director of Force Transformation, Office of the Secretary of Defense, statement before the Subcommittee on Terrorism, Unconventional Treats, and Capabilities, Armed Services Committee, United States House of Representatives, February 26, 2004.

[18] Lieutenant General James R. Clapper, Jr., "The Worldwide Threat to the United States and Its Interests Abroad," statement to the Senate Committee on Armed Services, January 17, 1995: <http://www.totse.com/en/politics/terrorists_and_freedom_fighters/wrldthrt.html>.

[19] David Price, "Lessons from Second World War Anthropology," *Anthropology Today* 18, no. 3 (June 2002), 19.

[20] Irving Louis Horowitz, ed., *The Rise and Fall of Project* Camelot: *Studies in the Relationship Between Social Science and Practical Politics* (Cambridge, MA: MIT Press, 1967).

[21] Ibid., 47–49, 232–236.

[22] Robert O. Tilman, "The Nonlessons of the Malayan Emergency," *Military Review* 46 (December 1966), 62.

McFate notes that Robert McNamara, the Secretary of Defense under Presidents Kennedy and Johnson, and the architect of American involvement in Vietnam, once admitted that he had never visited Indochina and that Vietnam had been a *terra incognita*—an unknown land. That was forcibly driven home by the the journalist Frances FitzGerald, whose 1972 book *Fire in the Lake*, traced the history of Vietnam and highlighted how President Johnson's belief that he could "horse-trade" with the Vietnamese, as if he were back in the U.S. Senate, showed a horrible misunderstanding of Vietnamese culture and society.

So, the article argues that, to be successful in Iraq and future wars, the U.S. military would have to do anthropology. Winning the "hearts and minds" of local citizenry thus requires the military to understand the local culture, use the indigenous social structure, and, above all, avoid imposing foreign norms on the indigenous people. Note how this advice resounds powerfully with the advice Robert Pape and his colleagues gave to stop suicide terrorism in Chapter 9— remove the occupying foreign element—in that case, forces.

You may feel some discomfort in reading how the author wants to use anthropological knowledge for military purposes. It sounds odd, but McFate thinks that future wars will not be about the enormous armies of powerful states, but will be smaller-scale affairs, sometimes with purely humanitarian goals, for peacekeeping, enforcing peace agreements, evacuating non-combatants from conflict and of course, fighting terrorism.

Anthropological Ethics

The author astutely closes with the observation that anthropologists are likely to be reluctant to help the military during war. Anthropologists are committed to helping the people they have studied, aren't they? McFate considers it their "prime directive."

Unfortunately, anthropology's record on that is less than stellar. As we noted above, anthropology at times has assisted the colonialist enterprise. Furthermore, the founder of the American Anthropological Association (AAA), Franz Boas, sometimes got into trouble because he exposed colleagues who were secretly assisting the intelligence community of the United States and he thought that was an abrogation of professional ethics. One of your activities will be to look at the statement of ethics of the AAA, and think about whether an anthropologist should, or should not, help the military of his or her country in a war effort.

CONCLUSION: WRAP-UP

Warfare, although in reality a form of politics to achieve the perceived self-interest of a governing entity, has all too often degenerated into a strident denunciation of "the Other," so that a state might convince its citizens to fight "the enemy" and kill them. (And to convince the relatives of soldiers who have been killed that the cause for which they died was worth it.) So, an encounter with "the Other" is the very definition of anthropology. Therefore, anthropologists have had to wrestle with the questions arising from a national war effort. Price concludes that anathropologists have to work to limit their wartime applications, even though he acknowledges that some of the activities of wartime anthropologists (in convincing Roosevelt not to execute the Japanese Emperor and to change propaganda that helped individual Japanese to think it possible to surrender) probably did help save lives on both sides. McFate's solution to the anthropologists' dilemma is to let military personnel do the anthropology after training by the professionals. That still leaves the anthropologist in a bind, because one might not want what they teach to be used in that kind of way. As Price pointed out, anthropologists have no way of controlling whether their recommendations are even heard by military and political authorities, let along get acted upon.

Anthropologists have always wondered whether warfare was just something that humans "naturally" do and so we have to accept it and deal with it. Anthropologists especially struggled during the Vietnam War as they saw so many of their students rejecting military service and even questioning warfare at all ("Make Love not War!"). Anthropology still does not understand fully the human tendency towards warfare. However, it is clear to a number of us that one major inducement to war is conflict over resources. All other appeals to motivations appear to be secondary to that "real" purpose for making war. However, as with most other forms of human behavior: would that it were that simple.

ACTIVITIES

General Activity: as a class, debate, from your Schema Activation Activity, *whether or not Americans in the United States are a "warrior people."*

Activity for Reading #26: in small groups, using the examples from the reading, debate the question: *should anthropologists assist in war efforts?*

Activity for Reading #27: in small groups, look at the AAA website and determine *what are the chief ethical considerations that an anthropologist must address in their work? Is McFate's characterization of the "prime directive" accurate?*

SOURCES

One of the most monumental collections of 19th c. anthropology was the work of Sir James George Frazer, a British classical scholar who wrote *The Golden Bough: A Study in Comparative*

Religion (which was retitled *The Golden Bough: A Study in Magic and Religion* in its second edition). It was most comprehensively published in its third edition between 1906 and 1915 in 12 volumes (with copious footnotes and references, many of them short ethnological descriptions by missionaries and colonial administrators). There are numerous one-volume abridgements (even online) but they do not have the extensive references of the original 12 volumes. Frances FitzGerald *Fire in the Lake: the Vietnamese and the Americans in Vietnam* Little, Brown 1972. Ruth Benedict's *The Chrysanthemum and the Sword* 1946 Mariner Books Reprint 1989. Carl von Clausewitz *On War*, originally published in 1832, has numerous editions including an online edition: http://www.clausewitz.com/readings/OnWar1873/TOC.htm. A recent anthropological treatment of war is Keith F. Otterbein *The Anthropology of War* 2009 Waveland Press. Another good collection is Jonathan Haas editor 1990 *The Anthropology of War* School of American research and Cambridge University Press. A much older treatment during the Vietnam War is *War: the anthropology of armed conflict and aggression* published by the American Anthropological Association in 1968.

Chapter 12

Revisiting the Nacirema; Taking Leadership in Addressing World Problems

OBJECTIVES

- Analyze the characteristics of American popular religion as another way to understand our own culture, what problems we might have, what problems we share with the rest of the world, and what to do about them.
- Determine the courses of action that we can take to address problems, as taking one at a time.
- Apply the cybernetic approach, deviation counter-acting of perturbations, to the issue of addressing world problems.
- Explain how an anthropological analysis of some cultural features, religion, for example, can lead to insight and a new understanding of our place in the world, as full global citizens.

KEY TERMS

Religion: as difficult a concept to define as culture: that collection of beliefs in every human society that are directed towards things invisible but thought to be numinous—that is, things that are beyond material understanding and endowed with conscious will. The original Latin word *religio* refers to the tendons in the leg that hold it together; so, it is a feature of human culture that binds people together and provides answers to life's questions and comfort in the midst of human suffering. Most importantly, religion carries out *rites of intensification*: ritual actions that unite people in a common outlook.

Fetishism: the word derives from the Latin verb *facere*, to make: endowing of an object or practice {called a *fetish*} with characteristics that inspire one to adoration, even worship of that object or practice. Recall that fetishes were featured in Reading #5, the Nacirema.

Cybernetic: a term derived from mid-20th century study of systems, in which there are deviation amplifying and deviation-counteracting forces, which work either to disturb the equilibrium of a functioning system (the former) or restore the equilibrium of a system that is changing (the latter). The word is from Greek meaning "characteristic of the steersman" with a cognate Latin word, which we have as "gubernatorial," so it has to do with the forces "governing" a system.

Globalization or Globalism: the increasing human interaction based on enhanced technologies of travel and communication that allow actors in all parts of the world to deal with each other quickly. The term is most focused on increased economic interaction, based on financial institutions that are deeply intertwined and interconnected with monetary standards (such as the Dollar or the Euro) that are fungible (exchangeable) world-wide. In tandem with the economic, social and cultural factors are also increasingly globalized.

Magic: activities or procedures used by humans to try and manipulate outcomes, usually involving the invoking of supernatural forces, or certain classes of rituals.

Potlatch: defined in Chapter 4.

SCHEMA ACTIVATION ACTIVITY

One theory of the origin of sports was suggested by a Greek scholar who suggested that the Olympic games began because animals were sacrificed to Zeus but the Greeks realized that none of the energy for hunting was used in getting domesticated animals for sacrifice. So, in order to appease the spirit of the animal, energy was expended in sports, which were part of the ritual: *Do you think that is very plausible and are sports a ritual? Why or why not?*

(Save these to share later in your discussion sections.)

INTRODUCTION

As a close of our exploration of anthropology and contemporary world problems, we juxtapose two rather different articles. The first harks back to the Nacirema we met in Chapter 2, trying to make sense of behavioral activities that appear secular, but seem to have some of the features of organized religion. The second piece briefly tries to suggest a good, reasonably rational approach to dealing with current world problems. The idea is that, first, we have to understand many complex issues, and anthropological methodology helps dig down to the essence of something. With that understanding, we can then think of possible solutions, by concentrating on the solution that is most likely to reverse a trend that has become problematic.

David Chidester

THE CHURCH OF BASEBALL, THE FETISH OF COCA-COLA, AND THE POTLATCH OF ROCK 'N' ROLL

What do we mean by "religion" in the study of religion in American popular culture? Consider this: "What has a lifetime of baseball taught you?" Buck O'Neil is asked in an interview for Ken Burns's television series on the history of the American national pastime. "It is a religion," O'Neil responds. "For me," he adds. "You understand?"

Not exactly, of course, because we have no idea what Buck O'Neil, the great first baseman of the Kansas City Monarchs in the 1930s, who served baseball for over six decades as player, coach, manager, and scout, means by the term "religion." What *does* he mean? As Ken Burns would have it, baseball is a religion because it operates in American culture like a church, "The Church of Baseball." Is that how we should understand "religion" in American popular culture, as an organized human activity that functions like the more familiar religious institution of the Christian church?

To complicate the matter, however, consider this: A religion is not a specific institution, but rather "a system of symbols." So says anthropologist Clifford Geertz; so too says Mark Pendergrast in his account of a new religion that was founded in America but eventually achieved truly global scope, the religion of Coca-Cola.

In his popular history *For God, Country, and Coca-Cola,* Pendergrast concludes that the fizzy, caramel-colored sugar water stands as a "sacred symbol" that induces "worshipful" moods which animate an "all-inclusive world view espousing perennial values such as love, peace, and universal brotherhood." [1] According to this reading, therefore, religion is about sacred symbols and systems of sacred symbols that endow the world with meaning and value. As Pendergrast argues, Coca-Cola—the sacred name, the sacred formula, the sacred image, the sacred object—has been the fetish at the center of a popular American system of religious symbolism.

But we can complicate things even further by considering this: "Let's Give It to 'Em, Right Now!" singer Joe Ely screams before the instrumental break in the Kingsmen's 1963 rock 'n' roll classic, "Louie, Louie." In the midst of the clashing, crashing cacophony, with lyrics that are unintelligible at any speed, we are struck by the strained screech of Ely's exhortation, "Let's Give It to 'Em, Right Now!" What kind of a "gift" is this?

In his book-length history of the song, which explores "the secret" of "Louie, Louie," rock critic Dave Marsh proposes that one useful model for understanding this kind of gift-giving appears in the ritualized display, presentation, and destruction of property associated with the potlatch ritual performed by indigenous American societies in the Pacific Northwest. This analogy with a Native American ritual, Marsh argues, can illuminate what he calls the "socioreligious" character of "Louie, Louie" in American culture. In this sense, however, religion is not an institution; it is not a system of symbols; it is the gift.

Church, fetish, potlatch—these three terms represent different theoretical models for analyzing religion in American popular culture. By examining their recent deployment in popular accounts of baseball, Coca-Cola, and rock 'n' roll, I hope to explore some of the consequences of these theoretical models for the study of religion. Among those consequences, I will highlight the force of metaphoric transference in theory building; the implications of these three metaphors—representing the institutional formation of the church, the powerful but artificial making of the fetish, and the nonproductive expenditure of the potlatch, respectively—for our understanding of the character of religion; and the ways in which the very term "religion," including its definition, application, and extension, does not, in fact, belong solely to the academy but is constantly at stake in the interchanges of cultural discourses and practices.

THE CHURCH OF BASEBALL

To return to the testimony of Buck O'Neil, baseball is a religion because it is an enduring institution governed by established rules. "If you go by the rules," he explains, "it is right." Baseball is a religion according to Buck O'Neil, then, because "it taught me and it teaches everyone else to live by the rules, to abide by the rules."[2]

This definition of religion as rule-governed behavior, however, is not sufficiently comprehensive or detailed to capture what Ken Burns presents as the religious character of baseball. The "church of baseball" is much more than merely the rule book. It is a religious institution that maintains the continuity, uniformity, sacred space, and sacred time of American life. As the "faith of fifty million people," baseball does everything that we conventionally understand the institution of the church to do.

First, baseball ensures a sense of continuity in the midst of a constantly changing America, through the forces of tradition, heritage, and collective memory. As Donald Hall suggests, "Baseball, because of its continuity over the space of America and the time of America, is a place where memory gathers."[3] Certainly, this emphasis on collective memory dominates Burns's documentary on baseball. But it also characterizes the religious character of the sport in American culture as a whole. Like a church, Major League Baseball institutionalizes a sacred memory of the past that informs the present.

Second, baseball supports a sense of uniformity, a sense of belonging to a vast, extended American family that attends the same church. As journalist Thomas Boswell reports in his detailed discussion in "The Church of Baseball," his mother was devoted to baseball because "it made her feel like she was in church." Like her church, Boswell explains, baseball provided his mother with "a place where she could—by sharing a fabric of beliefs, symbols, and mutual agreements with those around her—feel calm and whole."[4] Boswell draws out a series of analogies between baseball and his mother's church: both feature organs; both encourage hand-clapping to their hymns; both have distinctive robes and vestments; and in both everyone is equal before God. Although his analogy between the basepaths of a diamond and the Christian Cross seems a bit strained, Boswell provides sufficient justification for asserting that his mother regarded her attendance of baseball games as roughly equivalent to belonging to a church.

Third, the religion of baseball represents the sacred space of home. In this respect, baseball is a religion of the domestic, of the familiar, and even of the obvious. As Boswell explains:

Baseball is a religion that worships the obvious and gives thanks that things are exactly as they seem. Instead of celebrating mysteries, baseball rejoices in the absence of mysteries and trusts that, if we watch what is laid before our eyes, down to the last detail, we will cultivate the gift of seeing things as they really are.

The vision of reality that baseball affords, therefore, is a kind of normality, the ordinary viewed through a prism that only enhances its familiarity. While many religions point to a perfect world beyond this world, Boswell observes, baseball creates a "perfect universe in microcosm within the real world." [5] By producing such a ritualized space within the world, baseball domesticates the sacred and gives it a home.

Fourth, the religion of baseball represents the sacred time of ritual. "Everything is high-polish ritual and full-dress procession," Boswell notes. The entire action of the game is coordinated through a ritualization of time. But baseball also affords those extraordinary moments of ecstasy and enthusiasm, revelation and inspiration, that seem to stand outside of the ordinary temporal flow. His mother experienced those moments of "ritual epiphany" in church, according to Boswell, and "[b]asically, that's how she felt about baseball, too." [6] Through ritual and revelation, baseball provides an experience of sacred time that liberates its devotees from time's constraints.

In these terms, therefore, baseball is a church, a "community of believers." Certainly, the church of baseball is confronted by the presence of unbelievers within the larger society. As Thomas Boswell reports, his father failed to find his rightful place among the faithful in the church of baseball: "The appeal of baseball mystified him, just as all religions confound the innocent bewildered atheist." [7] Like any church, however, baseball has its committed faithful, its true believers. The opening speech of Annie Savoy in the film *Bull Durham* can be invoked as a passionate statement of religious devotion to baseball. "I believe in the church of baseball," she declares. The religion of baseball, however, promises a freedom beyond guilt. Although she observes the analogy between baseball and the Christian church, which is supported by the curious equivalence between 108 beads on the rosary and 108 stitches on a baseball, Annie Savoy proclaims baseball as a church in its own right. "I've tried them all, I really have," she concludes, "and the only church that truly feeds the soul, day in, day out, is the church of baseball." [8]

"What nonsense!" an unbeliever might understandably conclude in response to all this testimony about the church of baseball. Baseball is not a religion. It is recreation; it is entertainment; supported by the monopoly granted to Major League Baseball, it is very big business. All this religious language merely mystifies the genuine character of the sport in American society.

For all the apparent mystification, strained analogies, and improbable statements of faith, however, the depiction of baseball as a church represents a highly significant development in attempts to locate religion in American popular culture. In earlier anthropological accounts, especially those produced by the anthropologist-from-Mars school of cultural anthropology that gave us the "Nacirema" tribe ("American" spelled backwards), baseball registers as "magic" rather than "religion."[9] For example, a frequently anthologized article titled "Baseball Magic" records the magical techniques employed by baseball players to manipulate unseen forces and control events.[10] Using various kinds of amulets for good luck, players engage in specific practices—never stepping on the foul line, always spitting before entering the batter's box—that appear, in Freudian terms, just like "what are called obsessive acts in neurotics." In their magical practices, baseball players display an obsession with "little preoccupations, performances, restrictions and arrangements in certain activities of everyday life which have to be carried out always in the same or in a methodically varied way."[11] Although Freud held that such "obsessive acts" characterized the practice of both ritual and magic, the author of "Baseball Magic" implicitly upholds the familiar analytical distinction between the two. Instead of interpreting baseball as religion, however, he highlights its superstitious practices of magic.

This account of baseball magic raises two theoretical problems. First, by characterizing baseball as magic, the author pushes us back to the basic opposition between "religion" and "superstition" that has been crucial to the very definition of religion in Western culture. The ancient Latin term *religio,* indicating an authentic, careful, and faithful way of acting, was defined by its opposite, *superstitio,* a kind of conduct that was allegedly based on ignorance, fear, or fraud. In these terms, "we" have religion; "they" have superstition. But only rarely has the inherently oppositional character of the notion of "religion" been recognized: Thomas Hobbes, for example, observed that the "fear of things invisible is the natural seed of that, which everyone in himself calleth religion; and in them that worship or fear that power otherwise than they do, superstition," and the linguist Emile Benveniste observed that "the notion of 'religion' requires, so to speak, by opposition, that of 'superstition.'"[12] Baseball magic, therefore, is not religion. It is a repertoire of superstitious beliefs and practices that stands as the defining opposite of authentic religion. From the perspective of the anthropologist who stands outside and observes, baseball magic is clearly something very strange that "they" do; it is not "our" religion.

The second problem raised by the argument of "Baseball Magic" is that its author recalls the tension between the individual and society that has long characterized academic reflections on the difference between magic and religion. Following Emile Durkheim's classic formulation, magic is essentially individualistic and potentially antisocial. Unlike religious ritual, which affirms and reinforces the social solidarity of a community, magic manipulates unseen forces in the service of self-interest. As Durkheim insisted, there can be no "church of magic." Accordingly, if baseball is magic, there can be no "church of baseball."

Ken Burns intervenes in these theoretical debates by reversing their terms. Simply by presenting baseball as religion rather than magic, he represents the game as an authentic religious affirmation of the traditional continuity, uniformity, and solidarity of American society. Adopting a functional definition of religion, Burns documents the ways in which baseball operates like a church by meeting personal needs and reinforcing social integration. In fact, his implicit theoretical model of religion seems to be informed by the kind of functional assumptions found in J. Milton Yinger's definition of a universal church as "a religious structure that is relatively successful in supporting the integration of society, while at the same time satisfying, by its pattern of beliefs and observances, many of the personality needs of individuals on all levels of society." [13] Like a church, with its orthodoxy and heresies, its canonical myths and professions of faith, its rites of communion and excommunication, baseball appears in these terms as the functional religion of America.

Of course, this account of the church of baseball is positioned in a historical moment of great public disillusionment with the professional game. Feeling betrayed by both greedy players and arrogant owners, many devotees have become apostates of the religion of baseball. In this context, the phrase "church of baseball" shifts from metaphor to irony; it becomes a figure of ironic displacement as collective memory is transformed from commemoration of an enduring tradition into nostalgia for a lost world. From this vantage point, the continuity and uniformity of baseball tradition, the sacred time and sacred space of the baseball religion, can only be re-created in memory.

THE FETISH OF COCA-COLA

A very different theoretical model of religion is developed in Mark Pendergrast's *For God, Country, and Coca-Cola*. Drawing upon the familiar definition of religion provided by Clifford Geertz, Pendergrast proposes that Coca-Cola is a religion because it is

> a system of symbols which acts to establish powerful, pervasive, and long-lasting moods and motivations in men by formulating conceptions of a general order of existence and clothing these conceptions in such an aura of factuality that the moods and motivations seem uniquely realistic.[14]

To his credit, Pendergrast does not force his history of Coca-Cola into the mold of Geertz's definition. Rather, he allows the major actors in the drama to evoke their religious moods and motivations in their own voices. Here, I will mention only some of the more striking examples.

From the beginning, the beverage was enveloped in a sacred aura: its inventor, John Pemberton, referred to one of Coca-Cola's original ingredients, cocaine (which remained in the mix from 1886 until 1902), as "the greatest blessing to the human family, Nature's (God's) best gift in medicine" (27). During the 1890s, Coca-Cola emerged as a popular tonic in the soda fountains that a contemporary commentator described as "temples resplendent in crystal marble and silver" (16). Eventually, however, the blessings of Coca-Cola moved out of the temple and into the world.

Company executives, advertisers, bottlers, and distributors displayed distinctively religious moods and motivations in relation to the sacred beverage. Asa Candler, the Atlanta entrepreneur who started the Coca-Cola empire, was described by his son as regarding the drink with "an almost mystical faith" (68). Candler eventually "initiated" his son "into the mysteries of the secret flavoring formula" as if he were inducting him into the "Holy of Holies" (61). Robert Woodruff, who became president of the company in 1923, "demonstrated a devotion to Coca-Cola which approached idolatry" (160). Harrison Jones, the leading bottler of the 1920s, often referred to the beverage as "holy water" (146). Even the bottle itself was a sacred object that could not be changed. At a 1936 bottlers convention, Harrison Jones declared, "The Four Horsemen of the Apocalypse may charge over the earth and back again—and Coca-Cola will remain!" (178). Archie Lee, who assumed direction of Coca-Cola advertising in the 1920s, complained that the "doctrines of our churches are meaningless words," but he speculated that "some great thinker may arise with a new religion" (147). Apparently, Archie Lee, along with many other "Coca-Cola men," found that new religion in Coca-Cola.

Throughout the second half of the twentieth century, the Coca-Cola religion inspired a missionary fervor. At the first international convention, at Atlantic City in 1948, an executive prayed "May Providence give us the faith . . . to serve those two billion customers who are only waiting for us to bring our product to them" (238). Delony Sledge, an advertising director in the early 1950s, proclaimed, "Our work is a religion rather than a business" (261). Obviously, the Coca-Cola Company has imagined its enterprise as a religious mission.

Coca-Cola has also assumed religious significance for the consumer, having "entered the lives of more people," as one executive put it, "than any other product or ideology, including the Christian religion" (406). In the jive vocabulary of the 1930s, Coca-Cola was known as "heavenly dew." But the religious significance of Coca-Cola extends far beyond such playful invocations. Coca-Cola gave America its orthodox image of Santa Claus in 1931, by presenting a fat, bearded, jolly old character dressed up in Coca-Cola red; it became the most important icon of the American way of life for U.S. soldiers during World War II; it represented an extraordinary sacred time—the "pause that refreshes"—redeemed from ordinary postwar routines of work and consumption; and from the 1960s on, it promised to build a better world "in perfect harmony." One indication of the popular religious devotion to the drink was the public outcry at the changed formula of "New Coke" in 1985, which caused one executive to exclaim, "They talk as if Coca-Cola had just killed God" (364). In these profoundly religious terms, as editor William Allen White observed in 1938, Coca-Cola became a potent symbol of the "sublimated essence of America" (198).

Although the popular religion of Coca-Cola has pervaded American society, it has also been global. Represented in over 185 countries— more countries, Pendergrast notes, than are in the United Nations—the Coca-Cola Company has extended its religion all over the world. As company president Roberto Goizueta put it: "Our success will largely depend on the degree to which we make it impossible for the consumer around the globe to escape Coca-Cola" (397). The 1980s film *The Gods Must Be Crazy* suggests precisely this impossibility of escaping the religion of Coca-Cola, with its absurd parable of Coca-Cola's effect among a remote community of Bushmen in southern Africa. As Pendergrast notes, the film opens with "the totemic bottle fall[ing] out of the sky onto the sands of the Kalahari Desert, where it completely transforms the lives of the innocent Bushmen as surely as Eve's apple in Eden" (406). Here we find Coca-Cola as a sacred sign: a sign subject to local misreading, perhaps, but nevertheless the fetish of a global religion, an icon of the West, a symbol that can mark an initiatory entry into modernity. Through massive global exchanges and specific local effects, the religion of Coca-Cola has placed its sacred fetish "within arm's reach of desire" (376) all over the world.

"What utter nonsense!" a skeptic might justifiably conclude after reviewing this alleged evidence for the existence of a Coca-Cola religion. Coca-Cola is not a religion. It is a consumer product that has been successfully advertised, marketed, and distributed. In the best tradition of American advertising, the Coca-Cola Company has created the desire for a product that no one needs. Even if it has led to the "Coca-colonization" of the world, this manipulation of desire through effective advertising has nothing to do with religion.

In the study of popular culture, however, the religious character of advertising, consumerism, and commodity fetishism has often been noted. "That advertising may have become 'the new religion of modern capitalist society,'" Marshall W. Fishwick has recently observed, "has become one of the clichés of our time."[15] Advertising-as-religion has transformed "commodity fetishism" into a redundant phrase. In the symbolic system of modern capitalist society that is animated by advertising, the commodity is a fetish object.

As a model for defining and locating religion, the fetish raises its own theoretical problems. As William Pietz has shown in a series of articles, the term "fetish" has been a focal point for ongoing controversies in Western culture over what counts as authentic making. From the Latin *facere,* "to make or to do," the term has carried the semantic burden of indicating artificial, illicit, or evil making, especially in the production of objects of uncertain meaning or unstable value. In this respect, the fetish is not an object; it is a subject for arguments about meaning and value in human relations.

As a modern dilemma, the problem of the fetish arises in complex relations of encounter and exchange between "us" and "them." On the one hand, the fetish is something "they" make. Recalling the evil making— the *maleficium*—of black magic, Portuguese traders on the west coast of Africa in the seventeenth century found that Africans made *fetissos,* objects beyond rational comprehension or economic evaluation. Likewise, for generations of anthropologists, the fetish was an object that "they" make, a sign of their "primitive" uncertainty over meaning and inability to evaluate objects. On the other hand, Marx, Freud, and their intellectual descendants have found that the fetish is something "we" make—the desired object, the objectification of desire—something integral to modern subjectivities and social relations.[16]

Drawing upon this ambivalent genealogy of the fetish in Western culture, Michael Taussig has recently emphasized the importance of "state fetishism" in both making and masking the rationality and terror of the modern political order.[17] This recognition of the role of fetishized making in the production and reinforcement of the state resonates with recent research on the making of those collective subjectivities—the imagined communities, the invented traditions, the political mythologies—that animate the modern world.[18] All of these things are made, not found, but they are made in the ways in which only the sacred or society can be produced.

Unlike the historical continuity and social solidarity represented by the church, therefore, the fetish provides a model for religion in which religion is inherently unstable. As an object of indeterminate meaning and variable value, the fetish represents an unstable center for a shifting constellation of religious symbols. Although the fetishized object might inspire religious moods and motivations, it is constantly at risk of being unmasked as something made and therefore as an artificial focus for religious desire. The study of religion in popular culture is faced with the challenge of exploring and explicating the ways in which such "artificial" religious constructions can generate genuine enthusiasms and produce real effects in the world.

THE POTLATCH OF ROCK 'N' ROLL

As if it were not enough to bestow religious status on baseball and Coca-Cola, we now have to confront the possibility that rock 'n' roll should also count as religion. Certainly the ambivalent relations between rock and religion have often been noticed. As Jay R. Howard has observed, "Religion and rock music have long had a love/hate relationship."[19] On the one hand, rock 'n' roll has occasionally converged with religion. Rock music has sometimes embraced explicitly religious themes, serving as a vehicle for a range of religious interests, from heavy metal Satanism to contemporary Christian evangelism.[20] On the other hand, rock 'n' roll has often been the target of Christian crusades against the evils that allegedly threaten religion in American society. From this perspective, rock music appears as the antithesis of religion: not merely an offensive art form but a blasphemous, sacrilegious, and antireligious force in society.[21]

Rock's ambivalent relationship with religion is obvious. Less apparent, perhaps, is the inherently religious character of rock 'n' roll, and yet attempts have been made to theorize rock 'n' roll as religion. For example, rock 'n' roll has given rise to "a religion without beliefs"; it has given scope for the emergence of a new kind of "divinely inspired shaman"; it has revived nineteenth-century Romantic pantheism; rock music, concerts, and videos have provided occasions for what Durkheim called "ecstasy ritual"; and a new academic discipline—"theomusicology"—has included rock 'n' roll in its mission "to examine secular music for its religiosity."[22] From various perspectives, therefore, rock 'n' roll has approximated some of the elementary forms of the religious life.

In one of the most sustained and insightful analyses of the religious character of rock 'n' roll, Dave Marsh's book-length cultural analysis of the archetypal rock song, "Louie, Louie," explores the secret of its meaning, power, and rhythm, the "sacred duh duh duh. duh duh."[23] He issues a daunting assessment of all previous attempts to address his topic: the "academic study of the magic and majesty of duh duh duh. duh duh," as Marsh puts it bluntly, "sucks" (77). To avoid this condemnation, we must proceed not with caution, but with the recklessness that the song requires. We must say, with the song's African-American composer Richard Berry, who first recorded "Louie, Louie" as a calypso tune in 1956, "Me gotta go now," and see where that going takes us.

As Dave Marsh follows the sacred rhythm of "Louie, Louie," especially as it was incarnated by the Kingsmen in 1963, he dismisses previous attempts to explain the secret of the song's appeal as the result of effective marketing or the intentional mystification produced by its unintelligible lyrics. In rejecting economic and rhetorical explanations, Marsh advances an analysis of the secret of "Louie, Louie" in explicitly religious terms. His analysis uncovers layers of religious significance that are all associated with a "gift." Although his discussion is inspired by the dramatic prelude to the instrumental break—"Let's Give It to 'Em, Right Now!"—it is also directly related to the power of giving and receiving in the history of religions.

The song might be regarded as if it were a divine gift. As Marsh's colleague Greil Marcus puts it, by the 1980s "the tune was all pervasive, like a law of nature or an act of God." Marsh plays upon this theme: If the song was a gift from God or the gods, "he, she, or they chose a vehicle cut from strange cloth, indeed—deus ex cartoona" (78). However, the sacred gift of "Louie, Louie," the hierophany of incoherence, three chords, and a cloud of dust, cannot be accounted for in the conventional terms of any orthodox theology. Accordingly, Marsh turns to a passage in the gnostic Gospel of Thomas that seems to capture the "holy heartbeat" of "Louie, Louie."

> Jesus said, "If you bring forth what is within you, what you bring forth will save you. If you do not bring forth what is within you, what you do not bring forth will destroy you."

Bringing forth all that is within them, the gnostic celebrants of "Louie, Louie" are saved—if not "eternally," as Marsh clarifies, then at least temporarily, during the liberating moment when they participate in the rhythm of the "sacred duh duh duh. duh duh" and the "magical incantation" of "Let's Give It to 'Em, Right Now!" (73–4).

Ultimately, however, the religious significance of the gift must be located in relations of exchange. Here a Native American ritual—the potlatch—provides a model for giving and receiving in which the gift assumes a sacred aura. From a Chinook term meaning simply "to give," the potlatch practiced by indigenous communities of the Pacific Northwest signifies the ritualized display, distribution, and sometimes destruction of valued objects at ceremonial occasions.[24]

Although potlatch has variously been interpreted in the ethnographic literature as religious ritual, status competition, a kind of banking system, or even a periodic outburst of "unabashed megalomania," Marsh focuses on three aspects. First, the gift is total. The potlatch demands giving "everything you had: your food, your clothing, your house, your name, your rank and title." As a ritual occasion for giving everything away, the potlatch demonstrates an "insane exuberance of generosity." Second, the gift is competitive. In ritual relations of exchange, tribes compete with each other to move to the "next higher plane of value." Third, the sacred secret of the gift is ultimately revealed in destruction. As the ritualized exchanges of ceremonial gift giving escalate in value, the supreme value of the gift is realized by destroying valued objects, so that, as Marsh concludes, "eventually a whole village might be burned to the ground in order that the rules of the ceremony could be properly honored" (79–80).

By an odd coincidence, the Pacific Northwest was home to both the Native American societies that performed the potlatch, and the rock 'n' roll bands of the early 1960s that played the song "Louie, Louie." In Marsh's account, both demonstrate the religious "secret" of the gift, especially as it was revealed in acts of conspicuous destruction, in ritual acts that "violated every moral and legal tenet of non–Native American civilization, encumbered as it was with the even stranger socioreligious assumption that God most honored men by allowing them to accumulate possessions beyond all utility in this life, let alone the next" (80). In these "socioreligious" terms, the "modern day electronic potlatch" of rock 'n' roll violates Euro-American religious commitments to capitalist production and accumulation, to property rights and propriety, by reviving the sacred secret of the gift.

In defense of the capitalist order, J. Edgar Hoover's FBI pursued a four-year investigation of "Louie, Louie" during the 1960s, in search of evidence of subversion and obscenity in the song and its performers. As Marsh recalls, Hoover's mission "consisted precisely of visiting the plague of federal surveillance upon any revival of the potlatch mentality" (80). But "Louie, Louie" survived this state-sponsored inquisition. Defying all attempts to suppress it, the song remains the archetype of the sacred gift at the religious heart of the potlatch of rock 'n' roll.

"What utter, absolute, and perverse nonsense!" anyone might conclude after being subjected to this tortuous exposition of the religion of rock music. Rock 'n' roll is not religion. Besides the obvious fact that it is a major part of the entertainment industry, rock 'n' roll is a cultural medium in which all the "anarchistic, nihilistic impulses of perverse modernism have been grafted onto popular music." As a result, it is not a religion; it is a "cult of obscenity, brutality, and sonic abuse."[25]

The model of the potlatch, however, refocuses the definition of religion. As exemplified most clearly by rituals of giving and receiving, religion is a repertoire of cultural practices and performances, of human relations and exchanges, in which people conduct symbolic negotiations over material objects and material negotiations over sacred symbols. If this theoretical model—religion as symbolic, material practice—seems to blur the boundaries separating religious, social, and economic activity, then that is a function of the gift itself, which, as Marcel Mauss insists in his classic treatment, is a "total" social phenomenon in which "all kinds of institutions find simultaneous expression: religious, legal, moral, and economic."[26] According to Mauss, the potlatch, as ritual event, social contest, and economic exchange, displays the complex symbolic and material interests that are inevitably interwoven in religion. Similar interests, Dave Marsh and Greil Marcus argue, can be located in rock 'n' roll.

In the performance of the potlatch, Mauss observes, the contested nature of symbolic and material negotiations becomes particularly apparent; the "agonistic character of the prestation is pronounced."[27] If contests over the ownership of sacred symbols characterize the potlatch, what is the contest that is conducted in the potlatch of rock 'n' roll? It is not merely the competition among musical groups, a competition waged in the "battle of the bands" that Marsh identifies as an important element of the history of "Louie, Louie." It is a contest with a distinctively religious character. In broad agreement with rock critics Marsh and Marcus, anthropologist Victor Turner proposes that rock 'n' roll is engaged in a contest over something as basic as what it means to be a human being in a human society. "Rock is clearly a cultural expression and instrumentality of that style of communitas," Turner suggests, "which has arisen as the antithesis of the 'square,' 'organization man' type of bureaucratic social structure of mid-twentieth-century America."[28] By this account, rock 'n' roll, as antistructure to the dominant American social structure, achieves the human solidarity, mutuality, and spontaneity that Turner captures in the term "communitas." It happens in religious ritual; it happens in rock 'n' roll.

This "agonistic character" of the potlatch of rock 'n' roll, however, is not only evident in America. As Greil Marcus has proposed, the potlatch might unlock the "secret history of the twentieth century."[29] Tracking a disconnected narrative that links Dada, surrealism, litterists, situationists, and performance art, Marcus rewrites the cultural history of the twentieth century from the vantage point of the punk rock that was epitomized in 1976 by the Sex Pistols. Surprisingly, perhaps, that revised history depends heavily upon a sociology of religion that is implicitly rooted in the foundational work of Emile Durkheim and extended by Marcel Mauss's seminal essay on the gift, but it is a left-hand sociology of religion that takes an unexpected turn through the world of the French social critic, surrealist, and student of religion Georges Bataille.

In his 1933 essay "The Notion of Expenditure," Bataille takes up the topic of the potlatch to draw a distinction between two kinds of economic activity: production and expenditure. While production represents "the minimum necessary for the continuation of life," expenditure is premised on excess and extravagance, on loss and destruction, or, in a word, on the gift. This alternative range of economic activity "is represented by so-called unproductive expenditures: luxury, mourning, war, cults, the construction of sumptuary monuments, spectacles, arts, perverse sexual activity (i.e., deflected from genital finality)—all these represent activities which, at least in primitive circumstances, have no end beyond themselves." While productive economic activity is directed towards goals of subsistence, gain, and accumulation, expenditure is devoted to achieving dramatic, spectacular loss. In expenditure, according to Bataille, "the accent is placed on a loss that must be as great as possible in order for the activity to take on its true meaning."[30] In the performance of the potlatch, especially when gift giving escalates to the destruction of property, Bataille finds a model of expenditure that informs his entire theory of religion.

As exemplified by the potlatch, religion intersects with rock 'n' roll because both are cultural practices of expenditure. The gift—as in "Let's Give It to 'Em, Right Now!"—reopens the complex ritual negotiations over meaning and power, over place and position, over contested issues of value in modern American society. In that context, religion in American popular culture is neither a church, nor a symbolic system revolving around a fetish. Beyond the constraints of any institution or the play of any desire, religion is defined as religion by the practices, performances, relations, and exchanges that rise and fall and rise again through the ritualized giving and receiving of the gift.

RELIGION IN AMERICAN POPULAR CULTURE

So now where are we? After this long journey through the religious contours and contents of baseball, Coca-Cola, and rock 'n' roll, we are still left with the question: where is religion in American popular culture? How do we answer that question? Where do we look? If we only relied upon the standard academic definitions of religion, those definitions that have tried to identify the essence of religion, we would certainly be informed by the wisdom of classic scholarship, but we would also still be lost.

In the history of the academic study of religion, religion has been defined, following the minimal definition of religion proposed in the 1870s by E. B. Tylor, as beliefs and practices relating to spiritual, supernatural, or superhuman beings.[31] This approach to defining religion continues to find its advocates, both among scholars and in the discourse of popular culture. The extraordinary athlete, for example, can easily become the focus of religion to the extent that he or she is regarded as a superhuman being. When Michael Jordan returned to basketball in 1995, his "second coming" was portrayed in precisely these superhuman terms. While *Sports Illustrated* recorded Michael Jordan's embarrassment at being regarded as the superhuman focus of religious regard—"When it is perceived as religion," Jordan complained, "that's when I'm embarrassed by it"—it also added that this reservation was expressed by "the holy Bull himself" about "the attention his second coming has attracted." Adding to the embarrassment, the same article quoted Brad Riggert, head of merchandising at Chicago's United Center, who celebrated the return of Michael Jordan by declaring that this "god of merchandising broke all our records for sales."[32] In this case, therefore, Michael Jordan—the "holy Bull," the "god of merchandising"—registers as a superhuman being that should satisfy Tylor's minimal definition of religion.

In a second classic attempt to define religion, Emile Durkheim stipulated in 1912 that religion was constituted by beliefs and practices that revolve around a sacred focus, a sacred focus that serves to unify a community.[33] In this approach to defining religion, which also continues to have its proponents, religion depends upon beliefs and practices that identify and maintain a distinction between the sacred and its opposite, the profane. That distinction between the sacred and the profane has also appeared in the discourse of American popular culture. For example, during the long and difficult development of a crucial new software product, Microsoft hired a project manager who undertook the task with religious conviction. According to the unofficial historian of this project, that manager "divided the world into Us and Them. This opposition echoed the profound distinction between sacred and profane: We are clean; they are dirty. We are the chosen people; they are the scorned. We will succeed; they will fail."[34] According to this account, therefore, the cutting edge of religion—the radical rift between the sacred and the profane—appears at the cutting edge of American technology.

Like church, fetish, and potlatch, these classic definitions of religion—belief in supernatural beings, the distinction between sacred and profane—are at play in American culture. As a result, religion is revealed, once again, not only as a cluster concept or a fuzzy set but also as a figure of speech that is subject to journalistic license, rhetorical excess, and intellectual sleight of hand.[35] For the study of religion, however, this realization bears an important lesson: the entire history of academic effort in defining religion has been subject to precisely such vagaries of metaphorical play.

As I have argued in detail elsewhere, the study of religion and religious diversity can be seen as originating in the surprising discovery by Europeans of people who have no religion. During the eras of exploration and colonization, Europeans found indigenous populations all over the world who supposedly lacked any trace of religion. Gradually, however, European observers found ways to recognize—by comparison, by analogy, and by metaphoric transference from the familiar to the strange—the religious character of beliefs and practices among people all over the world. This discovery did not depend upon intellectual innovations in defining the essence of religion; it depended upon localized European initiatives that extended the familiar metaphors already associated with religion, such as the belief in God, rites of worship, or the maintenance of moral order, to the strange beliefs and practices of other human populations.[36] In the study of religion in American popular culture, I would suggest, we are confronted with the same theoretical dilemma of mediating between the familiar and the strange.

The theoretical models of religion that we have considered allow some of the strangely religious forms of popular culture—baseball, Coca-Cola, and rock 'n' roll—to become refamiliarized as if they were religion. These models allow them to appear as the church, the fetish, and the sacred gift of the ritual potlatch in American popular culture. Why not? Why should these cultural forms not be regarded as religion?

The determination of what counts as religion is not the sole preserve of academics. The very term "religion" is contested and at stake in the discourses and practices of popular culture. Recall, for instance, the disdain expressed by the critic who dismissed rock 'n' roll as a "cult of obscenity, brutality, and sonic abuse." In this formulation, the term "cult" signifies the absence of religion, the opposite of "religion." The usage of the term "cult," however it might be intended, inevitably resonates with the discourse of an extensive and pervasive anticult campaign that has endeavored to deny the status of "religion" to a variety of new religious movements by labeling them as entrepreneurial businesses, politically subversive movements, or coercive, mind-controlling, and brainwashing "cults." In that context, if we should ever speak about the "cult" of baseball, Coca-Cola, or rock 'n' roll, we could be certain about one thing: we would not be speaking about religion.

The very definition of religion, therefore, continues to be contested in American popular culture. However, if we look again at the privileged examples considered above—baseball, Coca-Cola, and rock 'n' roll—they seem to encompass a wildly diverse but somehow representative range of possibilities for what might count as religion. They evoke familiar metaphors—the religious institution of the church, the religious desires attached to the fetish, and the religious exchanges surrounding the sacred gift—that resonate with other discourses, practices, experiences, and social formations that we are prepared to include within the orbit of religion. Why do they not count as religion?

In the end, we will need to answer that question. In this case, however, "we" refers to all of us who are in one way or another engaged in the professionalized and institutionalized academic study of religion. Participants in American popular culture have advanced their own answers. As a baseball player, Buck O'Neil certainly had an answer: "It's a religion." As a Coca-Cola executive, Delony Sledge definitely had an answer: "Our work is a religion." As a rock 'n' roller, John Lennon had his own distinctive and controversial answer: "Christianity will go. It will vanish and shrink. I needn't argue about that. I'm right and I will be proved right. We're more popular than Jesus now." [37] These claims from outside the discipline raise problems of definition and analysis which need to be addressed within the study of religion. In different ways, as I have tried to suggest, the terms "church," "fetish," and "potlatch" signify both the problem of defining religion and the complex presence of religion in American popular culture.

NOTES

1. Mark Pendergrast, *For God, Country, and Coca-Cola: The Unauthorized History of the World's Most Popular Soft Drink* (New York: Charles Scribner's Sons, 1993), 400.

2. Buck O'Neil, "Why Would You Feel Sorry for Me? An Interview with Buck O'Neil," in *Baseball: An Illustrated History,* ed. Geoffrey C. Ward and Ken Burns (New York: Alfred A. Knopf, 1994), 226–31, quotation from 231.

3. Quoted in Ken Burns and Lynn Novick, "Preface: Where Memory Gathers," in Ward and Burns, *Baseball,* xvii–xviii, quotation from xviii.

4. Thomas Boswell, "The Church of Baseball," in Ward and Burns, *Baseball,* 189–93, quotation from 189.

5. Ibid., 193.

6. Ibid., 189–90.

7. Ibid., 189.

8. See Joseph L. Price's essay in this volume for another account of this speech from *Bull Durham.*

9. See, for example, Horace Miner, "Body Ritual Among the Nacirema," *American Anthropologist* 58, no. 3 (1956): 503–7.

10. George Gmelch, "Baseball Magic," in *Conformity and Conflict: Readings in Cultural Anthropology,* ed. James P. Spradley and David W. McCurdy (Glenview, Ill.: Scot, Foresman, 1978), 373–83.

11. Sigmund Freud, "Obsessive Acts and Religious Practices," in *The Standard Edition of the Complete Psychological Works of Sigmund Freud,* ed. James Strachey (London: Hogarth Press, 1953), 9:117–27.

12. Thomas Hobbes, *Leviathan,* ed. Michael Oakeshot (New York: Collier Books, 1962), 69; Emile Benveniste, *Indo-European Language and Society,* trans. Elizabeth Palmer (London: Faber and Faber, 1973), 522.

13. J. Milton Yinger, *Religion, Society, and the Individual* (New York: Macmillan, 1957), 147.

14. Pendergrast, *God, Country, and Coca-Cola,* 400; further citations will be made in parentheses in the text. For Clifford Geertz's definition of religion as "a system of symbols," see "Religion as a Cultural System," in *Anthropological Approaches to the Study of Religion,* ed. Michael Banton (London: Tavistock, 1966), 1–46, especially 4.

15. Marshall Fishwick, review of Sut Jhally, *The Codes of Advertising, Journal of Popular Culture* 26, no. 2 (1992): 155–6, quotation from 155.

16. William Pietz, "The Problem of the Fetish, I," *Res: Anthropology and Aesthetics* 9 (Spring 1985): 5–17; "The Problem of the Fetish, II," *Res: Anthropology and Aesthetics* 13 (Spring 1987): 23–45; "The Problem of the Fetish, IIIa," *Res: Anthropology and Aesthetics* 16 (Autumn 1988): 105–23. For further development of the problem of the fetish in contemporary cultural analysis, see Emily Apter and William Pietz, eds., *Fetishism as Cultural Discourse* (Ithaca: Cornell University Press, 1993), and Patricia Spyer, ed., *Border Fetishisms: Material Objects in Unstable Places* (New York: Routledge, 1998).

17. Michael Taussig, "Maleficium: State Fetishism," *The Nervous System* (London: Routledge, 1992), 111–40.

18. See, for example, Benedict Anderson, *Imagined Communities: Reflections on the Origin and Spread of Nationalism* (London: Verso, 1991); Eric Hobsbawm and Terrence Ranger, eds., *The Invention of Tradition* (Cambridge: Cambridge University Press, 1985); Leonard Thompson, *The Political Mythology of Apartheid* (New Haven: Yale University Press, 1985).

19. Jay R. Howard, "Contemporary Christian Music: Where Rock Meets Religion," *Journal of Popular Culture* 26, no. 1 (1992): 123–30, quotation from 123.

20. See Robert L. Gross, "Heavy Metal Music: A New Subculture in American Society," *Journal of Popular Culture* 24, no. 1 (1990): 119–30; Davin Seay and Mary Neely, *Stairway to Heaven: The Spiritual Roots of Rock 'n' Roll* (New York: Ballantine, 1986); and William D. Romanowski's discussion of Contemporary Christian Music in chapter 5 of the present volume.

21. Bob Larson, *Rock and Roll: The Devil's Diversion* (McCook, Nebr.: Larson, 1967); Linda Martin and Kerry Segrave, *Anti-Rock: The Opposition to Rock 'n' Roll* (Hamden, Conn.: Archon Books, 1988); Dan Peters, Steve Peters, and Cher Merrill, *What About Christian Rock?* (Minneapolis: Bethany, 1986).

22. David Shenk and Steve Silberman, *Skeleton Key: A Dictionary for Deadheads* (New York: Doubleday, 1994), ix; Tony Magistrale, "Wild Child: Jim Morrision's Poetic Journeys," *Journal of Popular Culture* 26, no. 3 (1992): 133–44; Robert Pattison, *The Triumph of Vulgarity: Rock Music in the Mirror of Romanticism* (Oxford: Oxford University Press, 1987); Lisa St. Clair Harvey, "Temporary Insanity: Fun, Games, and Transformational Ritual in American Music Video," *Journal of Popular Culture* 24, no. 1 (1990): 39–64; Jon Michael Spen-

cer, "Overview of American Popular Music in a Theological Perspective," in *Theomusicology,* ed. Jon Michael Spencer (Durham, N.C.: Duke University Press, 1994), 205–17, quotation from 205.

23. Dave Marsh, *Louie, Louie* (New York: Hyperion, 1993), 74; further citations will be made in parentheses in the text.

24. For a useful review of literature on the potlatch, see Steven Vertovec, "Potlatching and the Mythic Past: A Re-evaluation of the Traditional Northwest Coast American Indian Complex," *Religion* 13 (1983): 323–44. See also Sergei Kan, *Symbolic Immortality: The Tlingit Potlatch of the Nineteenth Century* (Washington: Smithsonian Institution Press, 1989).

25. Martha Bayles, *Hole in Our Soul: The Loss of Beauty and Meaning in American Popular Music* (New York: Free Press, 1994), 12.

26. Marcel Mauss, *The Gift: Forms and Functions of Exchange in Archaic Societies,* trans. Ian Cunnison (London: Cohen & West, 1969), 1.

27. Ibid., 4.

28. Victor Turner, *Dramas, Fields, and Metaphors: Symbolic Action in Human Society* (Ithaca: Cornell University Press, 1974), 262.

29. Greil Marcus, *Lipstick Traces: A Secret History of the Twentieth Century* (Cambridge: Harvard University Press, 1989).

30. Georges Bataille, "The Notion of Expenditure," in *Visions of Excess: Selected Writings, 1927–1939,* ed. Allan Stoekly, trans. Allan Stoekly, Carl R. Lovitt, and Donald M. Lesie, Jr. (Minneapolis: University of Minnesota Press, 1985), 116–29, quotations from 118.

31. E. B. Tylor, *Primitive Culture.* 2 vols. (London: John Murray, 1870), 1:424.

32. *Sports Illustrated,* 10 April 1995, 92.

33. Emile Durkheim, *The Elementary Forms of the Religious Life,* trans. Joseph Ward Swain (New York: Free Press, 1965), 62.

34. G. Pascal Zachary, *Showstopper: The Breakneck Race to Create Windows NT and the Next Generation at Microsoft* (New York: Free Press, 1994), 281.

35. On the significance for the study of religion of the polythetic categories "cluster concept" and "fuzzy set," see Fitz John Porter Poole, "Metaphors and Maps: Towards Comparison in the Anthropology of Religion," *Journal of the American Academy of Religion* 54 (1986): 411–57, especially 428, and Jonathan Z. Smith, *Drudgery Divine: On the Comparison of Early Christianities and the Religions of Late Antiquity* (Chicago: University of Chicago Press, 1990), especially 50.

36. See David Chidester, *Savage Systems: Colonialism and Comparative Religion in Southern Africa* (Charlottesville: University Press of Virginia, 1996).

37. Quoted in Fred Bronson, *The Billboard Book of Number One Hits* (New York: Billboard Publications, 1985), 201.

Church, fetish, potlatch: a trinity of features that the author says reveal much about American popular culture. All three involve consumption, and so take us back to the problem of consumption covered in Chapter 4. Potlatches are defined in that Chapter.

Magic

Because the author deals with baseball, he has to cite a famous article (one that is in many anthropology readers and could easily have been in this one) by a former pro-baseball player, George Gmelch, who became a cultural anthropologist. The one point that tha author misses with his review of "Baseball Magic" is that Gmelch made it clear why there is magic in baseball: it is used when the activity is of high uncertainty. Fielding percetages are in the high 90%; batting averages are such that a person who is successful one time in three is a superstar. Therefore, there is little magic associated with fielding, but plenty with batting and pitching. That is certainly a feature of human use of magic, especially inasmuch as human life involves so much uncertainty that leads to suffering. It is one reason why religion is a comfort to humans.

Magic and religion are sometimes paired. A well-known 20th c. archaeologist, V. Gordon Childe, once quipped: "Magic is a way of making people believe they are going to get what they want, whereas religion is a system for persuading them that they ought to want what they get."

The Gift

Remember the activity you did in Chapter 3, to write down your thoughts on the motivations for gift-giving, and then what happened when Richard Lee tried to give the !Kung San people a gift? To anthropologists, the giving of gifts is one of the most nuanced of all behaviors demonstrated by humans. Gifts represent a total social phenomenon that impacts on many aspects of culture such as religion, law, morality and economics, as argued by Chidester, based on the work of Marcel Mauss.

The complexity of gift-giving among humans is somewhat ironic, given that one of the most characteristic features of being human is something which virtually no other animals do: share food freely and without compunction. The free sharing of food is perhaps the ultimate expression of *communitas*: the expression of human solidarity, mutuality and spontaneity which are, according to Chidester, prominent features of baseball, coca-cola and rock'n'roll. *Communitas*, if extended to the entire world human community, would make everyone a global citizen. What would the world really be like if "I'd like to buy the world a coke" (and the humanity behind that expression, ignoring the advertizing aspect) really were put into practice?

SOLVING PROBLEMS
CONSTRUCTING ALTERNATIVES
TO ECONOMIC GLOBALIZATION

by Jeremy Brecher

SOCIAL MOVEMENTS OFTEN FIND IT EASIER TO SAY WHAT THEY ARE AGAINST THAN what they propose. It is difficult to get beyond extremely general objectives such as peace, freedom, and justice. Alternatives to what exists may be conceived in terms of an ideal world in which such general objectives have been realized. But such utopias, while they may stimulate the imagination and motivate action, often have little connection to what currently exists. That makes it hard to see how they can actually be realized. They are often utopian in the sense of being based purely on what we might want the world to be, without taking into account what it currently is.

My emerging approach provided a means for formulating alternatives to what exists that are based on transformations of current patterns and on actions that make use of capacities that people already possess. This approach starts with the current situation and its problems. It asks what changes would be necessary to correct those problems. This approach is based on the cybernetic idea of counteracting or compensating for deviations from goals.

The next step is to ask what changes in existing patterns of action and coordination would be necessary to produce those corrections. This is, in effect, a thought experiment: "What if . . . ?" "What would be necessary . . . ?" We can try to imagine actions that are variations of what people already are capable of doing that would close the gap between what exists and what is desired.

As I began trying to understand globalization, I discovered that it involved both problems of domination and problems of disorder. As we saw in the chapter on "Domination: The Restructuring of Global Governance," the IMF, World Bank, WTO, and their regional equivalents imposed new forms of authority that had little or no accountability to those they affected. Their actions might result in the destruction of a community by a dam, or the doubling of the cost of water for a home through privatization, or the shutting of a region's farms or factories due to economic policies imposed on a national government.

But as we saw in the chapter "Disorder: Unintended Consequences," not all the problems of globalization result from such domination. Many result from uncoordinated side effects and interaction effects that were intended by no one. The race to the bottom is not anyone's intent; it is the result of myriad decisions taken simply to maximize profit. The same goes for global warming and the environmental contamination of the maquiladora region on Mexico's border with the United States.

Correction of both domination and disorder requires coordinated action by those affected and their allies. Both require that opponents make use of dependencies in order to force change. But the type of change that would solve the two kinds of problems is somewhat different.

In the case of domination, the solution is essentially to set limits on the capacity of actors to perform unacceptable actions. Such limits may be very specific: Critics of the World Bank and IMF have drawn up detailed lists of actions they should be prohibited from performing. Or such limits may involve general reductions in capacity, such as proposals for major reductions in the World Bank's budget. Or they may involve the ultimate limit on an institution—abolition.

Such restrictions raise the often difficult question, What will happen to the functions that are being restricted? There are several possibilities.

The functions can be moved to another institution. Some critics of the IMF, for example, propose that it be abolished and replaced by a new UN agency.

The functions can be decentralized. For example, Walden Bello proposed that the functions of the IMF, World Bank, and WTO be devolved to a network of regional organizations and specialized agencies dealing with topics such as health and the environment.[1]

The functions can remain in the present organization but be subject to new forms of accountability. These may be from below. For example, there are various proposals to give local communities affected by World Bank loans a veto power over them. The new accountability may also be to a higher authority. Some have proposed that the IMF and the World Bank be made subject to a revitalized UN Economic and Social Council.

Alternatively, the functions can simply be abandoned. The Bush administration proposed, for example, that the "rescue operations" of the IMF be severely curtailed. If countries became insolvent, the problem would simply be left to them and their creditors to resolve. Of course, the predictable result would either be even more catastrophic global financial crises or greatly restricted lending to countries that are poor credit risks. Some anti-globalization activists, notably David Korten, argue that the latter would be a desirable result, forcing a return to national self-sufficiency;[2] others see it as leading only to new forms of disorder and impoverishment.

In the case of disorder, solutions are likely to be rather different. They require the construction of new patterns of coordination where uncontrolled interaction reigns. Such new patterns of coordination require new practices, norms, rules, laws, and/or institutions. Formulating generally acceptable proposals for these has been much more difficult for the critics of globalization. However, without such new patterns of coordination, the result of change is likely to be nothing but more disorder.

A case in point is the race to the bottom. Abolishing the IMF, World Bank, and WTO would do little to reverse it. Competition would still drive corporations to search the world for cheap production sites and to press governments and workers for cheap labor, lax environmental protections, and subsidies. Solutions to problems of disorder must transform not just the actions of particular actors, but also destructive patterns of interaction.

In trying to figure out how to address the global race to the bottom, Tim and I (who by this time were sometimes being referred to as the "race-to-the-bottom guys") looked for a historical precedent. We started by considering the earlier race to the bottom that was once a common dynamic within national economies. Local workforces competed by accepting lower wages and sub-national governments competed by reducing public interest regulations, just as national workforces and governments do in the face of global competition today. In the late 1920s, for example, the garment industry ran away from high-wage, highly regulated, unionized New York City to low-wage, union-free towns in surrounding areas in states with little industrial regulation, notably my home state of Connecticut. (I learned about this process when I interviewed some of the garment workers who, as teenage girls half a century before, had organized the first unions in the companies that had run away to New Haven.)

In many industrial countries, the internal race to the bottom was successfully countered starting in the 1940s by a series of measures fought for by workers and their allies. Unions bargained for uniform wages in each industry. This removed wages as a factor in competition among companies. It also protected workers from having to accept wage cuts to keep their jobs from moving to lower wage locations. National laws setting minimum wages, maximum hours, and other labor standards established a floor under labor conditions. National policies used public employment and fiscal and monetary stimulus to promote full employment, thereby giving all workers more leverage at the bargaining table. To realize these conditions, workers fought for the basic democratic rights to speak, assemble, organize, bargain collectively, and participate in the political process.

We looked for parallel strategies for the global economy. An obvious starting point was labor organization. International labor cooperation, international solidarity support for workers struggles, and protection of labor rights worldwide formed a significant aspect of globalization from below. These were not only important for the sake of the workers supported, but also as critical means for reversing the race to the bottom.

While there was no global equivalent to national law, there were many possible means for setting minimum standards that could put a floor under labor conditions. The European Union's "social dimension" provided minimum standards for job security, occupational safety, unemployment compensation, union representation, and social security benefits. The Just and Sustainable Trade and Development Initiative, proposed by unions and social movement organizations in Mexico, Canada, and the United States as an alternative to NAFTA, described in detail a continental development treaty that would establish rights and standards for North America. The Maquiladora Coalition established a code of conduct for corporations in the US-Mexican border region. Such codes might start by being enforced by public pressure, but could ultimately be made enforceable by national laws, international institutions, and agreements among governments. (A similar process saw the labor standards fought for by civil society groups like the Women's Trade Union League in the 1920s embodied in US law in the 1930s.)

Proposals for a global equivalent to national full employment policies had to recognize that there were no global equivalents to national budgets, treasuries, or central banks. A starting point might be the elimination of policies of the World Bank, IMF, G-8, and US Treasury Department that prevent most countries from pursuing full employment by requiring that they run their economies to maximize exports to service their debts. (Some of these policies have indeed been modified in reaction to the Great Recession.) Increasing the buying power of the world's poor and working people via unionization and minimum labor standards would increase demand for worthwhile forms of economic development.

Some form of "global Keynesianism" could counteract global cycles of boom and bust. For example, the IMF once created Special Drawing Rights—"paper gold"—to support international liquidity. We advocated consideration of this tool—something that was in fact adopted on a massive scale in 2009 in response to the Great Recession. In the 1990s, the UN Development Program proposed a new global central bank "to create a common currency, to maintain price and exchange-rate stability, to channel global surpluses and deficits, to equalize international access to credit—and to provide the liquidity and credits poor nations need."[3]

Achieving such changes would require a global process of democratization. Global institutions like the World Bank, IMF, and WTO would have to be replaced or radically democratized. Global corporations would have to be brought under democratic control. The global economy would have to be reshaped to encourage rather than undermine democratic government at all levels. National and local governments would have to be recaptured from the global corporations. Participatory democracy would have to be pursued at a global scale.

Far from being mutually exclusive choices, these various changes could be combined. For example, the IMF and the World Bank could be put under a higher UN authority; many of their functions could be devolved to regional organizations and specialized agencies; and local communities could be given veto power over actions that affect them. Labor organizations could be organized locally and nationally but coordinate globally through global bargaining councils. Minimum labor rights and standards could be set by global institutions like the UN's International Labor Organization but monitored and enforced by local and national governments and by organized workers and communities themselves. A global central bank could operate primarily by coordinating national central banks and channeling resources to local development efforts. Such a multilevel program reflects my emerging approach: Social life is made up not of sovereign entities but of multiple interacting levels that can be subject to multilevel reorganization.

Notes

1. Walden Bello, "Reforming the WTO Is the Wrong Agenda," in *Globalize This!,* eds. Kevin Danaher and Roger Burbach (Monroe, Maine: Common Courage Press, 2000), p. 177ff.

2. David Korten, *When Corporations Rule the World* (Bloomfield, CT: Kumarian Press, 2001).

3. United Nations Human Development Program, *Human Development Report 1992* (New York: Oxford, 1992), pp. 78–79.

How do we address the world problems that we have explored in this book? This final article gives a small suggestion about how to do this, but even carrying that through seems an enormous challenge.

The author thinks that we should base our solutions on the resources we already possess. We look at the problems, think of what is necessary to correct them (in the cybernetic mold) and then do a "what if" thought experiment to see what changes would be necessary to make the correction.

Simple, right?

Globalism

According to Brecher, the crucial problems of the great interconnectedness of the world today, which we call globalism or globalization, are caused by two things: domination and disorder.

There is no doubt that some global institutions are dominant. Brecher cites the financial bodies of the International Monetary Fund (IMF), the World Bank, and the World Trade Organization (WTO) as entities that perpetuate the domination which has increased inequality in the world markedly. Brecher presents as a representative solution to the world problem of domination and inequality the modification or even abolition of those financial entities, or their subordination to the United Nations. How difficult that seems to be in the current political climate.

Multi-levelism

Brecher also thinks that strengthening labor organization around the world can help counteract the domination of the financial institutions. The main point is that social life should not be dominated by sovereign entities but there should be multiple-interacting levels, and a re-organized labor system, such as the Just and Suitable Trade Development Initiative between Canada, Mexico and the U.S., where delegates work to modify the unintended negative effects of the North American Free Trade Association (NAFTA). Brecher highlights the need to support such entities in their functions. If many institutions world-wide are geared to working in cooperation, the solutions required to meet the challenges of contemporary world problems can be addressed by these multiple levels of interacting institutions, whether they be governments, non-governmental organizations (NGOs), corporate entities, or cooperating individuals.

CONCLUSION: WRAP-UP

Hopefully, one important lesson this course has taught you is that there is often an underlying meaning to human behavior that goes way beyond the explanations people might ordinarily give for their actions. We see that many human activities can take on the aura of religious behavior; that is why there are so many different expressions of religious belief among humans. One thing that seems common to all forms of religion—it works to bind people into a community. The real lesson of anthropology today is the realization that what the world needs most in the effort to solve our common problems is to build a global community, to combat domination by some humans over others, accept the multi-level nature of our societies, and get our institutions to work towards the common good of respecting and working to further the human rights of every individual on the planet.

ACTIVITIES

General activity: as a class, discuss the Schema activation responses and address the question: *are sports a ritual?*

Activity for Reading #28: in small groups, pick one of the three American practices and discuss whether or not it is a "religion." How is Chidester correct or not correct in his view?

Activity for Reading #29: in small groups, briefly research the IMF, WTO and the World Bank and then pick one and consider three ways in which the institution might be modified in order to make it less dominating.

SOURCES

The quote from V. Gordon Childe is from his 1947 book *History*, published by Cobbett in London, p. 37. The source for the use of magic in baseball is George Gmelch 1971 Baseball Magic *Society* 8(8) pp. 39-41. For the Marcel Mauss book: *The gift: forms and functions of exchange in archaic societies* first English edition in 1954 translated by Ian Cunnison, Glencoe, IL: Free Press. A recent version is translated by Jane I, Guyer Chicago: Hau Books, 2015. The *Essai sur le don* was originally published in French in 1925, with the French reprinted in 1950. A good introduction to cybernetics can be found in Magoroh Maruyama 1963 The second cybernetic: deviation-amplifying mutual causal processes *American Scientist* 51 pp. 164-179. The theory of sports mentioned is from David Sansone 1988 Greek *Athletics and the Genesis of Sport* University of California Press: Berkeley. The anthropology of religion has a huge literature. One useful recent text is Winzeler, L. Robert 2008 *Anthropology and Religion: What We Know, Think, and Question* Walnut Grove: AltaMira Press.

Credits